GEOFFREY BEARD

DECORATIVE PLASTERWORK
IN GREAT BRITAIN

Frontispiece. *Mereworth Castle*, Kent:
The Entrance Vestibule leading to circular Hall under the dome.
Stuccoist: Giovanni Bagutti, *c.* 1723, working for the architect Colin Campbell

Decorative Plasterwork

in Great Britain

Geoffrey Beard

Phaidon

Phaidon Press Limited, 5 Cromwell Place, London SW7 2JL

First published 1975
© 1975 by Phaidon Press Limited

Published with the help of a grant
from THE PAUL MELLON CENTRE
FOR STUDIES IN BRITISH ART

ISBN 0 7148 1686 8

Printed in Great Britain by T. & A. Constable Limited, Edinburgh

CONTENTS

Preface

IT should not be claimed for plasterwork that it is as important a decorative medium as painting. Few publishers are prepared therefore, in present-day concerns with international editions, to issue a book dealing with plasterwork in Great Britain. It is to the credit of the Paul Mellon Centre for Studies in British Art that I have been allowed adequate space and enough illustrations to survey the present state of knowledge and to publish a detailed list of plasterers and their work. What, however, we have not been able to do is to allocate the vast number of photographs to the subject which Laurence Turner used in his *Country Life* book on plasterwork in 1927. There has been no conscious effort on my part to outdo or replace Turner's book, for the aim of anyone undertaking architectural research in the 1970s needs to be substantially different in emphasis from what was needed forty years ago. There is a concern now for names and details of work with the supporting references. We have tried within the economic framework for this book to give as much of this sort of evidence as possible.

It must be owned, however, that it has not been possible to publish every name in my files. Thousands of names from the records of the Worshipful Company of Plaisterers of London alone would have to be added. The list which does appear includes most of the plasterers who are likely to have worked in the great country houses. My own personal view, in any case, is that (one or two notable exceptions apart) it is difficult for one person to issue a complete dictionary. A dictionary of craftsmen *is* needed, and all of us would be royally served if only three or four of us would compile it.

Plasterwork is anonymous stuff, rarely signed, and few plasterers' names appear in the conventional, or unconventional, literature of art history about it. Thus the attribution of plasterwork to particular dates and craftsmen is a more than usually hazardous task. It has to be made against too sketchy a framework with appalling gaps in its structure, against the use of the same moulds and sources by many hands, and against the scant dependence of the plasterers on the usual pattern-books for their motifs. Patient research seems to add little to the existing books on the subject, except that, at the time when they were written, forty and seventy years ago, their authors were more concerned with the appearance of plasterwork rather than the why and wherefore of it all. I began this study because the late Margaret Jourdain, who had written a book on plasterwork in 1926, urged me in 1953 to give some substance to her earlier words 'the names of a few plasterers are recorded . . .' We know now that there were perhaps too many who were mediocre, and few who were talented.

In contriving and maintaining enchanted palaces 'of solidity, conveniency and ornament', as Sir Balthazar Gerbier has it, many noble patrons over the last 400 years have frequently met problems in balancing income and expenditure and almost beggared themselves. Plasterwork does not take kindly to having an inadequate roof over its head and is liable to crumble into subjection almost without a struggle or adequate warning. In all its complex parts, therefore, the one problem is created by the other, and the economic history of the country house, although imperfectly studied, is of vital concern.

As in the study of decorative painting, attention must be devoted to the small groups of foreigners—the *stuccatori* in this case—who left their homes, whether in Switzerland or in Denmark, early in the eighteenth century to come and work in England. There are slight clues, followed up in later pages, to suggest that one or two of them (Charles Stanley and Francesco Vassalli, for example) may have worked as masters or partners of English plasterers. Whilst my own researches, and those of others, have clarified the role of architect and craftsmen, these aspects of collaboration, as well as the domination of the scene in the seventeenth century by the Office of Works, have still to be fully resolved. Plasterers were concerned more with doing than recording, although the appearance of one letter from a Swiss stuccoist, Francesco Vassalli, leads one to hope that more documentation of this kind will come to light. Such prolonged studies as those being made by Dr A.A. Tait in Scotland, by Dr Andor Gomme on Midland houses and Dr Ivan Hall on those in east Yorkshire, may finally unearth the evidence which is always needed to give a firm basis for further attribution—the chance mention in a letter and the recommendation of good craftsmen to a relative or friend.

Whilst it has been my good fortune to unravel a few problems in this book, I am only too aware that in trying to follow the advice of Edward Stillingfleet not to neglect 'those who have written before me' but to deliver when possible my own judgments, I may have made errors. I shall be grateful to those who point them out.

G.B.

Acknowledgments

IT might have been easier for me, and more informative to the reader, if this book had been prepared for publication in 1977, fifty years after Laurence Turner had issued his *Decorative Plasterwork in Great Britain*. By then, however, I should have been an 'unconscionable time' in writing it. I was also inveigled into delightful conversations with friends—sirens to the unwary—in which unique knowledge was imparted, but at which everyone agreed that I should write it all down and give, if possible, the footnotes to the conjecture. My principal debt of gratitude is to Professor Giuseppe Martinola of Lugano who guided me through the churches and parish registers of the Ticino, the home of the *stuccatori* who came to England in the eighteenth century. Professor Peter Murray led me to consider the possibilities of research there, and Mr F. S. Stych helped with the many conversations with parish priests and stucco-workers and restorers, which took place in an Italian too fluent for me to do more than flounder behind. Professor E. K. Waterhouse and Mr Anthony M. Clark gave me the benefit of their extensive knowledge of the decoration and contents of churches and houses in Rome. The writings of Professor Henry-Russell Hitchcock and Mr Nicolas Powell helped me to examine for myself the activities of stuccoists in the German baroque and rococo churches.

Nearer home, in Scotland, I should not have found much without the invaluable help of Mr David Walker, Mr John Dunbar, Mr Andrew Broom, Miss Catherine Cruft and Miss Mary Cosh. By suggesting houses I should visit, ceilings and documents at which I should peer, and photographs it was necessary to know of, they have given some balance to a study which purports to be about plasterwork in Great Britain. Boundaries on research are not easy to erect. Dr Bernard Watney pointed out to me that certain Irish stucco-work by Bartholomew Cramillion was similar to figures in the 'girl in a swing' ceramic groups made probably at the Chelsea factory. Despite much assistance from Dr C. P. Curran, Dr Maurice Craig, the Hon Desmond Guinness and the Knight of Glin I have not, however, felt myself qualified to write of plasterwork in Ireland other than to discuss work by the Franchini brothers. They left England in the 1730s and stayed away for many years enjoying the enchantments of that hospitable land across the water which were similarly extended to me.

My former colleagues at the Manchester College of Art and Design did much over many years to provide help and information when I flagged and to temper my enthusiasm when it was misguided. By undertaking some of my duties they allowed me to accept a Harvard research fellowship in 1969. Although awarded for work on another subject, this took me to many museums and libraries in America, whose resources added snippets of information to this study. Similar help was generously extended by John Harris and Mrs Margaret Richardson at the Royal Institute of British Architects Library, by Morrison Heckscher at the Metropolitan Museum, New York, and by Miss Jean Preston and Miss Haydée Noya at the Henry Huntington Library in California.

My further obligation divides neatly into two groups—to those owners who kindly allowed me to see their houses and examine documents in their possession, and to everyone who provided references and services of many kinds. In the first category I am indebted to the Duke of Devonshire, the late Duke of Norfolk, the Duke of Northumberland, the Marquess of Exeter, the Marquess of Lansdowne, the late Earl of Bradford, the Earl of Coventry, the Earl of Egremont, the Earl of Scarbrough, Viscount Scarsdale, Sir Ralph Anstruther, Bt, Sir Gyles Isham, Bt, Sir Richard Sykes, Bt, the late Sir William

Worsley, Bt, Lord Brownlow, Lord Leigh, Lord Sandys, Mr Euan Cox, Mr A. Galliers-Pratt, Mr Huw Lorimer, and Mr and Mrs Simon Towneley. For many kindnesses and friendly encouragement spread over several years I am grateful to the Viscount Cobham, Mr George and the late Lady Cecilia Howard, and Professor and Mrs J.L. Clifford.

In checking references, moving boxes, climbing ladders, taking photographs and providing clues my friends were all very diligent. My former colleagues on the staffs of the Birmingham and Leeds Reference Libraries and Art Galleries gave willing and varied service over many years. The same helpful attitude characterized the assistance given by many County Archivists and Record Office staffs, the archivists and senior officials of several London banks, and the staffs of the Guildhall Library, Public Record Office, Bodleian Library, British Museum, Sterling and Bienecke (Yale) and Avery (Columbia, New York) Libraries. The architectural editors of *Country Life* patiently endured many questions and made helpful suggestions. I would thank in particular Mr John Cornforth and Mr Marcus Binney who concerned themselves about the 'ceilings man' with a care fashioned out of friendship and knowledge. Dr I. Grafe and Mrs Jenny Wright at Phaidon Press and Dr Christopher White at the Mellon Centre in London were similarly helpful.

For help of various kinds I wish to thank my wife Margaret, and daughter Helen, Dr L.O.J. Boynton, Mr Edward Croft-Murray, Miss A.W. Cutler, Dr Kerry Downes, Mr Michael Felmingham, Mr Brinsley Ford, Dr Eric Gee, Mr Christopher Gilbert, Dr Andor Gomme, Nicholas and Judith Goodison, Joyce and David Green, Mr Miles Hadfield, Mr Eric B. Inglefield, Mr Edward Ingram, Major T.L. Ingram, Mr Francis Johnson, Mrs P. Kirkham, Mr James Lees-Milne, Mr Arthur Oswald, Mr W. Salter, Mr Derek Sherborn, Mr Frank Simpson, Mr Francis Steer, Dr Damie Stillman, Mr Christopher Wall, Major Jim Williams, Dr Peter Willis, Mr R.B. Wragg and Mr Tom Wragg.

Mr Cecil Farthing, Mrs M.P. Harper, Mr A.F. Kersting and the late Mr Edwin Smith gave special help with photographs.

I have left to the conspicuous end my indebtedness to Mr Howard Colvin; over the last fifteen years, and in company with the late Rupert Gunnis, no plasterer I should know of eluded their net. The debt which architectural historians owe to these two scholars is incalculable. All I am able to do is to dedicate to Mr Colvin these inadequate pages, regretting that Mr Gunnis was never able to see them in their final form.

University of Lancaster   Geoffrey Beard

For
Howard
Colvin

CHAPTER I

Magnificent Building

The Three chief Principles of Magnificent Building,
viz. Solidity, Conveniency and Ornament.
Sir Balthazar Gerbier, 1662

A MONG the first questions that arise when considering 'magnificent building' of any period is the responsibility of the architects and craftsmen for its appearance, and the sources from which patrons obtained the money with which to live and build. It is easy to say that the money usually came from a number of specific sources. It is harder to trace the exact routes. Furthermore, the century that lies between Ben Jonson and Alexander Pope saw great changes in English domestic architecture, and alterations in the whole function and character of the English country house. Most of the great houses built before the Civil War followed a traditional pattern. No architect was employed in their construction, and the usual method was to build by contract between owner and master workmen, one or the other of whom supplied the plan. This plan might undergo considerable alteration while the house was actually in course of erection.[1] It has been pointed out that 'the household was in the nature of a large family'[2] and, as such, the great hall was a central meeting-point for members of the family, their servants and tenants. This requirement continued to dictate the design of a house so long as the relation of the lord to his dependents was in the custom of 'housekeeping' with all rooms intended for daily use.

Some houses in the Elizabethan period did not, of course, conform to this pattern. Houses such as Holdenby and Wollaton were designed for the reception of Elizabeth and her court, and the urge to build which gripped their owners was combined with their desire to display their own importance. Sir Christopher Hatton 'at Holdenby hardly used his new house, nor did he build it for use', and Wollaton was 'an extravaganza', an 'exceedingly pretentious palace' and 'an inflated bauble, an architectural symbol rather than a house'.[3] These judgments are in accord with Ben Jonson's attack on ostentatious houses built for show in his poem *To Penshurst*—'those proud, ambitious heaps and nothing else'.[4]

The deliberate striving after effect which can be seen at Wollaton was, however, a pointer to the future. The decisive changes which ultimately altered the whole style and character of the large country house came with the rise of the professional architect during the third decade of the seventeenth century and the more exact control over a wide group of craftsmen of varying ability. Inigo Jones, who designed the Banqueting House at Whitehall, the first purely Classical building to be erected in England, had a knowledge of Italian aims and methods, and the result, completed in 1622, was a building relying for its effect on form, proportion and symmetry. The example thus set by the Crown and its architect was soon to affect the design of the large country house, and after the Restoration it became usual to consider carefully the appearance and the function which the house would eventually have.

In some ways this was a change for the good, and many of the houses built during the later seventeenth and early eighteenth centuries display a genuine concern for beauty of form. But in some cases the break with tradition resulted in function being sacrificed to stateliness. The great hall declined in importance, and the great house was devised in a search for the grand and the imposing. In the Queen Anne house, built to be lived in, with functional considerations well in mind, the architectural revolution produced something admirable; its effects as seen at Chatsworth, Blenheim and Castle Howard are more questionable, and the quest for a style must be taken into consideration. The strength of native tradition and the new progressive trends towards the simplicity of the Palladian style combined to militate against the establishment of the baroque in England. Furthermore, the severity of the Civil War had done much to reduce an interest in Italian art and architecture in the minds of those normally best fitted to benefit from travel and contacts there. English exiles, wandering about the Continent, had more chance to learn about what was happening in France and the United Provinces; a too brief efflorescence of baroque was followed by a reaction in the form of Palladianism and Classical proportion and a belief in ancient truths. For a time, like all new fashions, Palladianism dominated the building scene as our statistics of house-building will show.

The Urge to Build

The new changes were not, of course, entirely the result of the rise of the architect,[5] nor of a widespread interest in architecture. It was all made possible and helped on by social changes and by developments in the economy of the great house itself. The decline in 'housekeeping' which took place in the early seventeenth century meant that, instead of meeting in a communal way, an owner made more use of intermediary officials in his dealings with tenants and servants. In this way he was cut off from direct contact with the humbler day-to-day activities of his estate.[6] Most important of all, the seventeenth century saw an alteration in the whole relationship of the great landowner to his country home. Until the time of the Civil Wars—and indeed long after—it was the centre of his life, and there his main activities were concentrated. Family papers such as the *Memoirs of the Verney Family* give a good idea how full and absorbing that life could be, not only for the country gentlemen himself, busy with building and with settling disputes among tenants, but also for his wife and daughters, who were occupied with the management of the house. 'The country house was still the scene, not merely of relaxation, but of business.'[7] But under Charles I a certain number of country families began to feel the lure of the town and the court,[8] and the split between the older generation who remained in the country and the younger generation who gravitated to the court is clearly marked. After 1660 the process was advanced to such an extent that the Earl of Rochester could say that 'when he came to Brentford the devill entred into him and never left him till he came into the country again to Adderbury or Woodstock'.[9] The process had also been given a sharp push by the new exciting life which seemed possible to the followers of Charles II when the king was newly restored to the throne. To build was one way to participate in the scene.

It has been shown that about 125 houses were built or altered in the period 1625-85, of which about eighty were in progress after 1660. A further count, based on published lists[10] for the period 1685-1710, shows the following result, with a total of thirty-nine houses in progress:

1685-90	1690-5	1695-1700	1700-5	1705-10
11	2	5	13	8

The urge to build was therefore maintained, and Sir John Summerson has shown[11] that of 148 houses built between 1710 and 1740 '21 are dateable to 1710-14, 22 to 1715-19, but no fewer than 50 to 1720-4 . . .'. The details of many of these buildings show the involvement of craftsmen of the Office of Works, and the sparse figures for the end of the seventeenth century are due to the major wars of 1689-97 and 1702-13. Public expenditure on war in these two periods increased from some £49 million (1688-97) to over £93 million (1702-13).[12]

Activity before 1710, such as it was, was encouraged by the prospect of the end of wars and the setting up of a stable regime. It was not, however, until after 1720 that a surge of building came, inspired by the revival in the ideas of Palladio and Inigo Jones which Lord Burlington and Colin Campbell had been encouraging from about 1715 onwards. This was also a period which saw considerable dominance of building activity by the officers and craftsmen of the Office of Works. We shall see how, after reforming themselves in 1714-15 at the accession of George I, they were in a commanding position by 1720. A survey of the period 1660-1720, when good plasterwork abounded, allows us to see the differences between the achievements prior to the accession of Charles II in 1660 and those after, and to see a span of sixty years of activity and experience, much of it commanded by the efforts of Sir Christopher Wren. These years equipped English architects and craftsmen for the challenge of new styles and the extraordinary demands for large houses which arose after 1720. But what of the cost of building?

Income and Costs

The Civil Wars and the aftermath provided many occasions for underestimating or exaggerating income, so that even the official *Proceedings of the Committee for Compounding, 1643-1660* may be open to question. Here is a source by which estimates of the wealth of certain individuals may be assessed.[13] The total value of the forty-one peers' estates was about £1,241,906, which gives an average of £30,920. Sixteen were above the average, the Earl of Thanet leading with an estate worth £150,000, the Earl of West-morland's £90,000 and, at the other end of the scale, the Earl of Norwich had an estate worth £3,300. The estates of ninety-three baronets totalled £1,033,588—an average of £11,114, with exceptions like Sir Thomas Lyttelton of Hagley, Worcestershire, owning an estate worth £45,000.

Statistics, however, are not easy reading and many factors can affect their compilation. It is seldom possible to arrive at an accurate figure for the whole income and, in these particular cases, the Civil War probably made some inroads into the funds they might have used for building. From 1642, when King Charles raised his standard at Nottingham, until the end of the decade there was little building activity, and a period of instability and distress set in. Exile, imprisonment and the sequestration of property, compounding for it at the equivalent of two years' rental, were all too familiar expressions of the official line, and the effect of the Civil War on house-building, whilst it can be surmised, is not easy to define. The 2nd Earl of Peterborough, who had joined the king at Oxford in 1643, suffered for his adhesion to the royal cause. His estates were sequestered for his delinquency and, though the dower of his wife was 'very useful to him', he needed to spend the years from 1650 to 1660 in the retirement of his own house at Drayton and contend with great debts.[14]

The Parliamentarians had difficulty raising money to carry on the government of the country. Church lands were being sold, and the question even arose whether the open space to the west of St Paul's Cathedral was available for building. Fortunately wise courses prevailed; a committee of the House of Commons was appointed to consider the whole question of building in London. It recommended in February 1657 that a fine should be imposed for every building upon a new foundation within ten miles of London not having four acres attached to it. By 1659 the total amount levied was £75,000, of which £41,000 had actually been paid.[15] Would that each private builder had access to such sources of wealth. He was driven to other measures, and Dr Nicholas Barbon, a seventeenth-century speculative builder, stated in his *An Apology for the Builder* (1685) that in his opinion much of the emigration to the New World, especially Jamaica, was due to the building restrictions.

The Marquess of Worcester was said to have lost £700,000 in the Civil War; he pressed hard on his bailiffs and receivers to raise money from rents and land and was thus able to restore the fluctuating economies of his estates; he then spent almost twenty years, from 1666 to 1684, altering Badminton House, Gloucestershire.[16] Compensation money for damage was occasionally available, and a new race of builders emerged with the leaders of the Commonwealth regime ready to invest in land and building. On the Royalist front the eventual Restoration of Charles II quickly advanced many peers, even if they did not always escape the recovery of arrears of excise. The Acts of General Pardon were selective in their terms, and useful sums of money were extracted for the king's use. These demands were compensated for by additions to capital, made in at least four ways; trade and overseas investment, the profits of office and rents from property which were lucrative enough if properly handled. From Tudor times houses had been built out of income, with a frequent use of land and freestone from decaying monasteries and hospitals.[17] What arose was frequently ostentatious and confused in style. Austere Cistercian houses decayed into weed-cracked ruins and succumbed to plunder in order that the ogee turrets, mullioned windows and wainscoted chambers of the houses of merchants and lawyers could rise. To the cost of these new houses was frequently added the great cost of entertaining Queen Elizabeth I as she progressed about the country. Her visit to the Earl of Leicester at Kenilworth in 1575 was said to have cost him £6,000.[18]

As far as we know the seventeenth-century kings inflicted their royal presence on their subjects less frequently. They saw them often enough at court and in official positions (which could be most remunerative for the holder).

On the Royalist front the Restoration of Charles II quickly advanced many who were sympathetic and loyal to the king during his exile. Two such were John Berkeley, created Baron Berkeley of Stratton, and Edward, Earl of Clarendon. Both built houses early in the 1660s. Berkeley was a colleague of Pepys on the Navy Board, and his various official appointments enabled him to acquire a considerable fortune; according to his own account he had made £50,000 by the year 1663.[19] His wealth must have been increased by his marriage; Lady Berkeley is described on his monument in Twickenham Church as 'A young lady of a Large Dowry & yet larger Graces & Virtues'. In addition to building Berkeley House, facing Piccadilly, he bought a large estate near Twickenham. In September 1672, John Evelyn dined at the house and recorded his opinion of it and its cost:

> 'I din'd at Lord John Berkeley's newly arriv'd out of Ireland where he had bin Deputy; it was in his new house, or rather palace, for I am assur'd it stood him in neare £30,000....'[20]

The Earl of Clarendon's house, called nobly 'Clarendon House', was of vast proportions. Both Evelyn and Pepys described its size and merits. The earl had allowed his architect Sir Roger Pratt £18,000, but Evelyn noted that Pratt 'had exceeded the original estimate more than three times...' and that at a later stage 'the Earl, his successor, sold that which cost £50,000 building, to the young Duke of Albemarle for £25,000 to pay debts . . .'.[21] The imagination of architects was apt to cause the cost of buildings to soar (as their creations took place). Lack of effective cost control caused Lord Nottingham to write to his neighbour Lord Normanby that being 'engaged in building is a pleasure your Lordship will not envy me when once you have tried it'.[22] The costly wars against France also caused an owner keen to build to try to effect some economies by using materials found on his estate. Architects were often annoyed to find that their newly emerged profession had to stand aside for the accomplishments of owners well versed in the architecture and with a keener knowledge of what they could afford. Although the 1st Duke of Leeds took advice from the London professional architect William Talman during the building at Kiveton, Yorkshire (1694-1708), he was constantly exhorting his steward to calculate his personal estate at various stages to see if it could stand the building costs. In 1694 they calculated the duke's personal estate 'besides leases & grants & household goods and furniture' to be £41,436 9s 10d. The house, over its fourteen years of construction and decoration, finally cost £15,028 18s 6d,[23] a sensible amount viewed against the capital available.

Where cash payments only represented part of the total cost, as at Appuldurcombe, Isle of Wight (1702-13), and Denham Place, Buckinghamshire (1688-1701),[24] little can be learned from the final payments recorded. It must also be recalled that the scale of costs was different from those of today and mean little when expressed in modern terms; no accurate comparison is thus possible. Perhaps more important than assessing what the money would do was where it came from. At a time of building it was needed in more than ordinary quantity.

Sources of Income

The economic history of the English country house has still to be written: a few essays are all that exist.[25] Income came usually from six sources:

1 the rent roll;
2 income from estate managements of crops, livestock, etc.;
3 investment in lotteries, mortgages and stocks;
4 marriage settlements;
5 income from official positions held;
6 income from a profession.

Certain royal houses were supported by the resources of the Treasury, and the wishes of Parliament were administered in day-to-day detail by the Office of Works and its officers. Apart from this exception of royal funds (and their occasional application to the building of a house such as Blenheim Palace, bestowed by royal favour), an owner was by and large dependant on the six sources of income cited. His rents were usually exacted in money or kind, the latter being particularly attractive in, for example, a period of rising grain prices. The management and sale of his crops, cattle and sheep, and timber were an important part of his daily activity, only outrivalled by a close attention to investments of all kind. Some, such as Lord Chandos, became rich men through office,[26] and the 2nd Earl of Nottingham, whose comment to Lord Normanby on building we have mentioned, made a clear profit of over £50,000 while Secretary of State at the end of the seventeenth century.[27] Even more remarkable in terms of audacity was John Aislabie, who, as Chancellor of the Exchequer at the time of the South Sea

Bubble in 1720, was accused of making large profits. He had been building a house at Studley Royal, Yorkshire, possibly with advice from Colin Campbell. It has been established[28] that some £32,344 of the profits he gained by his fore-knowledge of stock movement was invested in his estate. He was finally brought to account, his estates forfeited (reported in 1729 at £1,996,392 7s 3d), and work on his house halted.

Lord Burlington, who in 1717 had debts estimated at £23,000, tried a safer method of raising money. He submitted a bill to the House of Lords to free him from irksome restrictions in his father's will and to permit him to grant building leases on land near his London home, Burlington House, Piccadilly. He had position, did not need to grovel for sinecures, but needed, as did most of his contemporaries, money to build. From his account at Hoare's Bank he drew some £20,000 in the years 1721-6. His House of Lords bill had received the Royal Assent a year or two earlier, in 1718, but financial problems and law-suits[29] against his agents were to occupy him well into the 1730s. He went on building, however, at Burlington House and Chiswick and patronized Handelian operas and singers. In his account-book at Chatsworth he recorded in meticulous detail the vagaries of his South Sea stock, the assignment of mortgages, and the fluctuating, ever critical balance of money 'to hand'. True he had not gained the £100,000 which the 'repellent common-sense' of Sarah, Duchess of Marlborough, had skimmed from the South Sea Bubble enterprise, but neither did he have her many oppressive problems. It was enough that his banker regularly obtained lottery tickets for him and that, as with all London bankers, advice was freely available on the raising of mortgages at fair interest rates. Richard Hoare was always on the look-out for good mortgages and, when not in a position to take them up himself, would pass them on to his customers.[30]

From the late seventeenth century the attempts made by William III to raise money included lotteries,[31] of which there were nine organized by the State between 1694 and 1714. Managers were appointed who supervised the activities of the receivers, and together they directed a scheme which, although it may have benefited them personally, proved inadequate in raising funds for the nation. But the possible rewards to the individual for a £10 ticket were substantial. The maximum prize was often as high as £20,000; rewards needed to be attractive if any attempt was to be made at adjusting the national debt of some £40 million that faced the cabinets of George I.[32] Lotteries alone were not enough to raise large sums of money, but they were a popular investment and a number of Oxford and Cambridge colleges applied to their banks for tickets. Lottery tickets were a recognized banker's security; in 1751 there were supposed to have been 30,000 on pledge with London bankers. These bankers turned increasingly away from goldsmithing to become the principal agents for dealing with a patron's portfolio in a variety of stocks, his most considerable asset in raising capital by loan.[33] Their success may be measured by the 1,600 or so customers, mostly from the landed classes, who banked at Hoare's in the years from 1673 to 1718.

Whilst investment in stock, by both patron and successful craftsman, was widespread when house-building was very active in the early years of the eighteenth century, most investors were concerned with the various Indies and Turkey companies, the South Sea Company, the Royal Africa Company, Hudson's Bay Company, the York Buildings Company, and various governmental and insurance issues. When Sir Theodore Janssen employed Colin Campbell to build at Wimbledon, Surrey, in 1720 he not only, as befitted a governor, held South Sea stock but also had £117,390 6s 8d in his Bank of England account.[34] The financial misfortunes which befell Janssen on the collapse of the South Sea Company were only partly resolved when Sarah, Duchess of Marlborough, acquired his Wimbledon house and imperiously directed Lord Herbert and Roger

Overleaf:
II. *Arbury Hall*, Warwickshire: Saloon window 1786.
Plastered by W. Hanwell, assisted by G. Higham and Robert Hodgson.
Based on work in the Henry VII Chapel, Westminster Abbey

Morris, her architects; eventually she dismissed them,[35] and they were probably glad to go.

The holding of this South Sea stock was fraught with danger. John Aislabie, Chancellor of the Exchequer at the time of the bursting of the 'Bubble', should have been astute enough to avoid the dire financial disaster. He was of course deeply implicated, having increased his private fortune by his official knowledge. On 8 March 1721, with eleven resolutions passed in the House accusing him of corruption, he was expelled and committed to the Tower, and building at his Yorkshire house of Studley Royal was delayed for twelve years or so.[36]

The 'Bubble' was the result of nine years speculation by the South Sea Company (granted its charter in 1711) in opening up trade with the imagined area of fabulous wealth, South America. By 26 May 1720 the stock had risen to 485 and on 30 June the London banker Thomas Martin wrote 'this day at one end of the Coffee House South Sea stock was sold at 1000 . . . the other end at 920'.[37] By October it was at 185 and, although George I had become a governor, the 'Bubble' burst when the investors realized that the prospects of trade in the South Seas did not exist. Bankruptcies and suicides— the death of Postmaster General Craggs in 1721 was not without suspicion—abounded, and craftsmen, including of course plasterers, submitted bills which were to be long delayed before payment was made.[38]

One who got out with a good profit was Sir Robert Walpole, who had opposed the Government scheme for taking over the irredeemable securities. He published a pamphlet called *The South Sea Scheme Consider'd* and took advantage of the mania to buy, considered, and then reinvested the profits in safer stock such as insurance and the Royal Africa Company. With this he built Houghton, and did such diverse things as paying the Swiss *stuccatori* who worked in the Stone Hall, had his portrait painted with the Garter Star prominently displayed, and used Charles Bridgeman to design his park and plantations. 'My father', said Horace Walpole, 'never, I repeat it with truth, never had any money in the South Sea.'[39] But recent research has added facts to this sweeping and somewhat untrue assertion.

Marriage as a source of income, or for 'strengthening' the estate is much less easy to define than stock investment. Daughters were more important than younger sons for they were the means by which the great landed families made their alliances. Marriage was more dependent on finance than romance; it was a social and economic contract designed to protect private property and male inheritance. The case of Edward Wortley who, in 1710, tried to marry Lady Mary Pierrepont is a good example. Wortley was eligible and an ardent suitor, but Mary's father, Lord Dorchester, firmly insisted that the Wortley estate be entailed on the first son born to the marriage; when Wortley refused to do this (after all, his first born might be incapable of such a responsibility), Lord Dorchester would not allow the marriage. In the *Tatler* of 18 July 1710, Wortley's friend Richard Steele attacked the whole business of mercenary marriages and the auctioning of the lady to the highest bidder.[40] Well handled by father and attorney the marriage settlement could usually bring a good return in land and prospective rents through the wording of the small print which dealt with the forfeitures of land and money in case of death or infidelity.

At the beginning of Elizabeth's reign there was also the allied problem of wardship.[41] The Crown took possession of lands on the death of a tenant, and adult heirs redeemed them by paying fines. Minor children were made wards of the Crown, and it was the Crown which sold the wardship, to which the right of marriage was attached, to anyone wishing to buy. So wardship as well as marriage at this time frequently brought with it the funds by which houses could be afforded. But whatever the source of family wealth, many were in a position to advance the causes of architecture and building. The Earl of Northumberland was assiduous about his buildings at Syon and possessed foreign architectural books. Sir John Thynne, at Longleat, and Lord Burghley, at Theobalds and Burghley House, were equally active in building big houses[42] and were ready to entertain their queen amid the scented parterres and rush-strewn plaster and wood galleries.

In addition to the benefits of inherited wealth and marriage alliances, many had an extraordinary capacity for earning money through their own abilities. In the seventeenth century Sir Arthur Ingram (*c.* 1570-1642) gathered a large fortune when Secretary of the Council of the North by the granting to him of monopolies by James I, and he became one of the ablest and most unscrupulous financiers of the period. He founded the fortunes of the family who lived at Temple Newsam for two and a half centuries after he had acquired it in 1622 for £12,000.[43] Sir John Banks amassed a fortune from his financial operations, commerce and land-owning,[44] and in 1670 he made considerable alterations to the Carthusian priory at Aylesford, Kent. Sir Richard Newdigate, who was appointed Chief Justice in 1660, the year of Charles II's Restoration, was a successful lawyer with such a lucrative practice that, as well as owning Arbury, Warwickshire, he managed to buy back the family's former seat at Harefield and also bought Astley Castle. Ferdinando Gorges, who bought Eye Manor, Herefordshire, in 1673, was a Barbados merchant in sugar and slaves, and Thomas Foley, who completed Stoke Edith in the same county by 1702, was a prominent ironmaster. His father Paul, who acquired the estate from the Lingen family (who were impoverished in the Royalist cause), was later Speaker of the House of Commons and son of an earlier Thomas, also a prominent ironmaster.

This pattern continued throughout the eighteenth century and many of the 400 or so 'great landlords', whose incomes in 1790 averaged £10,000 each,[45] owed some of it to skill in industrial and commercial enterprises. By the time the nineteenth century was under way, a south Yorkshire ironmaster, Walter Spencer Stanhope, was rich enough to add a new wing to Cannon Hall, Barnsley, designed by John Carr; coal and iron enabled others to do the same. House-building was described by Maria Edgeworth as one of 'those objects for which country gentlemen often ruin themselves'. Only the deep national purse could stand building on the scale that George IV employed in transforming Buckingham House, although the 1st Marquess of Ailesbury spent about £250,000 on Tottenham House and the 6th Duke of Devonshire lavished a fortune on Chatsworth.[46] Some of this money may have come from town properties which increased in value and also from the expansion of both properties and country estates which added more names to the rent roll. The Earl of Verulam added wings to Gorhambury House at an expense of £11,000 raised by the estate steward. Verulam had six sons and four daughters to accommodate. When momentous issues such as the rescue of an estate from ill-fortune was in question the nineteenth-century man turned to marriage as had his forebears, the arrangement of which 'was liable to be taken out of the hands of the matrons. Necessity impelled an impoverished aristocrat to seek a bride of fortune.'

The country house thus became the hub of the landlord's existence; it was the place which gave his family status, sense of identity and achievement, and perhaps, in the novels of Jane Austen at least, permanence. Whilst there are not enough detailed studies of the financial side for comparisons to be made and exact conclusions drawn, it is obvious that large sums of money were necessary in order to build. These were provided in the ways we have outlined, and the spending of the sums available put a heavy responsibility on the men who superintended the building operations, calculated the various payments due, and arranged for the supply of materials.

CHAPTER II

Materials and Methods

Thou shalt set thee up great stones, and plaister them with plaister.
King James 1611 *Bible*, Deuteronomy, XXVII, 2

WHEN Bottom the weaver talked in Shakespeare's *A Midsummer Night's Dream* of creating a wall in the great chamber in which Pyramus and Thisbe were to meet, he touched on the problems discussed in this chapter—raw materials: 'Some man or other must present Wall; and let him have some plaster, or some loam, or some rough-cast about him, to signify wall'.

Raw Materials and Equipment

Although the divisions did not usually exist in practice, it is necessary for us to consider plaster and stucco as individual materials. Both stemmed from limestone, one of the oldest chemical substances known to man.

Plaster

The best kind of plaster is obtained from burning gypsum, the natural mineral form of calcium sulphate. It is found in most countries, but the large deposits under Montmartre became the best known, and gypsum from there, sent to England as early as the thirteenth century, became known as 'plaster of Paris'. The importance of such a basic material from abroad also led to extensive mining of deposits in Derbyshire and Nottinghamshire. The most widely used form of plaster was however composed of lime (calcium oxide).

In this state the lime was too caustic to be used for plasterwork and needed to be 'slaked', that is chemically combined with the right quantity of water in order to reduce the caustic quality of the lime, which might otherwise cause blistering and bubbling of the treated wall-surface. Indeed, Roman law forbade the use of lime unless it had been kept for three years, by which time the gradual absorption of moisture from the atmosphere would have slaked it.

The usual kind of English plasterwork was composed of slaked lime, sand, and a binding agent such as hair. Sometimes the finishing coat was in finer gypsum plaster. The plaster which was used for lining barns and outhouses was coarse, being a mixture of common lime and rough sand to which anything to increase the toughness might be added. An analysis made in 1955 of a sample of plaster dating from about 1620 from the cove of the 'Bird and Baby' Room at Sheriff Hutton Hall, Yorkshire, (Plate 13) gave the result[47] as shown in table overleaf.

This plaster was obviously made from dolomitic lime of a fairly high standard of purity. A quantity of hair was noted in the plaster, but it is unlikely that this accounted for the whole of the 0·87% recorded in the analysis as carbonaceous matter. When ignited there was a strong aroma of horses' hooves, typical of that lingering in a black-smith's shop. Whilst the hair could have accounted for some of the smell it is quite possible that gelatine derived from hooves had been incorporated with the lime to improve the plasticity and workability of the plaster.

Contents	%
Insoluble in Hydrochloric Acid	1·17
Iron and Aluminium Oxide	1·06
Calcium Oxide ('quicklime')	28·90
Magnesium Oxide	19·03
Sulphur Trioxide (normally driven off when making 'quicklime')	0·74
Carbon Dioxide	37·84
Combined water	9·16
Free water	0·99
Carbonaceous matter	0·87
	99·76

It would be difficult, however, to build a system of dating from comparison by analysis since so many different types of plaster are found, irrespective of the period in which the work was executed. One of the most unusual types,[48] of sixteenth-century date, was plastered over what appeared to be a backing of blue lias lime and coarse aggregate with a hard plaster setting coat $\frac{1}{8}$ inch thick. The ceiling under this was composed of one-inch oak boards nailed to the underside of the wood joists, with oak laths nailed direct to the boards. Theoretically it is all wrong but the work survives.

With materials such as these, and their own sophisticated variations, English plasterers could do work of the categories defined in Bess of Hardwick's account for work at Hardwick Hall. Abraham Smith's bargain with the Countess in 1581 indicated that his plasterwork should:

'be cast in such mould as Habraham shal mak, for the same he most beat, born and sift, cast, cleanse (for the same moulde) and p'fectly set the sayd frese and cornish so wyll, and workmanly finish in every respect as shall be lyked of by yor la [Ladyship] and to end the same work within a fortnight aftr Eastr next . . . in the year of our lord god 1581, and to hav a laborer fond at yor la charges of meat and drink for on[e] fortnight and he to have for the well and work manly finishing of his work xxvis viiid and at the end of the bargayne xxvis viiid in full payment of this bargayn'.

Of such 'stuff' was the great Hardwick frieze made (Plate 1).

Hair

The material added to give toughness to the plaster was usually hair from cows, bullocks and, for finer work, goats. Brick dust, straw, dung and gelatine were all variations, but in good quality work the accounts usually included a payment for hair. For the work at Holyroodhouse in 1674 'Robert Greenhorn, tanner' was paid 'for common hair at 6s 8d per stone and whyte hair at 2 lb sterling per stone'. He provided £65 10s 0d worth, and this would probably be added to the plaster at somewhere between one to two pounds of dry hair for each two to three cubic feet of plaster.[49] For the best work less hair was added, and the thin finishing coats might then possibly be akin to stucco. It is of little use comparing the payments for hair due to variations in the value of money, but the talented late seventeenth-century plasterer Edward Goudge used '48 pounds of white Kidds hair at 6d p. pound' for his work at Castle Bromwich Hall, Warwickshire, in 1689 (Plate 36). The hair was not mixed with the other constituents until the plaster was needed. The successful plasterer Thomas Clayton (*fl.* 1710-60), in a memorandum of 17 June 1753,[50] about his work at Blair Atholl, Perthshire, gives useful information about the preparation of materials, including the hair:

> 'first to order . . . Lime towards the Latter ende of the year to be put in a place that is thought Conveneant under cover so that it may be riddelled and seasond But not mixed with hare, other ways the hare would Rot and Be of No youse. Second to order fourtey or fiftey Stone weight of Hare to Be In Readiness for youse when Eaver wanted . . .'

This rotting of the hair and the various tensile strengths were the subject of a study made in 1897.[51] Plaster briquettes containing respectively manilla hemp, sisal hemp, jute and best goat's hair were prepared. The ends of the briquettes were supported, and weights suspended from the middle. The briquettes broke at the following weights:

Goat's hair	144½ lbs weight
Jute	145 lbs
Sisal hemp	150 lbs
Manilla hemp	195 lbs

The 1897 study continues: 'In another experiment with two barrelfuls of mortar, each of equal portions of sharp sand and lime one barrel was mixed with a measure of manilla hemp and the other of best goat's hair, with the usual quantity of water, and stored in barrels in a dry cellar. On examination nine months later, the hair mortar crumbled and broke, little hair being visible, the bulk having been consumed by the lime; the mortar containing hemp showed great cohesion, requiring effort to pull it apart, the hemp fibre showed little evidence of injury by lime.' Late in the nineteenth century sawdust was sometimes used as a substitute for hair in plaster and mortar. The resulting plaster was not as good, though it had its use for external plastering which had to withstand rough weather and frost.

Sand

For lime-plaster the sand needed to be sharp, gritty and free from any organic matter or staining agents. In this way body was given to the soft plaster and if the sand was good a uniform shrinkage during setting took place. If salt was present, as in sea sand, efflorescence—the white frothy blotches on plaster—appeared and the mortar was liable to retain moisture. To avoid this plasterers liked to work in a warm atmosphere. Their bills frequently mention the expense of burning coal or peat, not only to burn the gypsum to produce quicklime, but to heat the rooms, and, in the case of the workers at Holyroodhouse, to bake their fretwork (Plates 133-134). Clayton's bill of 1747 is again explicit about the fires:

> 'To 170 Lodes of peates furnished By me for Burning Stucco, and fyers in the dineing room at 3 pence per Lode.   £2 2s 6d'

For the external 'stucco' washed, sieved sand was used in a ratio of four or five to one of lime, and again hair was usually introduced as a binding agent. The architect Giacomo Leoni in his 1726 edition of Alberti's *Architecture* wrote that 'river sand is more tractable and better for Plaistering work', another reference to the use of sand which did not contain any salt. In 1613-15, sand for building at Bolsover Castle, Derbyshire, was obtained at a cost of a penny a load plus 8d a load for carriage. For work at Wrest, Bedfordshire, in about 1706 sand was delivered at one shilling a load.[52]

Laths

Laths, narrow flat strips of wood usually 1 or 1½ inches wide by 48 inches long, were used as a backing and a key to the first coat of plaster. They were usually set a short distance (perhaps ⅜ inch) apart and thoroughly wetted with clean water several hours before the plaster was applied. Oak, beech and white pine laths were used, secured by lath nails. Sufficient painted lathing was recovered in the reconstruction of Mary Somerville's house, Edinburgh, to permit reconstruction of the ceiling, which, when photographed at various stages, showed the method of lathing.[53] The laths were hand-split with the grain of the wood, but during the late nineteenth century increasing use was made of expanded metal lathing which met building bye-laws in a more satisfactory way.

Sir Balthazar Gerbier, in his *Counsel and Advice to all Builders* (1663), has this to say about laths:

> 'One hundred of Lathes will cover six yards of seeling, and lathing is worth six pence the yard, one hundred of Lime will lay ten or twelve hundred of Lathes . . .
>
> One Tun of Playster of Paris will lay twenty nine yards of Lath, work, three quarters of an Inch thick . . .'

The eighteenth-century plasterer Isaac Mansfield charged in 1733-4 at the rate of 2s 2d a yard for finishing on fir laths and 2s 6d yard for work on oak laths;[54] the latter were more durable and somewhat more expensive to obtain.

Stucco

In his *Lives of the Most Eminent Painters, Sculptors and Architects* (1550) Giorgio Vasari (1511-71), the Italian architect and painter, indicated a basic difference between plaster and stucco, namely the addition to slaked lime of marble dust instead of sand and hair. He writes:

> 'And wishing to demonstrate how stucco is mixed: you take small pieces of marble and powder them in a stone mortar. No other lime is used for this stucco save white lime made either from marble chips or travertine, and instead of sand the powdered marble is taken and is finely sifted and mixed in with the lime in the proportion of two parts of lime to one part of powdered marble. The mixture can be made coarser or finer according to the needs of the work being done.'

It was usual to make the stucco with a lime which had been tempered in water for several months prior to use. The lime then had to be dried, crushed and put through a fine sieve. The marble dust was then added, together with any other constituents, such as kaolin (china clay), lard, curdled milk, fig juice, or albumen, which 'fattened' the stucco, retarded its setting, and regulated shrinkage and cracking. Contemporary Swiss stucco-restorers with whom the present writer has talked say that the eighteenth-century stuccoists must have needed either to carry around with them the tubs containing the lime covered with water, or to be assured of a length of time on the site for the mixture to be well prepared. Support for this 'laying-down' of stucco is provided in one of the accounts for work by Thomas Clayton at Blair Castle, Perthshire, in 1748 (Plate 149):

> '. . . pay'd for takeing Stucco out of my Seller at Leath and Cary'ing it tow the Bote, 2s 6d'[55]

The stucco was moved from Leith near Edinburgh to Perth and stored at the house to await use by Clayton.

Armatures

Whilst ornament was cast solid in plaster without any reinforcement and in many cases still survives, the best work was strengthened with various forms of armature. Bess of Hardwick's accounts, as previously quoted, mention 'peeces of wood' to be nailed up in 1589 either as bracketting or for the small tree stems round which plaster was modelled in the forest work of the East Great Chamber at Hardwick. 'Three hundreth and a half' of nails were also provided for John Market in 1595 'to nayl up braddets for his cornish in yr galary. 11s. 1111d'.

In the baroque and rococo stucco-work of the Swiss churches of the Ticino, armatures of willow wood were used, and when *stuccatori* from this region came to England they modified this method, as at Sutton Scarsdale (1724) and Ditchley (1726) (Plate 52), and used wire and metal prongs or nails. These can be seen protruding from small, broken pieces at Ditchley and in clearer detail at the ruined house of Sutton Scarsdale, Derbyshire. The cartouches over the doors and over the fireplace have crumbled away to reveal the metal supports. In contemplating the smoothly flowing, sensuous relief figure of Diana shaped by Thomas Perritt and Joseph Rose, senior, at Nostell Priory, Yorkshire, in about 1745, it is difficult to realize that the raised leg is built on a wooden armature.[56] The Swiss *stuccatore* Giovanni Bagutti used the services of the Duke of Chandos's smith, Walter Husbands, in 1722. The latter's work presumably included the provision of metal armatures for the reclining figures of *putti* in the chapel at Cannons, now at Great Witley Church, Worcestershire. The life-size figures that Bagutti included in his work at such houses as Mereworth (frontispiece), Clandon and Moor Park (Plate 57) were also built on such frameworks.

In the early seventeenth century the large pendants which are a particular feature of Scottish plasterwork (Plate 122) were usually built around a wooden or metal core attached to the joists above. It was of course important to provide these supports, and Sir Roger Pratt constantly stressed that adequate brackets to hold the cornice and soffits be provided. During building at Kingston Lacy, Horseheath and Coleshill (Plate 24) in the 1660-70 period, Pratt had occasion to look carefully at the construction of ceilings. Brackets were provided at critical points and then they were lathed over and given two coats of plain plaster. This was smoothed and the various enrichments of the frieze or cornice cast in moulds and stuck on at the appropriate places. As the modillions were of some weight they were sometimes fastened with nails.[57] At Astley Hall, Chorley, (Plate 26) the plaster enrichments, dating from about 1666, are held by leather and lead strips.

Whilst plasterers learned about these methods of construction as part of their apprenticeship, they could also turn to the writings of Giorgio Vasari, who in his *Lives* (1550) gives stucco recipes and methods. He records that if work was required in bold relief the plasterer should fix nails or other suitable armature supports to hold the weight. When the job was a large, low relief he advocated that nails should be hammered in to the height required. This would hold the first rough coat of plaster, and while that coat was hardening work could proceed on finishing and smoothing of the whole.

Tools

In dealing with plasterwork over a long period it is inevitable that variations occur and prevent the description of a standard set of tools. We may start with the description of the tools given in Joseph Moxon's *Mechanick Exercises* (1703 edition). The illustration given by Moxon is reproduced here, but there were many common tools used also by bricklayers and tilers. Moxon lists ten main tools in use by plasterers: the numbers at the beginning of each description are those used to identify the tools in Moxon's illustration. Sometimes a number is repeated, but careful reading of the text and the location of the particular tool in the illustration given at the end of each description should prevent confusion.

'1. *A Lathing Hammer being the same as before in tyling, with which the Laths are nailed on with its head, and with its Edge they cut them to any length, and likewise cut off any part of a Qurter, or Joyst, that sticks further out than the rest* [top left].

2. *A Laying Trowel, to lay the Lime and Hair withall upon the Laths, it being larger than a Brick Trowel, and fastned its handle in a different manner from the Brick Trowel* [centre].

3. *A Hawke, made of Wood about the bigness of a Square Trencher with a handle to hold it by, whereon the Lime and Hair being put, they take from it more or less as they please* [top left].

4. *A Setting Trowel, being less than the Laying Trowel, with which they finish the Plastering when it is almost dry, either by Trowelling and brishing it over with fair water, or else by laying a thin coat of fine stuffe made of clean Lime, and mixt with Hair without any Sand, and setting it, that is to say, Trowelling and brishing it* [top left].

5. *A small Pointing Trowel, to go into sharp Angles* [top centre].

6. *Brishes, of three sorts, viz. A Stock Brish, a Round Brish and a Pencil. With these Brishes they wet old walls before they mend them, and also brish over their new Plastering when they set, or finish it, and moreover white and size their Plastering with them. The Pencil, or Drawing Tool is used in blacking the bottoms, or lower parts of Rooms &c.* [top right].

7. *Floats, made of Wood, with handles to them, which they sometimes use to float Seelings or Walls with, when they are minded to make their Plastering very streight and even, these Floats being some larger and some lesser than the Laying Trowels. Likewise they use Floats made to fit to Mouldings, for the finishing of several sorts of Mouldings with finishing Morter to represent Stone, such as Cornices, Facias, Archytraves &c . . .* [top right].

8. *Streight Rules of several lengths, to lay Quines streight by, and also to try whether the Plastering be laid true and streight, by applying the Rules to their Work* [bottom right].

9. *A Pale, to hold Water, or Whitewash, or White and Size* [bottom right].

10. *Some use a Budget or Pocket to hang by their sides, to put their Nails in when they Lath, and others Tuck and tye up their Aprons, and put the Nails therein.*'

Moxon continues: 'Having given you a Description of the several Tools and uses, there are some things yet remaining, which tho' they cannot be properly called Tools, yet they are utensils, without which they cannot well perform their Work.' He then lists: ladders, fir poles for scaffolding and putlogs, or seven-foot pieces of timber which lie from the scaffolding poles into the brickwork and support the ten-foot fir boards, of one- or two-inch thickness. The cords which tied these various poles and

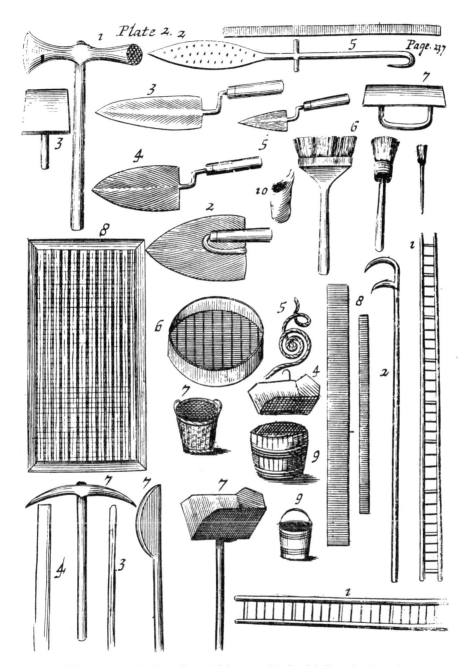

Plasterer's tools from Joseph Moxon's *Mechanick Exercises* (1703)

planks together were to be 'well pitched to preserve them from the weather, and rotting'. There were also sieves of several sorts 'to sift the Lime and Sand withal' and a 'loame-hook, beater, shovel, Pick Ax, Basket and Hod, which commonly belong to Bricklayers,

Labourers, and may be called the Labourers Tools'. A board and wire screen which acted as a larger sieve allowed the sand and rubbish to be separated from the lime.

In an inventory of Joseph Rose junior's workshops, made at his death in 1799 and used by the compilers of the sale catalogue[58] of his effects, the list of contents of the Coach House included:

'Lot 143   75 boards and 25 poles
  „ 144   ditto
  „ 145   ditto
  „ 148   4 crosses, 2 ladders, 4 tressels
  „ 149   ditto
  Lot 151   30 Poles, 7 doz Cords.'

In the house were 'brass drawing instruments, five foot rules, an instrument for drawing ovals, parallel scales, seven T squares and a pair of caliper compasses'.

By the nineteenth century scissors, screwdrivers, saws, folding-rules, spirit-levels, compasses, chisels, bradawls, plumb lines and pincers had increased the tool-kit to unwieldy proportions. In addition the skilled stuccoists always had large numbers of metal modelling tools with pencil- and wedge-shaped ends for making the lines and indentations needed in simulating human or animal features.[59]

Moulds

When Vasari wrote about moulds in the sixteenth century he described what was common throughout the following three centuries. Ornamental mouldings were made by making in reverse carved wood moulds, 'and some stucco which is semi-hard is beaten into the mould which has first been dusted with powdered marble. The stucco is beaten heavily until the ornament has been transferred to it when it is taken out and cleaned up. . . .'

Many plasterers made their own moulds but, from time to time, payments are found in house accounts to carpenters and blacksmiths for making moulds to precise measurements.[60] Samuel Pepys, on 10 February 1669, recorded in his diary the intricate business of the plasterers who cast heads and bodies in plaster. The frequent use of the same moulds, which in the sixteenth and seventeenth centuries were particularly expensive, made some identification of the plasterer a possibility; known through documentation to have worked at one house, he may be suspected at another by the use of the same moulds. This occurs frequently in Scotland and allows work at two houses to be credited to the same plasterer, James Murray. The use of identical medallions portraying Hector has been observed at Bromley-by-Bow, London, and Balcarres House. Other circular panels with heads of heroes, apparently cast from the same moulds, may be seen at Craigievar Castle, Aberdeenshire, Glamis Castle, Angus, and Merchiston Castle, Edinburgh.

The medallion heads at Towneley Hall, Lancashire (Plate 54) are known by documentation to be the work of Francesco Vassalli in 1729-30. Similar medallions of the same date appear at Mawley Hall (Plate 55), Lumley Castle (Plate 61) and in the Music Pavilion at Lancaster (Plate 63). It may reasonably be assumed that Vassalli worked at all three houses, and his work is noteworthy among that of the Swiss *stuccatori* for allowing almost certain identification by the use of a number of prominent motifs from common moulds. Thomas Perritt and Joseph Rose, senior, betray similar characteristics to Vassalli in their work at Temple Newsam House, Leeds, (Plates 76, 77) and Wentworth Woodhouse (Plate 97). Their use of medallions at houses which are documented as containing their work allows the plasterwork in the James Paine rooms at Nostell Priory (Plates 78-80), also in Yorkshire, to be attributed to them. Identical motifs also appear in the work in the Dining Room at Nostell Priory and at Ednam House, Kelso, Berwickshire. A letter of 30 April 1752, from William Windham to his agent shows that Rose incorporated four cast medallions of the seasons into his work at Felbrigg Hall, Norfolk. They still survive, frothed around with rococo embellishments.

For a mould designed to last and give repeated good impressions boxwood was often used, but examples have been found in yew-wood, soft blackstone and various close-grained hardwoods, as well as iron, plaster, wax and gelatine. A series of wooden moulds used by William Brown at Powderham Castle, Devon (Plate 87), in the 1750s were sold in 1960.[61] Brown incised his name on one of them, as a valued possession. Joseph Rose junior's premises in Queen Anne Street East, London, included a Mould Room, in which he stored wax moulds and a quantity of plaster casts and 'basso relievos', together with Casting Rooms and a Wax Room. All the impedimenta of his trade were here—the vases, crests, medallions, masks, figures, griffens and paterae betokening his dominance in work in Neo-Classical style.[62] From about the 1750s, when Robert Wood issued his books on the ruins of Palmyra (1753) and Baalbec (1757), plasterers such as Thomas Clark and Rose moulded identical ornaments to those in the Temple of the Sun at Palmyra. At Norfolk House, Osterley, Drayton, Bowood, Milton Abbey and elsewhere this particular ornament was used, thus the architect's knowledge of sources[63] allowed him to set out a replica pattern for the plasterer to copy. Wax or boxwood moulds were used because they lasted longer than other kinds of moulds without drying out.[64]

Following the use of wax moulds in the later eighteenth century, gelatine moulds were introduced in the 1840s, an innovation claimed by Monsieur H. Vincent. Their flexibility was useful in casting statues and plaques, and several pieces produced by this method were shown at the Great Exhibition in 1851. The only limitation gelatine moulds imposed was that, unless well cared for, they became (unlike wax or wood) hard and brittle. The gelatine was, however, easily obtained from the bones, hides and hooves of animals, and fresh moulds could be created to last for only a few jobs before being melted down.

Methods of Work

There is little documentary evidence about methods of work in the past, but from observation of surviving plaster and conversations with restorers and plasterers some facts can be pieced together. It was common for plasterers at most periods to be capable of working with plaster and stucco. The journeys of Inigo Jones and others to Italy in the seventeenth century, however, meant that an impetus was given to stucco modelling in England. The *stucco-duro* of Italy was an ancient art and excellent examples still survive. The great frieze at Hardwick Hall, Derbyshire, (Plate 1) appears to have been modelled in lime-stucco with metal tools. The panels in the nearby ruins at the old Hardwick Hall have been open to the sky for many years, as have the later panels at Sutton Scarsdale. Yet their hardness and durability has allowed them to survive neglect and the weather. When they were originally modelled there is little doubt that the stuccoist used the most flexible of his tools—his fingers—to work up certain expressions and stances. The indentations of nostrils, ears and eyes would be incised with wooden and metal pencil-like tools. The whole figure would be modelled over armatures and supports. It is reasonable to assume that the considerations proposed in the 1660s by

Sir Roger Pratt (and in the eighteenth century by James Gibbs) were those which faced most architects and plasterers in planning a ceiling design. Pratt wrote[65] about types of Italian ceilings and recorded his views on the major aspects of the work involved in the design.

> 'Of the several frets and divisions for ceilings
> (1) Breadth of the Soffit   (2) The Ornament of it
> (3) The form of the panels   (4) The beautifying of them
> (5) design   (6) colouring   (7) Panels and Plaster'

The various processes and methods may best be understood if we take Pratt's headings for our own discussion.

1. The Soffit, which in strict architectural terms may be regarded as the underside of an arch, lintel, etc., was in this context the rib-like arrangement of rectangles and ovals which appear, in particular, on ceilings of the 1640-1730 period. Soffits are most noticeable in the Palladian buildings of Inigo Jones,[66] in Wren City churches, interiors of the 1660s (Sudbury, Plate 29) and in eighteenth-century Palladian interiors which often copied the Palladio and Jones versions, as set out in the architectural pattern-books. Their breadth and arrangement were determined by Classical precedent or by structural requirements (and sometimes by both together). There is reason to think that large, involved arrangements required the plaster to be laid over a wooden framework 'bracketed' to the joists.

2. The decoration of the soffit or ribs usually involved the application of moulded ornamentation. At first, the ceiling arrangements in Elizabethan and Jacobean houses only called for a moulded rib of shallow relief (Plates 9, 11, 15) with bosses at the intersections. By the 1660s, when Sir Roger Pratt was writing, fruit and flowers were simulated in individual moulds and set up in a pattern held together by flexible armatures. This was a common procedure until the turn of the eighteenth century. The Palladian revival initiated and encouraged by Lord Burlington, Colin Campbell and Giacomo Leoni advocated a return to a simple enrichment of the geometric arrangement of ribs. Gilding was re-introduced as an additional effect. The division of the ceiling by deeply moulded ribs (Plate 30) gradually ceased, helped along by the gay ornaments of a free-flowing rococo and chinoiserie taste (Plates 79, 83). Some return to division was possible, however, with the deep indentations and pendants of the Gothic style (Plates 101, 102) and the rigours of Neo-Classicism (Plates 105, 110).

3. The form of the panels of which most ceilings were composed was usually decided by prevailing and fashionable moods, the dimensions of the room, and most of all by the desire to copy ancient originals. We have noted that the publication in 1753 of Robert Wood's *The Ruins of Palmyra* brought about a revival of coffered ceilings with small panels disposed in the same way as in the early Temple of the Sun. The Hall at Holkham, Norfolk, plastered *c.* 1759 by Thomas Clark, was inspired by Palladio's plan of a Roman Basilica for Barbaro's *Vitruvius* of 1567. Robert Adam's own book of measured drawings of Diocletian's Palace at Spalato, published in 1764, provided other sources for plasterers to copy. Those engravings by his friend Piranesi were spirited attempts at recapturing something of Imperial Rome; the trophies reappear at Syon, copied from both Piranesi and Le Roy's book on the ruins of Greece.

The Forum of Trajan, the Vatican *loggie* and the seventeenth-century decoration in such places as the Farnese Gallery and the Villa Pamphili and Villa Madama provided further inspiration. The centre of the 1730 ceiling at Clandon Park, Surrey, is based on the representation of Hector and Iole by the Carracci in the Farnese Gallery.[67] The

Drawing Room ceiling at Hatchlands (Plate 103) is based on the panels of the dome at the Villa Pamphili,[68] and the coffered and arabesqued interiors of the Etruscan Dressing Room at Osterley are derived from the Villa Madama and elsewhere by way of Piranesi's *Diverse maniere d'adornare . . .* (1769).[69]

4. The beautifying of panels, as Sir Balthazar Gerbier recorded in his *Counsel and Advice to all Builders* (1663), with 'all the members inriched according to the moulds therewith' was therefore one entirely dictated by the desire to be surrounded by memories of this ancient and largely mythological past. In the rich derivative work of the Swiss *stuccatori* almost every god and goddess is lolling in chariots or being borne away on the frozen mists of incised modelled clouds. Guido Reni's picture of Aurora, created for the ceiling of the Casino attached to the great palace which was then being built by the Borghese family on the Quirinal, was to become only one of many popular subjects for beautifying panels (and later Regency mirrors).

5. The design of these panels was therefore a more or less faithful version of some original picture—Vassalli's panel over the Hall fireplace at Hagley Hall, Worcestershire (1758) is after a lost picture by Carlo Maratti—or a version derived by consultation from an architect's drawing. Those by Edward Goudge (Plates 37, 38), James Gibbs (Plate 51), James Paine (Plate 80), or Robert Adam (Plates 104, 106) show that across the seventeenth and eighteenth centuries the main responsibility for laying out the ceiling plan and suggesting the arrangement in broad outline was the architect's or, as in the case of Goudge, the plasterer's, whose drawing (Plate 38) was then 'allowed' by William Winde as architect. Goudge was also capable of making all his own designs and based some of these on sources such as the 1676 English edition of Le Pautre's engravings,[70] entitled *A New Book of Fries Work*.

The relationship between sources and the final design is a close one, if at times difficult to untangle. A vast repertory of engraved designs by such masters as Francis Barlow, (engraved by Hollar, Plate 45), Gaetano Brunetti and Grignion was available to most plasterers. The Swiss stuccoist Francesco Vassalli wrote to Richard Towneley on 7 December 1730, claiming that 'since I have been in Italy, it is in my power to satisfy you more than I could have done before I returned into Italy . . .',[71] an allusion presumably to his obtaining ideas and engravings there to improve his design. A comparison of the designs for stucco-work in southern Germany and elsewhere[72] also provides many motifs discernible in English designs of the same period.

6. Plasterwork, with a few Elizabethan and Jacobean exceptions, was usually finished white or off-white throughout the sixteenth and seventeenth centuries. In the eighteenth century this practice continued until about 1760, with the occasional addition of gilding, as in the Temple of the Four Winds at Castle Howard, decorated in 1736, and possibly with the use of colour, as revealed by the recent restoration work at Clandon Park, Surrey, originally stuccoed in 1730. When the Dining Room from Kirtlington, Oxford-shire, (Plates 72, 73) was re-erected at the Metropolitan Museum, New York, in 1955 a microscopic examination was made of cross-sections of paint taken from various parts of the plasterwork and woodwork. The examination showed that the room, a construction of about 1745, had originally been painted throughout in a soft off-white, and this seems to have been common in the Ticino areas of Switzerland from which most of the *stucca-tori* working at Clandon, Kirtlington and elsewhere came. This, therefore, was the normal practice and one which, in the absence of precise documentary information—paint 'scrapes' are far from infallible—should be followed in restorations of period plasterwork.

After the introduction of complete decorative schemes by Robert Adam, Sir William Chambers and James Wyatt from about 1760 onwards, colour became more apparent.

The extensive series of Adam drawings at the Soane Museum are the best guide to what was allowable. In addition, the advice of Sir William Chambers in May 1770, to Gilbert Mason, a merchant at Leith, is worth quoting. In 'regard to the painting your Parlours,' he writes, 'if they are for Common use Stone Colour will last best & is Cheapest but if you mean them to be very neat pea green & white, Buff Colour & white, or pearl or what is called paris Gray and white is the Handsomest'.[73]

The Drawing Room from Lansdowne House, re-erected in the Philadelphia Museum of Art, was originally designed by Robert Adam in 1767. His drawing[74] shows a light green background with gold and green arabesques. The flowers are coloured and arranged in darker circles within cream diamonds. The background of the rest of the ceiling is not coloured and the decorations are in gold, green, blue and brown, with gilded mouldings. Adam's design for a ceiling for Sir Abraham Hume at Wormleybury, Hertfordshire,[75] indicates a return to the use of white ornamentation on a pale green background, brighter colours being used for the carpet designed for the room.

In the early nineteenth century, in addition to using colourful heraldry, the plasterer Francis Bernasconi was leading the way back to the austere lines of Gothic architecture (Plate 156). From the 1830s, however, spurred on by the polychromatic decoration of the Houses of Parliament, and guided by such patrons as John Talbot, Earl of Shrewsbury, gilded screens, Minton tiles, coloured and glazed brick and terracotta usurped the plasterer's art. This led to the great wealth of craftsmanship and colour displayed at Cardiff Castle and elsewhere by architects such as William Burges. He provided some of the most colourful interiors of the Gothic Revival.

In concluding his seven divisions Pratt wrote of 'Panels of Plaster'. He indicated that 'the way of finishing the curious part of them is generally this: first there is a boy who serves you with the enrichments; secondly a sticker, thirdly a cleanser'. This suggests the arrangement whereby the sticker stood on a scaffold near the ceiling and was served with individually moulded enrichments by the boy. The cleanser followed over the work with modelling tools making final adjustments to the pattern as the plaster or stucco slowly set. Various additions to the recipe and wetting the surface retarded this setting time.

Whilst a successful Neo-Classical plasterer such as Joseph Rose, junior, did much of his work from moulds in the 1760-90 period, he did also have to send men to work *in situ* by hand. Rose's letters of 1793-7[76] addressed to Lord Belmore at Castlecoole show his difficulties in persuading the 'ornament men' to cross to Ireland because of their fear of being press-ganged. He therefore suggested on 2 July 1793, that he get some part of the work modelled in London under his inspection. By March 1795, he was ready with eight packing cases containing the casts and moulds for the capitals and frieze in the Saloon. A man who was to do the parts 'that must be done by hand on the Ceilings' was sent over to work under the supervision of Rose's man, Richard Shires. Much of this work would involve the setting of moulded ornament in place and the trimming of excess plaster away to give sharp impressions. The Rose firm also used papier-mâché ornaments.

Guilds, Apprentices and Craftsmen

The art and mystery of plasterwork was kept going by men trained by apprenticeship. The requirements, however, for all trades did not show much divergence and a general statement will suffice. The system allowed masters to take apprentices for instruction for periods of seven to eight years. The vigour of the local centres may be indicated by the high number of 2,659 apprentices in all trades in the City of York in the late seventeenth century.[77] At Durham the various trade guilds also occupied an important part in the social life of the city. During the time of the seven-year apprenticeship the master taught the trade and set an example of good workmanship. When the apprenticeship was finished the test work was carefully examined by representatives of the company. Then, at three successive meetings, the apprentice was 'called'; if no one objected to his election he was sworn in as a member of his guild before the mayor at the borough court in Durham.[78]

The ordinances of most guilds were very similar. Those at Durham and York gave guidance on the regulations to which a master needed to adhere. He was not to absent himself from guild meetings, and he was to see that apprentice indentures were available to the guild's 'searchers'. He could be put out of his occupation and forbidden for ever to work within the city if he took 'any goods out of any good man or woman's place'. No master was to take any apprentice until he had been a freeman or brother of the 'mystery' himself for seven years, and thereafter he was not to take apprentices for a shorter term than seven years. There were also fines for default in workmanship or for the use of inferior materials. Although it could be said that the system was based on the rigid supervision of men and work, a great deal depended on the integrity of the guild officers. The seventh injunction, also followed in most London companies, 'not to have any more Apprentices but two', seems to have been observed. The overall effect was to limit, by conservative and safe approach, the capacity of business, to expand and become more efficient.

Rebuilding after the Great Fire of London in 1666 focused attention on the restrictive attitudes of the trade guilds. It was hopeless to expect that the City could be rebuilt solely by freemen of the City. It was necessary to allow all tradesmen from whatever part to work 'for the space of seven years next ensuing and enjoy the same liberty as the freemen of the City'. The monopoly of the trade guilds was broken and craftsmen of all kinds could flock to London and seek work. Master masons came from Taynton and Burford, the quarry districts of Oxfordshire, and the Isle of Portland. By 1670 the building trades complained that foreigners had come in from all parts of the kingdom. As well as the Plasterers', the Carpenters', Masons', Bricklayers' and Joiners' Companies presented a joint petition against foreigners working on the rebuilding without the necessary qualifications of apprenticeship. They also squabbled among themselves, and by 1672 the old quarrels about the allocation of tasks between joiner and carpenter had broken out again.

The official policy of expanding English trade led, however, to tolerant naturalization orders. All the protests went unheeded. Even the powerful Goldsmiths' Company could do little about the inrush of Huguenot goldsmiths leaving the Continent after the revocation of the Edict of Nantes in 1685. In the twenty-five years before 1710 some 120 French goldsmiths came to London. The new styles and engravings they brought with them fitted alongside the growing acceptance by English craftsmen of pattern-books and practical manuals of all kinds.

In 1700 Joseph Moxon, author of a number of such books and in particular *Mechanick Exercises*, a book applied to a number of trades, suggested that tradesmen should study architectural books. He listed a number he considered suitable, '*Sebastion Serlio* in Folio, Hans Bloom's *Five Collumns* in Folio, Sir Henry Wotton's *Element's of Architecture*', as well as Palladio and Vignola. With this sort of reading he pronounced that there would soon be more 'master-workmen that will contrive a Building, and draw the Design thereof, as well, and as curiously as most Surveyors: especially those Workmen who understand that Theorick part of Building, as well as the Practick'.[79] There is no doubt that whilst foreign competition was disliked by English craftsmen they would have to come to terms with it. We shall be able to see later in this study the increasing number of, in particular, decorative painters who came to England in 1710 to try their luck in the competition to select the artist who would decorate the dome of St Paul's Cathedral. The rivalry in all areas of activity taught British craftsmen to be competitive and to learn from example. They had to learn how to carve with dexterity in soft-wood and pin the work together in trophies and swags, how to manage the hard-setting Italian stucco or the niceties of rustication on stonework, the cutting and dressing of brick and the veining and marbling of paint to simulate more exotic materials. The apprenticeship system covered only a small part of this; in retrospect we can see that foreign competition hastened forward the slow process of learning new tricks.

Some, however, doubted the ability of English craftsmen to improve themselves. In a long statement in *An Account of Architects and Architecture*, which John Evelyn appended in 1664 to his translation of Fréart's *Parallèle de l'Architecture*, he wrote that he thought English 'Mechanicks' were impatient of direction and unwilling to recognize faults:

> '... For let one find never so just a Fault with a *Workman*, be the same of what *Mystery* soever, immediately he shall reply, Sir, I do not come hither to be taught my *Trade*. I have served an Apprenticeship, and have wrought e'er now with *Gentlemen* that have been satisfied with my work ...'

Evelyn did go on to admit that the craftsmen 'when once they arrive to a thorough Inspection and Address in their trades they pargon [paragon], if not exceed even the most exquisite of other Countries ...', and that 'our Smiths and *Joiners*, they excel all other Nations whatsoever'.

Whilst the same could be said of a number of plasterers, the humble abilities of the majority of craftsmen were pin-pointed by Sir Christopher Wren. Writing in 1694 to the Treasurer of Christ's Hospital he indicated the fundamental weakness in English training:

> '... our English artists are dull enough at Inventions but when once a foreigne pattern is sett, they imitate soe well that commonly they exceed the originall ... this shows that our Natives want not a Genius but education in that which is the ffoundation of all Mechanick Arts, a practice in designing or drawing, to which everybody in Italy, France and the Low Countries pretends to more or less.'[80]

Wren's words were heeded by the school, at least, and Bernard Lens was appointed as drawing-master. It seems, however, improbable that English interior decoration would have produced much of true interest without further stimulus by travel abroad and by the arrival of foreign craftsmen in Britain.

CHAPTER III

Wrought with Plaster, 1500-1660

Some men will have their walls plastered,
some pargeted and white limed, some rough cast,
some pricked, some wrought with plaster of
Paris...

William Hormann, *Vulgaria*, 1519

ON 10 March 1501, Henry VII granted a charter to the Worshipful Company of
Plaisterers of London, and the art and mystery of plastering was given formal
recognition. Prior to this date plasterwork must be considered as a means of lining flat
walls with a durable surface. We know little of any decorative work other than pargetting,
and what there was inside houses took the form only of the simplest of mouldings and
motifs, not dependent on any fashionable style, engraving or pattern-book. The great
period of timber-building, with its splendid roofs and sombre, wainscoted rooms, gave
little opportunity for the plasterer to display his art, and it was not until the late years
of Henry's reign that he became more important. What painted decoration there was
at this time has been shown to have been applied to wooden rather than plaster surfaces
or, as at Eton College Chapel in 1486, direct to the stone.[81] This was a situation which
by its limitation is seen in stronger contrast to that in Italy where firm traditions of
working the finer stucco had evolved. With the beginning of the sixteenth century and
the careers of Bramante, Michelangelo, Raphael and others fermenting into activity,
there was room for a revival of the techniques of modelled stucco in the decoration of
the great villas of the Renaissance.

The fine and informed taste which prevailed in the Medici Court in Florence led to
the grander scope of the Roman period of the High Renaissance under the pontificate
of Julius II, patron of Bramante, Michelangelo and Raphael. The Florentines again held
sway at Julius's death when one of their enlightened number, Cardinal Giovanni de'
Medici, a boyhood acquaintance of Michelangelo, acceded to the papal throne as Leo X.
The Vatican was filled with artists, musicians and performers of all kinds and the peace-
able pontiff encouraged a new interest in the Classical world. It sparked off feverish
excavations among the ruins, and Pope Leo put Raphael in charge of the search for the
buried remains of ancient Rome. In the excavation of the Golden House of Nero and the
Roman *thermae* they found not only rooms decorated in grotesque style but also many
modelled decorations in a hard, white stucco. Raphael's assistant Giovanni Battista da
Udine set himself the task of discovering the secrets of the stucco composition. Grotesques,
festoons, mythological scenes, heraldic weapons and trophies then appeared in paint and
stucco on many villa walls and principally in Raphael's *loggie* in the Vatican and in the
Villa Madama. Erected as the dream and passion of the Pope's relative, Giulio de' Medici,
the Villa Madama contains supreme achievements in paint and stucco, most of which
were completed by 1525. In magisterial terms Giorgio Vasari recorded in his *Lives*
(1550) that 'He [Giovanni da Udine] painted and worked all the stuccoes of the loggia
in the "vineyard" of Cardinal Giulio under Monte Mario...'. His work was completed
by the inventive and masterly grotesques of Giulio Romano, Giovanni Francesco Penni
and Baldassare Peruzzi.[82]

From the Udine workshops in Florence stuccoists left for Venice and, at the request
of Francis I, who was then decorating the new palace at Fontainebleau, for France. At

once the rivalry and vanity which existed between Francis I and Henry VIII came into sharp focus. With John Brown's painted decorations in his temporary Banqueting Hall Henry had sought to dazzle the French court at The Field of the Cloth of Gold in 1520. Soon after 3 June in that year the Governor of Genoa received a letter from his diplomatic representative Gioan Joachino, who wrote of a strange, extravagant building soon destined for ruin. 'Could I', he wrote, 'describe the fortress house raised at Guisnes by the King of England for his banquet you would be more delighted to behold such a structure, built to last a day and no longer. It appears to be that which it is not, and it is that which it does not appear to be.' By sunset its organ and fountains were silent, its brick-decorated cloth awnings in folded subjection. As far as we know it contained no stucco decoration, but what it did express was the distilled essence of rivalry, of attempts to outbid and impress, which enabled foreign decorative influences, such as those in stucco, to enter England in all their attractive variety. The Renaissance element, although a late arrival, was now to be reckoned with, but the Gothic style persisted in England.

When Henry VII died, his will ordered images of himself and his Queen in 'copure and gilt' to be carved and placed in the chapel of his name in Westminster Abbey. But his successor, wishing as we have seen to patronize Italian craftsmen, as Francis I was doing in France, brought over two sculptors in quick succession and accepted the design of 'Peter the Florentine', Pietro Torrigiano. At the same time encouragement was being given to Italian painters and workers by Cardinal Wolsey at Hampton Court. Here, on a site he acquired in 1514, the cardinal planned a house which was to declare his eventual position as Archbishop of York and later as a Cardinal and Lord Chancellor of England. Neither he nor much of his house survived his downfall in 1529 and the forfeiture of all his lands and goods. The only room at Hampton Court which now gives an idea of what the palace was like when the French ambassador and his vast retinue of 400 were entertained there in 1527 is Wolsey's Closet (Plate 4). The frieze above the wainscoting and the painted panels bear Wolsey's motto *Dominus michi adjutor* in composition ornament simulating stucco, and, above, dolphins, vases, mermen and mermaids surround rosettes, Prince of Wales's feathers and Tudor roses. With most of these the ceiling is elaborately panelled between low relief ribs of three-inch width.

It has been a popular theory to credit the work to Italians working for Wolsey. As he was in residence from 1514 to 1526 the work has been dated to 1525,[83] but it has also been pointed out[84] that the presence on cornice and ceiling of the Prince of Wales's feather encircled by a coronet might bring the work into line with a date later than 1537, when Prince Edward was born in the palace.

As the visual evidence presented by plasterwork of this early date is conflicting, it is necessary to remember that such problems always surround the dating of plasterwork. The long life of the moulds and the expense of creating new ones were inhibiting factors to the creation of new designs. The work of the Plaisterers' Company, however, went on, and among their Charters and Ordinances[85] is an illuminated genealogical tree which contains portraits of Henry VII, Henry VIII, shown as a youth in Milanese armour, with his sword pointed upwards, Edward VI, Mary and Elizabeth I. The rhyme which accompanies it records the help of the 'Fyve worthy Princes' and tells of 'Henry, the eight' that 'he is renowned farr, and neare'. Some of this fame is due to the other major task with which Henry VIII concerned himself, and which he saw partly completed before his death: the grand conception of Nonsuch Palace. It was planned by Nicholas Bellin of Modena,[86] who acted as adviser to the chief officers of the king's works, and no effort was spared to make it grand and enduring. The outside walls of the Inner Court were covered with moulded stucco panels. During the excavations at Nonsuch in 1959, thousands of fragments of these panels were found (Plates 2, 3). Two inches in thickness and showing the impression of wood-grain, it is surmised that they were moulded *in situ* with a backing sheet of planks and dowels and with armatures inserted to assist the adhesion of the relief parts of the designs. John Evelyn saw the panels on 3 January 1666, when he visited Nonsuch:

'I supped in Nonsuch House . . . at my good friend's Mr Packer's and took an exact view of the plaster statues and bass-relievos inserted betwixt the timbers and puncheons of the outside walls of the Court; which must needs have been the work of some celebrated Italian. I much admired how they had lasted so well and entire since the time of Henry VIII, exposed as they are to the air; and pity it is that they are not taken out and preserved in some dry place; a gallery would become them. There are some mezzo-relievos as big as the life; the story is of the Heathen Gods, emblems, compartments, etc. . . .'[87]

The riches of the stucco-work at Fontainebleau were an obvious inspiration to the workers at Nonsuch. Among the modellers who had gone to work in France in 1531 was Primaticcio, fresh from training in the workshop of Giulio Romano. He worked at Fontainebleau for forty years and his activity and example were soon to inspire emulation at Nonsuch. The surviving accounts, however, only contain the names of William Kendall and Giles Gering, who lead a team of twenty-four mould-makers in 1541, in which year the Inner Court at Nonsuch was probably finished.[88] The one important omission from this list is the name of the painter and *stuccatore* Nicolo Bellin of Modena who had worked under Primaticcio at Fontainebleau. He provided the link whereby the Renaissance style, in all its jumble of Italian and French pattern, transferred to England. There was at Nonsuch, however, much that was straightforward Tudor Gothic in style, even if a sight of Bellin's carved and gilded panels of slate, which covered the timber framework between the stucco panels, would have led one to think of 'the perfection of Roman antiquity'. In this phrase the many statues and casts at Nonsuch were described by Paul Hentzner, a German traveller who visited the palace in 1598.[89]

That the Italian influence had also come to interest provincial patrons is evidenced by the loggia at Horton Court, Gloucestershire, built in 1521 for William Knight and containing four stucco heads of Roman emperors set high on the inner wall. The loggia looks onward to the time when the big houses of Elizabethan and Jacobean venturers incorporated not only Renaissance ideas of symmetry but also—as at Hatfield, Charlton and Bramshill—the well-proportioned loggias that suggested the white stucco and rich, grotesque painting of villas under a hot Italian sun.

It was not far to the next step—the appearance of houses, such as Longleat, with four symmetrical fronts, and the repertory for the plasterer could now include the strapwork ornamentation that Rosso Fiorentino took as an idea from Italy to incorporate in his Gallery at Fontainebleau in 1535. Before long the Fleming Cornelis Floris was filling the pages of his pattern-books with interlaced strapwork, and the Elizabethans prepared to abandon themselves to a riot of robust and vulgar styles. These compounded together might lightly be regarded as an individual expression of Mannerism,[90] but a self-conscious interest in Late Gothic Perpendicular persisted, and this does much to counter the belief that everything odd at this time must, in consequence, be labelled 'Mannerist'.[91] In an assessment of the building and decoration of the sixteenth century it is as much the vanished houses, or those ruins such as Kirby or Hardwick Old Hall, which leave the period without precise outlines—the obscurity of the Elizabethan silence.[92] By its severance from Rome, England could boast few 'gorgeous, sumptuous superfluous buildings', despite all the opportunities which the decoration of such houses gave to artists intent on furthering their skills. One which did was Longleat, but even here we are not exactly sure that one of the first of the English plasterers, Charles Williams (who, as he testifies, had travelled to Italy and would therefore have learned the mystery of stucco), was employed. It has often been assumed he was the 'connyng plaisterer' referred to in a letter from Sir William Cavendish to John Thynne. The text of parts of three letters[93] at Longleat explains the matter. In one, Williams writes to Sir John Thynne, then building at Longleat. His undated letter is endorsed 'August 1547'.

> 'In his right humble wise shewyth & wisshi the encrease of dayly wourship unto youre good mastershipp Youre faithfull Oratour Charles Williams of this his natyve contrey of Englonde That where as the same yo[r] Oratour hath travayled the contrey of Italy as far as Cissill which is beyonde Roome above three hundreth myles knowing the most parte of all the nottable Citties there That is to say Myssina, Calabria, Napulls, Roome, Florence, Bolonia, Farrara, Padooa, Venice, Verona, Bresse and Mylan, besydes many other goodly townes and castelles There contynuyng in the long the space of XII yeres, Where was constrayned to learne these Qualities following:
>
>> Imprimis, A maker of Gally disshis and pavements for the same, after the maner of Italye: And also can make style glasses, fynally can bothe paynt and also wryt bothe the maner of Italye, and this said realme of Englonde.
>
> The whiche said Oratour have thought hit good in his foresaid most humble wise, to desire youre mastershipes favour at the contemplacion hereof, or the premisses to be tenderly considered that is to saye to receave the same your Oratour to your service, or elles to preferr him unto the right honorable Lorde Protector, for the whiche so doyng youre said poure Orator shall daylie pray to all mightie God, for yor contynuall healthe and dayley worshippe long to endure.
>
> To the right worshipful S[r] John Thynne.'

Apart from this letter from Williams there are two letters from Sir William Cavendish and his wife 'Bess of Hardwick'. Sir William wrote on 30 March 1554 or 1555:

> '... Sir I understand that you have a connyng plaisterer at Longlete w[h] haith in your hall and in other places of your house made dyverse pendaunts and other prettye thynges.[94] Yf yo[r] busynes be at an ende or will by the next sommer after this that comyth in I woold pray you that I myght have hym in to Darbyshere for my hall is yet onmade. And therefore nowe myght he devyse with my own carpenter howe he shuld frame the same, that it myght serve for his worke...'

At the time when Bess wrote her letter, on 25 April 1560, Sir William had died, a fact which she had momentarily forgotten since she signed the letter 'Elizabeth Cavendysshe', which she then corrected with the surname of her next husband, Sir William St Loe.

> 'After my very hertie comendations... Thies are even to desire you to spare me your plaisterer that flowered your halle whom I wold gladly have furthwith to be sent either to my howse at Chattesworthe whiche way Mr Hyde can instruct hym or elles to London that I may sende him downe with all spede myselfe... I pray you yf your man can not be had to spede me yet some oother where wherein you

shall doo me great pleasure for that my howse is much imperfit in that respect and lacks mete men for the same . . .

    From Bromham the XXVth day of Aprill 1560.

Your assuryd frende

seynt Lo

Elyzabeth ~~Cavendyssche~~'

This would be for work at the Elizabethan Chatsworth, of which 'no vestige . . . has ever been discovered'.[95] In conception it was far from the Italian work at Nonsuch, but this cannot be said about work at Loseley, Surrey. The fireplace there, dating from 1562-8 (Plate 5), was probably copied from one at Nonsuch and was probably 'even executed by one of the Nonsuch stucco-workers perhaps from a design by Bellin of Modena'.[96]

Apart from the Hardwick accounts and those for the King's Works, records citing payments to plasterers in the Elizabethan period are scarce. The agreement[97] for plastering at Lady Sheffield's house near Blackfriars Bridge in 1576 shows that Ralph Belle, Richard Brigge and Thomas Brown 'citizens and playsterers of London' were in the usual way working with 'lyme and haire' and were to receive £27 for their work in two instalments of £13 10s 0d. It was a small, typical transaction the exact nature and appearance of which has long been lost to us.

One of the best ceilings of this date to survive is that at Sizergh Castle, Westmorland. In reproduction it is seen above the Inlaid Room which was removed from the castle to the Victoria and Albert Museum in 1891. The room is dated about 1575 and the design of the frieze and ceiling is based on the repetition of the demi-figure of a winged cherub and shallow ribs in a geometrical pattern interspersed with goats and stags, heraldic shields, and intertwined acorns.[98] The decoration we have noted at Loseley is copied at many houses[99] but with less detail. Shallow decoration, the royal coat-of-arms and the 'E.R.' initials appear. At Gwydir Castle, Caernarvonshire, the overmantel plasterwork of figures and heraldry bears the date 1597 and at Plas Mawr in the same county caryatid figures are surmounted by the date 1580. After about 1620, dates are rarely encountered as part of a relief decoration. A return to the rich decoration of Loseley is encountered at South Wraxall Manor, Wiltshire, with its vaulted ceilings of about 1590 and a great fireplace bearing figures representing Prudence, Justice, Geometry and Arithmetic, and at Stockton House in the same county, with plasterwork dating from about 1600.

Much of this work would be by plasterers trained by members of the London Company. They had gone from strength to strength and on 10 February 1597, Queen Elizabeth had granted them a confirmation charter.[100] It must have gladdened the hearts of John Jackson (the Master), Hugh Capp (the elder warden), and Patrick Browne (the younger warden) to be able to enter the words 'her Maties Ltrs Pattents' into their Charter and Ordinance Book. Throughout the Elizabethan period, however, the one problem which the plasterers continually had to face was intervention with their normal tasks by bricklayers and tylers. Entered in the back of the same ordinance book is the account of the 'settlement of dispute between Companies of the Bricklaiers & Tylers, and Plaisterers by Lord Mayor & Court of Alderman meeting at Guildhall' 3 March 1579. It was agreed that:

> 'The Bricklayers unlett yt bee in the Queen's Works and upon tiling.
> The Bricklayers not to meddle in any wise with haire. Can rough cast, pargett walls with Lyme & Sand so that it be without haire. And that it shal be further Lawfull for them to pargett all chymneys both within & without.'

These elaborate instructions continue for many pages, but in essence what was decided was that if 'the owner will have the same done with Lyme and hayre, Then the Playsterers to doe the same. And if he minde to have it done with Lime and Sande Then the Brick-layers to do it . . .'. The matter was still giving trouble as late as 1613 when, on 1 June 1613, the plasterers petitioned that 'the Bricklayers doe dailie practice . . . the proper and peculiar Labor and worke belonginge to the said Plaisterers to the defraudinge and inconvenience of his Maties subjectes . . .'. Such disputes, however, were not usually encountered by the City of London plasterers only.

One of the best documented of the late Elizabethan houses is Hardwick Hall, Derby-shire, the creation of the much-married Elizabeth, Countess of Shrewsbury—'Bess of Hardwick'—and her architect Robert Smythson.[101] Born in 1520 at Hardwick, Bess was married by the age of twelve to the young squire Robert Barley, but greater wealth came when she married Sir William Cavendish in 1547. With the money he obtained as one of the Commissioners for the Dissolution of the Monasteries she had the means to build the old Chatsworth, and as an accomplished needlewoman she sketched it out in an embroidery which survives at Hardwick. In 1557 Sir William died and after a short widowhood Bess donned her marriage robes again to marry the Grand Butler of England, Sir William St Loe. We have already noted their employment of the 'Longleat plasterer' at Chatsworth, but Sir William lived but a short time to enjoy the results. Three years after his death in 1565 Bess married George Talbot, Earl of Shrewsbury, a statesman of great influence and the custodian, soon after their wedding, of Mary, Queen of Scots. This charming but sad ward may have been a partial source of the jealousy and quarrelling in which Bess and her husband indulged. In 1584 she left him and once again the manor house in which she had been born became her home. Inevitably the building craze returned and she began to build a new house at Hardwick. Lord Shrewsbury's death in 1590 left her mistress of an ample fortune and an undiminished urge to build.

The first mentions of plasterwork in the accounts[102] include work for the old Hardwick Hall which lies near to the present building. On 26 May 1579, 'Jhon, plasterer' was paid money for 'the plasterer that he brought with him frm Kenelworth, III wieks at Vd a day'. This must refer to Kenilworth Castle, which Queen Elizabeth had visited in 1575 and which contemporary accounts describe as 'a stately pallace . . .'. Two plasterers working at Hardwick came to occupy prominent positions—Abraham Smith and James Hindle. The latter was paid in 1587 for work 'with plaster and lyme and hare'. We have already noted Smith's 1581 agreement with the Countess. The plasterers named in the list of plasterers who worked at the house, some twenty-one in number, did so for between 4d and 6d a day as contrasted with the lump sum she paid to him. By October 1597, Bess could move into the house and the old Hardwick slipped gradually into unhindered decay.

Smith's great hunting frieze in the High Great Chamber (Plates 1, 6) based on designs of the Flemish painters Martin de Vos and Nicholas de Bruyn, and the strapwork fire-place in the entrance hall, with its heraldry of life-size stag supporters and coronet-bedecked arms, ranks among the most spirited achievements of Elizabethan plasterwork. With his scaffolding, hurdles, rope, wicker-baskets, limestone burnt on the ground, and special white lime from Crich for whitewashing,[103] Smith was able to continue decorating and repairing the plasterwork at Hardwick until Bess died in 1608. He probably came locally from Ashford and it is recorded that in 1592 he had been given, 'against his wedding, xl.s' (£2). If a search could be continued beyond the registers of Ashford and Bakewell and if his name were more unusual and thus easier to trace, we might discover the burial-place of this master of his craft.

As the years of Elizabeth's reign rolled boisterously away, plasterwork became more complex. The date of each creation, however, was often recorded by figures inserted in a frieze or panel. The chimneypiece in the Long Gallery at Gawthorpe Hall, Lancashire, a simple affair when compared with the later chimneypieces in the dining and drawing rooms at Langleys, Essex, has the precise date of 1603 inserted into the design. The Langleys work can be dated only by stylistic features to about 1620. The appearance of books by Abraham de Bruyn (1584), Wendel Dietterlin (1598) and Jan Vredeman de Vries (1563) did much to increase a more sophisticated repertory of ideas, and an increasing use of Biblical themes, citations of tests and allusions to Classical knowledge became common. This is particularly apparent in the plasterwork at Boston Manor House, Middlesex (Plates 12, 14, 16). Built for the widow of Sir William Reade (a stepson of Sir Thomas Gresham) in 1622—the date appears on the heads of the rainwater pipes—the house had splendid plasterwork in the State Drawing Room and State Bedroom.

The plasterwork at these houses is unsurpassed both for these Classical allusions and for its overall richness. The Five Senses (Plate 16), the figures of Peace and Plenty, the strapwork, cartouches and coats-of-arms are interlaced with an assurance which heralded the increasing skills of plasterers. Some of this may be traced to the new mood of patrons who were following the ideas and journeys of the young Inigo Jones and the opportunity provided for new buildings. Some credit is also due to the knowledge imparted by the Elizabethan plasterers who had known the workers at Nonsuch or at least the manner in which they worked. Two of the most accomplished were Richard Dungan, who worked at Knole, the great house of the Sackvilles, and at the Tudor palace of Whitehall, and James Lee, who worked at Hatfield House.

It has sometimes been assumed[104] that the rich decorations of the state apartments at Knole (Plate 9) may date from the earldom of Richard Sackville who succeeded to the title in 1609. But much work was certainly initiated by his grandfather, Thomas, Earl of Dorset, Lord High Treasurer to James I. Thomas's account-book[105] records large payments to Richard Dungan from 1605 to 1607 for 'ffresse and plaistering work', the carriage of plaster of Paris and 'for fretts & other worke done at Knoll'. The flat interlaced ceilings above the painted staircase and in the Cartoon Gallery, the Ballroom, the King's Room and the Reynolds Room are surely his work. That Dungan was a very competent plasterer is shown by his employment, at about the same time (1606-9), at Whitehall Palace, where, charging at the rate of about seven shillings a yard he provided the ceiling in the Banqueting House for £303 6s 0d.[106]

James Lee worked on the great house which Robert Cecil, first Earl of Salisbury, built at Hatfield in Hertfordshire. Begun in 1607 the house was complete by 1612. Materials were assembled from many sources, including Italy, and French, Dutch and Italian artisans, in addition to hundreds of local labourers, gathered to embellish the house. Venetian craftsmen did a mosaic portrait of Cecil under instructions from the English ambassador, Sir Henry Wotton, and the carver John Bucke did screens for the hall and staircase. Lee's plaster ceilings have now disappeared, but a good deal of the panelling and joiner's work survives to indicate by its quality the standards expected of Lee and the other craftsmen.[107]

Although Knole still stands as an incomparable standard for plasterwork of the period, the unknown work in the panelled room from the Old Palace of Bromley-by-Bow, now in the Victoria and Albert Museum, is worth study.[108] The Bromley ceiling is planned in intersecting squares and quatrefoils, and eight pendants hang from the points of intersection. Circular medallions are surmounted by wreaths and winged cherubs' heads, and full-faced, bearded busts represent three of the Nine Heroes or Worthies. Each medallion, inscribed 'IOSUE. DUX', 'HECTOR. TRO' or 'ALEXANDER', is repeated twice. The centre quatrefoil has the shield of James I bearing the royal arms. A similar medallion to that of 'Hector. Tro', and with the same inscription, is found at Balcarres House, far away in Scotland. The Bromley work, which dates from 1606, may also be compared with the 1620 ceiling at the Vicarage, Tottenham, Middlesex,[109] a house built for a London barber-surgeon, Joseph Fenton,[110] and with the ceilings dated 1599 at Canonbury House, Islington. The geometrical arrangements are slightly different and other medallion heads appear, but the overall treatment allows comparison of the three.

The source of the design in the elaborate overmantel in the State Drawing Room at Boston Manor was identified in 1924[111] as one of the patterns of grotesque ornament engraved by Abraham de Bruyn (Plates 12, 14). The plasterer closely followed de Bruyn's decoration around the oval centre, but replaced de Bruyn's central scene of the rescue of Andromeda by Perseus with his own dramatic rendering of the story of the sacrifice of Isaac. The tablet below bears, instead of the name 'Andromeda', the words 'In the mount of the Lord it shal be seene'.

Modellers of the time also used herbals and emblem books. Geoffrey Whitney's *A Choice of Emblems*, issued in 1586, was an immediate success and was used as a basis for many kinds of decoration. The twenty-one panels in the long gallery at Blickling Hall, Norfolk (1620) are taken out of Henry Peacham's emblem book *Minerva Brittana or a Garden of heroical Devises . . .*, of 1612. Decoration in the gable ends of the gallery at Little Moreton Hall, Cheshire, rely on devices in Read's *Castle of Knowledge*, printed by Reynold Wolfe in 1556.

At Bolsover Castle, Derbyshire, the unusual plasterwork in the Star Chamber (Plate 15) has a central device which betokened the interest in another form of expression—the emotional poem printed in a diamond shape.[112] We also find at Bolsover and elsewhere the use of plaster called *glacis* as a durable paving for the floors of the rooms.[113] At Sheriff Hutton Park, Yorkshire,[114] John Burridge and Francis Gunby, plasterers from York, made diamond devices on the ceilings, and Burridge set his plaster foliage within the precise geometry of the ribs of the Bird and Baby Room and the Oak Parlour (*c.* 1620) (Plate 13). The human figure in stylized form joins the birds and beasts on the ceilings at Lanhydrock, Cornwall (Plate 17). Henry Peacham's recommended imitation of 'the Antique', which he defined as 'an unnatural or disorderly composition for delight's sake, of men, birds, fishes, flowers etc., without (as we say Rime or Reason), for the greater variety you show in your invention, the more you please' is well observed in this Cornish house, in a ceiling formerly at Emral Hall, Flintshire, a fantasy of men and beasts (Plate 18), and in a number of houses in the West Country. Some of those in the High Street at Barnstaple and Forde House in Devon are as interesting as any in Britain. Other similar work is at Heringston and Golden Farm, near Wiveliscombe, Somerset. Some of this work was probably by John and Richard Abbott, members of a family of Devon plasterers, whose descendant John Abbott II (1639-1727) inherited their ideas and put down a great variety of sketches in a notebook. This, together with some of John's tools, has survived[115] and gives a unique idea of the activity of a provincial plasterer and the influences which formed his style.

At Lanhydrock, Cornwall, the twenty-four sections of the Long Gallery ceiling (Plate 17) illustrate events in the history of the Old Testament, from the Creation to the burial of Isaac. It was probably worked in about 1635, but no record of the exact date or the plasterer's name has survived. The pendants are unusual: small, sculptured figures are encased within a framework obviously built on metal armatures which terminate in a hook to support a lamp.

Pendants of this elaborate kind and date—a development from the flat medieval boss—can be seen at Rushton Hall and Canons Ashby, Northamptonshire, and are found extensively in Scotland. The succeeding years saw the pendant gradually decline in favour as a decorative motif. By the outbreak of the Civil Wars it had gone altogether. A late example may be seen at Nettlecombe Court, Somerset (*c.* 1645), and there are a few of eighteenth-century date, principally those in neo-Jacobean style at Audley End, Essex (Plate 101). They also reappeared in 'Jacobethan' work of the nineteenth century.

Styles and moods, however, could not continue in a ferment of activity while the Civil Wars were taking their toll.[116] We have already noted their effect on fortunes in Chapter I, and the inscription over the west door of Staunton Harold Church, Leicestershire, is indicative of the deep despair which gripped not only the Church but all men of vision and intellect at this time. Sir Robert Shirley did the 'best things in the worst time', and the resilience and brevity of memory gradually blurred over this period.

Building and decoration therefore went on apace at the cessation of the war. At Wilton, the Wiltshire home of the Earls of Pembroke and Montgomery, the Double Cube Room was 'largely, if not entirely executed during the Commonwealth'. Whilst the complex interior of Wilton[117] contains a vast amount of painted and carved decoration, the plasterer's work is less in evidence. His function was to provide the flat and coved surfaces on which Emmanuel de Critz and Edward Pierce painted the legend of Perseus. The rooms were redesigned by Inigo Jones and John Webb after a fire in 1647-8 caused, according to John Aubrey, 'by airing of the roomes'. In the small ceilings, such as that of the Little Ante-Room, an accomplished mood suggesting rococo, but shy as a too-early guest, emerges. A number of designs[118] for ceilings at Wilton survive and that illustrated here (Plate 19) is inscribed in the hand of John Webb 'for ye vault of ye Ceelings of ye Roomes East and West end, Wilton 1649'.[119] The plasterer is unknown. The work seems beyond the competence of many of the London plasterers of the day and bears no relationship to ceilings by Joseph Kinsman or John Grove, two of the best men of the 1650 period.

The elaborate plaster decoration at Forde Abbey, Dorset, (Plates 21, 23) is again by an unknown hand. Its author may be Richard or John Abbott but, compared with the ceilings of similar date at Coleshill (unfortunately destroyed by the fire of 1952), they show less assurance and knowledge of Classical precedent. It seems possible that the Coleshill ceilings were the work of the elder John Grove, whom Sir Roger Pratt employed at a slightly later date at Clarendon House, Piccadilly. Coleshill was designed by Pratt for his cousin George, 1650-62,[120] and its competence set the tone for fifty years.

Although Inigo Jones also gave advice about the building of Coleshill, and although a Palladian-style design by John Webb for a chimneypiece in the house exists in the Burlington-Devonshire Collection at the RIBA Library (iv, 2), the house was not derived from a form of Jones-Palladianism. A later owner, Sir Mark Pleydell, has recorded that 'Pratt and Jones were frequently here and Jones was also consulted about the ceiling'. There are similarities between this ceiling and that in the Queen's House at Greenwich, and touches of Italy could be discerned in the heads of Roman emperors[121] in the niches of the Hall and stiff swags and twenty shields in the cornice of the Saloon (Plate 24). The credit for the design of the interior, however, must go to Pratt, and it may be recalled that the death of Jones in 1652 and his association with so few grand interiors, Wilton apart, do little to encourage attribution in his direction. Close parallels can be seen with the essentially English ceilings at Thorpe Hall, Northamptonshire, a house designed between 1654 and 1656 by Peter Mills.[122] As a leading London architect, Mills was acquainted with Pratt, and he, Wren and Hugh May were appointed surveyors to supervise the rebuilding of London after the Great Fire of 1666.

There was still a stiffness in the plasterwork of this time, and the beasts, caryatid figures and emblazoned heraldic shields of these years betrayed a preoccupation with pattern-book and lineage. Whilst the influence of Pratt was encouraging a concern for Classicism, he was quick to point out that it was not necessary 'to proceede to a rash and foolish imitation' of Italian models. In any case, money was scarce because of the long rigours of the Civil War. John Webb received some commissions from Commonwealth leaders but regular work for the plasterers had to wait for the Restoration of the king and the return of the court from its exile abroad.

CHAPTER IV

The Beste Masters, 1660-1702

Mr Goudge will undoughtedly have a good deall of worke for hee is now looked on as the beste master in England in his profession.

Captain William Winde
to Lady Mary Bridgeman,
8 February 1690

IN the history of plasterwork decoration the period which commences with the accession of Charles II in 1660 and ends at the death of William III was remarkable for the way in which craftsmen threw off the stylistic rigours of the Jacobean age. In this the Office of Works played an important part, and an outline is given here of the work undertaken by the Master Plasterer and his colleagues. In addition to royal work—and some chronological overlap becomes necessary to follow Wren's work at St Paul's and Greenwich—the Surveyor-General was also busily engaged in building the City churches. Opportunities were also available to craftsmen for work in the great houses of discerning noblemen. The high decoration of the Italian and French painters favoured in these households provided a constant challenge to the plasterers. Firstly, however, there was need to put their affairs in order, and the Worshipful Company of Plaisterers, with a solemn inward look, declared:

'Whereas this Court taking notice of the great debts that now lyes upon this Company wch hath been occasioned by unnecessary expences upon large dynners . . . from this day forward there shal be noe more feasting at the Hall or any other place at the Companys Charge . . . July 1660. . . .'[123]

Apart from feasting, however, one problem which the upsurge of activity brought to the surface was bad workmanship. From vigilance undertaken on the Company's behalf 'the beste masters' emerged, but in October 1655, these attempts at improvement received a setback when the Master of the Company himself, Joseph Kinsman (the plasterer of the fine ceilings at Ham House, Surrey in 1637-8), was fined 5s 'for bad worke'.[124] Vigilance was also needed to ensure that plasterers did not take apprentices before their own apprenticeship of seven years was served, that they did not have more than two apprentices, and that they did not take the work away from carpenters. The restriction on the number of apprentices severely limited the effective growth of the trade and may have been one of the factors which led plasterers such as Edward Goudge and later Isaac Mansfield finally to end their trade. There were many insistent demands on a patron's money occasioned by war or the new vogue for decorative painting. As for the plasterer, he had to pay for his supplies of hair, lime and other materials with more promptness than he was paid for his fret-work ceilings. It was therefore useful to be in active employment, and work on the royal residences was in plenty, even if sometimes delayed. By 1657 the most able plasterer seemed to be John Grove, and the Worshipful Company appointed him as its Renter-Warden. Within seven years he was ready to seek and be given the post of Master Plasterer to the organization which controlled work for the king, the Office of Works. His letters patent were enrolled on 1 August 1660.[125]

The Office of Works

The history of the Office of Works, which prior to 1814 was solely concerned with the maintenance of the royal palaces, is in process of being written by a team of writers. Whilst some work has been published on parts of the medieval period, only brief statements have appeared about the organization after 1660. The manuscript sources are voluminous and have probably done much to deter any single author from attempting the task. It soon becomes apparent in examining these documents that to isolate all references to the plasterers is meaningless, unless some idea of the organization and building programmes in progress is given.

The Principal Officers

The three principal officers of the Office of Works were the Surveyor-General, the Deputy Surveyor-General and the Comptroller. They were backed up by a clerical staff, the Paymaster and his deputy, eight Master Craftsmen, and clerks of works and itinerant clerks to deal with each property. These officials gathered together huge teams of other craftsmen and labourers when needed. Such a position of importance as the Surveyor-General commanded caused it to be eagerly coveted by many aspirants. In May 1660, John Webb (1611-72) petitioned the king, and indicated that he could ably succeed the suspended Surveyor, John Embole. He had been brought up by Inigo Jones, had married Jones's niece, was one of the commissioners to regulate building in London and, at Jones's death in 1652, he had been left almost without a rival in the architectural field.

Webb, however, was not alone in looking for royal favour and Hugh May (1622-84) and Sir John Denham (1615-69) were equally anxious to be given the post of 'Surveyor-General of His Majesty's Works'. Webb thought little of Denham and, in a frankness typical of the age, larded his own petition with proposals to reorganize the Office of Works. But despite his protestations the post was given in June 1660, to Denham. Webb for his part prepared to slip into retirement, but one of Denham's first tasks was to appoint Hugh May as Paymaster of the Works. We shall see that the office of Surveyor-General was again to elude May at Denham's death in 1669.

In trying to obtain the Surveyor-Generalship, Webb had poured scorn on Denham's 'possible' ability in architecture, having perhaps in mind that he was rather a poet of some accomplishment. He forgot that Denham had lent the king money during the exile abroad. Denham for his part was not a Surveyor-General of great architectural ability, and there was a certain irony in the fact that he should decide not to dispense with Webb's ability and recalled him to design the Charles II building at Greenwich as part of a proposed palace for the king. By May 1664, Webb was being referred to as Denham's deputy, and in November 1666, he was placed in charge of the works at Greenwich Palace. After four years work under Denham, Webb again petitioned the king. Denham was in ill-health and about to appoint a Deputy Surveyor. Webb was concerned to press his case hard. But Denham recommended Christopher Wren, an active member of the Royal Society and a member of the commission appointed to supervise the rebuilding of London. When Denham died in March 1669, the natural successor to the post of Surveyor-General seemed to be Wren.

On 15 December 1668, the Court at Whitehall announced that it had made Wren Surveyor-General. Both Webb and May had been finally passed over for the leading post, but May was made Controller at Windsor Castle. Wren's post, confirmed by patent on 28 March 1669, was to bring him into close contact with the king and queen, the Privy Council, the Lords of the Treasury, and not least the Master Plasterer, in the person of John Grove.

Wren's forty-nine years as Surveyor-General were busy, and not always untroubled. Considerable problems of personal antagonism were created in June 1702, when William Talman was displaced as Comptroller by John Vanbrugh (1664-1726). In private practice Vanbrugh had already won the confidence of the 3rd Earl of Carlisle and ousted Talman in the earl's favour. Carlisle, as First Lord of the Treasury, was anxious to bestow honour on the architect who had provided him with such a noble plan for Castle Howard (Plate 47). He not only saw to Vanbrugh's appointment to the Office of Works but also made him Clarenceux Herald in the College of Arms. Vanbrugh was to remain as Comptroller of the Works until his death in 1726, but in 1716 he had needed to exercise some tact in being appointed Surveyor of the Works at Greenwich in place of the ageing Wren. From this time Wren could be held to be in retirement. Wren's deputy at St Paul's, the architect John James, also took over more responsibility at a time when Wren was excusing himself more and more from active participation in Works affairs.

This improvement in James's status made his colleague and rival Nicholas Hawksmoor jealous. Although Hawksmoor had been 'discovered' by the plasterer Edward Goudge working in Yorkshire and brought to Wren's attention, his abilities[126] had often been overlooked. He had certainly been appointed Secretary to the Board of Works in March 1715, and Wren had appointed him Clerk of the Works at Greenwich in 1689 against the superior claims of James. This time the positions were reversed.

But all eyes were turning now beyond the squabbles of Hawksmoor and James to the post of Surveyor-General. The tussle came when William Benson (1682-1754), a man of slight architectural and Parliamentary experience, decided he would like the post. He persuaded the Ministry of George I to appoint him; the strategies he deployed may be traced in the minute-books of the Office of Works and the Treasury. The thrust was clean and precise. Wren was supplanted, and as soon as Benson had taken office in April 1718, he appointed his brother Benjamin as Clerk of Works in place of the faithful Hawksmoor. The Scottish-born architect Colin Campbell was appointed Deputy Surveyor and Chief Clerk (Plate 70).

This was political jobbery at its worst, even if we ignore for a moment the real abilities of Campbell. Fortunately Benson's competence was not equal to the tasks he assumed, and after declaring certain buildings in and about the House of Lords to be in danger of collapse his abilities were soon checked. A Committee of the House proved his allegations to be wrong and the discredited Benson, censured also in a long letter from Wren, was relieved of his recently acquired post on 17 July 1719. Wren hoped now that he would be allowed to retire peacefully to his house in St James's Street, Westminster and the house which Queen Anne had granted to him on Hampton Court green. In travelling from Hampton to London he contracted a cold and died on 25 February 1723.

Benson's dismissal meant that Campbell had also gone into disgrace with his master. On 24 August 1719 Sir Thomas Hewitt, Surveyor-General of His Majesty's Woods and Forests was appointed as Surveyor-General of the Works. Sir John Vanbrugh (he had been knighted in September 1714), Nicholas Dubois and Grinling Gibbons, the successful Wood-Carver to the Crown, were made Commissioners on 10 October 1719. During the years from 1662, when exact procedures for the conduct of the Office of Works were formulated,[127] until its reorganization in 1715, these officers, in their varying degrees of importance, were in control of the activities of a large group of craftsmen, including the plasterers at work under the day-to-day supervision of the Master Plasterer.

The Master Plasterer

At Wren's succession as Surveyor-General in 1668 there was little need to replace any of the Master Craftsmen to the Crown whom Denham had appointed or reappointed in 1664.[128] When John Grove died in 1676 he was succeeded as Master Plasterer by his son John. The other Master Craftsmen were Edward Marshall (Master Mason), John Davenport (Master Carpenter), Thomas Kingwood (Master Joiner), Isaac Corner (Master Bricklayer), Thomas Bagley (Master Glazier), Henry Phillips (Master Sculptor), Peter Brent (Serjeant Plumber) and Robert Streeter, senior (Serjeant Painter). All of these posts were held for life against letters patent, unless the holder committed serious offences of fraud, treason or constant bad workmanship. The Master Glazier, Thomas Bagley, for example, had been in royal service since 1634. All that Wren decided to do was to draw up fresh contracts and to replace Denham's Comptroller, Francis Wetherid, by Hugh May.

The Master Plasterer John Grove, assisted by his son, was soon at work on Secretary Bennett's lodging, the queen's Privy Chamber and other royal works. They also found time, as we shall see, to work at Clarendon House and elsewhere for Sir Roger Pratt and for Wren. A long recital of names and payments and speculations about identity is easy to compile from the thick Works account-books, each of which measures some $16 \times 12 \times 6$ inches. What perhaps seems of greater use and interest is to give brief accounts of each of the major buildings at which Grove and his colleagues worked.

Official Projects

The royal properties which were maintained structurally by the Office of Works were those in Whitehall and Hampton Court. The Parliament buildings around Westminster and, within the Wren period, those buildings at Greenwich, Chelsea, Audley End, Newmarket and Kensington (from 1689) were also supervised.

Whitehall to 1685

Evelyn records in his diary for 27 October 1664, a conversation with Charles II when he had presented the king with copies of his translation of Fréart and his *Silva*. 'I presented him with both, and then laying it on the window-stool, he with his own hands, design'd to me the plot for the future building of Whitehall, together with the rooms of state and other particulars. . . .' A large number of seventeenth-century drawings for the Whitehall Palace have survived, for the notion of its creation had been cherished not only by Charles II, but also by his father. The drawings,[129] distributed between Worcester College, Oxford, Chatsworth and the British Museum, are firstly in the hand of John Webb and fall into two groups. They show that in the first scheme the palace was to be realized in accordance with Inigo Jones's ideas of the 1630s.[130] The second scheme was recast by Webb and moved away from Jones's conception. Charles I, however, did not live to build it, and when his son took up the idea, as related by Evelyn, only Jones's Banqueting House (1619-22), with its great wooden painted ceiling, had been completed, a fragment of a greater conception. It seems certain, however, that Wren, before working on the palace, informed himself what all the early ideas amounted to. He also had the continuity of the craftsmen, many of whom had worked for Jones, Denham and himself.[131]

The first volume of accounts of the Office of Works opens with payments for work at Whitehall and the Tower. John Grove, senior, was in charge of the plasterers and had under him John Martin, father of the proficient Edward Martin who was working at the Tower, and ten other master plasterers. It is interesting to note that 'George Dunstervile' was paid fifty shillings for twenty-two days work. He is presumably the plasterer who did much of the superb work at the Palace of Holyroodhouse in about 1676 (Plates 133, 134). It is work of a high order because it succeeds with the full-size representation of a human figure (Plate 136). These were not often introduced—even Grove had not yet done so—and Sir Roger Pratt had lamented that few workmen could be found to perform 'so great an undertaking'.

By 1669 Whitehall was the chief royal palace in London, a sprawling complex of buildings partly Tudor and partly Stuart in date. When the rebuilding was contemplated Wren made drawings, but only two of these, now at All Souls College, Oxford, have survived, and none of the work they represent was carried out. It was to be 1685-6 before Wren built a long, new wing for James II containing a suite of apartments for the queen, a Roman Catholic Chapel for his use, and some offices. Meanwhile Charles II had other work for the craftsmen under Wren's control.

Newmarket

In 1668 the king began to feel that a new King's House at Newmarket was necessary if he was to enjoy the royal sport of horse-racing there in any style or comfort. One of the first tasks which had faced Inigo Jones when he succeeded Simon Basil as Surveyor in 1615 was to enlarge the King's House there by a lodging for Charles, Prince of Wales. It is not certain that Wren himself had anything to do with the new House, which was erected by William Samwell (1628-76) in about 1668, but the craftsmen of the Works were employed there, and he must have had exact knowledge of its progress from the regular meetings held to authorize all accounts. At these meetings, however, the emphasis at this time was on the extensive works the craftsmen were conducting at Windsor Castle.

Windsor Castle

The antiquity of Windsor appealed to the king, and its dramatic siting on a hill-top afforded scenic and picturesque possibilities beyond those of any royal palace in England or in the France of his rival, Louis XIV. He had appointed Hugh May as Controller of Works at Windsor in 1673—perhaps to atone for the architect's understandable disappointment at Wren having been made Surveyor four years earlier. May rebuilt the block on the north side with brick with stone dressings and this contained most of the new state rooms. He was careful not to disturb the general character of the medieval buildings, but it was the interiors which were important. In the course of about nine years the king was to spend at least £190,000 on the new works, and under May's direction Antonio Verrio was to spread his frescoes across the plaster of twenty ceilings, three staircases, the chapel and the hall. Most of these decorations were swept away in the work Sir Jeffry Wyatville did about 1824 for George IV.[132]

The entrance to the royal apartments was made by two staircases named after the king and his queen. The Queen's Great Staircase was built first and stood in a painted hall. As the first grand painted staircase executed in Great Britain it must have had a tremendous visual impact on visitors entering from the low, columned vestibules. On its plastered walls Verrio painted the stories of Phaethon's sisters changing into trees and Cygnus being changed into a swan. Bronze statues heightened in umber and gold stood in niches and, in the dome far above, Apollo granted Phaethon permission to drive the fiery chariots of the sun. The King's Staircase was surrounded by a painted version of the 'Four Ages of the World' and the giants battled far overhead. Grove must have felt that no mere plasterer could equal such a great decorative scheme. The riches of the baroque churches of Rome, with their ceilings decorated with a riot of athletic *putti* garlanding each other with stucco festoons, were still far away from English plasterers' eyes.

The joiner and plasterer were required at Windsor mostly to provide coved ceilings. This allowed Verrio and his assistants to paint the ceilings and sweep them down towards the walls as an extension of the room space. It was also possible to open them up by painting a simulated sky, as Veronese had done in the Palladian villas near Vicenza. By 1677 the wood-carvers had also moved into the state rooms to work under the super-intendence of Grinling Gibbons and the Master Sculptor and Carver in Wood to the Works, Henry Phillips. Their work in these rooms complemented the theme of Verrio's ceiling-paintings. Painter and carver were here triumphant.

Fortunately for the plasterer no painted ceilings were used in the City churches. Needle spires were rising fast, a symbol of hope after the crushing losses in the Great Fire. The flames had destroyed some eighty-seven churches but twenty-two more remained more or less intact. These could now be modified and brought into use.

The City Churches

By 1670, after endless delays and squabbles, Parliament had decided to rebuild fifty-one of the eighty-seven churches destroyed. Work began during 1670 and lasted, as did the work on St Paul's, well into the eighteenth century. John Grove, junior, was employed as plasterer at many of the churches and together with his partner Henry Doogood worked at forty-three City churches. The extensive researches which the Wren Society[133] have conducted render it unnecessary to do more than analyse a few of the facts about plasterwork in the churches.

Grove and Doogood, as stated, did the bulk of the work to the value of £8,060. To leave it there, however, is to deny credit to a handful of others—John Combes, Robert Horton, Thomas Meade, Robert Dyer and John Sherwood, who between them worked at another ten churches. Minor work was done by another seven plasterers, including Widow Rowe, one of the few women who had taken over and continued her husband's business at his death. At St Stephen's Walbrook, Grove and Doogood did work to the value of £494 12s 8d and worked alongside the competent masons Thomas Strong and Christopher Kempster and the wood-carver Jonathan Maine, whom Wren also employed at St Paul's.

Some idea of the plasterer's problems in working in a City church can be gained from studying the charges for rebuilding the Church of St Mary le Bow. In 1671 Matthew Bankes, the Master Carpenter to the Works, provided the ribs and roofing for the oval ceiling and all the bracketing that the plasterer, John Grove required. Grove charged £10 for the 'high Scaffolding', and the enriched ribs which ran down the middle of the ceiling extended to almost forty yards in total length, at a rate of 5s 5d a foot. The great modillion cornice, of the same length and over four feet in girth, was charged at 5s 6d a foot. Grove's men had the laborious task of doing '1500 yds of whiting' at 2d a yard, a part of the final bill of £298. It was at this church that Grove, senior, had also worked.

In July 1674, when the younger Grove was engaged on the City churches, Wren reported to the Treasury that over £1,000 was owing to Grove for plastering work done on behalf of the Office of Works. Grove, senior, in his petition recommending his son to succeed him as Master Plasterer,[134] indicated that his son had worked on the 'Kings Works and many Publique buildings' and that he was sober, diligent '& as skilful in his Art as any of that profession'. Grove, junior, was a Vestry member at St Mary le Bow and it was perhaps natural that he should recommend that any work there should be done by Doogood and himself. As for Doogood, we notice him early in Wren's career, in 1663, when the architect designed Pembroke College Chapel, Cambridge. Doogood was to collaborate with Grove again when Wren designed the Library at Trinity College, Cambridge. Here they were paid at the rate of 9s a yard for their fretted ceilings. The bracketing to hold the work was done by the Cambridge joiner Cornelius Austen, who also made the cedar bookcases. But again the final touch of enrichment was done by a craftsman more eminent than any of the plasterers; Grinling Gibbons carved the coats-of-arms. Gibbons and Grove, junior, were to be involved again during the same years at St Paul's Cathedral.

St Paul's Cathedral

By 1672 the old church of St Paul's, which had been severely damaged in the Great Fire, was demolished by the use of gunpowder and its foundations were dug up. There was need for haste. Wren had prepared designs and a model for a new St Paul's was made by William Cleere, the master-joiner he had employed when building the Sheldonian Theatre, Oxford, from 1664 to 1669. The model was shown to the king in November 1672, and approved by him. When it was shown to the Commissioners, however, Sir Roger Pratt, who wanted to rebuild St Paul's himself, voiced their objections. He made a powerful case and Wren was forced to start work on what is commonly called the 'Great Model Design' after Cleere's second and imposing model. This was made of oak, to a scale of half inch to one foot and was over twenty feet long. The Serjeant Painter finally gilded several parts of it and cleaned and coloured parts to resemble stone and lead. The Master Plasterer John Grove, senior, plastered the inside of the dome and lantern. The published accounts[135] show that he charged £1 and that he provided 'workmanship, lime and hair'. In all, the joiners spent almost 800 days in seeing that this model was fully worthy of the designs Wren had prepared.

The king gave his commission to rebuild the church on 12 November 1673—he knighted Wren two days later—and, by August 1674, the Great Model was finished. By May 1675, the 'Royal Warrant for the Design Chosen' had been issued, and the foundation stone was laid on 21 June of the same year. The building was not finished for another thirty-five years and its progress not only shaped Wren's career but also forced a final division between painter and plasterer over the major decorative schemes; this did not happen until the dome was complete.

As early as 1673 Wren had realized the problems inherent in the design of a dome which, in order to be seen above the houses, might have to look cavernous within. He deduced over the years that there must therefore be two domes, the outer one to present a bold silhouette and the inner one proportioned to the interior space. There were of course great problems in structurally relating the two, but they were as nothing to the problems which arose over the internal decoration. Wren's son, in the *Parentalia*, said it had been his father's intention to cover the inside of the dome with mosaics. An engraving by Hulsbergh of a section of the great model of 1673 shows a coffered interior to the dome,[136] presumably of plaster. The Commissioners, however, meeting on 3 March 1709, ordered that the inside of the dome should be painted and that designs and proposals for this should be submitted to them on 5 April 1709.

On the day appointed, the Commissioners met and considered designs submitted by Thornhill, Pellegrini, Catenaro, Berchet and Cheron. The announcement of the competition had brought many of these painters to London, eager to fill the dome of St Paul's with swirling and colourful pictures. Thornhill and Pellegrini emerged as leaders from the first round of the competition by the superiority of their designs. They were commissioned to paint specimens in fresco in model cupolas, and presumably one of the plasterers prepared the surface inside the models. It was perhaps a foregone conclusion that no Roman Catholic decorator would be given the task of painting the dome, and although Wren is said to have preferred Pellegrini's work he was over-ruled in favour of Thornhill. Thornhill added little life and warmth to Wren's interior—the Commissioners had unfortunately ordered that the work be done in monochrome—but it finished the cathedral in an adequate way, to their minds at least.

In these years plasterwork in the cathedral had passed out of Grove's hands, since he had died in 1708. Chrysostom Wilkins was in charge of the many plasterers and from 1708 to 1710 he received over £1,802. The bulk of the plain plasterwork had been needed in the earlier years, and significantly Henry Doogood received some £2,617 from 1687 to 1707. Thornhill's paintings were put on to plaster provided by Wilkins's team of ten men, among whom was a younger Doogood. For his 'Extraordinary Care, Pains & Attendance in Plastering the said Inside Cap of the Dome' he was given, in October 1708, a gratuity of £50 above the £443 10s 10d which he had charged for work on the dome and the vaults.[137]

Winchester

Wren's preoccupation with St Paul's did not cause him to neglect his main job as Surveyor-General. One of his tasks was to build a palace at Winchester for Charles II. When the work at Windsor Castle was at its height, just after 1680, the king started to think about another palace. A fire at the prince's lodging at Newmarket had caused the king, according to the invaluable John Evelyn, to become 'more earnest to render Winchester the seate of his autumnal diversions . . .'. It was intended that the palace should be composed of a central block with pedimented entrance and dome and cupola, flanked by two forward-projecting wings. An equestrian statue of the king was to stand in the enclosed forecourt. The contracts were made and work started.

Early in 1684 John Grove, junior, visited the site and then returned to enter into agreement with Henry Doogood to do the plastering work. By their contract of 29 January 1685[138] they were, as usual, to find all the plasterers and labourers and to perform the work in the 'best workmanlike manner'. To do this it was estimated that they would need 140 loads of laths, lath nails, 210 loads of lime at 12s 6d a load, 280 loads of sand at 5s a load and 3,600 bushels of hair at 5d a bushel. The cost of materials totalled £597 8s 4d. The work was to be done speedily, and in compensation for the journeys and proper supervision of the task they were to receive an extra penny for every yard completely finished and approved by the officers of the Works. The complete finishing implied, as the contract stated, that the work should be done from mortar well mixed with hair, and that the ceilings, when set, should be free of cracks. The absence of signatures to this contract was probably due to the death of King Charles II in 1685, which meant that the shell of the palace was never completed within the lifetime of most of the craftsmen involved. Although the roof had been finished over all but the centre pavilion, the new king, James II, considered that work should not continue at Winchester. He needed the men of the Works at Whitehall.

Whitehall: the Chapel

It is a matter of history that the Catholic court of James II, on which decorative painters like Antonio Verrio depended for patronage, was short-lived, and that in 1688 the king had to flee abroad. His reign, however, had brought with it his own fearless demands for a splendid Roman Catholic chapel. Wren, as son of a Dean of Windsor, tried to plan the sanctuary on Anglican lines, but to no avail. Begun in May, 1685, the chapel was built and decorated so swiftly that it was in use by the following year. This achievement affords a little insight into Wren's efficiency in supervising the often tardy Works organization. The chapel was erected, with a Privy Gallery and other buildings in the Whitehall Palace scheme, near to Inigo Jones's Banqueting House. But the great fires of 1691 and 1698[139] reduced the palace to ruins and only the Banqueting House, by its massive construction and the special exertions made at the time, was saved.

The mason's work on the chapel was entrusted to Thomas Wise and the carpentry was placed in the hands of the Master Carpenter Matthew Bankes, who chose his oak and spruce deals with care. The Master Bricklayer, Morris Emmett, had so many labourers at work that his lists extend to almost two pages in the accounts.[140] James Groves, John's brother, came in to assist his brother-in-law Bankes with the carpentry, and then the joiners assembled. William Emmett, a very skilled worker in the City churches, and John Gibson raced ahead to get work ready. William Ireland was impatient to be glazing the building, and a further skilled joiner, Roger Davis (who was to work at Burghley House and Chatsworth), was engaged. The Serjeant Plumber Charles Atherton, the Serjeant Painter Robert Streeter, and the Master Plasterer John Grove, junior, and his partner Henry Doogood hastened about their various tasks.

Grove and Doogood charged for ninety-two and two-third yards of fret-work on the great staircase, in the ceiling of the lantern and on the ribs of the chapel. The mouldings, large flowers, shields and trophies in the panels, and the ceiling behind the altar provided a rich foil to the other decorations. They prepared '95 yds of ceiling for the Paint^r with Kids Haire' at 20d a yard. This would give a smooth white finish for Verrio's paintings. But whereas they were to receive £49 17s 4d for their work (apart from a further payment of about £7 for the altar ceiling area), Verrio was only willing to do his work for £1,250. However, by the time that he had completed his *Assumption of the Blessed Virgin according to their Tradition*, the *Salutation* over the altar and the many colourful worlds of figures on the walls, he had charged £1,700.

In the chapel there were to be two organs, a throne and many enrichments in wood and marble, for which Grinling Gibbons and his fellow-craftsman from Antwerp, Arnold Quellin, charged £1,800. The altar-piece in the chapel was to have fifty workmen employed on it. With such a large and talented labour-force at work, the chapel was soon finished and the first service was held there on Christmas Day 1685. John Evelyn had visited it several times while building was proceeding, and his diary description of 29 December 1686, when the chapel was open to public use, gives a vivid picture of the rich decoration of the interior and the mysteries of the Roman ritual. He concluded with his disbelief that he should ever witness such things in a king of England's chapel.

Wren's position at this time must have been very difficult. The Queen's Chapel at St James's Palace had been denuded to furnish this new Roman Catholic chapel in

Whitehall. Matters came to a head in 1688 when the queen moved to the palace on the eve of the birth of Prince James Edward. Many of the most influential men in the country decided to invite William, Prince of Orange, to come over and ascend the throne. He landed at Torbay in November 1688, with his Dutch Guards and moved into Whitehall Palace. James II left hurriedly for Rochester and France and, although persuaded to return a few days later by his Catholic supporters, finally abandoned his dreams to settle popery in England and left again for France. The Monmouth rebellion had earlier tried to overthrow him and there were bitter memories of his persecution of those involved. The Roman Catholic services were discontinued at the chapel early in 1689, and at the snuffing of these candles Verrio's employment as a decorative painter seemed also at an end. He could hardly serve a Protestant master. The plasterers, for their part, had no such troubles of conscience.

Hampton Court

Within a few months of William's accession war was declared against France, but this did not prevent the king from ordering Wren to prepare schemes to adapt the old Tudor palace at Hampton Court. At this time Talman was appointed Comptroller of the King's Works. He and Wren were at once busy. The account of riding-charges for Hampton Court, 1689-91, shows that in two years Wren visited it on 308 days and Talman on 300. Nicholas Hawksmoor, 'Surveyor's Clerk', also accompanied one or other of the officers on 303 occasions. Work proceeded steadily for a short time only, with the usual Master Craftsmen and their men in attendance, but there is also some evidence to show that the talented plasterer Edward Goudge had interests there.

Goudge worked, as far as is known, entirely for private patrons, and it will be noted that as well as plastering he also did building-work. Writing to Lady Mary Bridgeman on 17 December 1689,[141] the architect William Winde says that Goudge has been delayed in attending to plastering at Castle Bromwich in Warwickshire on account of illness and of 'his goeing to Hampton Court, wher hee is Imployed about yᵗ worke'. A footnote to the letter records what we know from other sources that 'a great parte of Hampton Court, now building, and at Kensington, is fallen dowen . . .'.

In 1689, while building was proceeding slowly at Hampton Court because of the scarcity of both money and Portland stone, there occurred a disastrous building failure. Part of the great trusses of the roof on the Privy Garden front collapsed and carried away the floor over certain rooms near the Cartoon Gallery. Wren and Talman were called to a meeting on 21 December 1689, and said they would give a report in writing. When both officers were questioned on their reports early in the New Year, Talman tried to use the opportunity to belittle the Surveyor. The altercation dragged on until the king, upon hearing Wren's evidence, ordered the works at Hampton Court to proceed.

As the house rose steadily, Queen Mary, who had a passion for building, decorating, gardens and arrangements of porcelain and flowers, asked Wren to complete Charles II's Fountain Garden. But after her deeply mourned death in December 1694, the king lost interest and work ceased. At about Christmas of the previous year Wren had estimated that it would take £35,315 to complete the new quadrangle at the house. It was not until 1699, when the country was no longer at war with France that the work went ahead. The king had reassumed his interest in making improvements to the house and gardens, but the acute lack of palace accommodation after the Whitehall fire of 1698 was perhaps the most pressing cause for resuming work.

In November 1690 and again in October 1691, John Grove presented bills for work ranging from bare lathing with oak laths in various garrets to finishing ceilings for painting with kid's hair. There was also the mysterious 'Frenchman' for whom masons were employed in 'Squaring and laying two stones' for him 'to beat his plaster on', and in providing a shed for the 'Frenchman to burne his Plaister in'. A payment in the accounts[142] to 'Mr. Nadue' for plastering work done in the Queen's Closet in the Water Gallery to the value of £50 would seem to refer to this. Finally Antonio Verrio was prevailed upon to decorate the palace with paintings that emerged as complicated allegories[143] sweeping across the kid's hair plaster surfaces.

Kensington Palace

A building project which proceeded concurrently with the work at Hampton Court was the construction of Kensington Palace. In June 1689, the king bought the Earl of Nottingham's house in Kensington, and the work of adding to it began at once. The king did not like living at Whitehall, and work at Hampton Court had only just begun when the building failure occurred. As if this were not enough for the Works to cope with, anxious as it must have been without knowledge of the new king's moods, the additional buildings at Kensington also fell down in November 1689. Fortunately for Wren the queen intervened. She wrote to the king in December that she had often gone over to Kensington to hasten the workmen. She wanted to take up residence quickly and the pressure on them, she insisted, had brought errors in the work, but the hand of God had also intervened. It was to be at Kensington that the queen died in 1694, and the whole history of its building was contained in the previous five years. The decorations by William Kent and others came long after the king's own death in 1702.

In the Kensington Palace contracts book, 1689-95,[144] it was stated that the stairs were to be of elm and the joists and floors of oak or yellow fir. The oak doorcases were to be seven feet high and the floors in the queen's rooms were to be prepared with extra care. The carpenter's work was to be done so that the joiners and plasterers would not be hindered in following.

The joinery in preparing the wainscoting for rooms at Kensington was done by Henry Lobb and Alexander Fort. After them came the carvers, Nicholas Alcock and William Emmett, who were old friends of the Works. Gibbons was the Master Carver and Robert Osgood and Gabriel Cibber were the sculptors. As John Grove was busy at Hampton Court, such plastering as was needed was entrusted to Henry Margetts, a plasterer employed on occasion by William Talman, as at Kiveton in Yorkshire. Wren's riding-charges show that he visited the house on 384 days and the total in the account-book came to nearly £66,000. This Pay Book differs, however, from the Declared Accounts,[145] which continue until 1696 with a final total of almost £81,000.

Greenwich Palace

Unfortunately, Kensington lacked the attractions of a palace by the river. The old Tudor palace at Greenwich had fallen into disrepair during the Commonwealth, but King Charles II liked a residence near the river. The Queen's House at Greenwich, designed by Inigo Jones, was too small to house the court. John Webb, who took over, intended that the palace should consist of two blocks at each side of an open court running down to the river. Only the west wing was built but a number of drawings, some for plaster-work,[146] survive. These depict the usual arrangement of wreathing foliage set around an oval or rectangle composed of moulded ribs. A plasterer of Grove's competence could follow such designs with ease.

Greenwich was always assured of popularity while London was growing in size and population, and the officers of the Works were constantly engaged in work there. In 1694, twenty-five years after the completion of Webb's wing for Charles II, the idea was conceived of converting the site and buildings of the royal palace for the use of disabled and superannuated seamen. The idea met with royal approval, the king possibly recalling that before her death the queen had expressed great interest in a renewal of building at Greenwich and had opposed the then current idea of pulling part of the palace down. The only alternative to this seemed to build, and the work went on. Between 1696 and 1698 all the foundations were dug and serious building began, including a start in August on Wren's Great Hall. It was not finished until November 1704 or ready for Sir James Thornhill's nineteen years of painting which began in 1708.

The plasterwork was to be entrusted to Henry Doogood, Grove's partner. Although Grove might benefit from this commission, he was careful not to have his name linked with it in the contract because he was being paid a salary as Master Plasterer. John Evelyn, who acted as treasurer, kept the accounts with meticulous care. The abstract of payments made from June 1696 to July 1699,[147] shows a total expenditure of over £36,000, of which almost a third was for mason's work. This sum had been raised by gifts from the king, subscriptions and free gifts, levies on seamen and fines on French smugglers. The money continued to flow in and kept pace with the expenditure. By the end of 1704 accommodation was available for the first pensioners, and the first forty-two arrived in March 1705; by December 1708 there were 350.

One of the most interesting parts of the sprawling complex of majestic buildings at Greenwich is the Painted Hall. It had been started in 1703 and was originally intended as the hospital refectory. By 1708 it was decided that it should be embellished with decorative paintings. The work was entrusted to Sir James Thornhill, by then the best-known English painter of great murals. He started work in the Lower Hall in the same year.

The long and involved negotiations Thornhill had with the 'Grand Committee' at Greenwich has been told elsewhere.[148] The plastering at Greenwich was carried on after Doogood's death in 1707 by James Ellis and Richard Wetherill. The latter seems to have struck up a similar relationship with David Lance, Grove's successor as Master Plasterer, as Doogood had done with Grove. This says much for Wetherill, for he had been one of Lance's competitors (along with Chrysostom Wilkins and John Coombs) for the post of Master Plasterer.[149]

By May 1712 Thornhill had advanced far enough with his painting to ask the Board to appoint qualified persons to inspect his painting. He also asked for some money to encourage him along. By May 1714 he was ready to clear his scaffolding away but, disillusioned by the small amount of money made available against his total bill, he ceased work.

As early as 5 February 1713 John James had laid before the Grand Committee a proposition to use Derbyshire plaster-stone 'proper for laying the Painting on' at the upper end of the Hall at the rate of £5 a ton. 'Mr Hurst', an otherwise unrecorded Derbyshire plasterer, was to arrange this, and on 2 July 1713 James brought Hurst's bill of £33 13s 6d to the Committee. He was paid, but Thornhill still waited. In the meantime, Vanbrugh had been appointed Surveyor at Greenwich and one of the things he looked into was Thornhill's incomplete painting of the Hall. After endless memoranda without any decision Thornhill was beaten down in price, and by late 1717 he was ready, perhaps with some weariness, to bring his great work to a conclusion. It took him a further ten years. By this time he was in his early fifties, the officials of the Office of Works were ignoring him, and he was having to argue with them over the payment of small bills. The decorative painting jobs at Kensington Palace they gave to William Kent.

At Grove's death in 1708, the post of Master Plasterer to the Works had gone, as we have noted, to David Lance. His appointment was reconfirmed on 27 May 1715,[150] during the reorganization of the Works after the accession of George I. Lance submitted plans for further work at Hampton Court on 6 March 1716, and his proposals[151] show his method of working. First, a coat of lime and hair was laid and then scratched to make a good key for the second coat. This was to be 'proved' (levelled) with a twelve-foot rule and 'floated' (smoothed). The 'stuff' (plaster) was to be of good quality, 'well wrot in the best manner', beaten six times, and then a coat of 'stuff' of black hair was laid, the whole being finished with a coat of plaster made with white hair. Lance and Wetherill seem to have submitted separate prices for the work, and a price was then allowed which they accepted. This price, in all but two cases, was the same as they asked: needless to say, the two exceptions were at a lower price. A terse rider was attached that there must be 'in all the said worke not above one Load of good Sharp Sand to one hundred of Lyme, and not less than 10 Bushell of good Black Hair to the same'. The Office of Works had been in existence for 350 years and had gained enough experience to ensure that the clauses of its contracts were carried out, at least by plasterers.

Private Patronage

Apart from his official work John Grove had found time for private work, particularly for the architect Sir Roger Pratt at Coleshill and Clarendon House. John Evelyn had visited Clarendon House during building and had pronounced it 'the first Palace in England'. Grove did work there to the considerable value of £2,082 'whereof the fret ceilings came to about £820 besides bracketing, which I conceive came almost to as much more'.[152] Pratt had previously compared the rates of Edward Martin and Arthur Toogood, the Master of the Plaisterer's Company in 1663. They, as 'plaisterers just within Bishopsgate' wanted 6s to 7s per yard for work only. Grove on similar work for the Office of Works was charging about 5s 6d to 6s per yard. He and his son also worked for Hugh May at Cassiobury and for Sir Robert Hooke at the Royal College of Physicians and, as we have seen, the younger Grove was commissioned by Wren to work in many of the City churches and at St Paul's Cathedral.

Two plasterers of this period, whose work was very accomplished but whose London work is almost unknown, were Robert Bradbury and James Pettifer. Their one known work outside London is at Sudbury Hall, Derbyshire, which they did in 1675-6. It is full and rich (Plates 27-9) and deserves close attention. The house was begun by Mary Vernon in the reign of James I, but was far from finished when she died in 1622. It then stood empty as a partly completed shell until after the Restoration, when Mary's great-grandson, George Vernon, completed it. In doing so, he had the good sense to use excellent carvers, plasterers and painters.[153]

In 1675-6 Bradbury and Pettifer provided the ceilings of the Drawing Room, the Parlour, the Staircase Well and Hall (Plates 27, 28), the Queen's Bedroom, and that of the 138 feet long Gallery. They charged at the rate of 6s a yard, which contrasts well with the charges of plasterers which Pratt considered when commissioning plasterwork at Clarendon House. Whilst to some eyes the plasterwork which Bradbury and Pettifer provided was florid and all-enveloping, the exuberance of decoration was at least confined to the spaces provided in the design. Nothing strayed beyond the limits set down by the moulded ribs, although the plasterwork on the centre of the Parlour ceiling looks as if it was disturbed by Laguerre's later ceiling painting. Using wire, parchment or leather strips the delicate swirling work was set into place with such skill that in 1927, when Laurence Turner wrote his book on plasterwork (before the discovery of the accounts), he thought 'the four well modelled amorini in the corners of the [staircase] cove [to be] evidently by an Italian modeller, for no English plasterer could have developed so suddenly the ability to model the human figure . . .'.

In the seven compartments of the Long Gallery ceiling there are curling flowers and foliage, shells, emperors' heads, horses galloping from cornucopiae, and dragons and wild boar. After their work at Sudbury we hear no more of Robert Bradbury, but James Pettifer (who should not be confused with James Petiver, d. 1698) went on to work for Wren in the City churches and succeeded Dan Morris as Plasterer to Christ's Hospital in 1698.

The long years of apprenticeship which all craftsmen undertook produced another competent plasterer in the person of Edward Martin (or Martyn). Apprenticed to his father John in 1648 he was free of the Worshipful Company of Plaisterers by 21 September 1655. He could not, however, avoid getting into trouble with its officers. In 1657 he was fined for arrears and, although he became Beadle of the Company in 1660 (and its Master in 1699), he was fined for bad workmanship in 1671 and 1685, along with James Pettifer. The indictment read that he had done work 'not well ordered in the setting done by him att the Ld Bellasis house in the Pell Mell'. This stood on the site of 31 St James's Square, London.[154] Martin is, however, known for good ceilings in the country—at Arbury Hall, Warwickshire (Plate 30) and Burghley House, Northamptonshire (Plate 32).

Wren also seems to have been connected with the work at Arbury. In 1674 he wrote to the owner, Sir Richard Newdigate, about the doorway to the stable building, and he probably also supervised the erection of the house chapel. Martin agreed with the owner on 28 January 1678, to do the chapel ceiling and a closet ceiling for the sum of £48 'besides comeing and going and goat's hair'. The Arbury ceiling shows the technical advances made by plasterers at this time in moulding deeper ribs and applying decorative foliage to them. The room provides, with its wainscoting and ceiling, the sort of setting which Wren had created in many a City church vestry. Martin had worked for Wren at St Nicholas Cole Abbey, Queenhithe, alongside John Sherwood.

Martin was also to work for the Earl of Exeter. The south front of Burghley House, the earl's home in Northamptonshire, had been damaged in the Parliamentary assault on the house led by Cromwell in 1643 when the 4th earl was a minor. The 5th earl, whose wife was a sister of the Duke of Devonshire for whom Chatsworth was rebuilt and decorated, was a notable traveller and a lover of architecture and painting. It seems probable that he turned to the architect William Talman to supervise the alterations he planned at Burghley. The architect visited the house in August 1688, but some work, including plasterwork, had already begun prior to this date (Plate 32).

With the mass of documents at Burghley House only partially sorted and arranged, it is useful that the seventeenth-century bank account of the 5th earl survives in the ledgers of Child's Bank (Glyn, Mills & Co.), London. It is an unusually full one, and a rare feature is that the occupation of the payees is given. The accounts indicate that 'Mr Martyn, Playsterer' was being paid for work. On 1 July 1682 he received £50, and on 14 February 1683 a further £100. Martin was moving in distinguished company.

The wood-carvers at the house included Grinling Gibbons, Jonathan Maine and Thomas Young. Maine was the talented Oxford carver with a long list of work to his credit, including woodwork at Trinity College, Oxford, and St Paul's Cathedral. Young also worked at Chatsworth. Martin went on to succeed Henry Cromwell as Master of the Plaisterers Company in 1699.

There is no doubt that one of the most important plasterers at work in the late seventeenth century was Edward Goudge. He did not owe his fame, however, to any connection with the Office of Works or with Sir Christopher Wren. As far as can be established, his name does not appear in the records of the Worshipful Company of Plaisterers and his origins and apprenticeship details are unknown. He was principally employed by the architect Captain William Winde (?-1722), whose career has been detailed in recent years.[155] Winde was born at an unknown date before 1647, in Holland, of English parents. He came to England at the Restoration and married into the Bridgeman family, for whom he later remodelled Castle Bromwich Hall, Warwickshire. His first known commission, however, was work for his principal patron, the 1st Earl of Craven, at Hampstead Marshall, Berkshire.

Hampstead Marshall was one of the first houses to be designed after the Restoration. Lord Craven employed as his architect Sir Balthazar Gerbier, to whose books on building we have referred. In fact, one of Gerbier's dedicatory epistles in his *Counsel and Advice to all Builders* is addressed to Lord Craven. Unfortunately, within a year or two of commencing work for Lord Craven, Gerbier died and was buried at Hampstead Marshall Church in 1667. The epitaph on his monument states that he 'built a stately pile of Building in the years 1662 to 1665 for the Rt Hon William Earl Craven at Hampstead Marshall'. Even before Gerbier's death William Winde was journeying to the house, and the drawings for the house in the Bodleian Library[156] include some by Gerbier, Winde and the craftsmen employed there over some twenty years. These were the mason Thomas Strong, the carver Edward Pearce and the plasterer Edward Goudge.

Winde as the 'Master William Wine' of one of Gerbier's dedicatory epistles, has his career documented further on the fly-leaf of a letter-book of his client Lord Craven. This, together with some eighty letters traced by the present author in 1952, gives an idea of the patronage he attracted and of the casual way he attended to the buildings under his supervision. One of Winde's 'performances' (Walpole's phrase in his *Anecdotes of Painters*) was to attend to the rebuilding of Combe Abbey, Warwickshire, for Lord Craven between 1679 and 1684.

The Bodleian letter-book faithfully records the progress made—the timber for flooring, the sawing of it, the 'Right draufts of the whole designe' and, unfortunately, Winde's surprising inattention to the task in hand. Some of this attitude also appears in the work he did for his Bridgeman relatives in 1685 and later. On 6 March 1682 Lord Craven writes in the hope that Winde will be able to come to Combe to see the foundations laid, but by 10 July 1682 he is still awaiting the designs. He remonstrates that he has not heard anything from Winde and that the workmen are idle, not knowing how to proceed without instruction. They will have to be discharged, he fears, if positive directions are not forthcoming. The interchange of letters preserves details which might not otherwise have been set down. The owner tells Winde on 5 February 1683, that sufficient timber has been sawn for the stairs and that it is lying in water 'to fetch out the Sapp . . .'. The letters also imply that Pearce and Goudge were at the house, and that it was Winde and Pearce who recommended Goudge to Lord Craven's attention. The plasterer was also Winde's choice when he was called on to work at Hampstead Marshall and at Castle Bromwich.

The system which Gerbier advocated in *A Brief Discourse concerning . . . Magnificent Building* (1662), by which the Master Workman kept his men 'under a certain regular proportion of pay, to hinder them from spending their wages too fast and to run to other works . . .' does not seem to have been followed with much diligence by Winde. He placed great reliance on the skill and acumen of his master craftsmen, but inspected all designs. The signed drawing made by Goudge for the Dining Room ceiling at Hampstead Marshall (Plate 38) is endorsed across the centre 'June 22th: 1686. This Drauft for the Dineing Roome att Hampstead Marshall marked A allowed of by me Wll. Winde.'

For fifteen years after 1685 Winde gave spasmodic attention to the detail of the alterations his relatives were planning at Castle Bromwich Hall, Warwickshire. Goudge was one of a group of craftsmen among whom the principal figures, in addition to himself, were the master carpenter Jonathan Wilcox (who was also much employed by Wren), the joiner Robert Aiscough, the sculptor John van Nost and the decorative painter Louis Laguerre. In July 1686 Winde instructed Goudge to 'prepare the draughts for the Severall Roomes' at Castle Bromwich and to provide estimates of the cost. These seem to have been accepted, but it was two years before the plasterer was at work there. He also needed to be properly introduced to Lady Bridgeman. Winde therefore wrote to her on 12 July 1688:

> 'This bearer is Mr Edward Gouge & is the Person I recommended to yr Ladp att Bromingen. he dide the frett seallings att Combe and I will assure yr Ladyp no man in Ingland has a better Tallent in ye way (of plastering) than himselfe. He has bine employed by mee this 6 a 7 years, is an excellent drauffteman and mackes all his desines hime selfe. . . .'

By 1688 Winde was advising his client that the plasterer and joiner would soon be finished and that as their 'hands is in they may aforde it cheaper than if they where to come againe . . .'. Winde was preoccupied with his service in King William's army and often wrote on his letters the words 'in camp'. He was, however, concerned when Goudge tried to charge more for his work than agreed, but tried to justify the situation by writing on 8 February 1690:[157]

> 'Mr Goudge will undoughtedly have a good deall of worke for hee is now looked on as the beste master in England in his profession, as his worke att Combe, Hampsted & Sr. John Brownlowes will Evidence. . . '

This is confirmation of Winde's known attendance at the first two houses, both Craven properties, but the latter reference is valuable in suggesting Goudge as the author of the fine plasterwork at Belton House, Lincolnshire, (Plates 40, 42) which Sir John Brownlow had had decorated in 1686-8. It also hints to us that the master mason in charge of the work there, William Stanton, a statuary of some note, was possibly supervised by Winde.

This valuable unpublished correspondence between Winde and his cousin Lady Mary Bridgeman gives a good idea of the attention necessary to the remodelling of Castle Bromwich Hall (Plate 36) and of Goudge's movements. In the letter indirectly referring to work at Belton, the Brownlow house, Winde goes on to state that 'Mr Goudge is employed by ye Earl of Clarendone att his house at Swallowfield where I believe hee will have above a 12 monthes work', and in a letter dated only by the year '1691', he mentions the plasterer still being at the 'Earle of Clarendon'. The Berkshire house of Swallowfield was erected in 1689-91 for Henry, 2nd Earl of Clarendon, by William Talman. Some of the work there had been delayed by Goudge's illness, and Winde also indicates that the plasterer had needed to go, as we have stated, to view the fall of building work in 1689 at Hampton Court. A reference to 'Mr Gouge at the Duke of Somerset' implies that Goudge worked shortly afterwards at Petworth, Sussex.

As well as being a successful plasterer Goudge supplemented his income by acting as a clerk of works for buildings, particularly those being altered in London for Thomas Coke of Melbourne in 1698. Coke, who later became Vice-Chamberlain to Queen Anne and George I, married Lady Mary Stanhope in 1698. While he was away after his marriage his house in St James's Place was enlarged by adding the adjoining house. Goudge was in charge of the work and wrote that he did not approve of the way this was to be done. He therefore prepared a design of his own. The humdrum nature of his duties included taking care that the household necessities were ready, such as 'jack, jackwheel, spits, racks, boiler, stoves, cistern etc . . .'. Within three years Goudge was to ask Coke in a letter of 25 March 1702 for 'some sort of business . . . that may be a livelihood for that which I am in at present is prejudicial to my health'. He was soon to be finished as a plasterer, and the last we know of him is his statement later in the same letter of 25 March.

> 'I suppose Sir, I need not tell you that for some years past, for want of money occasioned by the War, and by the use of ceiling painting, the employment which hath been my chiefest pretence hath been always dwindling away, till now its just come to nothing. . . '[158]

Looking back across the few recorded facts of his life we have some reason to be grateful to Goudge in architectural terms. George Vertue records[159] that the plasterer had gone to 'Justice Mellust's' house in Yorkshire in the late 1670s to do fret-work ceilings and had discovered the young Nicholas Hawksmoor working as a clerk there. He took him to London where Hawksmoor, because of his 'early skill and genius' for architecture, entered Wren's service. As for Goudge, his letter of 11 October 1690 to Lady Bridgeman indicates that he was then living 'next doore to the Bore's head in Queen Street, near Bloomsbury Market'. The letter also states his charges. For whiting fret-work he required 9d a yard, and for plain work 1½d. Grove and Doogood charged 2d for whiting plain work. His assistant's travel expenses were also charged.

We have noted that in one of Winde's letters he had indicated that Goudge was working for the Duke of Somerset at Petworth. A further letter from Goudge to Lady Bridgeman of 27 April 1691 says that his assistant 'Mr Lance is at the Duke of Sumersetts att Pettworth in Sussex'. Goudge was also working at Chatsworth in 1696-7, principally in the Gallery.

One of the last enterprises with which Winde's name has been connected was the building of Ampthill Park, Bedfordshire, which John, Lord Ashburnham, undertook with John Lumley's assistance, between 1704 and 1707. In his letter-book[160] Lord Ashburnham copied his letters to his agent Brian Fairfax, and three to Winde. In them, Fairfax is asked to consult Winde about Louis Laguerre's charges for painting the Great Hall at Ampthill and about statues, and to establish Jean Tijou's rates for iron gates and balusters. Whether Fairfax successfully accomplished all this is not recorded and Lord Ashburnham turned directly to the architect. On 11 July 1706 he wrote to Winde with the dimensions of the great Hall and asked again about the statues and rates for ironwork. Winde's life, however, was a busy and erratic one, and both Lady Bridgeman and Lord Ashburnham often waited impatiently for replies to their letters. We have seen how work at Combe Abbey almost came to a halt for lack of Winde's instructions.

On 15 October 1706 Lord Ashburnham wrote again. Winde's advice was needed concerning the nature and manner of plastering the Great Hall to make it fit and proper to be painted by Laguerre. It is doubtful if this was done by Goudge, as his lament of 1702 seemed to imply he was ceasing his plastering work partly on account of the activities of painters such as Laguerre. It is not known whether Winde went on to employ Goudge's assistant David Lance, who in any case was to become even busier when he became Master Plasterer to the Works in 1708.

As Goudge was lamenting his lack of business, other plasterers worked on. One of these was Henry Margetts, who was employed by the Duke of Leeds. As one of the leading politicians of the late seventeenth century, Treasurer of England, Lord President of the Council, and an active supporter of the Prince of Orange, Thomas Osborne (1620-1712) was soon made Duke of Leeds. Although described by contemporaries as a 'thin, ill-natured ghost' and 'a gentleman of admirable natural parts, great knowledge and experience . . . but of no reputation with any party', he amassed a considerable fortune and in the later years of his career spent large sums on building and decoration at Kiveton in south Yorkshire. The elevation of the house[161] is endorsed 'For ye D. of Leeds at Keiton in Yorkshire'. The duke seems to have consulted William Talman, Comptroller of the Office of Works, but Talman is nowhere mentioned in the many documents[162] about the house, which was erected by Daniel Brand of Westminster and his son Daniel. A house with eleven bays, slightly smaller than that planned by Talman with fifteen bays, was erected, and from Brand's accounts it can be calculated that some £10,344 4s 6d was spent on the structure in eight or nine years (c. 1694-1702), decoration apart.

After the main structure had been erected, the decorators gathered. The house must have presented to contemporary eyes a very lavish scene. There were twenty-four chimneypieces, that in the Great Dining Room being largely composed of purple marble. Louis Laguerre painted scenes from the story of Cupid and Psyche, and Louis Hauduroy provided fifty-six painted panels over doors and chimneypieces. The staircase balustrading was probably by Jean Tijou, and, as at Dyrham and Honington, gilt-leather panels hung in the lower vestibule. Some twelve feet high and ranging in width from a foot to 4 ft 6 in wide, they would vie for attention with Jonathan Maine's spirited wood-carving, which was also to be found over the altar of the house chapel. The plasterwork throughout was by Henry Margetts. He received £372 16s 6d for his work. By 1702 the house was almost complete and was encircled in 'workmanlike manner' with an iron fence made by Tijou's follower, John Gardom of Baslow. With a new century and a new queen, the duke paid Child's, his bankers, on 26 June 1702 'for 4 Coronetts for Queen Anne's Coronation for himself, his wife, his son Carmarthen & his wife £36 8s 10d'. Regrettably Kiveton itself was demolished in about 1812.

Another important house, part of which was designed by Talman in 1698 is Dyrham Park, Gloucestershire. After his work on Thoresby House, Nottinghamshire, (1684) and his design for the south front of Chatsworth (1687-96). Dyrham was erected as a great rectangular block three storeys high with the roof concealed by a heavy cornice and, as at the earlier Chatsworth, by a balustrade. Statues and urns were used to soften the impressive outline. With Dyrham to show, and after his appointment in 1689 as Comptroller to the Works, Talman[163] was a much sought-after but temperamental architect. He had come to the notice of the owner of Dyrham, William Blathwayt, in 1692, just after Blathwayt had inherited the Wynter estates at his wife's death.

Building on the west front at Dyrham was the first to go ahead, to the designs of Samuel Hauduroy, a member of a Huguenot family working at various decorative tasks in England. Supervision of the day-to-day building was put in the hands of Edward Wilcox, a master carpenter who had worked for Talman at Hampton Court and Kensington Palace, and the son of Jonathan Wilcox, who had done similar supervisory work for William Winde. John Povey and Robert Barker, 'joiners of the Parish of St Martin-in-the-Fields, London', agreed to do the joinery work of the Great Staircase and the Great Balcony Room. In 1704 Thomas Porter, also of London, came to do the plasterwork, but some of the decorative effect on the staircase was obtained by the veining done by Hauduroy to simulate marble.

Blathwayt's opinion of his agent and his craftsmen was not a high one. In 1701 he commented that 'these people want stirring up roundly and not to be overfed with money'. Porter, along with the rest, was paid as late and as little as possible. The money was reserved to buy books, pictures, gilt-leather hangings and china, and to order, through colonial contacts, timber and garden plants from America. But by 1702, when William III died, Blathwayt's sources of money were diminishing. He lost his post as acting Secretary of State and three years later, in 1704, he was dismissed from his post as Secretary at War. In 1707 he suffered the final indignity of being deprived of his position of Secretary to the Lords of Trade. Perhaps for these reasons the interior decoration of Dyrham, in plaster and paint, is restrained, and there are no grand staircase paintings such as Thornhill had painted for Blathwayt's friend Paul Foley at Stoke Edith House, Herefordshire, in 1705.

Talman's country house practice was not extensive and it had suffered a setback when Vanbrugh replaced him as architect at Castle Howard in 1699. His work at Drayton Park, Northamptonshire, merits examination because the contract survives.[164] Dated 24 August 1702, it is between Sir John Germain and Benjamin Jackson. Particular mention is made of the decoration of the façade of the house: heads, vases and flames or pineapples on pedestals being specified. The plasterwork inside the house has a restrained look. Plaster decoration in precise geometrical panels is found in the King's Dining Room, and in lighter swags and scrolls in the chapel which Lady Betty Germain fitted out again after the mob spoiled it in 1688, when James II fled from England. Her father, Henry, 2nd Earl of Peterborough, had been persuaded to turn Roman Catholic by the king. Again, the ironwork seems to have been provided by Jean Tijou and the paintings were done by Gerard Lanscroon (*fl.* 1677-1737), a pupil of Verrio, who also painted staircases at Powis Castle and Burley-on-the-Hill. By 1704 the main structure had been almost completed, but as the Lanscroon paintings are dated 1712 many more years must have been spent on decoration. The house has rooms dating from the late seventeenth century, with marquetry floors, carved and gilded ceilings, red brocade wall-coverings, and plasterwork by William Rhodes in rooms dating from 1771-2 (Plate 114).

The late seventeenth-century plasterwork at Drayton is in the assured style of a London plasterer, and one who had connections with the Office of Works. It was done by George Worrall, Master Plasterer for over forty years, but the work was far removed in style from the jolly friezes to be found at Denham Place, Buckinghamshire. Sir Roger Hill, High Sheriff for the county and a Member of Parliament, began to rebuild his house at Denham in 1688. He had William Stanton, fresh from his work at Belton, to supervise the work. Stanton received £5,000 at Belton but the most he raised at the more modest Denham was about £214. The London plasterer William Parker was employed, and he and his patron were obviously lovers of the drawings of Francis Barlow (as engraved by Hollar) for his *Several Wayes in Hunting*. The Drawing Room frieze (Plates 43-6) provides as charming a decoration as can be found anywhere in Great Britain. Parker was no mean performer and imbued the cupid in the centre of the Tapestry Room ceiling with a freedom only recaptured by the Italian *stuccatori* forty years later. He is presumably the William Parker who appears in the Plaisterer's Company lists until 1693. At Denham he received £273 11s od for his work. Parker is an example of those plasterers to whom it would be impossible to credit work. Fortunately the precise record[165] for Denham survives, but it is tempting to ascribe to him the 1691 ceiling at Fawley Court.

Work in a similar 'vernacular' style may be found at Eye Manor, Herefordshire, Clarke Hall, Wakefield (Plate 35), and Astley Hall, Lancashire (Plate 26). The Great Hall and Drawing Room ceilings at Astley are fantasies; the plaster figures intertwine with scallop shells, palm-branches and gay festoons in a flamboyant display which suggests the rim of a Dutch-style silver salver with its heavy *repoussé* work. The idealized flowers and ginger-bread styled motifs which appear at Clarke Hall are probably the work of a local plasterer. Properly handled and controlled these ceilings could have been as successful as those at Melton Constable, dated 1687 (Plate 34). The work at Eye Manor is similar in part to the plasterwork at Holyroodhouse. This has led to the suggestion that the same plasterers were employed. Reference has been made[166] to the similarity which the panels of scrolling acanthus at Eye Manor have to those depicted in *The Art of the Plasterer*, a book reissued in about 1680 by the younger Edward Pearce.

Whilst London plasterers may have been involved at Eye Manor they were almost certainly employed at Holme Lacy, the Herefordshire home of the Scudamore family. The master mason at Holme Lacy was Anthony Deane, who contracted to build the house in 1674 to the approval of Hugh May. He also worked at Horseheath Hall, Cambridgeshire, to the designs of Sir Roger Pratt, who would undoubtedly employ London craftsmen. Although he gave up this work he probably continued to work with them. Whether John Grove or George Dunsterfield and John Houlbert ever travelled from London to work at Holme Lacy we shall perhaps never know. Documents about the Scudamore family have gradually come to light over the years in repositories as far apart as Birmingham Reference Library and the Folger Shakespeare Library in Washington, DC, but no plasterer's agreement has been found. The wood-carvings[167] by Grinling Gibbons are now mostly at Kentchurch, Herefordshire.

The last years of the seventeenth century had allowed, by the elusive development of taste, a finer plasterwork (in technical terms) to appear in England than ever before. The workers, however, could not rid themselves of stiff, geometric borders and a hesitation at handling lifesize figures. The competition to paint the dome of St Paul's in 1709-1710 undoubtedly focused the attention of many Venetian artists on England. Some of the *stuccatori* working in Bavaria and in the villages on the Swiss-Italian border also saw an opportunity to increase their area of activity by moving to England. One of their earliest patrons seems to have been Sir John Vanbrugh, soldier, dramatist and, seemingly by accident, an architect. The durable stuff composed of lime and ox-hair was to be banished for a few years by an exuberant froth of stucco, which was to be mounted plane upon plane and fashioned into dexterous scrolls, mask-faces and caryatid figures. The 'heathen Gods, Emblems, Compartiments &c' which John Evelyn had seen at Nonsuch in 1666 and pronounced 'must needes have been the work of some excellent *Italian*...' had come at long last in plenty to England, with the *stuccatori* themselves to fashion them.

CHAPTER V

Adorned with Stucco, 1702-1760

He built himself a house which he adorned with
Stucco work . . .

William Aglionby,
Painting illustrated in three dialogues, 1685

IN the first few years of Queen Anne's reign Swiss stuccoists reached England and were soon employed in the decoration of houses throughout the country. They were born in Italian-speaking Switzerland and, having Italian names, were invariably referred to in England as 'Italians'. At this time, efforts were being made to attract decorative artists into England. In 1707 Charles Montagu, 4th Earl and subsequently 1st Duke of Manchester, went as Ambassador Extraordinary to Venice. The main purpose of his mission (which failed) was to obtain the Republic's support against Louis XIV. From an artistic point of view the significant thing to emerge was that the duke brought back with him to England in 1708 the decorative painters Giovanni Antonio Pellegrini (1675-1741) and Marco Ricci (1673-1729). There is no direct evidence that the duke sought out stuccoists in addition to painters, but presumably the word had swiftly gone abroad that patrons and work were available in England. The painters in particular came eagerly to try their luck in the competition to paint the dome of St Paul's.

It has often been assumed that James Gibbs was responsible for the introduction of the *stuccatore* Giovanni Bagutti and his partner Giuseppe Artari to England. This, however, does not seem likely in Artari's case. Gibbs was in Italy, and in Rome in particular, from 1703 to 1708. Bagutti, the son of Andrea Bagutti was then in his twenties, having been born at Rovio on 14 October 1681. A 'House of the Bagutti' survives in the village. He could have met Gibbs (or equally the Duke of Manchester) and have been invited to England. Artari was born at Arogno, near Lugano, a few miles away from Bagutti's birthplace, towards the end of the seventeenth century. It would seem unlikely for Gibbs to be involved with a stuccoist then in his teens, and he did not employ either Artari or Bagutti until the 1720s. We also now know that Bagutti was at Castle Howard in 1710. It would seem likely that, after possible introduction to England by Gibbs, the Duke of Manchester or the Venetian painters, Bagutti returned to Rovio and Arogno and persuaded Artari to join him in England.

The Duke of Manchester, the Earl of Carlisle, who was then building Castle Howard, and Sir John Vanbrugh, their architect, were all members of the Kit-Cat Club, and presumably decided among themselves the nature of the decoration the Venetians were to undertake. At Kimbolton Castle, then being remodelled by Vanbrugh for the duke, there is no decorative plasterwork of this period, but Pellegrini painted some fine murals there. The architectural history of Castle Howard has been given careful attention over the years, and the present author has also written at length elsewhere on the building documentation.[168]

Lord Carlisle spread the expenses for building Castle Howard over some thirty-six years, but by the midsummer of 1737 he had spent £78,240 2s 10d. When negotiations with certain London craftsmen broke down he turned to the capable workers of the nearby city of York, aided by a number of itinerant foreigners. Several chimneypieces were provided by William Harvey; Josiah Kay, the royal locksmith, provided brass locks, keys and hinges; and John Bagnall of York (and later Richmond) did the plain plasterwork and 'whitening throughout all the whole building'.

The most important item to emerge from a study of the accounts is the first recorded employment in England, during the years 1710-12, of the *stuccatori* Giovanni Bagutti ('Mr Bargotee') and 'Mr Plura'. It seems reasonable to assume that they provided the stucco fireplace and the scagliola niche in the Great Hall (Plates 47, 48). The accounts relating to this have not previously been published in full; they read:

Feb 10th 1710

	Mr Bargotee, Italien.	
	Given him upon Acct of woork.	25. 0. 0.
	Pd Jno Storey, Labee, for attending him to ye 8 Febry	
	1710.　　　　£33. 19. 0.	7. 8. 0.
	Paid Jno Storey from ye 8 Febry to ye 31 March	1. 16. 0.
June	Pd ye Labs for attending him	2. 19. 0.
	Pd Mr Bargotee	20. 0. 0.
	Labourers	2. 10. 0.
	Given Mr Bargottee	10. 15. 0.
	Labourers	1. 4. 6.
	Paid for 7 Load of Hull Plaister	3. 5. 0.
	Labourers	2. 7. 6.
	Pd Labourers	1. 7. 6.
	Pd Is[aac] Mansfield for wha he did & pd upon Acct.	2. 13. 0.
	Given Mr Bargotey	10. 15. 0.
	Given Mr Plewra	34. 8. 6.
March	Given Mr Plewra when went to London	10. 15. 0.
1711/12	Given Mr Plura	34. 11. 0.
	Given Mr Bargottee	10. 0. 0.
Aug 1712	Pd Mr Plura & Bargote in full of all work done to this day	156. 07. 0.

Further payments in the Building Book for 1711 bring the total received by these two stuccoists to £321 17s 0d, in contrast to the £105 2s 6d paid to Isaac Mansfield. Mansfield was a competent plasterer who settled at York in 1704 and moved from one important job to another, including Blenheim.

When Artari joined Bagutti in England they first worked as partners, with the older Bagutti taking the main responsibility. In the 'Book of Strangers dining at Cannons',[169] the home of the Duke of Chandos, the entry for New Year's Day 1722, records the visit of 'Mr Bagutti, his Partner Mr Artree'. On three other occasions it was Bagutti who introduced '1 Stranger', possibly Artari, to dine at the Officers' Table. When Bagutti and Artari worked together for Lord Mildmay at Moulsham Hall, Essex, and under the superintendence of the Venetian architect Giacomo Leoni, it was noted that the 'agreamt was only with Mr Bagutti and Mr Altari who did the Bustos & Figures assisted him'. They seem to have stayed together until a little after 1730 and to have done their most important work for Vanbrugh, Gibbs, Campbell, Leoni and Francis Smith.

For the years between 1710, when Bagutti was at Castle Howard, and about 1720, when he decorated the chapel at Cannons, no other work by Bagutti is recorded. He may have done work on a staircase off the Long Gallery at Wentworth Castle, Yorkshire, in about 1715 but these are the dark years. There was also plenty of work in progress in the churches of southern Germany which commanded the attention of many of Bagutti's fellow stuccoists.[170] It was work for James Gibbs in 1720 at the Octagon House, Twickenham which brought Artari and Bagutti together. They were to work for him again at St Peter's, Vere Street (1723-4), at St Martin-in-the-Fields, London (1724-5), and Ditchley, Oxfordshire (1725) (Plate 52). They may also have collaborated in the decorations at The Mynde, Hereford (Plate 50), and Clandon Park, Surrey (Plate 67).

The many drawings by Gibbs in the Ashmolean Museum, Oxford—one is illustrated here (Plate 51)—show his ability to indicate exact detailing to the stuccoists. The drawings for work at Fairlawne and Gubbins do much to reinforce the theory that many of the instructions to the stuccoist came from the architect. There is of course no doubt that they were also capable of their own decorative schemes. These might well be misunderstood jumbles of mythology with unconsidered hordes of gods and goddesses agape at the feats of Hercules, but a market for such subjects abounded. Gibbs in his *A Book of Architecture*, 1728, describes the St Martin's ceiling (dated 1725) as 'enrich'd with Fretwork by Signori Artari and Bagutti, the best Fret-workers that ever came into England'. Colin Campbell, who employed Bagutti at Mereworth (frontispiece), wrote 'the ornaments are executed by Signor Bagutti, a most ingenious artist'.

Despite this flow of commissions, however, and more work for Gibbs at the Senate House, Cambridge, Bagutti did not achieve wealth from his labours. In May 1725 Lord Chandos informed his agent that there was 'a poor man I employ'd to finish the inside of Cannons. I owe him £650 . . .'. York Buildings stock was to be sold to raise the money; £350 was to paid at once to 'this person, Mr Bagutti', and he was to wait for the other £300 'till the end of next week. Pay him today if you can.' After the work at Moulsham in 1730-1 Bagutti's name appears less frequently. But there is reason to think, by the endorsement 'For Mr. Baguti att More Parke near Rikmonsworth in Hertfordshire' on the back of a Gibbs drawing possibly for work at Down Hall or Stowe, that he was responsible for both the exuberant plasterwork at Moor Park, Hertfordshire (*c.* 1732), with its life-size figures (Plate 57) and that represented on the drawing itself.

Apart from Bagutti, most of the *stuccatori* at work in England came together in 1725 to work together at Ditchley, the Oxfordshire house that Gibbs designed for the 2nd Earl of Lichfield. Principally these were the brothers Giuseppe and Adalbertus Artari, Francesco Vassalli and Francesco Serena. The existence of two stuccoists surnamed Artari at work in England was suggested by the mention in the Ditchley records of 'the two Mr Artares' and the inclusion on the Sutton Scarsdale rising-plate of the name of an 'Albert Artari'. The situation was confused enough to lead the present author to record[171] that the two people were Giuseppe and his father Giovanni Battista, whose third Christian name is given by some sources as 'Alberti'. The Arogno parish registers which the author subsequently searched then indicated the birth of Giuseppe's brother Adalbertus—the 'Albert' of the English records—on 8 October 1693. His father emerged firmly enough as Giovanni Battista born in 1664, not as usually stated in 1660.

The record of 'The Italian Plaisterer's Account for worke done by them in severall rooms att Ditchley'[172] in 1725 lists a number of items with their prices. The account reads:

'Imp For doing the Basso relieves in the Hall & the Brastheads with the flowers in the four corners of the ceiling	£26. 5. 0.
for the 9 Bustos	16. 16. 0.
for finishing the Salloon entirely	105. 0. 0.
For doing the six Images over the pediments	21. 0. 0.
For doing the four eagles in the Hall	4. 4. 0.
For the four roses in the Ceiling	2. 2. 0.
For the Festoons under the Bustos	10. 10. 0.
For doing the Drawing roome ceiling	15. 15. 0.

Some of this work no longer survives. For example, the nine Bustos now include some of later date, and the four eagles have left their outline on the wall but have been replaced by lion-mask lights of a Regency flavour. Ditchley, however, still boasts superb stucco-work and is carefully maintained by the Ditchley Foundation. The receipts in the archives are often signed by Giuseppe Artari and 'francesch Vassallij' for 'worke done by me & my partners'. Serena was paid for the 'Basso relievo done in the Hall'. The Ante Room contains splendid work by Vassali. Over the door is a superb mask face and the family coat-of-arms. The wall panels represent Minerva and Diana. The hound on a delicately held leash quivers for activity and is watched from above by Flora and, at the four corners of the ceiling, by medallion heads in cartouches supported by *putti*.

At about the same time, 1724, Vassalli and Adalbertus Artari were working for Francis Smith (who was to supervise many buildings for Gibbs) on a rebuilding of his own design at Sutton Scarsdale, Derbyshire. The lead rising-plate formerly at the house, but now lost, recorded that 'Francis Smith of Warwick, gentleman architect' was in charge and that in addition to carpenters, joiners, plumbers, upholsterers and lock-smiths, 'Albert Artari, gentleman and Francis Vessali, gentleman, Italians who did stuke work' were there. They were assisted by 'Joshua Needham of Derby, gentleman plasterer'.

Francesco Vassalli was born at Riva St Vitale, within a dozen miles of his friends Artari and Bagutti. The family had been settled in the village since the fourteenth century, and there is still a 'House of the Vassalli' in the village, now used as a cobbler's shop. The shoes are mended below ceilings and before a fireplace abounding with fine stucco. Interestingly enough, the Via degl'Inglesi (Street of the English) runs at the back of the house. The best documented of Vassalli's commissions is in England also: the work he did for Richard Towneley at Towneley Hall, Burnley 1729-31. He had an assistant named Martino Quadri (or Quadry), and stuccoists of that surname worked in the churches of the Swiss valleys around Riva St Vitale.

One of Vassalli's letters, containing his account relating to the Towneley work, has survived. It reads in translation:

> Most Respected Sir,
> Having written a letter to you during the past month of July to which I have received no reply, I do not know to what I should attribute the reason for this &c. Perhaps you are dissatisfied with me for not having finished your hall before this time. Wherefore, if the reason lies here, I am very glad that it is within my power to win back your favour, in that, since I have been in Italy, it is in my power to satisfy you more than I could have done before I returned into Italy. I hope you have procured everything for the completion of the above-mentioned work, for, at the beginning of February I shall be at Towneley to finish all, and in everything which you may condescend to require of me you will find me ever ready to execute your most esteemed orders. At present I am at Ask near Richmond in Yorkshire, the hall of which I have decorated with 5 rooms, the hall *c.* 47 feet in length, and 30 broad, *c.* 30 high.
> I conclude by subscribing myself always
> Your most humble servant
> Fran: Vassalli
> Aske the 7th [?] day of December 1730

While in Italy, Vassalli was presumably working and obtaining ideas and engravings which allowed him to think that 'since I have been in Italy it is in my power to satisfy you more than I could have done before I returned into Italy . . .'. His account shows that at Towneley he charged £126 for the Hall (Plate 54) and £21 for the 'ornaments on the stairs'.

The letter was written from Aske Hall, near Richmond in Yorkshire. Unfortunately

Vassalli's work has not survived there. The style of his Towneley work, with its dominant medallions, suggests, however, that he may have worked for Giacomo Leoni on a number of northern commissions, including Lyme Park, Lathom and Bold Halls, and Knowsley. The east part of the south front at Knowsley, dated 1732, closely follows Plates III and XXXVIII in Leoni's edition of *Palladio* (1715). The Lyme Park archives[173] not only include two letters from Leoni but record the friendship of the owner, Peter Legh, with the owners of Knowsley (Lord Derby) and Bold (Peter Bold). The Stucco Room at Knowsley (dated 1733) was stated by two nineteenth-century writers to contain medallion heads. Writing in his *History of the House of Stanley* (1840) William Willis records that in the Stucco Room were 'the head of the great philosopher Locke and other celebrated characters'. William Pollard, in *Stanleys of Knowsley* (1868), states that there were 'beautiful medallion heads of the twelve Caesars in *basso relievo*'.

These references to medallions touches on the one possibility of eventually isolating the work of the Swiss *stuccatori*, in England. Given a few more discoveries of exact documentation (as in the case of Towneley Hall) the task would of course be simpler. If we assume the Knowsley work to be Vassalli's—because of the medallions and because the architectural design is attributed to Leoni, who favoured employing *stuccatori*—may we deduce that the stucco medallions at the Music Room, Sun Street, Lancaster, and Lumley Castle, Durham, denote his presence there also? At least seven of the Lumley medallions are of Roman Emperors and that of 'Otho: Imp' appears also at Lancaster (Plates 61, 63). Sir John Clerk of Penicuik visited Lumley in 1738 and recorded that it 'is now very much ornamented & is indeed a very fine place'.[174] It should, however, be borne in mind that Peter Nicholson, in his *Practical Builder* (1848), writes that certain Italian *stuccatori* (who are otherwise unrecorded)—'Catezzi, Philip Danielli and Franconi [Franchini?] worked in County Durham, and at the castles of Bishop Auckland, Lumley and Hutton about 1760'.

Some of this seems like a confused story, or at least it creates one, but there may be some truth in these nineteenth-century statements. Seven years earlier than Nicholson, William Howitt recorded in his *Remarkable Places* (1842) that 'two Italians came over on purpose to do the room for Lord Richard Lumley', the owner of Lumley Castle. Howitt also described the Swiss-style stucco-work at Hylton Castle, near Sunderland, but the wings containing the seventeenth- and eighteenth-century work were later destroyed. The Charles I room in the palace at Bishop Auckland has a ceiling of the 1730s, and there is also good rococo work at Wallington, where the Franchinis certainly worked, and at Croxdale and at St Helen Hall, St Helen Auckland. It is as well to remember, however, that the English plasterers Perritt and Rose seem to have worked for James Paine as far north as Kelso and may be responsible for the Auckland ceiling. The additions at St Helen Hall may be by Paine. The Croxdale ceilings have the usual incised, modelled clouds but again the work could be by Perritt and Rose or by Giuseppe Cortese. Another Italian, Francesco Consiglio (see List), also needs to be noted.

We have noted that Francis Smith, through the work at Ditchley and Sutton Scarsdale, was well acquainted with the capabilities of both Artari and Vassalli. Apart from the Ditchley work, where he was acting for Gibbs, there is no record of Smith's employing any of the other *stuccatori*, such as Bagutti or Serena. Some consideration must be given in this light to the stucco-work at Stoneleigh Abbey, Warwickshire, and Mawley Hall, Shropshire, a house firmly attributed to Smith. It has been recently established[175] that Artari was working for Smith in 1737-8 at Trentham Hall, Staffordshire, and that Vassalli was employed there in 1751. Unfortunately, this work was in part of the house which was reconstructed in the late eighteenth century and again by Sir Charles Barry in the late 1830s before final demolition in 1910. Both Stoneleigh and Mawley, however, whilst surviving, lack the documentation which has been preserved about the demolished Trentham. Speculation about the authorship of the stucco-work on stylistic grounds therefore needs to be cautious.

The house at Stoneleigh was enlarged with a west wing designed by Smith in 1714. The original estimate survives but does not mention the interior decoration. The parish registers at Cubbington, two miles away, record that the house was finished in May 1726.[176] The stucco-work presumably dates from about 1724-5 and may be compared with the work at Sutton Scarsdale, at least by means of photographs. The Derbyshire house, a poignant ruin (work started in 1973, under the Department of the Environment, to make it safe) with stucco still clinging to its shell, was fortunately visited by Margaret Jourdain, whose illustrated account appeared in *Country Life* in February 1919, a few months before the sale of fittings. It would be rash to insist that the work at Stoneleigh is by Vassalli and Artari, but it comes into the category of their known style, with its lavish use of mythological panels. We know at least that the Birmingham locksmith John Wilkes worked at both houses—the rising-plate records his name at Sutton Scarsdale and he signed a lock at Stoneleigh. May it be assumed that most of the craftsmen went on to Stoneleigh from the Derbyshire house? Thomas Broval, the joiner at Sutton Scarsdale, was originally from Warwick, and had presumably worked on many occasions for Smith, who owned a large house and marble-yard in Warwick.

The stucco at Mawley Hall (Plates 55, 56) can be dated to about 1730, some six years after the work at Stoneleigh. The large medallions on the staircase walls are in similar style to those by Vassalli and Quadry at Towneley Hall. It is also possible to isolate motifs which appear at Ditchley. In the absence of documents applying to the work at Mawley—a fire destroyed all the house records in 1808[177]—it seems likely that two or more of the stuccoists joined forces to decorate the house. The busts in niches at the head of the staircase (Plate 56) recall work at Barnsley Park, Gloucestershire (Plates 58-60) which Rudder, the Gloucestershire county historian, pronounced in his history (1779) to be 'by the best Italian Masters'.

Barnsley Park was built in 1720-1 for Henry Perrot, a Member of Parliament for Oxford, and a frequenter of the circle of friends surrounding James Brydges, 1st Duke of Chandos. The house seems to have been complete by 1731 and was possibly designed by John Price (?-1736), an obscure, almost legendary, architect-builder employed by the Duke of Chandos. In 1714-15 the duke had employed many stuccoists at Cannons, his house in Middlesex, but he knew Bagutti and Artari well. This is not a good basis on which to attribute the work at Barnsley Park, but it is all we have—again no contemporary documents appear to have survived. There were, however, few stuccoists in England at this period other than the Italians skilled enough to produce the convincing decorations to be seen at Barnsley Park, and Rudder's attribution of the work to them seems to be near to the truth. Nevertheless it has been suggested that Charles Stanley, the Danish-born stuccoist, could be responsible. His work has long been known, but is masked by an atmosphere of riddles and unanswered questions.

Simon Carl Stanley was born in Copenhagen of an English father and a Danish mother on 12 December 1703. Recent researches by a Danish scholar, noted at the end of this book, have done much to chart his career there. In 1718 he was apprenticed to the stuccoist J. C. Sturmberg and in 1721-2 assisted him on ceilings which still survive at Fredensborg Castle. Here he was also working in the company of Italian stuccoists,[178] particularly the talented Carlo Enrico Brenno (1688-1745). The style of Brenno's work at Clausholm and Fredensborg tempts one to believe that he also worked with Stanley in England, but there is no evidence of this, and a careful study of the Fredensborg ceilings does not help to identify Stanley's later work. What evidence does survive indicates that, after further study in Amsterdam under Jan van Logteren, Stanley left in 1727 for England and was soon working with the sculptors Peter Scheemakers and Laurent Delvaux. Later, instead of leaving for Italy with his two friends and the painter Pieter Angelis, he stayed to work at Eastbourne, and it is here that the story becomes a little more involved.

English houses, as the illustrations in this book show, are rich in plaster decoration, but few can surpass Compton Place, built for Lord Wilmington at Eastbourne. The State Bedroom ceiling in particular is one of the most opulent examples in England. In a Danish biography of Charles Stanley, written by A.F.Busching in 1757, it is stated that he worked in England for almost twenty years (1727-46) 'and ... with fame for My lord Willnington in Eastbourne, Sussex, and for My lord Maynard in Essex ...'. Since Stanley signed the monuments to Thomas Maynard at Hoxne, Suffolk, and to the Maynard family at Little Easton, Essex, Katharine Esdaile assumed in 1937[179] that Stanley must have executed 'sculptures' for Lord Wilmington. Finding no relevant monument or portrait bust she thought that Stanley was responsible for the elaborate plaster ceilings at Compton Place, which indeed in terms of relief are almost 'sculptured'. However, the evidence now available warrants more caution in attributing the work to Stanley alone.

The main ceiling at Compton Place (Plate 68) commemorates in bold relief, after Titian, the amours of Venus and Adonis, and two small reliefs show Paris and Helen and Diana with Endymion. In the border, with its sphinx-like figures, modelled *putti* and elaborate shells and foliage, richness abounds, but the dominant impression is left by the centre panel. Venus has alighted from a shell-like coach drawn by fluttering birds. All around are the swirling modelled clouds, which Mrs Esdaile suggested were Stanley's most recognizable characteristic, but which appear in work by most of the Italian *stuccatori*. A re-examination of the account-book, which mentions the 'plasterers' collectively, and of a vast amount of correspondence and vouchers has revealed, however, that Stanley was not solely responsible for the plasterwork.

On several occasions Lord Wilmington's gardener, William Stuart, and his agent, Thomas Willard, are explicit in their letters about the progress of work. The main building, designed by Colin Campbell, was built by John Lane, and he expected to finish his work by 1 May 1728. A few weeks earlier, on 8 April John Hughes, the competent London plasterer who had worked for Lord Burlington, visited the house and the gardener reported that Hughes 'thinks of sending some of his men shortly to worke ...'. The vouchers for the years 1723-7 preserved at Compton Place make it clear, however, that Hughes had already been employed to work on the old house. John Burnett, 'Hewe's man', had been paid for a visit he made to the house 'with Mr Campbell' on 19 November 1726. By June 1728 Hughes had four men at work on the new house, and on 14 July Stuart, the observant gardener, informed his master 'The German plasterers say they have almost don here'. We do not know if Stanley was one of the German plasterers in Hughes's service. On 28 July 1728 Stuart reported to his master that the joiners and carvers were at work in the Gallery, the carpenters and painters likewise, but that 'the German plasterers are gon from Bourn today, to co[ll] fains [Colonel Fane's] ...'. By 11 August 'Mr Hughes's men (the plasterers), are all gon'.

It is brief mentions of this kind in correspondence which extend the sketchy evidence on which the attribution of plasterwork is based. Colonel John Fane, later 7th Earl of Westmorland, was continuing the decoration of his house at Mereworth, Kent, which

Colin Campbell had designed for him in 1722. Although the stucco-work at Mereworth is by Bagutti, as Campbell records in *Vitruvius Britannicus*, the Germans from Compton Place probably provided enrichments to Francesco Sleter's decorative paintings in the Long Gallery. Documents in the Dashwood collections at the Bodleian Library, Oxford, however, show that Sleter was still working, under Leoni's supervision, at Mereworth as late as 1739. The problem remains, but meanwhile the following conclusions can be drawn from the Compton Place documents and Busching's biography of Stanley:

1. No payment to Stanley occurs throughout Lord Wilmington's personal account-book in which payments to the woodcarver (James Richards) and other craftsmen appear.
2. If Stanley did work there he would have to be one of the 'German' plasterers working under Hughes and in consequence cannot be given sole credit for the plasterwork.
3. Some connection, as yet untraced, existed between Lord Wilmington and Stanley (as the Danish biography records) because it was in Eastbourne that Stanley married on 21 May 1730. Busching recorded that Lord Wilmington paid Stanley so well for his work that he was able to marry his Eastbourne landlady's daughter, Anne Allen.

What Stanley did at Eastbourne, apart from getting married, is open to some doubt, and the rest of his work in England is not well documented. He is said to have worked at Barnsley Park, Gloucestershire (Plates 58-60), at Hall Place, Maidenhead, at Honington Hall, Warwickshire (Plate 69), at Easton Neston, Northamptonshire, and at Stratton Park, Hampshire (the work of this date being destroyed in 1790). It should be said that all these are attributions. He certainly worked at Okeover, Staffordshire (Plate 74) and with Thomas Roberts at the Radcliffe Camera, Oxford. It is of course likely that during a residence of twenty years in England, out of which came only two monuments known from his hand, stucco-work, possibly at many of the houses noted above, would form his chief occupation.

There is a more precise reference in Volume 3 of Neale's *Seats . . .* (1823)—'Saloon, Alto Relievo in Stucco, Stanley'—which suggests that Stanley did the plasterwork at Langley Park, Norfolk (Plate 75) in the 1740s. But by October 1746, as the correspondence preserved at Okeover Hall between the architect and owner of Okeover, Joseph Sanderson and Leak Okeover respectively, makes clear, Stanley had dashed back to Denmark 'without any formal leave of his friends . . .'. At Okeover he had provided a stucco ceiling of Bacchus and Ariadne as well as marble chimneypieces and the gilding of a picture frame. Stanley's connections with John Sanderson[180] are still obscure, but it is obvious that the relationship was one of active business. One of Sanderson's letters, dated 16 October 1746, indicates that Stanley had passed over some money, 'a large sum due to him for Mr Barrington'. This may mean that Stanley had been working for Lord Barrington at Beckett Park, Berkshire, as there is no monument by him in the church at nearby Shrivenham.

This account of Stanley has taken us long past the chronology it is necessary to follow in these pages. The principal plasterer at work in the 1720s was Isaac Mansfield, who started his life in poverty and ended it as a bankrupt. When his father Samuel, who had worked as a plasterer at Sudbury, died in 1696 Isaac found himself cut off with a shilling. The reasons are not clear and Isaac went away from Derbyshire to York. By 1704 he was a freeman there and his active career was finally crowned when he became Sheriff of the city in 1728 and 1729. Mansfield must have spent some of these years in

London, perhaps through his connections with Sir John Vanbrugh and James Gibbs. In 1710 he had worked at Castle Howard alongside Bagutti and Plura, and he seems to have been first employed by Gibbs (again alongside Bagutti) in 1725 at the Senate House, Cambridge. At this time Isaac was in practice with his son, another Isaac. Isaac, senior, subscribed to the third volume of Campbell's *Vitruvius Britannicus* in 1725, and three years later father and son subscribed to Gibbs's *A Book of Architecture*.

One of the most important commissions which came in 1725 to Mansfield (who was then living in a London house near to Gibbs in Henrietta Street) was his work at Blenheim Palace, particularly in the Long Library. Hawksmoor wrote on 23 December 1725 to Sarah Duchess of Marlborough:

> 'I presume Mr Mansfield has near upon finnished great part of the Gallery by this time and I hope to your Satisfaction . . .'.[181]

The letter makes it clear that the mouldings—or bracketing—had been set out for Mansfield, and that he should be urged to take care 'in the performance of the foliage and other enrichments . . .'. The ceiling is laid out in ovals and lozenges in the best City church tradition, and rises into a splendid hexagonal framed dome at the south end (Plate 49). After the Gallery was finished Mansfield moved on into the chapel where another fine ceiling was set in to rival Rysbrack's great towering monument to the Duke of Marlborough. The duchess wrote in May 1732 that 'the Chappel is finish'd and more than half the Tomb there ready to set up . . .'. Although carved by Rysbrack it was designed by William Kent, the versatile architect whom Mansfield had probably known when working for Kent's patron, Lord Burlington, at Burlington House, Piccadilly in 1720-1. Before the work they jointly did for Frederick, Prince of Wales, could it be that Mansfield worked again for Vanbrugh at Grimsthorpe Castle, Lincolnshire?

There is, to the present author's knowledge, no precise documentation on the plaster decoration of Grimsthorpe. The chapel ceiling is a puzzling feature for, although dated by some to after 1726, its layout,[182] with the typical treatment accorded to a ceiling by such a worker as Edward Goudge, is in the style of the mid 1680s. The decoration of shells and foliage in the centre may possibly have been added later. Another explanation is to allow that the chapel is by Hawksmoor—the researches of Dr Kerry Downes show that there were drawings of the chapel in the architect's sale[183]—and that a slightly old-fashioned layout was followed in the 1720s and abandoned at Vanbrugh's death in 1726. It is interesting to recall that the Master Plasterer at this time was still David Lance— he was succeeded by George Worrall in March 1725—and that Lance was trained by Edward Goudge. Indeed, it may have been Lance who did the plasterwork for Hawksmoor on the staircase ceiling at Easton Neston, Northamptonshire (1702). Speculation of this kind is, however, of little use and we must move, in Mansfield's career at least, to firmer, documented ground—his work for Frederick, Prince of Wales.

In 1730 the prince took a lease of Kew House and shortly afterwards William Kent, 'our architect', was employed to redesign the house and its interior. An extensive series of vouchers relate to the work.[184] Christopher Cass and Andrews Jelfe were the successful and experienced masons whom Kent chose to do the main stonework. For the interior decoration Isaac Mansfield was the plasterer, and James Richards, the Master Carver to the Crown, and John Boson did the wood-carving. Mansfield's work was done over oak laths, and he had fifteen plasterers assisted by seven labourers, engaged on the task. A number of hard, durable plaster floors (at 4s 10d a square yard) were put in, but it was the enriched ceilings (at 1s 6d a foot) which would attract the visitor's eye. Some nineteen master craftsmen did all the work of erection and decoration, and the cost of

Mansfield's plasterwork was only £625 8s 9¼d out of a grand total of £9,463 18s 11¾d. By 1733 all was finished and paid for.

Whilst royal employment may be thought to have been the ambition of all plasterers, it brought little lasting success to Mansfield. In the careful scrutiny which the Duchy Office and William Kent kept over the craftsmen employed by the prince details of Mansfield's eventual bankruptcy are recorded.[185] At his death in 1739—his will was proved on 22 January—his widowed sister Alice Milhum was granted administration rights. She had a sorry task, for a Commission of Bankruptcy had been recorded against her brother on 9 December 1738. Mansfield was then living in the Parish of St James, Westminster, and his main creditors were Leonard Phillips of Scotland Yard, a timber merchant and John Mackreth of Westminster, a lime merchant. Without laths and lime no plasterer could pursue his craft, and his goods were seized in settlement. By 1740 his sister had probably cleared up the miserable affair, and she was given a letter of attorney a few days before Christmas to collect £34 2s 0d for 'plasterwork done for His Royal Highness'. Although we may not know how to disentangle the careers of Isaac from his son Isaac, we are at least certain that William Kent turned to other plasterers.

The architect, decorative painter, landscape gardener, man of letters, and delightful friend and correspondent of a host of *literati* that made up the man known as William Kent was no mean performer. He had worked for Sir Robert Walpole when the Prime Minister was building his imposing mansion of Houghton. Whilst that great man was also a fearful force to be reckoned with, he took a keen interest in and probably enjoyed the work of the decorative artists he engaged. In describing Artari's stucco-work for the Stone Hall at Houghton, Dr J.H.Plumb remarked that 'a well-concealed bawdy joke in the stucco dado could never have been made by Artari without Walpole's permission'.[186] There is also ample evidence in Burlington's and Pope's letters that Kent was the dearly loved 'card' of a wide circle and that he had also worked alongside Artari at Ditchley. When he took on architectural work in his own right he had, as we have seen, employed Isaac Mansfield as plasterer. Indeed, it may well be that the plasterwork done for Kent at Raynham Hall, Norfolk (Plate 71) is Mansfield's work, but after Mansfield's death Kent turned to Robert Dawson who had been Mansfield's foreman. He employed Dawson at Lord Pelham's house in Arlington Street and at Lady Isabella Finch's imposing house at 44 Berkeley Square. The daring 'flight' of the staircase at No. 44, praised by Walpole, is too well known to need much description or an illustration here. Dawson enriched the console brackets beneath each landing, and draped his swags, shells and oval and circular panels with an assured touch. He also compartmented the front drawing room ceiling for Kent to paint with subjects in grisaille. Within five years of the completion of the work in 1743 Kent was dead and laid to rest in 1748 in the vault at Chiswick House. To his patron at Berkeley Square, Lady Isabella Finch, he bequeathed his 'veined Alabaster Vase with brass ornaments gilt . . . together with my four models of Newton, Lock, Woollaston and Doctor Clark . . .'.

While Kent was engaged on his commissions in London Charles Stanley, the plasterer, was working in Oxfordshire. In 1742 Stanley, William Wilton, Jonathan Crook and Giuseppe Artari had submitted estimates for doing the plasterwork at the Radcliffe Camera, Oxford designed by James Gibbs. As Gibbs had engaged Artari on commissions since the 1720s it would seem natural that Artari should do this further work. His estimate[187] was the lowest of the three whose price was recorded. In addition to Artari, however, 'Charles Stanley & Thos Roberts' were engaged, and they agreed to do eight ceilings . . . 'Ornamented with Stucco according to a drawing made by Mr Gibbs at £35 each'. Their rates of work varied between 2s 2d and 2s 6d a foot and Stanley finally received £232 18s 10d for the work he and Roberts completed. This connection between Stanley and Roberts may suggest that together they were responsible for the stucco decoration of nearby Kirtlington Park, built by William Smith to the designs of John Sanderson.

The Dining Room from Kirtlington (Plates 72, 73) was re-erected at the Metropolitan Museum of Art, New York in 1955. The plaster medallions which remain at the house —those in the Library—are subjects from Aesop's *Fables* (like those at Nuthall Temple, Nottinghamshire, demolished in 1929, and at Heythrop House, Oxfordshire). Those at Kirtlington are based, as is the earlier work by William Parker at Denham Place (Plates 43-45), on the engravings in Francis Barlow's books. In 1778 Mrs Lybbe Powys said the work at Heythrop was by 'the famous Roberts of Oxford' and it seems possible, therefore, that Roberts (who was born in 1711 and had a son and nephew who were also plasterers) worked at all these three houses, and that he improved his skill at working in stucco by his collaboration with Stanley. The ceiling decorated by Roberts in the Senior Common-Room at St John's College, Oxford, with its meticulous attention to the detail of a great variety of shells, shows him to have been a worthy challenger in techniques to the enigmatic Stanley.

The main years of Roberts's activity lay in the period 1740-60 when the rococo mood of decoration persisted. The engravings of Brunetti and Hubert Gravelot and the activities of a group of artists and craftsmen meeting at Slaughter's Coffee House in London did much to make the style a popular fashion. The story has been examined elsewhere,[188] but our concern is with the plasterers who realized it all in swirling plaster, set with a swagger and verve high on wall and ceiling. London apart, no active centres existed for good craftsmanship other than York and Bristol. At York the principal plasterer for rococo-type work was Thomas Perritt (1710-59).

The Perritt family had long been settled in York and Thomas's father, Jonathan, was a bricklayer there. By 1738 Thomas had been made a freeman of the city, and in 1744 was employed with his father in cleaning various rooms and colouring the stucco-work at the Assembly Rooms. The stucco-work had been completed some ten years earlier by John Bagnall. Perritt's first main commission had come, however, in 1741 from the 7th Viscount Irwin. It was to provide plaster ceilings at Temple Newsam House, Leeds, principally in the imposing Long Gallery and adjoining Library. The Long Gallery ceiling, for which Perritt received £190 10s 9d of his total bill of almost £420, presented an iconographical problem until 1974, when Jacob Simon identified the figures in eighteenth-century dress portrayed in the medallions in the design as George I, George II and his Queen, their children and children-in-law. These are mentioned in the accounts as '13 Medals at 10s 6d each. £6 16 6d.'[189] Two of them are illustrated here (Plates 76, 77).

What is of more interest to us is that a receipt for £10, dated 27 June 1745, was signed on behalf of Perritt by 'Jos: Rose'. This one clue led to a search of the York Apprenticeship registers and to the discovery that Perritt took Joseph Rose, senior, one of the most accomplished of all plasterers and head of an important family of plasterers, as his apprentice on 16 October 1738. On this occasion Perritt was described as 'Plaisterer and worker in Stucko'.

Perritt's principal commissions, given to him by James Paine, have been described and illustrated elsewhere.[190] One of them, Nostell Priory, bears brief re-examination especially as the architect's drawing for it is now illustrated here (Plate 80). All the 'evidence' on stylistic grounds—the medallion heads, the stance of figures and the way they are disposed—point to the conclusion that the Nostell work is by Perritt and Rose. There is, however, no precise manuscript material to confirm this and indicate the cost.

What is beyond doubt is that at Nostell the plasterers rose to exceptional heights of competence (Plates 78, 79). Paine was so pleased with their work at this time that he recorded in his book on the Doncaster Mansion House (1751) that the stucco ornaments were 'executed by Mr Rose and Mr Thomas Perritt' and were 'inferior to none of the Performances of the best *Italians* that ever work'd in this Kingdom'. At Nostell they certainly showed what they could achieve.

Apart from his work for Perritt—whom he seems to have left when he came out of his apprenticeship in 1745—Rose worked at Cusworth Hall, Yorkshire, and probably at Cowick Hall and Denton Park in the same county. In addition, he was joined by his brother Jonathan for work in south Yorkshire at Wentworth Woodhouse (Plate 97) where similar medallion heads to those at Temple Newsam and Nostell appear. Joseph was then living at Doncaster, where he had taken two apprentices, Richard Mott and John Wright, but he later moved to London. In 1752 he went to Norfolk to work at Felbrigg Hall for William Windham and under Paine, being represented in part of the commission by George Green, possibly a relative of the Luke Green whom he had employed at Cusworth eight years earlier.

Whilst Paine designed excellent rococo-style ceilings and superb room settings for Perritt and Rose to execute (and more can be attributed to them as research proceeds), they did not quite match in skill of execution the work at Norfolk House, London. In 1960 Norfolk House was described and illustrated in detail in the *Survey of London* (volumes XXIX-XXX). It need only be said here that the house was designed for the 9th Duke of Norfolk by Matthew Brettingham, senior. The house was demolished in 1938 and the collections dispersed, but fortunately the Music Room was saved and re-erected at the Victoria and Albert Museum, London (Plates 85, 86). Careful descriptions of this room have been published.[191] The absence of all but one account-book firstly led to the reasonable speculation that the plasterwork was probably by William Collins, who worked later for the Duchess of Norfolk at Worksop, a house she was having built to James Paine's designs.

The prototype of the Music Room ceiling at Norfolk House was that of the Banqueting Hall in Whitehall by Inigo Jones. But the eight compartments which surround the central oval are filled with very accomplished rococo plasterwork, richly gilded. The names of the persons who carried out this work remained unknown until December 1968, when the Duke of Norfolk's archivist, Francis Steer, made a special search of the Arundel Castle archives on behalf of the present writer. The plasterer's and carver's accounts were found and prove that the plasterwork was done in 1755 by Thomas Clark, who later became Master Plasterer to the Office of Works, and that the richly gilded wood-carving is by John Cuneot. Clark's bill for work on the 'Principal Floor' amounted to £225 7s 8d and included 'Scaffolding, Colouring and adding to Ornaments—according to Mr Bora's Directions'. An 'Ornament Plaisterer' was employed for forty-five days, assisted by seven plasterers, two labourers and two boys. Fine lime and hair and nine hods of stucco were used as well as 'prepared Plaister of Paris'. A sum of £3 15s 6d was also paid 'for different degrees of Colour'. The Entablature in the Great Room was also decorated by Clark 'according to Mr Bora's Design'. Cuneot's bill, amounting to a staggering total of £2,643 3s 8½d, included a sum of £35 7s 0d for gilding the Music Room ceiling. In summary, therefore, everything in carved wood on the walls seems to be the work of Cuneot and, as one would expect, everything in plaster and stucco on the ceiling is by Thomas Clark, guided by Borra.

Not a great deal is yet known about Borra's connection with the work at Norfolk House, his previously recorded English activities having been associated with Stowe House,

Buckinghamshire.[192] It is assumed that he is the Giovanni Battista Borra who accompanied Robert Wood and his friends Dawkins and Bouverie on their journeys to Asia Minor. Here he helped to make the surveys and the drawings which were finally engraved by Fourdrinier and produced by Wood on their return in his books *The Ruins of Palmyra* (1753) and *The Ruins of Balbec* (1757).

Horace Walpole was at the opening of Norfolk House in 1756 and, like everyone else, spent much time 'gazing in the air' as he looked at the 'delightful' ceilings, many of which, in view of Borra's connection, were an early attempt at emulating those at Palmyra. Isaac Ware, however, in his book *A Complete Body of Architecture*, was to deprecate the representation of wind instruments, flowers and books of music on ceilings straggled over with meaningless C's and O's and tangled semi-circles. Such decoration was nevertheless to appear on many more occasions (Plate 83), and it has been shown[193] that Ware himself designed rococo interiors in Woodcote Park, Hertfordshire, and Belvedere, Kent, as well as those in Chesterfield House, London. Drawings made by Vardy, Lightoler and the Hiornes at this time also show enriched coves in stucco or chiaroscuro and delicate swags of flowers or fruit carved in wood or plaster. It was all contrived with a sense of balance and tension—the 'wanton kind of chace' which Ware mentioned. The ceiling of the Court Room of the Foundling Hospital in London and that in the library of Christ Church, Oxford, show how William Wilton and Thomas Roberts respectively handled the sensuous mood in plaster.

Clark, the creator of the rococo plasterwork at Norfolk House, had a successful career, and yet he first comes to our notice for bad workmanship. The Worshipful Company of Plaisterers tried in a desultory way to control the quality of work done by its members by fining them for bad work. They maintained a 'Work Quest and Fine Book'[194] from 1653 to 1761. It might be expected that this would provide many details of houses and plasterers' names, but it was kept in a very casual manner. It does, however, indicate that on 'Search Day, August 20th, 1742' Thomas Clark was fined 'for bad workmanship in washing, stopping, whitening at his Majesty's Palace of Saint James for which said offence we believe he ought to be fined in the Sum of £4 os od'. At that time Clark was working under the direction of the Master Plasterer, George Worrall. His first major commission was, however, in Norfolk, where he worked for Thomas Coke, 1st Earl of Leicester, at Holkham Hall (Plate 95).

The story of Lord Leicester's Grand Tour, his collection of rare books, manuscripts, pictures and statuary, and his dedication in erecting Holkham to Classical pattern has been delightfully told in recent years.[195] The general idea of the house 'was first struck out by the Earls of Leicester and Burlington, assisted by Mr W.Kent', but the final realization was entrusted to Matthew Brettingham, senior. He and Clark were to be associated at a later date at Norfolk House. At Holkham, Clark's main task was to create the coffered panels of the Great Hall ceiling, probably based on a drawing by Inigo Jones or John Webb probably in Lord Burlington's collections and derived, in its other parts, on the plates which appeared in Desgodetz's popular book *Les Edifices Antiques de Rome*, such as those of the Temple of Peace. Lord Leicester and his friends Lord Burlington and William Kent were concerned that the main features of the house should be adapted or copied from such sources or from the designs by Jones or Webb in Burlington's possession. Clark worked at Holkham over many years providing plasterwork (some of it gilded) of great competence. He was working in the Saloon by 1753, but his great achievements in the Hall were not completed until after 1759, ten years after it had been roofed. It was in that year that Lord Leicester died, but by 1762 the house was more or less finished, owing much to Brettingham's supervision.

Although the rococo and Gothic styles of the 1750s were divergent from their sources, they had much in common with each other and reflected the taste of the age which saw their fulfilment. They did not conform to simplicity or regular pattern, and decorative elements adorn them both. The Gothicists looked back to an English medieval past, and the exponents of rococo to a world of present fantasy, the sprite-like touch of which was to enhance for a time even Gothic itself. In the 'amazing super-abundance of taste' which prevailed few could say what taste really was or what the word signified, but all strived to produce their versions of it in the interiors they created. None was more diligent than a small group of patrons—Horace Walpole, George Lyttelton and James Harris among them—and the plasterers they employed. Often the concern was with atmosphere rather than structural stability, as exemplified by the ruinated castle which the architect Sanderson Miller (1717-80) erected for Lyttelton in 1748 at Hagley, Worcestershire.

Miller was in demand for ruins, their erection and repair, but he found time in 1754 to rebuild the Great Hall of Lacock Abbey, Wiltshire, with plasterwork in suitable fan-vaulted medieval style, and to supervise the Gothic decoration of the chapel at Wroxton Abbey, Oxfordshire (Plate 81). He had wanted to design a Gothic house for his friend George Lyttelton at Hagley. The final plan, with borrowings from John Chute, a member of Horace Walpole's Committee of Taste, and from Miller's ideas was said by Walpole to have been stolen from the concept of the Walpole family home of Houghton, Norfolk. Certainly the interior of the house at Hagley was decorated, not by Miller's favourite 'Gothic plasterers', Robert Moor and Richard Huss, but by Francesco Vassalli (Plate 98), an Italian stuccoist who knew little of the long survival of Gothic in England.

Wren and Hawksmoor had retained the Gothic form for certain ecclesiastical and collegiate projects, and Sir John Vanbrugh had redesigned the staircase ceiling at Audley End, Essex, in a Jacobean Revival style in 1720. William Kent, at a time when he was employing Isaac Mansfield for his work at Kew, introduced imitation Jacobean-style ceilings in rooms in the George II Gateway at Hampton Court in 1732. It can be seen therefore that Gothic in the mid-eighteenth century was certainly a survival, and that Horace Walpole, much as he approved of Gothic, was a champion rather than an inventor of it. At Strawberry Hill, which he started to Gothicize in 1749, he was able to please his own taste and realize his own visions. These included rooms with Gothic wallpapers copied from the screen of Prince Arthur's tomb in Worcester Cathedral, library book-cases designed, with scarcely any adaptation, from the Hollar engraving of the choir of old St Paul's, and fan-vaulted ceilings worthy of Henry VII's Chapel.

The continuance of the Gothic style was assured during Walpole's lifetime, and it found in Batty Langley, as well as in Miller and his friends, an important literary champion. The architects Henry Keene and James Essex worked in the styles advocated by Langley, and there were occasional later essays in Gothic building by Capability Brown, Robert Adam and James Wyatt. Henry Keene (1726-76) was for a time Surveyor to the Dean and Chapter of Westminster and thus had plenty of opportunity to revere and restore earlier styles of architecture. His most famous Gothic essay, in which Westminster elements appear, was for Sir Roger Newdigate at Arbury Hall, Warwickshire. When Sir Roger returned from the Grand Tour in 1742, he seems to have begun the transformation of Arbury, a project which went on until his death in 1806. All the principal rooms, with the exception of the Wren Chapel (Plate 30), were either completely or partly redecorated in the Gothic manner. The Dining Room has its fine fan-vaults and the bow window-bay of the Saloon, is one of the most notable examples of the plasterer's art, revealing a sugar-icing delicacy in all its complex parts (Colour Plate II).

Other architects who turned their attention to Gothic work were George Shakespear and John Phillips of London. They worked for the antiquarian James West at Alscot, Warwickshire, where they created Gothic plasterwork and woodwork. The author of the plasterwork in James Harris's house in The Close at Salisbury is unknown. Harris is praised on his monument of 1780 in the Cathedral for his great learning. Some of this he applied to the decoration of his house, which in the 1750-60 period was given a delightful Gothic library with a chimneypiece decorated in rococo mood surmounted by Gothic arches, and a stylish window-bay with deep leaf ribs.

The elusive rococo style, which like the Gothic, made a short-lived contribution to English interior decoration, also had some exponents who were used to its vagaries in churches and houses abroad. The Italian stuccoists, whose activities were so important in the 1730s, had a second flowering in the 1740-60 period. Principally the later commissions of Artari and of the two Vassallis must be considered, as well as those of Giuseppe Cortese and the Franchini brothers.

The Franchini were skilled *stuccatori* from Mendrisio, Switzerland, whose work in England is surrounded in mystery. Mr John Cornforth, however, discovered a note by the Duchess of Northumberland[196] among the Northumberland archives at Alnwick Castle which indicates that the plasterwork at Wallington, Northumberland, is by the Franchini brothers. The wife of the 1st Duke of Northumberland was an inveterate country house visitor and diary-writer of great wit, and there is no reason to think that, with her considerable capacity for recalling detail, she would mention the Franchini if some other *stuccatori* had been involved in decorating at Wallington. Mr Cornforth has also indicated to the present author that the documentation implies that one of the brothers was also employed by the duke in the early 1750s, perhaps in the gallery at Northumberland House. The plasterwork at Wallington bears comparison with work by the Franchini brothers in Ireland,[197] where they were to purvey a flamboyant style of baroque mixed up with forms of rococo and to achieve a skilful depiction of the full-size figure. A third Franchini, otherwise unrecorded, has been noted working for the architect Daniel Garrett.

We have to seek hard for Vassalli in these years. In 1736 he had been given a commission, in preference to Artari, to decorate the Temple of the Four Winds at Castle Howard in stucco and scagliola. Artari, for his part, made rare appearances in the 1740s at Trentham Hall, Staffordshire, Wimpole Hall, Cambridgeshire and Castle Hill, Devon. There is no doubt that both stuccoists worked on commissions at houses and churches abroad, and details of those which are known are recorded in the List of Plasterers in this book. In summary it may be said that plasterwork in these years was monopolized by a dozen or so good English plasterers, with some commissions wrested from their hands by foreigners such as Vassalli, Artari and, particularly in the north, Giuseppe Cortese.

Cortese's name first appears on the back of a drawing which came to light among drawings by Colin Campbell presented to the Royal Institute of British Architects Library in 1967. It allows speculation that he was in England by the late 1720s, although his first recorded commissions were at Studley Royal and Gilling Castle in Yorkshire.

John Aislabie had finished his house at Studley Royal with advice from Colin Campbell and Roger Morris by about 1730. After his death in 1742 decoration was continued by his son William. Cortese's name first appears in 1745 in the surviving documents.[198] He wrote a letter on 15 August 1745, asking that his man Tadei, who was decorating the house at the time, be given £10. Cortese worked sporadically at the house for several more years, but in 1752 he submitted a Bill of Work and expressed his hope that William

Aislabie would 'remember all tis Alteraivo wich was all done by your Order'. His quaint attempts at mastering English were to be commended, his work even more so. Unfortunately it was all destroyed by the fire which gutted Studley Royal (except the Stable Block) in April 1946, and can only be partially assessed in the photographs accompanying the description of the house in *Country Life* in 1931.

Cortese's work for Lord Fairfax at Gilling Castle (now the preparatory school to Ampleforth Abbey) luckily survives, and careful and sympathetic care is taken of the building and energetic searches are constantly made in the surviving documentation about it.[199] The researches of Father Hugh Aveling and Father James Forbes have established that the 'new building' of Gilling was in progress by 1738 and that the gallery was complete by 1740-2. In 1747 more building was in progress and Cortese was at work there. He decorated the summer house in the grounds in 1751, and in 1757-9 was employed on the Temple and in the Hall. All the work done at Gilling in the 1750s—like that done at the house acquired by the Fairfaxes in York in 1759—was under the supervision of the successful northern architect John Carr. It may be at Gilling that Cortese forged a connection with Carr's usual plasterer, James Henderson of York. The latter was to act as one of Cortese's executors when the *stuccatore* died in 1778, and he may well have learned many tricks from Cortese as Roberts did from Stanley and Joseph Rose may have done from John, the other Vassalli. Cortese's other work in Yorkshire (Plate 100) was done mainly between 1760 and his death in 1778, by which time he was living at Wakefield.

Between 1736, when he was at Castle Howard, and the 1760s Vassalli appears only four times: in 1751 at Trentham Hall, Staffordshire, in 1753 at Petworth House, Sussex, in 1758 at Hagley Hall, Worcestershire, and in 1763 at Shugborough Hall, again in Staffordshire. There is some reason to think that, as well as the two Artari brothers, there were two Vassalli relatives, Francesco and Giovanni (or John). In 1758-9 a 'John' Vassalli signed receipts for work done at Croome Court, Worcestershire, a house which three years later was to be extensively remodelled by Robert Adam and the Rose family of plasterers. A further bill at Croome, unsigned but in a similar hand, records that 'Stucco work by hand & Plaisterer's work' was done in 1761 to the value of £299. It may not be too fanciful to suggest that John Vassalli was employed by the Rose firm—Joseph Rose, senior, had worked with a 'Signor Pedrola' at Ormesby, Lincolnshire, in 1755—and there is slight evidence to show that Rose, senior, had also visited Italy, as his nephew Joseph was to do in 1766. The relationship between Vassalli and the Rose family may have been similar to that referred to some years later in the correspondence between the Jesuit Father Thorpe and Henry, 8th Lord Arundell. A letter of 1775, relating to work at Wardour Castle exclaims: 'they [English plasterers] certainly work very well in stucco yet they now offer a young [Italian] lad £300 p. an. and all expenses of journey, diet and lodging, if he will agree to work stucco in England for five years'.

Artari's career in the 1750s is also obscure. There is, however, slight reason to think that he was responsible for the stucco-work at Ragley Hall, Warwickshire (Plate 96). The Hall, with its rich decoration, is one of the last and least known works of James Gibbs, who in the early 1750s was engaged by the 1st Earl of Hertford to complete the unfinished house. The stucco-work in the Hall, at least, does not seem to have been carried out until 1756. When Dr Richard Pococke visited the house on 28 September 1756 he recorded that it was 'just new modelled and embellished with ornaments in stucco'. The slight evidence for Artari's authorship is suggested by references to him three years later in the Earl of Hertford's letters to Horace Walpole, now preserved in the British Museum. On 14 July 1759 Hertford writes:

'. . . if your building and Press can spare you for a day I shall be glad to meet you in town about the middle of next week, and shall hope you will call at Snr Artario's to see the Design you fixed on for my Saloon in Colours.'

Two months later, on 1 September Hertford writes again:

'. . . I propose bringing back with me Sn^r Artario's design for the Saloon as I am inclined to have some parts of it altered which I think far from being perfect.'

By 13 December 1760 he reports that 'my new painted ceiling' is finished, 'not ill, nor very elegantly'. These letters refer to the Red Saloon, which is usually regarded as the later work of James Wyatt. There is no doubt that Wyatt did do extensive work at Ragley. Our only concern here is to suggest that Artari, one of Gibbs's favourite plasterers, did all the stucco-work, and was retained for later work in a more Neo-Classical vein. But again the exact and undisputed documentation is lacking.

Lastly in this chapter, which is almost entirely given over to the activities of the Swiss *stuccatori*, there is need to examine some work of 1759 done by George Richardson (*c*. 1736-1813) at Kedleston, the Derbyshire house erected by Robert Adam for Lord Scarsdale, 1760-4. It has been shown[200] that Richardson had accompanied James Adam on the Grand Tour, and had entered the service of the brother architects as a draughtsman.

In his *A Book of Ornamental Ceilings, in the style of the Antique Grotesque*, which Richardson issued in 1776, dedicated to Lord Scarsdale, Richardson stated that he had been 'for 18 years draughtsman and designer to those eminent Masters Messrs Adam of the Adelphi'. Before setting out for his travels in Italy and Dalmatia he provided the design for the ceiling of the Great Hall ceiling at Kedleston. Some of the work itself seems to have been done by the plasterer Abraham Denstone,[201] who was also to do plain plastering there two or three years later under the supervision of Joseph Rose. Some touches were also added to Richardson's scheme by Joseph Rose, who charged £29 0s 6d for decoration over the chimneypiece. As a tribute to Richardson both Rose, junior, his father and his uncle subscribed in 1776 for copies of Richardson's book. It showed much that was in 'the best manner', with its depiction of honeysuckle, the husk, 'and other ornaments of graceful contour'.

Robert Adam was now back from his Grand Tour, ready to launch a style and ferment everyone into action. The *stuccatori*, by now elderly and out of touch with the vogue of the new Classicism, left for sunny lands or quietly died, unknown and unmourned. Only Vassalli—perhaps John Vassalli—worked on at Shugborough in the early 1760s.

CHAPTER VI

Classical Composition, 1760-1830

As you seem'd fully determin'd, when here, to have the Front of your House in St James's Square done with Mr Liardet's Stone Paste . . .
Robert Adam to Sir Rowland Winn, 6 July 1774. (Nostell Priory Archives, C3.5(1)9)

IN the previous chapter we have summarized some of the main achievements of the *stuccatori* and suggested that there may have been two Artaris and two Vassallis at work in England. Some further light on the activities of John Vassalli is shed both by the receipts which he signed for work at Croome Court, Worcestershire, and by the work that he did at Petworth, Hagley Hall, and Shugborough. A common link between Hagley and Shugborough is to be found in the employment of both Vassalli and the architect and painter James Stuart. The correspondence of George Lyttelton, the owner of Hagley, particularly his letters to Mrs Montagu (now at the Huntington Library, California), throws light on the work going on at Hagley. Three letters add to the fragments of information in similar letters to other friends which Lilian Dickins and Mary Stanton printed in 1910 under the title *An Eighteenth Century Correspondence*.

Vassalli—whether Francesco or 'John' is not clear—had obviously finished his stucco-work at Hagley by 1758 (Plate 98). James Stuart was then engaged to build 'a true Attick Building, a Portico of six Pillars'. This was the Doric Temple of Theseus, as important to the early history of the Greek Revival in British architecture as Sanderson Miller's ruinated castle elsewhere in the grounds is to the story of the Gothic revival. Stuart was then to paint a Flora and four zephyrs on the Tapestry Room ceiling in the main house. Lyttelton told Mrs Montagu in one of his letters that the ceiling was 'ornamented with Flowers in Stucco, but has spaces left for these Pictures'. Stuart thought that all the stucco-work at Hagley was 'very well done'.

The house was ready by September 1760, the foundations having been laid in 1754. The Temple, begun in 1758, was delayed in building, since Lyttelton was probably diverting most of his money to building the main house to Sanderson Miller's design. By the autumn of 1762, however, the Temple was finished, and in that year it was approved by Robert Adam on a swift visit to Hagley. What was more important to Stuart was that on 15 October 1762, he brought Thomas Anson of Shugborough over to Hagley.

The Hon. Thomas Anson inherited all his brother's possessions in 1762. During the remaining eleven years of his life he employed Stuart to erect an interesting and important series of monuments in neo-Greek style in the park at Shugborough and to embellish the house. There was also a London house (15 St James's Square) which Stuart designed for Anson. The visit which Anson and Stuart made to Hagley was obviously one of exploration in preparation for the work at Shugborough. It was therefore natural that, being pleased with Vassalli's work there, Anson should invite the plasterer to work at Shugborough. In 1964[202] the present writer attributed the Shugborough work to Vassalli, and it was therefore pleasant when documentation emerged in 1966 which confirmed this.

In 1763 Philip Yorke, who a year later became the 2nd Earl of Hardwicke, visited his friend Anson at Shugborough and in the letters which he wrote to his father he referred to Vassalli's work there[203] (Plate 99). On 21 August 1763 he wrote that Shugborough had received many embellishments since his first visit in 1748 and that 'Versalli's Stucco here is twice as good as his Performances at Hagley not to mention the Superiority of the Designs . . .'. In another letter Philip described the house in detail and enthusiastically remarked 'The Stucco Ceilings by Versalli (who lives in the neighbourhood) are the best I ever saw, particularly that in the Great Room, which is a copy of Guido's Aurora'. He did not like the 'Pictures in Stucco', the paintings by Stuart in stucco frames in the vestibule, the colouring of which Yorke found hard and raw. This was proof enough of Vassalli's work, but further confirmation is found in the manuscript *Journal of an Excursion into Wales, etc.* by Sir Joseph Banks.[204]

Before turning to the activities of Robert Adam and his rivals and their employment of the Rose family we must consider the work of two other plasterers, Thomas Roberts of Oxford and Thomas Stocking of Bristol. We have seen that Roberts had an association in the 1740s with Charles Stanley, and that he had produced competent work during these middle years at St John's College, Christ Church and elsewhere in Oxford. In February 1761 a fire broke out at Roberts's workshop in Oxford, and much of his work was destroyed. By 1764 he had recovered enough to do his best-known work in the Great Parlour at Rousham, Oxfordshire where he provided attractive frames for the pictures. Roberts was helped by his son William and his nephew James. After his father's death in 1771 William was in partnership with James for a time. Then he finally severed his connections with plastering to take over the licence of a public-house at Hounslow, Middlesex.

Plasterwork in the west country at this time was usually done by Joseph Thomas and Thomas Stocking. It has perhaps not previously been noticed that Thomas Stocking had a son also named Thomas who was apprenticed to his father in 1765. Stocking's best-known work is at Corsham Court, Wiltshire, where he carried out the decoration of the State Rooms and the Library. Paul Methuen, the owner of Corsham, recorded in his Day Book, 1761-2, payments totalling £105 9s 0d to 'Stocking, stuko man', and the book, continuing the list of payments until 1766, shows that Stocking received £570 in all, of which £390 was probably for the Gallery ceiling. This has a coffered design, and the coves are decorated with bold serpentine scrolls. The centre of each side is marked by a medallion modelled in relief. That of the 'Birdcatcher' is particularly attractive. At Corsham, Stocking was working to the instructions and design of Capability Brown. The design, however, was not one which Brown created with Corsham in mind: he had offered it to William Constable, who, however, never used it for his Yorkshire house, Burton Constable, near Hull.

It has been pointed out[205] that the stucco decoration work at Corsham has no affinity with work being done in London in the early 1760s. But similar work, mostly by Stocking, was being done in Bristol at the Assembly Rooms (1756), the Royal Fort (*c.* 1760) (Plates 91, 92), St Nicholas Church (1768, destroyed by bombing in 1941) and the Roman Bath at Arno's Castle, now transferred to Portmeirion. Methuen did, however, patronize London craftsmen for his other decorative work at Corsham. The king's brass-founder, James Palmer, provided the cast and chased ormolu door-furniture and the fashionable and arrogant John Cobb provided the 'extra neat Inlaid Comode' and a pair of *torchères* which are among the leading examples of their kind. In 1770 'Mr. Adams' was paid for the designs for the four pier-glasses in the Picture Gallery. The mirrors are most elegant, with two female figures surmounting the glass and holding a further oval glass in a foliated frame. An added attraction is the reflection of Stocking's plasterwork or, if Mr Methuen was recording with precise knowledge, stucco-work.

The history of stucco decoration in the Adam period must be considered in the light of two important factors: firstly, the development and use of many different kinds of plasters at this time, and secondly the legal action by which the Adam brothers sought to establish their claims to the use of patent stucco. The work done by the *stuccatori* in England had familiarized English plasterers with stucco, and their bills frequently include the specific mention of stucco, as opposed to plaster containing hair and other organic material. The old Renaissance recipes for compositions of stucco or cement by Alberti, published in 1485, were restated when Leoni issued his English translation of Alberti in 1726. Various experiments were also made in England, and some even tried to protect themselves by taking out patents.

Isaac Pyke, who was Governor of St Helena in 1717, spent much time in having a tomb ten feet high and seven feet broad built in memory of his wife. The mortar he used and the experience he gained enabled him to report to Edmund Halley, Vice-President of the Royal Society, 'of a method of making the best mortar'.[206] From this development, David Wark, a clergyman, claimed in his specification of 1765 (patent no. 834) that he had 'a composition of stone paste made with oils and various other things' and that this could be used to cover walls, roofs and domes and even to line water-cisterns. Charles Neville, who lived in Lincolnshire, claimed in July 1744 to have a 'Lime Stucco Plaster, Morter Cement made from Cockle, Oyster and other sea shells by grinding, pounding or burning the same'.[207]

Neville's claim in particular is an interesting one, but makes us go back in time to the period of Wren and Vanbrugh to understand it. In the *Parentalia* volume of reminiscences about Wren, his son records that stucco of cockle-shell lime, 'which becomes as hard as *Portland* stone', was used at St Paul's Cathedral. This must have been a favourite material of the time, but when Vanbrugh wrote to the Duchess of Marlborough on 19 June 1716,[208] he indicated that 'the Plaistering done at Blenheim is all after the Dutch manner which nobody is got into the practice of here in England; but it is well worth what it costs more than our manner being as much difference as between fine paper and coarse, besides it being much more lasting'. Dr Katharine Fremantle has kindly tried to establish for the present writer what this 'Dutch manner' means.

When Sir James Thornhill travelled in the Low Countries in 1711 he described a merchant's house in Rotterdam, the home of Jacques Meijers, and noted that 'the passage leading to this room is hard like stone done with cockle shell lime, very delicate'.[209] Vanbrugh must have been referring to stucco-work made from cockle shells, of the kind that became popular in the United Provinces under the influence of Daniel Marot, the Huguenot designer, but it is clearly a difference in technique to which he is referring. The use of shells to make plaster was common in the west part of the Dutch republic in the eighteenth century. All this may seem at some distance from the later kinds of stucco, but the various patents often cite earlier methods and materials, as we have noted in the case of Wark's patent of 1765, which relied on Isaac Pyke's earlier work.

The most famous of the compositions was that which 'John Liardet of Great Suffolk Street in the Parish of St Martin-in-the-Fields in the City of Westminster, Clerk,' claimed to have invented. In his specification of patent (1773. No. 1040) he said he had invented 'A Composition or Cement for all the Branches concerning Buildings to which the same is applicable, with a Grease for Frictions, preserving Steel, Iron and Various other Uses'. It contained drying oil, absorbent matter, solid material such as gravel, sand and 'white or any coloured lead'. It was its use that led to a legal dispute.

The facts are set out in two rare pamphlets, *Observations on Two Trials at Law respecting Messieurs Adams's new invented Patent Stucco* and a *Reply* thereto, published in 1778.

Having purchased both Wark's and Liardet's recipes, the Adam brothers were in a position to prosecute anyone selling a similar composition, particularly one resembling Liardet's, which was easy and practical to use. In a short time they were forced to proceed against the architect John Johnson of Berners Street. He claimed to have improved on a composition previous to that of Wark, Liardet or, as it was now called, 'Adams's new invented patent Stucco' and had proceeded by patent (1777. No. 1150) to manufacture it. The case was heard in the King's Bench before the Lord Chief Justice, Lord Mansfield, a fellow Scot and friend of the Adam brothers, who had worked at Kenwood for him.

The present writer has previously summarized the evidence[210] but a number of points may be observed, particularly in the evidence given by architects and plasterers. Johnson had made bold claims: his composition would ornament houses and buildings both without and within, and would 'adhere to surfaces that are wet as well as those that are dry, at any season of the year'. Six architects—Taylor, Paine, Mylne, Dance, Sandby and James Stuart—were examined. Strangely enough, Stuart claimed no experience in stuccoes, but said that when it was applied to Thomas Anson's house at Shugborough it had failed. The general consensus of opinion was, however, that stucco 'promises to be better than any thing hitherto known before'. Joseph Rose, the principal plasterer called to give evidence, said it was much superior to anything he knew, 'and in all his experience he was never taught to do such a thing before'. Support for the superiority of the Adam stucco continued, with the mason John Devall, the younger, saying that it was 'the best he ever heard of'. By 'mature consideration' the jury found for the Adam brothers, who could then tighten their hold on the market for providing panels and bas-reliefs, festoons, griffins and mask-heads, and all the impedimenta of their all-pervading style.

Among the plasterers employed regularly by the Adam brothers were the family firm of Joseph Rose & Co. and William Collins. The dictionary entry in this book for the Rose family surveys the most important commissions in which they were involved. With Joseph Rose, senior, working principally for James Paine, and his nephew, Joseph, for the Adam brothers, Sir William Chambers and James Wyatt, the family exercised an almost complete monopoly over English plasterwork in the 1750-90 period. The principal years of their activity coincided with the important new influence on artistic training which came with the foundation of The Royal Academy Schools in 1768.

We have seen (chapter II) that hitherto training in England for the crafts consisted of apprenticeship, with examinations carried out by the Livery Companies to determine proficiency. There was no organization which set a standard in design or encouraged individual lines of experiment or development. In the early eighteenth century Sir Godfrey Kneller and Sir James Thornhill supported an academy which was continued by Thornhill's son-in-law, William Hogarth. This St Martin's Lane Academy had influential members in the history painter Francis Hayman, the engraver Hubert Gravelot, the talented sculptor Louis François Roubiliac, and silversmiths, seal engravers and painters who have been noted as an important influence in the advancement of the rococo style.

The Academy did not, however, have much effect on the training of students, and a deteriorating situation over the next twenty years brought the final presentation of a memorial to King George III, signed by twenty-two artists and architects. Adam was not one of the signatories but his rival William Chambers was, and the list also included the signatures of many of the decorative painters whom Adam patronized, such as

Cipriani, Angelica Kauffmann and Francesco Zuccarelli.[211] The gracious patronage which resulted from the presentation of the memorial founded the Royal Academy and laid down the basis for its schools. Of the 1551 pupils admitted in the period 1768-1830, almost half (771) were painters, and the remainder consisted of architects (247), designers (3), draughtsmen (4), engravers and sculptors.

Perhaps one of the most significant names for our purpose to appear in these lists was that of Joseph Rose, junior (1745-99) who was to take his place in the family firm of plasterers as one of Robert Adam's most dependable craftsmen. Born in March 1745, he was baptized on 5 April 1745 at Norton, Derbyshire. By 1768 he was on a visit to Italy with influential companions, including the landscape painters James Forrester and George Robertson, Mr and Mrs Richard Dalton, a Miss Robinson, Gavin Hamilton, Peter de Angelis and Joseph Nollekens the sculptor. Dalton had been sent to Italy by George III to collect pictures for the royal collections. Returning to England, Rose entered the Royal Academy Schools in 1770. He married in 1774 and was admitted as a member of the Worshipful Company of Plaisterers in 1775. In the previous year his uncle had been made Master of the Company. The Rose family had already served Robert Adam from as early as 1760 and Joseph, junior, was probably present at most of these early commissions despite being still in his teens.

Details of the expenditure incurred in the execution of a few of the forty-five or so commissions with which Adam concerned himself in the 1760-90 period can be traced. The expenditure at Croome, Kedleston, Syon and 20 St James's Square has been set out on a previous occasion.[212] Adam prospered; his bank account showed a balance of £6,620 in 1764, the year it opened at Drummonds Bank, and by 1771 it was over £40,000. Success had come his way, but did it come to his craftsmen? In the case of the Rose family and the important cabinet-makers, sculptors and decorative painters, there seems little doubt that their incomes were considerable. An examination of the wills of Joseph Rose, senior and junior, and the bank accounts at Drummond's of the cabinet-maker John Cobb, and the sculptor Henry Cheere show that this was so. Joseph Rose, senior, was in a position to leave £6,000 each to his nephews, and Cobb's account shows a steady £5,000-£6,000 annual income. In his first will of 3 February 1774 Cobb left his wife Mary Cobb 'one half of a fortune amounting to upwards of £12,000 which I have on the 3 per cent funds'. By his second will of 17 July 1776 he had increased this to £22,000. It may well be that the provision of classic order and discipline paid a craftsman well, even if fertility of invention had to be sacrificed to the rule and precedent of Neo-Classicism, and there was always the wish to avoid the fate of bankruptcy which had befallen Mansfield and others such as the cabinet-maker Samuel Norman.

The family firm of Rose did the plasterwork at most Adam commissions, but they were not always meticulous with their accounts. In September 1777 Robert Adams examined those which Rose had submitted for work at Nostell Priory, Yorkshire. He indicated to Sir Rowland Winn, the owner, the plasterer's dependence on their judgment[213]

> '. . . we have put such prices as are rather under than above the ordinary allowance . . . Mr Rose left it altogether to be settled by us. Nor did he ever see the bill till it was in the State it now is'.

The work at Nostell had been done over a long period, and the accounts also included work done at Sir Rowland's London house, 11 St James's Square. John Adam wrote to Sir Rowland on 6 July 1774, that as he was determined to have the front of the house done 'with Mr. Liardet's Stone paste', two drawings were being sent. One showed it plain; the other tempted by showing pilasters and other ornament. The plain version would cost £180, the decorated above £500. As it was then July Sir Rowland was advised how favourable the weather was for such work and informed that the paste was ready. Sir Rowland chose the ornamented front, the design for which is preserved in the Soane Museum, London. A letter written by Rose to Sir Rowland on 20 August 1777 reveals that a failure occurred later in the external stucco and that the misfortune came about because the 'usual and necessary preparations' (covering the cornices and other projections with lead and securing the joints of the coping) were not made by Sir Rowland's men. He was willing to take a deduction, however, to satisfy this important client of his architect master.

At both Kedleston, Harewood and Nostell, Rose was content to see work by Sir Henry Cheere's pupil William Collins (1721-93) incorporated. This London plasterer and sculptor had built up a successful business making plaster casts and devising bas-reliefs for insertion in niches and mounting over doors and chimneypieces. In addition, he could provide composition panels and medallions for mounting on the exterior of the house. He does not seem to have had any connection with Sir William Chambers's principal plasterer, Thomas Collins.

Sir William Chambers's bank account started (at Drummonds Bank) as a joint one with Thomas Collins. The latter, born in 1735, had been apprenticed to his uncle William Wilton, a well-known London plasterer and father of Joseph Wilton R.A., the sculptor. He owned joint leases on property with Chambers and in 1770 alone there were payments of £1,420 to him in the account. When Chambers died in 1796 Collins was appointed an executor and trustee. He lived to reach the age of ninety-five and died in 1830. His obituary in the *Gentleman's Magazine* (3 May) says of him: 'he became a desirable member of the society of Dr Johnson and Sir William Chambers...', an indication of the levels to which a competent craftsman could rise, but which few attained.

In his work for Chambers at Somerset House, Collins came up against the arguments over payment set in hand by the two partners Thomas Clark and Charles Clarke. We have seen that Thomas Clark, was successful and that he had become Master Plasterer to the Office of Works. He seems to have taken Charles Clarke as his Clerk and Measurer in 'about 1772 and at leisure times'. Clarke 'worked at the plastering business as journeyman'. He then moved for a time into the service of another plasterer, known only by the name Bever, and finally returned to become Thomas Clark's partner. After their work at Somerset House in 1782 had been assessed by James Paine a reduction in costs was suggested. Thomas had just died and in 1783 Charles Clarke published a pamphlet, *The Plaisterer's Bill for Works ... at Somerset House*. In it he retails his background and in the 7th injunction strikes out. Sir William Chambers, architect of Somerset House, had favoured Collins's plasterers despite the fact that Clark had been, in the words of the pamphlet, 'the Kings patent plaisterer and had always been employed to do all public works under government'.

Besides the two partners themselves Clarke declared that on the site they had one clerk attending to the men, two others copying drawings and writing out accounts, and a labourer at the yard packing and sending off materials. They were using wax moulds and there was considerable waste of wax, which was costing 2s a pound. With great fervour Clarke punched out his message to leave their bill alone. The final accounts[214] show that Thomas Clark, as senior partner, received £1,176 8s 6d. The Collins firm, with work continued for it by John Papworth after 1784, received almost ten times as much. The composition ornaments were on this occasion, however, provided not by William Collins but by James Thorpe. The ever-present Joseph Rose received over £1,100.

Sir William, therefore, was faithful to his earlier statement. In May 1757 he had written:

> 'An architect from the nature of his employment must have many dependants among Artificers. His Bussiness is to penetrate into the capacities of all and to Employ each according to his talents . . .'[215]

The main names apart, it was the general dissemination of pattern-books and the increasing awareness of the advantages of travel which gave provincial craftsmen their chance. In 1771 William Rhodes, for example, provided a ceiling for the Saloon at Drayton House, Northamptonshire (Plate 114) using Robert Wood's book on Palmyra (1753) as the basis for the work. The work supervised by Thomas Farnolls Pritchard of Shrewsbury in the counties of Shropshire and Herefordshire has been recently established.[216] It may have included designs for the plasterwork at Tong Castle (now demolished) and Croft Castle. The plasterer here is most likely to have been Joseph Bromfield of Shrewsbury, who is credited with the delicate work in the Lion Hotel, Shrewsbury, now thought to have been one of Pritchard's late works. Bromfield also did the delicate festoons in the Saloon and Library at Hartlebury Castle, Worcestershire in 1782. Vassalli may also have worked for Pritchard at Tong and at Hatton Grange, Shropshire—the decoration has similarities to that at Hagley—but it is unwise for us to speculate too much without the exact documentation. One last word might imply that Pritchard also employed or worked with the Warrington plasterer Thomas Oliver. Oliver did the plasterwork at Tabley, Cheshire, 1762-7, and may have also worked at Tatton Park nearby. At Tatton, Pritchard's dining room, with its fine plasterwork, survives amongst the later work of Samuel Wyatt.

It was inevitable that, apart from Sir William Chambers, there should be other rivals and claimants to Adam's position, and that they should all have their favourite teams of craftsmen. Two such were James and Samuel Wyatt. They came from a long line of architects, carpenters and master builders, and their father Benjamin was a builder and timber-merchant. James and Samuel were to pursue architectural careers which over-lapped on what to us seem many confusing and relatively unknown occasions. There is no doubt that all the members of the Wyatt family—there were at least four brothers who were architects—passed business and work to and fro between themselves. They also employed Midland craftsmen, as well as London firms such as Joseph Rose & Co., and they were on good terms with the important Birmingham manufacturer Matthew Boulton and his partner James Watt.

As well as designing Heathfield House for Watt, Samuel Wyatt was involved with the design of Soho House for Boulton (1789). He wrote on 10 July 1798 'Pray have you got proper sand to dredge [throw] upon the paint for your house. We could find none in Staffordshire when at work upon Shugborough'.

In an earlier letter, dated 8 July 1783 (now in the Wyatt papers at the Birmingham Assay Office) he outlined his movements to Boulton and mentioned his presence at Heaton Hall, Manchester:

> 'I shall not be able to leave here [Heaton Hall, Manchester] before Thursday, when I shall go to Mr Wilbraham Bootle's on my way to Lord Harrowby's . . .'.

This indication that Samuel Wyatt was at Heaton draws attention to the fact that whilst his brother James had provided the design in 1772 he had no small part in the erection of the house for Sir Thomas Egerton. Both James and Samuel were to employ Joseph Rose to do plastering—James had met him in 1770. Rose, who had worked with Vassalli for James Stuart at Shugborough—a reason for believing that the *stuccatore* was perhaps in Rose's employ—did the Great Drawing Room ceiling at Shugborough in the early 1790s for Samuel Wyatt.

James Wyatt had first come to the attention of polite society in 1770 when he erected a copy of the Pantheon in London. He had travelled to Italy in company with the Earl of Northampton's Embassy to Venice, and may have gained access to such an entourage by the intercession of the earl's secretary, Richard Bagot. The Bagots of Blithfield were an old Staffordshire family and were later to employ Wyatt's favourite Gothic-style plasterer, Francis Bernasconi, to decorate their house.

In the 1780s James Wyatt turned his attention to Gothic. As a late rival to Robert Adam's Classical work Wyatt had enjoyed a successful if ill-organized, practice. At Milton Abbey, Dorset, Sheffield Park, Sussex and Sandleford Priory, Berkshire, there is Gothic work to his design. He will be best remembered in this context, however—apart from his major, but now destroyed essay of Fonthill Abbey, Wiltshire—for his activities at Lee Priory, Kent, for Thomas Barrett between 1782 and 1790. The most important rooms were on the first floor, particularly the Library (Walpole enthused to his friend Mary Berry that 'it is the most perfect thing I ever saw') and the 'Strawberry Room', now re-erected in the Victoria and Albert Museum, London (Plate 117). For the Pantheon plasterwork, however, Wyatt turned to Joseph Rose, whose sketch book (in the possession of the Earl of Harewood) includes drawings for the work. This early association between Wyatt and Rose was pursued on later occasions and particularly during the important commission at Castlecoole, Wyatt's most important Irish house, begun in 1790.

We have mentioned previously Rose's difficulties in getting men over to Ireland without trouble from press-gangs. The Castlecoole records allow us to see, however, one of the reasons for the plasterer's success. In addition to the attention to detail which he gave to his business and the quality of his work, his success owed much to his firm but polite manner, as one of his letters to the Earl of Belmont shows:

> 'If your Lordship has the least wish for my bill to be looked over by Mr Wyatt I will give him a copy. I only mention this as I wish you to be perfectly satisfied before you pay the balance of £593.'

This figure was part of a total bill of £2,249. His day bills were delivered weekly and in this case he did not charge for drawings. The fact that he had all the earl's correspondence, with copies of his own replies, and the letters from his men at the house, together with his 'memorandums' of money received, enabled him to resist firmly the earl's weak protests that he had charged too much for the 'Staircase that was intended to be plain'. There was no redress to Rose's reply of 8 December 1797: 'I have your Lordship's letter from Bath ordering me to make designs for the ornaments which you approved of when you came to town . . .'.

At Castlecoole, scagliola work[217] was provided by Domenico Bartoli, who fell on hard times and suffered 'very great distress for want of money'. Whilst scagliola and Coade stone[218] were decorative materials which could take the place of plasterwork, they were frequently used in conjunction with it. The *stuccatori* had known how to prepare scagliola, and Bagutti had used it in 1710, and Vassalli in 1736, at Castle Howard. The work for Adam and Wyatt was usually done by Giuseppe and Domenico Bartoli. For a time a Bartoli (probably Giuseppe) was in partnership with John Richter of Newport Street, London. Richter had taken out a patent in 1770 (No. 978) for his invention of 'an Art or Method of inlaying Scagliola or Plaister in and upon Marble and Metals to imitate flowers, trees, fruits, birds . . . and all sorts of ornaments'. Bartoli and Richter were recommended by Sir William Chambers in 1773 as able to 'imitate almost any sort of marble'.

Apart from Bartoli's financial troubles, James Wyatt was also losing money. Joseph Farington, in his somewhat unreliable diary, records that Wyatt lost £2,000–£3,000 a year 'from mere neglect in respect of order in his accounts'. At his death he owed £900 to Joseph Dixon, his draughtsman, and £2,000 to his plasterer, Bernasconi. His house in Foley Place, London, was heavily mortgaged and his widow was granted a pension of £100 a year. The pace of life had quickened but the discerning patron of the time was looking back to the medieval castles of Edward II and was bent on copying them. Bernasconi's Gothic plasterwork, carried out in composition, came into its own, and success also attended Sir Robert Smirke (1780–1867), the architect for whom Bernasconi principally worked in the early years of the nineteenth century.

The Bernasconi family were probably descendants of the stuccoists of that name who settled at Riva St Vitale, Vassalli's birthplace. Bernato Bernasconi worked at Claydon, Buckinghamshire, in the 1770–80 period, but was described as 'a poor man with a large family'. Francis Bernasconi, who was probably Bernato's son, was more important by reason of the success which came to Sir Robert Smirke, the architect for whom he principally worked. His son, also named Francis, was made a freeman of the Plaisterers' Company on 9 November 1805 and then presumably joined in the business. Their recorded commissions show them working all over the country from Kent to Herefordshire and even in Scotland (Plate 156).

Although the Plaisterers' Company admitted 465 freemen between 1763 and 1830,[219] the trade of plasterer was gradually yielding to the competition from papier-mâché and the introduction of new kinds of compositions. There were also contenders for Bernasconi's monopoly, although little success attended most of them. Exceptions included John Baily, who did a great deal of work for Sir John Soane. He also came to the notice of the architect Peter Nicholson, who mentioned 'Bailey's composition' in his dictionary.[220] John Rule worked for Nash in the Gothic style in Durham, and Henry Holland was credited with the introduction of French workmen skilled in various pressed-paper techniques—*carton-pierre*—made from moulds. As early as 1767 Isaac Ware had written of the 'old deception of stampt paper, instead of carved wood' which was 'coming up with all the rage of fashion'.[221] Curiosity rather than fashion probably prompted Dr Johnson to call at Charles Clay's Birmingham factory in 1774, intent on seeing the manufacture of articles in papier-mâché. By the first quarter of the nineteenth century C. F. Bielefeld was assured of a ready market for his book on papier-mâché, *Gothic Ornaments* (1835), and he wrote several volumes advocating the use of the material, one of them even recommending it for portable buildings (1840). By 1858 White and Parlby had patented a method of producing ornaments direct from moulds and Bielefeld had begun to make the fibrous slabs with which the ceiling of the Reading Room at the British Museum was lined.

The dictionaries of architecture and building magazines issued in the early nineteenth century abound in details of patent stucco compositions.[222] Indeed, the word 'compo' seems to have been first popularly applied to Parker's Roman Cement[223] patented in 1796. The best known, however, because of its use throughout Westminster Palace, was Keating's patent cement, which was finally called Parian cement. By 1861 even this superior material was replaced by the various fireproof cements of which the brand patented in 1861 by A. G. Barham of Bridgewater was one of the best. This superseded the use of plasters containing lime and hair and did not crack or swell. It dried and hardened rapidly and could be painted or papered almost at once. Other fireproof plasters were patented by Hitchins in 1877, and Johnson introduced a fireproof wire lathing, a development which had started in the 1840s. These developments must, however, await telling in the many studies in progress which will provide an even wider knowledge and appreciation of nineteenth-century architecture. Within a few years we shall know much more of the Greek Revival[224] in England and of the detailed history of the Houses of Parliament. Facts and deductions which lie buried in the pages of *The Builder* and similar magazines will also become more generally available.

CHAPTER VII

Plasterwork in Scotland

The bearer is sent with four of My Lord Dukes
Carts to Bring home the Hair His Grace bespoke
from you for the Stucco work . . .

Alexander Inglis, October 1742.
Hamilton MSS., Box 127

OF recent years Scottish architectural history has emerged from a long period of neglect enlivened only by the great volumes on castellated and domestic architecture by MacGibbon and Ross (1887-92). That this is so is due in large measure to the researches of a number of architectural historians to whose work tribute has been paid in the Preface to this book. They recognize that anecdote must give way to fact and that criticism and judgment of good and bad is essential. In this they are aided by the patient and careful investigations carried out by the staffs of the National Register of Archives for Scotland, the Scottish Record Office and the National Library. There is no doubt that this final chapter on Scotland owes a great deal to those efforts. There is equally no doubt that many more problems, at which it is yet only possible to hint, will be solved in the not too distant future by the same scholars. The author of the present book has not presented detailed descriptions of Scottish ceilings that are illustrated in Bankart's and Turner's books on plasterwork. What is of more concern is to point out what documentation has come to light since their books were issued in 1908 and 1927 respectively.

The union of the Crowns of England and Scotland in 1603, and the establishment of a link between the two royal houses opened the way for English ideas and craftsmen to enter Scotland more freely than hitherto. In Scotland ideas from south of the border mingled with a wide repertory of ideas bearing the marks of association with Scandinavia, France and the Low Countries. It all did much to enliven the sombre, fortified castles and tower-houses,[225] and plasterers and plasterwork were among the forces which brought this about. With a verve and swagger alien to the scene they covered all before them, and even superb painted decoration disappeared on occasion beneath their oak laths and well-beaten lime.[226] In this creamy-white froth of plaster Scotland was provided with more exuberant animals, demi-gods, well-fashioned pendants and proud heraldry, and, within the eighteenth century, a finer form of rococo than almost anywhere else. At the same time Scotland seemed to produce few good plasterers of its own, and artistic temperament had always to contend with a Presbyterian frown. Landowners were easily persuaded that England, or anywhere but Scotland, had a superior style and technique to offer.

A convenient starting-point for the history of Scottish plasterwork is, in fact, in England: the important ceiling of Bromley-by-Bow, *c.* 1606, now in the Victoria and Albert Museum, London. The quatrefoils are occupied by full-faced bearded busts of three of the Nine Heroes, each repeated twice. The same layout of panels and the appearance of Hector occurs again in Fife at Balcarres House. Some documentary help in the quest for evidence indicating the presence of English plasterers in Scotland is provided by the accounts of the Masters of the Works as they relate to Edinburgh Castle in 1617. Prior to publication Mr John G. Dunbar, one of the editors, has kindly given me details of the payments set out there:

'February 1617

Item to Johne Johnstoun and his man plaisteris in consideration of his paynes in comeing fra York to his work—xlib.' [£10]

In June of the same year a further item appears relating to the moulds which were used:

'9 June 1617

To James Murray for careing muldis to the plaisterers from Kellie—xls.' [40s]

Kellie Castle, Fife, has been added to over a long period of time, and work of 1676 is illustrated here (Plates 129, 130). In one of its rooms medallion heads appear, one of which is dated 1617. May it therefore be assumed that the work at Kellie and Edinburgh Castle, in view of the use of the same moulds, was by John Johnstoun from York?

At Glamis Castle, the plasterer who worked for the 2nd Earl of Kinghorne in about 1620 is identified again by use of the same moulds at Muchalls Castle, Kincardineshire (1624), and Craigievar Castle, Aberdeenshire (1625). At Craigievar, the hall is vaulted in stone and covered with rich plasterwork. The magnificent panel of the royal arms was paid for by William Forbes, a merchant trading at 'Dantzick' who bought the unfinished castle in 1610 and altered it during the following sixteen years. Muchalls may have been intended as a dower-house for the Burnets of Ley, whose family seat at Crathes is only twenty miles away. It was Sir Thomas Burnet who paid for the fine ceilings put in as part of his remodelling of the house, 1619-27.

The early work at Pinkie House, Midlothian, *c.* 1613, with its delicate floral and heraldic motifs contained within a complex array of moulded ribs, is copied again at Winton Castle, East Lothian (Plate 123). Documents at Winton record payment to 'John Quhytte' for the plasterwork. He may have been a relative of the Alexander White whose receipt survives to record his work for Thomas Dalyell at the House of the Binns, near Linlithgow. A number of the patterns here are identical with those at the Mansion House, Auchterhouse, near Dundee, remodelled for the Earl and Countess of Buchan in the 1620s. The Binns has a great single pendant in the King's Room (Plate 122) and four more in the High Hall and Sea Room. Part of the work is dated 1630, and the plasterer presumably moved there after his work for Lord Buchan. Some iron moulds survive at the house.

Pendants of the elaborate kind found at the Binns, Auchterhouse, Winton, Glamis and elsewhere usually developed from the form of the medieval roof boss. Some of the most attractive examples are to be seen in Scotland. At Auchterhouse, there are twenty-three pendants on the Drawing Room ceiling alone. The display is one of the best in Scotland, and it was repeated in a nineteenth-century copy at Cortachy Castle. When the upper storey at Auchterhouse was refloored in about 1930, a work carried out with care for the late Mr W.H. Valentine, the beams which carry the drawing-room ceiling showed traces of having formed part of an earlier painted ceiling.

The 1640s were troubled times in English and Scottish history, and no great relief came until the Restoration of Charles II in 1660. At the end of the Civil Wars John Maitland, afterwards Duke of Lauderdale, was released from prison and again took up his friendship with the king, whom he had loyally served at the Battle of Worcester. He was appointed Secretary for Scotland, and in 1672, at the death of his wife, he took the swift and important step of marrying again. Neither Maitland nor his second wife, the former Lady Elizabeth Dysart, had long to wait for the conferment of the title of duke and duchess. As befitted his rank, Lauderdale not only remodelled Ham House, Surrey, but employed Sir William Bruce (*c.* 1630-1710) to do the same for him at

Thirlestane Castle, Berwickshire, and for the Crown at Holyroodhouse. Some of the letters they wrote to each other have survived and tell a little of the work.[227]

In March 1671 the duke wrote to Bruce, who had been appointed overseer of the Royal Works in Scotland, about obtaining furnishings from Holland, and requesting him to send 'the draught of the Kings palace at Holyroodhous to the end his Maj[te] may declare his pleasure about it . . .'. A later letter of 4 May excitedly declares the duke as being 'up to the elbows (if I live) before I have done with it'—the 'it' referring to building on the grand scale. Bruce was also remodelling his own house at Balcaskie, Fife, at the time. The ceilings there (Plates 125, 126) are among the most interesting in Scotland, and together with those created at Thirlestane (Plate 128) and Holyroodhouse (Plates 133, 134, 136) are by the English plasterers John Houlbert and George Dunsterfield, whom Lauderdale sent north. The friendly correspondence which the duke and his architect exchanged, however, mentions that the 'Dutch Men who are Excellent Jo'n [joiners] & have made all my Shapies & lynenings of my Rooms at Ham' were travelling north. In another letter 'Germane' joiners are mentioned in mistake for the Dutch men. They were to be sent by sea to Newcastle and then by land to Thirlestane. The English plasterers most likely came to Scotland by a similar route.

Some indication of the movements of Houlbert and Dunsterfield in Scotland is provided by the Thirlestane documents[228] and that referring to the work carried out during the same years (1671-8) at Holyroodhouse, where a new series of State Apartments was intended. The two plasterers went to Thirlestane in 1674, possibly to join Thomas Alborn, the Glasgow plasterer who, with his apprentice William Lindores, also did 'several sorts of Plaisterwork' with them at Holyroodhouse but worked independently at the palace and castle at Stirling and probably at Kinross House. At Thirlestane both Houlbert and Dunsterfield signed receipts, but the largest amount of money was paid to Alborn, who presumably engaged the London plasterers for the intricate work done from 1674 onwards.

Houlbert and Dunsterfield then moved to Holyroodhouse, where the accounts show that the two men were in partnership, Dunsterfield having worked previously under John Grove in London. Between May and October 1674, Robert Greenhorn, a tanner, delivered a great quantity of common hair and finer white hair for their use, and Andrew Paterson, a wright, made 'several plaister moulds'. Since he was paid £101, 'several' probably meant all the moulds which were used. Lime from Pitlessie, forty miles to the north-east of Edinburgh, was to be used for the work. Houlbert and Dunsterfield then had all they needed. It was probably owing to the intervention of Bruce or Lauderdale that the human figure appears modelled in the Holyroodhouse plaster (Plate 134). Sir Roger Pratt had indicated how ill-suited to this sort of work English plasterers were, and it is significant that the portrayal of the figure is absent in the London work of the same period. Bruce had travelled in the Low Countries and France in about 1663, and it has been suggested that he may have brought back current architectural treatises, such as Le Muet's *Manière de bien bastir*, 'whose second edition (1647) includes at least one set of engravings incorporating all the main features seen at Holyroodhouse'.[229]

By December 1675 Houlbert and Dunsterfield had been paid some £1,564 for the work done 'since coming to Scotland to work at the said Pallace'. The accounts also show some £1,100 being paid to Thomas Alborn. It is also possible to form from these accounts some idea of the conditions under which the plasterers worked. In 1674-7 153 loads of coal were provided for them to bake their plaster and for warming the rooms 'for putting up the work in the winter tyme'. By 1677 only Houlbert's name was appearing in the accounts, and on 11 March 1679 he was paid £271 10s 0d for 'the plaister work of the roof and corneishes of the great . . . stair on the south-west corner' (Plates 133, 134). The fact that the plasterwork was baked, the large payment for moulds and the appearance of the finished work show that most of it was moulded on tables at ground level and then fixed into position. Both at Holyroodhouse and at Thirlestane (Plate 128) there are deep ribs and an exuberant display of flowers and foliage.

When Holyroodhouse was completed in 1678 Bruce turned to his private practice. Lauderdale's health had begun to fail and he was forced to resign. By 1682 he was dead,[230] but Bruce was to be active for another thirty years. He moved from Balcaskie to live at Kinross House, Kinross-shire (Plate 127), where building went on for several years. Elsewhere in Scotland exuberant plasterwork was being done at Brodie Castle, Moray (Plates 131, 132), Whittingehame Tower, East Lothian, Arbuthnott House, Kincardineshire (Plate 135) and in Edinburgh itself. It is all characterized by a flamboyant display of caryatid figures and strange creatures of the deep sea. Again, a close parallel may be seen between some of this decoration and Dutch silver of the same years. We also know that at Wemyss Castle, Fife, a Danish plasterer, John Nicoll, was at work in 1672-3, and this is another indication of the strong foreign influences which were at work on Scottish decoration. English influence is hardly discernible in the work in Scotland of the architects Sir William Bruce and James Smith, although William Adam does seem to have imitated Vanbrugh and Gibbs. It has also been observed that at the beginning of the nineteenth century England could produce little to compare with the neo-Greek buildings in Scotland.[231]

Towards the end of his life Bruce gave a plan to Charles Hope for the building of Hopetoun House, West Lothian. In later years Hope, who became the first Earl of Hopetoun, called in William Adam (1689-1748) to revise the layout of the main façade and forecourt. This, together with a mention of James Smith (*c.* 1646-1731) as having 'really the best skill of them all',[232] introduces the two architects who gave employment to plasterers in Scotland in the first half of the eighteenth century. Their careers have been assessed elsewhere, and some of Smith's drawings came to light in 1967.[233] Adam probably served under William Bruce at Hopetoun, and Smith had known Bruce when as a master mason he had helped in the erection of the new work at Holyroodhouse. But neither is recorded as having much to do with each other. It was 1721 before Adam signed his contract for the Hopetoun work, and the only plasterwork which survives there is the splendid rococo work done under the supervision of his sons Robert and John Adam, *c.* 1752-4 (Plate 150). There is, however, a group of houses which shows the 'descent' of Scottish plasterwork through the hands of William Adam and the plasterers Samuel Calderwood, Joseph Enzer and Thomas Clayton.

Samuel Calderwood was born in London in about 1687, and apprenticed to the plasterer Robert Dyer in 1701 for seven years. Dyer had worked for Wren at St Andrew's, Holborn, from 1686 to 1692, but he was presumably dead by 1704 when Calderwood's apprenticeship was transferred to John Winterburne. It is not unrewarding to compare Calderwood's early work in Scotland with Dyer's work in London[234] as the same heavy foliage and repertory of motifs appears at Drum House, Edinburgh, designed by William Adam. It would seem that Calderwood met Adam on the architect's visit to London, made with Sir John Clerk in 1727. Sir John was concerned about the decoration of his house of Mavisbank, Midlothian, and for the festoons in stucco Adam recommended Calderwood's services. He indicated that he had engaged Calderwood for one year— 'he is now to begin at Drum and as 'tis near Mavisbank if you please he shall also begin at your Lordship's house. In this weather he can be putting up the bracketing and lathing.'[235] Adam also wrote that Calderwood's 'man' was equally good. It is tempting to assume that this 'man' was Thomas Clayton, but no documentary evidence has yet been traced to support this. On stylistic grounds it is certainly possible.

On the ground floor of Drum House—or 'Somerville House', as it was called in William Adam's *Vitruvius Scoticus*—Calderwood was allowed to spread his stucco embellishments to greater advantage. The Hall chimneypiece (Plate 142) is his work and, with its profusion of overspilled trophies, recalls those at Blair Castle, Perthshire (Plate 147) and Mawley Hall, Shropshire. The common source may be merely an engraving or a liaison which Clayton, the creator of the Blair work, may have had with Francesco Vassalli, the possible author of the Mawley work. The slight evidence for this is discussed later. At the same time Clayton worked in the 1740s at Drum House on the decoration of the rooms on the first floor, and would know Calderwood's work there, either as an observer or as an apprentice who had worked on it. Calderwood also worked for Adam at New Hailes, Midlothian, a house originally erected for his own use by James Smith.

In 1730 Adam came to decorate Dun House, near Montrose—a house for which he had drawn plans as early as 1723—and the plasterwork assumed a more varied appearance. The Saloon has a coved ceiling and at each end, in the cove, a stucco display of figures, animals, flags and sea-creatures. It is worthy of the *stuccatori*, and one idly wonders whether they did indeed come to work at the house for Adam (who, as an architect, had visited London and knew Lord Burlington and his use of stucco[236]) and for a patron, David Erskine, Lord Dun, an eminent judge who had been educated in Paris. We shall probably never know this, but it is equally likely that Joseph Enzer, who was Adam's plasterer at Arniston House, Midlothian, and Yester House, East Lothian, and who was said to be Dutch, worked there instead.

Enzer worked in the stuccoed hall at Arniston in about 1730 (Plates 137, 138). By 1738 he was married, but there is no reason to think that his wife, Helen Erskine, was of Lord Dun's family. When his daughter Susan was born in 1739 he was described as 'plaisterer at Yester'. This statement is supported by his account-book of 1736-9, for his work at Yester House. The house was started by James Smith in about 1715, and the shell was complete by 1723 when John Macky visited it. Later work was supervised by Alexander Macgill, and William Adam's connection with the house dates from 1729 until his death in 1748. His sons John and Robert then took over the work and completed the Saloon on the first floor.

Enzer's account-book records that he arrived at Yester on 14 June 1736 to set up the scaffolding on the Great Staircase. He stayed about ten days to do this and then returned on 16 August with his apprentice Philip Robertson. He continued to work at Yester until 4 December when he left for Edinburgh. He was away until 7 March when he returned alone. As the summer came, with good weather for plastering, Robertson was joined by two other apprentices, Francis Nicols and Daniel Ross, and even by 'a soldier', Abraham Lester, who worked there for eighty days. The amount of work done can be imagined from the total of days worked by each apprentice. Robertson did 544 days while Nicols worked longer, for 611 days. The superb plasterwork, with its curious baroque overtones on the staircase and in the ground-floor Dining Room, is therefore documented work by Enzer. His accounts show payments for wire for use as armatures in the capitals and ornaments. The hair and plaster came from London, and some 19½ tons of chalk at 10s a ton was used. Much of the progress made in the work in the 1730-48 period can be followed from fourteen of William Adam's letters to the Marquess of Tweeddale in the family archives.[237] In that of 5 July 1743, we are told that 'poor Joseph Enzer died last week'. The Saloon at Yester was unfinished at the time of Bishop Pococke's visit in 1760 and may be attributed to Thomas Clayton, working under Robert Adam's supervision. Clayton was the plasterer who from the early 1740s was the force to be reckoned with, and who gave to Scotland some of its finest plaster decoration.

We have no knowledge where or when Clayton was born but it was probably in about 1710. We do not know to whom he was apprenticed, but there is no doubt that, like Samuel Calderwood, who may have been his master, he was an Englishman and probably born and trained in London.[238] The name Clayton is, however, common in the Newcastle area. He is first recorded in 1740 as working in Scotland for William Adam at Drum House and Holyroodhouse. His work at the last house has vanished, but there are many mentions of Clayton in the Hamilton manuscripts[239] for the 1740s which show that he worked for the Duke of Hamilton both at Holyroodhouse, Hamilton Palace, Lanarkshire, and the imposing garden building of Châtelhérault at Hamilton.

The 5th Duke of Hamilton and Brandon had been friendly with William Adam for some years. The duke had acted as a witness when James Adam was baptized at Edinburgh in July 1732. On 7 April 1740 he wrote to William Adam and urged him to come as soon as he could to Hamilton 'from the infected City of Ed^n to the wholesome Air of your own Child the Kennell, and revell in the delights of yr owne production . . .'. The letter also stated that Clayton would be in attendance in about three weeks. This was obviously to start work on the Hamilton apartments at Holyroodhouse. The letters recently discovered in the Hamilton archives show, however, that work did not start until September. Clayton had charcoal-burners lit in each room to prevent the stucco, kept in its tubs of water, from freezing. It was to be applied in the usual fashion in three coats built up from the coarse first scratch layer to the fine thin top coat. This final coat was made from rich lime which had been slaked, sieved and allowed to stand for at least four months. For a perfect finish pounded white marble, the 'marble meal' mentioned by Wren,[240] was added.

The duke's letter of 1740 to Adam seems to imply that the garden building of Châtelhérault at Hamilton Palace was complete in structure. It was dated by two travellers to 1732, but we now know that the interior stucco-work (Plates 143, 144) was not done until the winter and spring of 1742-3. Amusingly, the architect had dubbed the complex of pavilions (built after the model of the citadel of Châtelhérault in Poitou) 'the Dogg Kennell'. In the *New Statistical Account* the Rev. William Patrick quotes its local name of 'Wham', and this clue, allied to one more tenuous, indicates Clayton as the creator of the stucco-work.

In November 1968 and July 1969 Miss C.H.Cruft traced in the Hamilton registers and other records preserved at the Scottish Record Office not only the details of the birth of three sons, Thomas Varsallis, Archibald and James[241] to Clayton and his wife (Elizabeth, née Wilson), but also several puzzling facts about other members of the family. This has enabled a conjectural pedigree to be constructed in the Select List of Plasterers at the end of this book, but it may be some years before all the parts of the puzzle are found and put in place. In the entry for Thomas Varsallis Clayton, born at Hamilton on 8 March 1743, his father was described as working 'at the Whahn', the name (in its variant of Wham) for Châtelhérault. What is, however, of equal importance is the inference which can be drawn from the Christian names of Clayton's son: Thomas Varsallis. Miss Cruft has suggested that 'Varsallis', a more than unusual name, would be the nearest a Scottish clerk of the time would get to 'Vassalli'. Is this suggestion of a possible link between Clayton and the *stuccatori* Francesco or John Vassalli borne out in the style of the stucco-work itself?

If we look carefully at the Châtelhérault work[242]—unfortunately only in photographs, for severe damage by subsidence and fire reduced the chances of saving it—one or two significant things are apparent. First, the large medallion heads over the doors in the upper room (Plate 143) are very reminiscent of Francesco Vassalli's work at Towneley Hall, Burnley, a well-documented example of 1730 (Plate 54). Furthermore, such medallions are probably unique in Scottish plasterwork at this period. Secondly, the small rosettes on a diapered backbround surrounding the reclining huntress on the centre of the West Pavilion ceiling are completely consistent with the style of the *stuccatori*. There is also the significant fact that Clayton showed facility for working in both plaster and stucco, and he may well have learned the latter technique from a foreigner.

In continuing this supposition the final and most fragile link between the two plasterers is arrived at by a process akin to thinking out loud. When the 5th Duke of Hamilton died in 1743 Clayton was employed by his son, the 6th Duke. There was work to do at Hamilton Palace itself. In 1752 the 6th Duke married Elizabeth Gunning. Her sister Maria married the 6th Earl of Coventry. This connection alone does much to show why one of Robert Adam's first English commissions in 1760 was at the Earl of Coventry's Worcestershire home of Croome Court, and why most of the portraits of the earl and his family are by the Scottish portrait-painter and friend of the Adams, Allan Ramsay. Maria only lived nine years after her marriage. She died in 1760, as Mrs Delany records, from clogged pores from the over-application of make-up. We know, however, from the dates on receipts at Croome Court that she would see the partial completion of the stucco-work which was done at the house in 1758-61 by John Vassalli. It seems quite likely that Vassalli would have been recommended to Lord Coventry by the Duke of Hamilton, his brother-in-law, if he, or his father (?) Francesco, had already worked with Clayton for the duke at Hamilton Palace. This, however, is only guesswork but it may, for the moment, be regarded as a possibility that Clayton was assisted, in the 1740s at least, by one of the Vassallis.

When Clayton's third son James was baptized at Hamilton in April 1747, the baptismal entry stated that Thomas Clayton was 'working in Stucko at the Palace'. Unfortunately mining subsidence later damaged the palace and it was demolished in 1936. Clayton's stucco-work was fortunately illustrated in *Country Life* (14 June 1919). It might be assumed that the other decorative work in the palace was done by some of the same craftsmen whom William Adam had engaged at Holyroodhouse.[243] The fact that rococo decoration is present, however, probably means that part of the work was carried out after Adam's death in 1748.

By this time Adam's two elder sons, John and Robert were taking an increasing share in the responsibilities of the family business. It was natural enough that they continued the contact with Clayton and that some interesting work ensued. Clayton was also diligent about his business, and consideration must now be given to his major commissions of the late 1740s and the 1750s, including his work at Blair Castle for the Duke of Atholl, in Glasgow, and at a group of other houses including Dumfries House, Inveraray Castle and Hopetoun House, near Edinburgh. The year 1747 was a busy one for Clayton. By the summer of the year he had started work for the Duke of Atholl at Blair Castle, and he may have done some work for Lord Minto at his home in Roxburghshire.

On 12 December 1746, Clayton submitted an 'Estamate of Stucco work to the Right Honorable Lord Minto'. Unfortunately, we do not know if he was given the commission as Lord Minto had also solicited other estimates[244] from John Bagnall of Gilling—the plasterer who had worked at Castle Howard and the York Assembly Rooms—and James Carmichall of Edinburgh. Bagnall was highly recommended to Lord Minto by Gilbert Waugh of Kirkleatham. In his letter of 23 September 1743 Waugh says Bagnall was one 'commonly employ'd by Gentlemen in this Country'. Waugh also pointed out that Bagnall's work was done well and cheaply—he was charging 5d to Clayton's 6d for 'plain ceiling'—and that, apart from 'having his own meat in the house', his servants were lodged elsewhere. He recommended the use of Carlisle alabaster, a ton of which would suffice for the materials for eleven yards of stucco-work.

The three-year gap between Waugh's letter and Clayton's estimate might suggest that Clayton was chosen. However, Bagnall's estimate is dated only nine days earlier than Clayton's, 3 December 1746. Carmichall's tender is an insignificant scrap of paper dated 14 February 1745. The octagonal Drawing Room (for which there is a drawing, probably by William Adam) and the Dining Room at Minto House do contain work which may be Clayton's. It is also worth noting that Bagnall's estimate gives the prices he charged per foot or yard, whilst Clayton's not only did this but set out the prices to be finally charged for each part of the work, totalling £78 10s 0d. Although such small commissions were doubtless welcome to Clayton, the sum paid to him for the work at Minto pales into insignificance against the £1,840 or so which he received for his work at Blair Castle, Perthshire, in the period 1747-57.

The turreted and battlemented walls of Blair Castle rise in stark whiteness from a gently undulating green park. The castle was remodelled for James, 2nd Duke of Atholl, and we are fortunate in having a mass of surviving documentation. That for the house and furniture has been used in the accounts of its history and decoration.[245] The letters and accounts from Clayton allow the progress of the stucco-work to be followed here in detail. On 17 July 1747 Clayton had submitted his prices for work in stucco and plaster. Agreement was presumably reached, for the 1747-51 account shows that Clayton's men arrived at the castle in August 1747. John Cowchar and William Clow, presumably from Edinburgh (where Clayton had his yard), and labourers and lads were set to work. Three boxes of tools were sent to them. The decoration was carried out slowly and carefully but the two principal rooms, the Dining Room and the Great Drawing Room, seem to have been stuccoed in 1751-2 and 1755-6 respectively. It is hard to give exact dates as the two main accounts, whilst very detailed, are rendered at the end of four-year periods.

The Dining Room (Plates 145, 147, 151) at Blair is one of the finest rooms in Scotland. Originally built as a banqueting hall by the 3rd Earl of Atholl in the middle of the sixteenth century, it was remodelled some 200 years later for the 2nd Duke. The marble mantelpiece was provided by Thomas Carter in September 1751—he waited until April 1753 to be paid—and above it Clayton put a great array of stucco trophies (Plate 147). He charged for 170 loads of peat for burning stucco and for fires in the Dining Room while he and his men worked. Seven letters in addition to the accounts not only provide information about the work at Blair but also give a few insights into Clayton's other work and the journeys he undertook. In a letter of 19 October 1753 Clayton wrote that he had brought a good many hands from England and would bring more if the duke's future plans for work warranted it. He was being urged in the letter he was answering to provide a duplicate design of the Dining Room ceiling. This was presumably to show to the painter Thomas Bardwell (1704-67), who provided paintings on canvas of the Four Seasons for insertion into the roundels left at each corner. In his earlier letter of 21 May 1753, Clayton indicates that he has been down in London and must leave for the 'West Counterey', the area around Glasgow.

In Glasgow Clayton had work on hand for Allan Dreghorn (1704-64) who, besides designing his own house at 130 Clyde Street, also designed the Parish Church of St Andrew's. The Glasgow City Minutes of 9 March 1753 show that the city fathers entered into a contract with 'Thomas Clayton, stucco worker in Hamilton' to finish the ceiling and entablature of the church by 1 January 1754 for a payment of £487. Clayton was to pay for the stucco, lime, sand, hair, and other materials, and carriage. The Clyde Street house, now a warehouse, has one very elaborate ceiling of 1752 which is presumably Clayton's work.[246]

The next letter, dated by Clayton 'Hamilton 3 Janry 1754' shows that he was again away in the 'West Country'. He at last encloses the design for Bardwell's use. There is then an unfortunate gap in the chronology of the Hamilton manuscripts until 29 January 1756. A letter of this date, itself of no great significance, encloses a memorandum which reveals that by this time the flat ceiling of the Grand Drawing Room was finished, together with its cornice. 'Only the cove and frieze remains undun', Clayton stated. The Grand Drawing Room work is itemized in Clayton's account. His charges totalled £217 8s 9½d for 158 yards of plain ceiling, 85 ft 6 in of 'Palmyra Cornice'—evidence for his use of Robert Wood's book *The Ruins of Palmyra* (1753) as a source—512 ft of plain moulding, 765 ft of enrichments, 917 ft of ornament and 346 ft of Corinthian cornice. All this adds up to an impressive achievement, and the rococo swirlings and cartouches in the corners of the cove frame the heavy square and hexagonal panels forming the centre of the ceilings.

A comparison with the earlier work in the Dining Room shows a surer feel for rococo motifs and an absence of reclining stucco figures—the two over the pedimented Dining Room doorway look as accomplished as any by the best *stuccatori*. The two-tier chimney-piece has Corinthian columns and a scroll pediment, and the entire treatment is more in accord with what the Adam brothers had done at Hopetoun a year or two before. By March 1757 Clayton's lads John Oliphant, James Clow and Will Rid were busy cleaning all the work, and sheets had been laid over the floors to protect them from dust and small fragments of stucco. On 15 May 1757 Clayton was paid his second account of £635 7s 10d rendered to 10 July 1756. Some ten years' work at an average yearly payment of £180 had been satisfactorily concluded.

We have said that during the ten years when Clayton was working at Blair (1747-57) he also attended to other commissions. On 5 November 1753, he had written to the Duke of Atholl's factor that he was endeavouring to make himself capable of carrying two or three jobs forward at once. He resisted the duke's suggestion to work by the day, preferring instead to prepare an estimate and receive the amount stated in convenient sums at regular intervals. His good relationship with the young Adam brothers persisted, and in about 1753 he went to do some work for them at Hopetoun House, within a few miles of Edinburgh.

In 1745 the Countess of Oxford set out from Edinburgh to visit Hopetoun House. In a document found in 1914 at Welbeck Abbey, her home in Nottinghamshire, and now preserved at Hopetoun, she observed that it was 'a very fine and large free stone House situated on a Hill above the Firth of Forth . . . Here are a great many valuable pictures and Bustos, but are not put yet in order, the House being not quite finished . . .'. Lady Oxford was of course referring to the work of William Adam at Hopetoun. After 1750 his sons Robert, James and John completed the work.

It has been revealed in detail by Mr John Fleming[247] how the house was started soon after 1699 by Sir William Bruce. Twenty years after the building of the first house the Earl of Hopetoun employed William Adam to enlarge and complete the exterior. His design, as it appears in *Vitruvius Scoticus*, gave rise to the curved colonnades and forward pavilions to north and south. His final account of some £2,116 was receipted on 11 September 1731. It was left to William's sons to deal with the interior decoration, a situation not unlike that which they were to follow at Mellerstain in Berwickshire. While the work at Hopetoun was proceeding (1754-8) Robert Adam went off with the earl's younger brother, Charles Hope, on the Grand Tour. He obtained furniture in Italy and possibly sent from Rome the design for the chimneypiece in the Red Drawing Room executed in 1756 by Rysbrack.

In the Yellow Drawing Room at Hopetoun, Clayton provided delicate rococo swags in the cove, some twenty feet above the floor. His simple frieze with shallow rococo swirls snakes along above the yellow damask and the gilded picture-frames. In the Red Drawing Room, a noble room some 44 ft long, 24 ft wide and 22 ft 7 ins high, the stucco-work flows over ceiling and cove (Plate 150). This is Clayton at his best and shows his complete mastery of the rococo style. It was done in 1754, a year earlier than Clark's fine work at Norfolk House (Plates 85, 86). Adam and Clayton would know of several sources for the ornaments. William Delacour (*c.* 1700-67),[248] who had issued his *Books of Ornament* from 1741-3, may well have had something to do with the formation of the very accomplished and sophisticated rococo motifs which acted as a basis for the decoration of these ceilings. Some years after the completion of the work, in 1758, he was in Scotland working under John Adam in Edinburgh.

That Clayton undoubtedly gave satisfaction by the quality of his work at Blair (and elsewhere) is pin-pointed by his request to the Duke of Atholl to be recommended to the Duke of Argyll. The two dukes were friends, and Atholl had set a fashion among his circle for both building and forestry. When the 3rd Duke of Argyll succeeded to the title in 1743 he abandoned as a home the old fifteenth-century keep, and by 1746 had started the building of the present Inveraray castle. His architect was Roger Morris, with William Adam as 'Intendant General'. The plan of the foundations is dated 3 May 1745 and work on the grand project went on from this time until delayed by William Adam's death in 1748 and that of Morris in 1749. Adam's sons John and Robert had worked as his assistants and they were asked to carry on the work after his death.

Clayton wrote to the Duke of Atholl on 15 October 1753 requesting that, as the Duke of Argyll's house would be ready soon, he might be recommended there. No reference occurs in the Inveraray documents to Clayton, nor before 1755 to plastering. However, there is among the Saltoun papers[249] an estimate drawn up by Clayton in September 1756, of charges for plastering and stucco-work for the Duke of Argyll. The Argyll historian Miss Mary Cosh, kindly shared the results of her researches[250] with the author of this book before the publication of her volume on Inveraray. In 1755 plain plasterwork was done by John Johnstone in the castle kitchen—prosaic work lining the flues and oven vents. By August 1757, the plasterers had finished more, similar plain work and the scene was set for the main decoration. Clayton had obviously hoped to be considered for this, but there is no record that he was. In any case, much of the work of this period was swept away when Robert Mylne (1734-1811), architect descendant of generations of Master Masons to the Crown of Scotland, altered the castle between 1770 and 1782.

On 31 October John Adam specified which rooms at Inveraray were to be decorated with plaster and stucco. The accounts for 1757 and the following year show that some £326 was paid to the plaisterers and to the suppliers of Irish limestone. During the winter of 1758 the remainder of the rooms on the principal storey were lathed by the chief wright, George Haswell. In 1760 the name of a plasterer first appears in the accounts: Joseph Enzer's erstwhile apprentice, Philip Robertson. There is then a gap until Mylne's work, which we shall mention shortly.

After the completion of Clayton's work at Dumfries House in 1756, his name disappears from documentary records and he cannot with confidence be identified among others of the same name who will be mentioned. The bills for the stucco-work at Dumfries House, as well as those for the chimneypieces, are missing. Sir John Stirling Maxwell did, however, see all the bills in 1938 and stated in his book on Scottish houses that the stucco-work was by Clayton. As for the attributed work, much of it can only be hazarded. The ceilings at Glendoick House, Perthshire (Plate 148) may have been done by Clayton in about 1750, but the Morisons seem almost as likely. The Glendoick historian, David Walker, has indicated to the present writer that the ceiling at Pirn (destroyed in 1950) by Alexander Morison was close enough in design structure to cast some doubt on his attribution of Glendoick to Clayton. The twisted frond which was a favourite Clayton device was also on the Morison ceiling. It again raises the question whether Alexander Morison ever worked for Clayton, despite the fact that his father Thomas Morison had established a business before his death in 1748. Such imponderables will occupy attention for some time to come, especially as the same twisted frond does occasionally appear in the work of Joseph Rose, senior, notably at Felbrigg Hall, Norfolk, where Rose was working under James Paine's supervision in about 1752.

The career of the Adam brothers as it relates to their work in the Neo-Classical style is comparatively well documented.[251] In Scotland their plasterwork is adequately represented by the decorations at Mellerstain and Paxton House (Plate 154), both in Berwickshire. On 11 September 1725 the date cut on the foundation plinth of the east wing at Mellerstain, William Adam inaugurated a great scheme to provide Lady Grisel Baillie with a new house.[252] Adam built the two wings, but for years there was nothing to connect them, although a design for the centre block exists which may be by Alexander Macgill. Then, in about 1770, Robert Adam put in the centre block, drawings of which exist, and blended the whole together in battlemented style. In contrast with the severe exterior, the interior is decorated with stucco-work of a high quality (Plates 153, 155). Some of Adam's designs for the ceilings, dated 1770-3, are at Mellerstain whilst others are at Sir John Soane's Museum, London. They show that the usual combination of moulded composition and printed roundels and the use of dark colours such as purple were being advocated. Unfortunately no documents or accounts survive to reveal the plasterer's name.

Adam-style plasterwork in Scotland is something of an enigma purely in that the identity of the people who did the work is often uncertain. The younger Thomas Clayton seems to have done most of the important commissions, but at houses such as Mellerstain the work can only be attributed to him. The case appears to be similar to that of Joseph Rose, senior, and his nephew Joseph, who did all the work for the Adam brothers in England. Joseph Rose, senior, like Thomas Clayton, senior, worked mainly in the rococo style. The younger generation, however, were more ready to work in the Neo-Classical mood.

There is no direct evidence that Thomas Varsallis Clayton, who had been born in 1738, became a plasterer. But there was a 'Clayton' who, with Stephen Coney, decorated two ceilings in Sir Lawrence Dundas's house in Edinburgh, and the 'Mr Clayton' who worked at Inveraray Castle in 1781-2, and the 'Thomas Clayton' who entered into a contract on 12 March 1785, to do the ceiling of the dome at the Register House in Edinburgh. Miss Cruft's researches have also shown that this Thomas Clayton, or another of the same name, was a plasterer and died in Edinburgh in October 1793.

The work which Clayton and Coney did for Sir William Chambers in 1771-2 at Sir Lawrence Dundas's house in St Andrew Square, Edinburgh, is noted in a reliable source. George Richardson, whom we have noted as draughtsman to the Adam brothers, issued his *Book of Ceilings* ... in 1776, and 'Mr. Clayton' was a subscriber. Richardson stated in the book that the ceilings in the Drawing Room and Dining Room were by Clayton and Coney. A glance at the later work at Inveraray[253] (Plate 152) and that at the Register House[254] shows that Clayton, junior, was a thoroughly competent craftsman. He presumably did much Neo-Classical work in Scotland.

The Inveraray accounts are useful in recording the names of a few other plasterers in the late eighteenth century. James Hutchison was paid for unspecified work in August 1782, and in 1795 Robert Buchan repaired the ceiling of the billiard room. Buchan seems to have been a Glasgow man, since his travelling charges are paid to that city. The work done at the castle in the 1780s for Mylne, the architect in charge, also shows the use of papier-mâché and other pressed ornament. As early as June and August 1773, Mylne had mentioned 'a design for ornamenting the ceiling of a circular dressing-room, be-speaking the papier machice for it in London, and sending the same to Inveraray'. In 1772 a certain McConnie, a Scottish enough name, was paid for a 'Cornice Mould of Stucco' and much of the work of the late 1770s was done in this material. However, an account of Mylne's, which, apart from its quotation in 1893,[255] is otherwise unknown, recorded that by 1781-2 plasterwork in casts, models and moulds was being provided by 'Mr Papworth' (John Papworth) and artificial ornaments by 'Mr Jacques'.

Although Scotland does not abound in good Neo-Classical work there is competent plasterwork at a number of houses.[256] Unfortunately, nothing is known of the plasterers but the seeker of fine examples of plaster decoration should consider the work at Leuchie, East Lothian, a good example of about 1770, and the excellent ceilings at Scotstoun, Peeblesshire, dating from about 1765. At Pitfour Castle, near Perth, there is a Robert Adam wing which has a fairly elaborate Drawing Room ceiling of about 1785 which was probably designed by the Adam Office. Duchal House, Renfrewshire, has plasterwork of about 1760. Duff House, Banffshire, an imposing house designed in the mid 1730s by William Adam, contains decorative work completed years later. There are two good ceilings on the ground floor and fine plaster work in a cove above the first floor ceiling. This can only be seen by climbing up through a hatch but the rococo arabesques in the corner are similar to work at Dumfries House. It may well represent the early style of John and Robert Adam, as more effectively displayed at Hopetoun House (Plate 150).

The chronology of all interior decoration is not easy to determine in the absence of accounts. This is more than true for plasterwork, but in Scotland it is possible to see in sharper focus the changes that took place over the years from Neo-Classicism to the neo-Greek style. As it developed from the early efforts of Playfair and Hamilton to the later achievements of Simpson, Thomson and others, the neo-Greek style made a distinguished contribution to European architecture. It is not our task to chronicle this, but the facts which are becoming available about the buildings of Edinburgh, Glasgow and Dundee, for example, will in due course extend our knowledge of the decoration of their interiors. This is particularly true of the information provided in the inventory volumes issued by the Royal Commission on the Ancient and Historical Monuments of Scotland. There the patronage offered by commerce is placed alongside that of a more personal kind.

Although the Gothic style in Scotland is not often noteworthy for quality, the Entrance Hall at Taymouth Castle, Perthshire (Plate 156) is impressive enough. Scottish plasterers probably regretted that the commission, of about 1810, was given to Francis Bernasconi. This may have occurred because one of the two architect brothers chosen—Archibald Eliot—lived in London from about 1806 and was familiar with Bernasconi's work there. With its centre block looking surprisingly like Smirke's Eastnor Castle, Taymouth[257] comprises an interesting group of buildings ranging from William Adam's west wing, remodelled in 1838-9 by James Gillespie, to William Atkinson's east wing, flanking Eliot's centre block. Bernasconi's account for all the Gothic plasterwork was on the princely scale of £6,120 2s 3d. Much of it survives in the rooms of the central block.

With a Scottish tenacity of purpose John Gillespie Graham (*c.* 1777-1855), who started life as a joiner, became a leading Scottish architect, married well and enjoyed a most successful practice. His castellated houses show his ability to devise imaginative Gothic residences. At Achnacarry House, Inverness, which he started in about 1802, he decked the rooms with simple, pierced friezes coloured at the back, and provided a central medallion only where the chandelier would hang. There is a sharp contrast between this cool, austere work and the opulent work which he did at Taymouth with the Crace family of decorators. In between, Graham could practise a dignified Classical style, as his columned and porticoed houses in Moray Place, Edinburgh, show.

The Calton Hill Terrace scheme which W.H.Playfair (1789-1857) carried out in Edinburgh brings to notice the architect who did a considerable amount of public building in the city, including the National Gallery. Playfair also remodelled the interior of Floors Castle, near Kelso, sweeping away whatever plasterwork Sir John Vanbrugh and William Adam had placed there in about 1720. The plasterwork is therefore good nineteenth-century 'Jacobethan', but it pales against the most impressive work in this style, that designed for Falkland House (1839) by William Burn (1789-1870), a talented pupil of Sir Robert Smirke. His designs for plasterwork at Carstairs, Lanarkshire, are also stylish in a form of Tudor Gothic.

In Glasgow the architect Peter Nicholson (1765-1844) had an extensive practice. Good plasterwork done under his supervision still exists in Laureston House, Carlton Place. Archibald Simpson (1796-1847) was Nicholson's counterpart in the Aberdeen area. It is, however, at Strathcathro, Angus, that Simpson's talents are seen at their best. The interior of the house, built between 1827 and 1830, is a rich mixture of decoration, but as much in paint as in plaster. Elsewhere in Angus, Cluny Castle, designed by John Smith, had elaborate Graeco-Renaissance work in the Drawing Room of 1836-40 and a round room with a tent ceiling. David Hamilton (1768-1843) designed Keir House, which has interesting plasterwork. At Pitlochry, the House of Auchleeks has good, early nineteenth-century work of rather unexpected detail, but the architect and plasterer are not known.

These, however, are the terse notes of inventory compilers and they do not make for easy reading here. What may be said in conclusion is that Scottish plasterwork provides as many rich and unexpected examples as any in England or Wales. There is an assurance of technique—from the rich, pendanted ceilings and heraldic scenes of the seventeenth century, to the sun-burst Apollo motifs to be found one hundred years later at Blair Castle, Touch House and Kippencross House. Although nineteenth-century architecture in Scotland is not usually out of character with that found in England, great turreted houses such as Dunrobin and Brodick castles never fail to amaze the eye. But even here the intertwining plasterwork in the long Dining Room at Dunrobin, so closely resembling seventeenth-century work, was put up under the supervision of the eminent English architect Sir Charles Barry. That at Brodick, rich with ribs in geometrical patterns, was done just as well and with superb assurance in about 1844 by the Scottish architect Gillespie Graham. Mock baronial and heavily derivative it may all be, but it has a flourish and swagger which captivates the heart of even the Sassenach.

Notes

1. Sir John Summerson, *Architecture in Britain, 1530 to 1830*, 5th ed., 1969, pp. 24-7.
2. J.A. Gotch, *The English Home from Charles I to George IV*, n.d., p. 5.
3. Summerson, *op. cit.*, p. 38.
4. *Oxford Book of Seventeenth Century Verse*, 1958, p. 162.
5. Barrington Kaye, *The Development of the Architectural Profession in Britain*, 1960, pp. 39-53.
6. This process is described in detail by Gladys Scott Thomson, *Life in a Noble Household, 1641-1700*, 1937, Chs. VI-IX.
7. G.M. Trevelyan, *England under the Stuarts*, 1925, p. 6.
8. David Mathew, *The Age of Charles I*, 1951, p. 286.
9. A. Clark (*ed.*), *Aubrey's 'Brief Lives'*, 1898, II, p. 304.
10. In H.M. Colvin, *A Biographical Dictionary of English Architects, 1660-1840*, 1954. The 1625-85 figures were established by John Cornforth and Oliver Hill, *English Country Houses: Caroline*, 1966.
11. Sir John Summerson, 'The Classical Country House in Eighteenth-Century England', *Journal of the Royal Society of Arts*, July 1959, p. 540.
12. P.M.G. Dickson, *The Financial Revolution in England, 1688-1756*, 1967, p. 10.
13. E.L. Klotz, & Godfrey Davis, 'The wealth of Royalist Peers and Baronets during the Puritan Revolution', *English Historical Review*, 58, 1943, pp. 217-19.
14. N.V. Stopford Sackville, *Drayton*, privately printed, 1939, p. 9.
15. N.G. Brett-James, *The Growth of Stuart London*, 1935, p. 121.
16. Child's Bank, London. Bank accounts of Marquess of Worcester, created 1st Duke of Beaufort in 1682.
17. H.J. Habbakuk, 'The Market for Monastic Property', *Economic History Review*, 2nd series, x, No. 3, 1958.
18. Lawrence Stone, 'The Anatomy of the Elizabethan Aristocracy', *Economic History Review*, XVIII, 1948, p. 6; *The Crisis of the Aristocracy, 1558-1641*, 1965, p. 100; *Family and Fortune, Studies in Aristocratic Finance in The Sixteenth and Seventeenth Centuries*, 1973.
19. H.B. Wheatley (*ed.*), *Pepys' Diary*, entry of 12 October 1663.
20. E.S. de Beer (*ed.*), Evelyn's *Diary*, entry of 25 September 1672. Evelyn, however, was not always accurate in such matters. He estimated the cost of the Sheldonian Theatre, Oxford, as £25,000 instead of half that amount (Wren Society, XIX, p. 91).
21. Evelyn, *Diary*, *op. cit.*, entry of 18 September 1683.
22. J.H. Habbakuk, 'Daniel Finch, 2nd Earl of Nottingham, his House and Estate', in *Studies in Social History . . . ed.* J.H. Plumb, 1955, p. 93.
23. Yorkshire Archaeological Society, Leeds. Duke of Leeds MSS., Box 32. Building agreements and Analysis of Expenditure.
24. L.O.J. Boynton, *Appuldurcombe House, Isle of Wight* (Ministry of Public Buildings and Works guide-book), 1967, pp. 12-13; John Harris, 'The Building of Denham Place', *Records of Bucks*, XVI, pt. 3, 1957-8, pp. 193-6.
25. T.S. Ashton, *Economic Fluctuations in England, 1700-1800*, Ch. II, 'Building', 1959; Habbakuk, 'Daniel Finch . . .' *op. cit.*; J.H. Habbakuk, 'Economic Functions of English Landowners in the 17th and 18th Centuries', *Explorations in Entrepreneurial History*, VI, pp. 92-101.
26. Godfrey Davis, 'The Seamy Side of Marlborough's War', *Huntington Library Quarterly*, XV, No. 1, November 1951, pp. 21-44.
27. J.H. Habbakuk, 'Daniel Finch . . .' *op. cit.*, p. 145.
28. Kenneth Darwin, 'John Aislabie, 1670-1742', *Transactions, Yorkshire Archaeological Society*, XXXVII, Pt. 147, 1950, pp. 318-19.
29. London County Council, *Survey of London*, XXXII, 1964. The author has also examined the private account-book and financial books of Lord Burlington in the Chatsworth archives.
30. *Hoare's Bank, A Record*, 1955, p. 26; A.W.B. Simpson discusses the complications of mortgages in *An Introduction to the History of the Land Law*, 1961, pp. 226-9.
31. C.L. Ewen, *Lotteries and Sweepstakes in the British Isles*, 1932.
32. P.M.G. Dickson, *The Financial Revolution in England, 1688-1756*, 1967, pp. 79-80.

33. D.M.Joslin, 'London Private Bankers, 1720-85', *Economic History Review*, VII, No. 2, 1955, pp. 167-86.

34. Bank of England, Ledger 45 (1718-20), 21 May 1720.

35. David Green, *Sarah, Duchess of Marlborough*, 1967, pp. 263-4.

36. Geoffrey Beard, *C. Life*, 10 August 1961, based on Studley Royal MSS., Leeds Reference Library; Dickson, *op. cit.*, p. 173.

37. Martin's Bank, London, Letter Book (1714-21), 30 June 1720.

38. *Inventories and Particulars of the Late Directors of the South Sea Company*, 2 vols., 1721, gives bills from craftsmen which were at that date unpaid.

39. Horace Walpole, *Letters* (Toynbee edition) XIII, p. 77.

40. Rae Blanchard, 'Richard Steele and the Status of Women', *Studies in Philology*, XXVI (1929), p. 343; J.H.Habbakuk, 'Marriage Settlements in the Eighteenth Century', *Transactions, Royal Historical Society*, XXXII, 1950; R.Halsband *Life of Lady Mary Montagu*, 1960.

41. J.Hurstfield, *The Queen's Wards: Wardship and Marriage under Elizabeth I*, 1958; H.E.Bell, *An Introduction to the History and Records of the Court of Wards and Liveries*, 1953.

42. Eric Mercer, *English Art, 1553-1625*, 1962, pp. 12-16; Lawrence Stone, *The Crisis of the Aristocracy, 1558-1641*, 1965.

43. A.F.Upton, *Sir Arthur Ingram*, 1961.

44. D.C.Coleman, *Sir John Banks, Baronet and Businessman*, 1963.

45. G.E.Mingay, *English Landed Society in the Eighteenth Century*, 1963, p. 26.

46. F.Thompson, *History of Chatsworth*, 1949, Ch. IX; David Spring, *The English Landed Estate in the Nineteenth Century: Its Administration*, 1963; E.M.L.Thompson, *English Landed Society in the Nineteenth Century*, 1963.

47. The author is indebted to Mr W.Salter of Leeds, a practising plasterer with great experience of period work, for details of this analysis and for much advice on methods and materials.

48. Restored by G.Jackson & Sons Ltd. in 1960. Information kindly communicated by Mr C.W.Symonds.

49. We have no contemporary evidence, only the estimate made in 1897 by William Millar in *Plastering, Plain & Decorative*, 1897, p. 297.

50. Blair Atholl MSS., 40 II D(4) 32.

51. Millar, *op. cit.*, p. 106.

52. Melbourne MSS., Thomas Coke's Garden Notebook, 1706, 'Prices of building att wrest in Bedfordshire, Duke of Kent'.

53. M.R.Apted, *Painted Ceilings of Scotland, 1550-1650*, 1966, Plates 93, 94.

54. Duchy of Cornwall Office, Vouchers, IV, 1733-4, p. 229.

55. Blair Atholl MSS., 40 II D(4) 37.

56. Information kindly communicated by Mr W.Salter of Leeds, who restored the ceiling, c. 1950.

57. R.T.Gunther, *The Architecture of Sir Roger Pratt*, 1928, pp. 80-1.

58. See note 62 below.

59. Millar, *op. cit.*, pp. 87-9, Plates CII, CIII. Millar's basic tool-kit in 1893 consisted of 58 items.

60. Holyroodhouse, 4 September 1674, 'To Andrew Paterson, wright, for several plaister molds, £101', R.S.Mylne, *The Master Masons to the Crown of Scotland and their Works*, Edinburgh, 1893, p. 195.

61. About eighty of these moulds, including the signed one, were sold by B.T. Batsford Ltd., in 1960. There is a small collection of moulds at the Geffrye Museum, London.

62. Christie's catalogue of the Joseph Rose sale, 10, 12 April 1799.

63. Damie Stillman, *The Decorative Work of Robert Adam*, 1966, pp. 34-6; *C. Life*, 22 September 1966, p. 703.

64. Millar, *op. cit.*, p. 217.

65. R.T.Gunther, *The Architecture of Sir Roger Pratt*, 1928, pp. 58, 67.

66. The ribs of the ceilings of the Banqueting House, Whitehall, the Queen's House, Greenwich, and the Queen's Chapel, St James's, were entirely made of carved wood. The author is indebted to Dr Maurice Craig for this information.

67. Illustrated in J.R.Martin, *The Farnese Gallery*, 1965, Plate 45. The Clandon ceiling is illustrated in the present author's *Georgian Craftsmen and their Work*, 1966, Plate 51.

68. Damie Stillman, *The Decorative Work of Robert Adam*, 1966, Plates 118, 119.

69. Stillman, *op. cit.*, Plates 46, 47.

70. Gervase Jackson-Stops, 'French Ideas for English Houses, The Influence of Pattern Books 1660-1700', *C. Life*, 29 January 1970, pp. 261-6.

71. Lancashire County Record Office, Towneley MSS., (DDTO/Q10).

72. Edoardo Arslan (*ed.*), *Arte e Artisti dei Laghi Lombardi*, II, 1964; Henry-Russell Hitchcock, *Rococo Architecture in Southern Germany*, 1968.

73. British Museum, Add. MS., 41,133, 21 April 1770.
74. Soane Museum, Vol. II, No. 83; Stillman, *op. cit.*, Plates 134, 135.
75. Soane Museum, Vol. 14, No. 22.
76. Joseph Rose's letters at Castlecoole were copied for the author by the late Lady Dorothy Corry, following two visits made in her company to see the plasterwork there in 1956.
77. Victoria County History, *The City of York*, ed. P.M.Tillott, 1961, pp. 167, 217.
78. C.E.Whiting (*ed.*), *Durham Civic Memorials*, Surtees Society, CLX, 1945, p. xvii.
79. Joseph Moxon, *Mechanick Exercises, Applied to the Art of Bricklayers-works*, 1700, p. 16.
80. Wren Society, XI, p. 74.
81. Edward Croft-Murray, *Decorative Painting in England, 1537-1837*, 1962, I, p. 159.
82. Renato Lefevre, *Villa Madama*, Istituto Poligrafico dello Stato, n.d., p. 64; Frederick Hartt, *Giulio Romano*, 2 vols., Yale University Press, New Haven, Conn., 1958.
83. Laurence Turner, *Decorative Plasterwork in Great Britain*, 1927, p. 2.
84. Croft-Murray, *op. cit.*, p. 21.
85. Guildhall Library, London, MS., 6132.
86. The whole career of Bellin in relation to Nonsuch is set out by Martin Biddle, *Jnl. British Archaeological Association*, XXIX, 1966.
87. John Evelyn, *Diary*, ed. E.S.de Beer, 1955, entry of 3 January 1666.
88. John Dent, *The Quest for Nonsuch*, 1962, p. 49. Kendall was replaced by Gering as 'overseer of certain of our white works' at Christmas, 1544.
89. Paul Hentzner, *A Journey into England in the Year 1598*, 1957, p. 27.
90. N.Pevsner, 'Double Profile, a Reconsideration of the Elizabethan Style as seen at Wollaton', *Architectural Review*, March 1950, pp. 147-53; *The Planning of the Elizabethan House* (inaugural lecture at Birkbeck College, London), 1960.
91. Eric Mercer, *English Art, 1553-1625*, 1962, pp. 31-2, sets out the counterclaims against Mannerist influences.
92. Mark Girouard, *Robert Smythson and the Architecture of the Elizabethan Era*, 1966, pp. 15-17.
93. Longleat MSS., 'Records of the Building', I, p. 271 (letter from Charles Williams); II, p. 87 (letter from Sir William Cavendish); II, p. 129 (letter from Lady Saint Loe).
94. This would be for the 'second' Longleat: Girouard, *op. cit.*, pp. 53-4.
95. Francis Thompson, *A History of Chatsworth*, 1949, p. 23; Basil Stallybrass, 'Bess of Hardwick's Buildings and Building Accounts', *Archaeologia*, Vol. LXIV, 1913.
96. Biddle, *op. cit.*, p. 112, n. 7.
97. Public Record Office, E 210/10340.
98. Victoria and Albert Museum, Panelled Room booklets, IV, *Sizergh Castle*, 1928, p. 24.
99. At Levens Hall, Westmorland, *c.* 1570; Holcombe Court, Devon, *c.* 1590; and Haddon Hall, Derbyshire, *c.* 1570.
100. Guildhall Library, London, MS. 6143B.
101. The reasons for thinking that Smythson is responsible for the general design for Hardwick are set out by Girouard, *op. cit.*, p. 121.
102. Stallybrass, *op. cit.*, p. 356, note 46.
103. Abraham Smith's materials are noted in the Hardwick accounts, Stallybrass, *op. cit.*, p. 385.
104. Christopher Hussey, 'The Spell of Knole', *Country Life Annual*, 1961, p. 28.
105. Kent County Record Office, U 269, A1/1. 'A Booke of severall Accompts of Tho: Earle of Dorsett', 1607.
106. Eric Mercer, 'The Decoration of the Royal Palaces, 1553-1625', *Archaeological Journal*, CX, 1953, p. 151. This Banqueting House was burnt down in January 1619, and Jones designed the new one with a carved wooden ceiling.
107. Lawrence Stone, 'The Building of Hatfield House', *Archaeological Journal*, CXII, 1955, p. 121.
108. Ernest Godman, 'The Old Palace of Bromley-by-Bow', London County Council, Greater London Survey, Monographs III, 1902.
109. L.Turner, 'A Middlesex Jacobean Plasterer', *C. Life*, XXXV, p. 919.
110. His name and the date 1620 is inscribed in plaster on a first-floor ceiling.
111. Margaret Jourdain, *English Furniture and Decoration of the Early Renaissance*, 1924, pp. 26-7; *English Interior Decoration*, 1950, p. 23.
112. Girouard, *op. cit.*, p. 36.
113. *Transactions, Thoroton Society*, 51, 1947.
114. Christopher Gilbert in *C. Life*, 8 September 1966.
115. At Devon County Record Office. See also *C. Life*, 2 March 1940, pp. 222-5, and *Transactions, Devonshire Association*, XLIX, 1917, and 89, 1957, pp. 124-44.

116. A group of Commonwealth houses which provide an exception to this comment were discussed by Professor Geoffrey Webb in *RIBA Journal*, XI, 1933.

117. Christopher Hussey, six articles in *C. Life*, May-August 1963; H.M.Colvin, 'The South Front of Wilton House', *Archaeological Journal*, CXI, 1955, pp. 181-90.

118. Noted by Colvin, *op. cit.*, p. 188, fn. 2 at RIBA, Library, and at the Ashmolean Museum and Worcester College, Oxford.

119. First noted and illustrated by W.G. Keith, *Burlington Magazine*, xxii, January 1913, p. 219, Plate I. The drawing is now in the Ashmolean Museum, Oxford.

120. R.T.Gunther, *The Architecture of Sir Roger Pratt*, 1928; H. Avray Tipping, *English Homes*, iv, i, 1929.

121. Pratt noted the prices of 'Hubarts Plaster heades' in his memoranda, Gunther, *op. cit.*, p. 157.

122. H.M.Colvin, 'The Architecture of Thorpe Hall', *C. Life*, 6 June 1952, pp. 1732-5.

123. Guildhall Library, London, MS., 6122/2, July 1660.

124. *Ibid.*, 9 October 1655.

125. P.R.O., Works, 5/1; 5/145; *Calendar of Treasury Books*, I, 1660-7, p. 463.

126. Kerry Downes, *Hawksmoor*, 1959.

127. P.R.O., Works, 6, 368/2.

128. P.R.O., Works, 5/5.

129. Margaret Whinney, 'John Webb's Drawings for Whitehall Palace', *Walpole Society*, XXXI, 1946.

130. Sir John Summerson, *Inigo Jones*, 1966, pp. 128-34.

131. Wren Society, VII, p. 72.

132. Edward Croft-Murray, *Decorative Painting in England*, 1962, pp. 240-1; W.H.St John Hope, *Windsor Castle*, 1914. Derek Linstrum, *Sir Jeffry Wyatville, Architect to the King*, 1972, pp. 170-200.

133. Wren Society, X, pp. 45-53.

134. *Ibid.*, XVIII, p. 40.

135. *Ibid.*, XVI, pp. 202-7.

136. *Ibid.*, XIV, Plate III.

137. *Ibid.*, XV, p. 169.

138. *Ibid.*, VII, pp. 42-3.

139. *Ibid.*, VII, pp. 80-1.

140. *Ibid.*, VII, p. 96, citing P.R.O., Works, 5/33. The author has also used the details in P.R.O., Works, 5/54.

141. Earl of Bradford, Weston Hall MSS., Box 18/4.

142. Wren Society, IV, p. 25.

143. Edgar Wind, 'Julian the Apostate at Hampton Court', *Jnl. of the Warburg and Courtauld Institutes*, III, 1939-40, pp. 127-37.

144. P.R.O., Works, 5/146.

145. Wren Society, VII, p. 174.

146. H.M.Colvin, '*Royal Buildings*', RIBA, Drawings series, 1968, Plate 13.

147. Wren Society, VI, p. 33.

148. Croft-Murray, *op. cit.*, pp. 73-6.

149. *Calendar of Treasury Books*, 1708, XXII, 1950, p. 133.

150. P.R.O., Works, 6/11, pp. 41, 171.

151. P.R.O., Works, 4/1, 6 March 1716.

152. R.T.Gunther, *The Architecture of Sir Roger Pratt*, 1928, pp. 145, 156.

153. Christopher Hussey, *C. Life*, 15, 22, 29 June 1935; John Cornforth and Oliver Hill, *English Country Houses: Caroline*, 1966.

154. *Survey of London*, XXIX, 1960, p. 198.

155. H.M.Colvin, *A Biographical Dictionary of English Architects, 1660-1840*, 1954, pp. 682-7; Geoffrey Beard, *C. Life*, 9 May 1952, pp. 1408-11.

156. Bodleian Library, Gough Drawings, a.2. Some have been reproduced by H.M. Colvin, *Architectural Drawings in the Bodleian Library*, 1952, Plates 2-6, and by John Cornforth and Oliver Hill, *English Country Houses: Caroline*, 1966, pp. 142-3.

157. Earl of Bradford, Weston Hall MSS., Box 18/4.

158. The Goudge letters at Melbourne, Derbyshire, are noted in *Historical Manuscripts Commission, 12th Report (Earl Cowper)*, Appendix 2, pp. 375-9; Appendix 3, pp. 3-4.

159. *Vertue Notebooks*, III, p. 51, Walpole Society, XXII.

160. East Sussex County Record Office; Rupert Gunnis, 'Letters of the first Lord Ashburnham', *Sussex Archaeological Collections*, 88, 1949, pp. 3-4.

161. RIBA, B4/5.

162. Yorkshire Archaeological Society Library, Leeds, Boxes 32, 33; summarized by Geoffrey Beard, *Leeds Arts Calendar*, No. 46, 1961, pp. 4-11.

163. M.D.Whinney, 'William Talman', *Jnl. of the Warburg and Courtauld Institutes*, XVII, 1955, pp. 123-39; John Harris, 'The Hampton Court Trianon Designs of William and John Talman', *ibid.*, XXIII, 1960, pp. 139-49.

164. The contract is printed in *Archaeological Journal*, CX, 1953, p. 189.

165. John Harris, 'The Building of Denham Place', *Records of Buckinghamshire*, XVI, Pt. III, 1957-8, p. 193.

166. Christopher Sandford, 'Notes on Eye Manor', *Transactions of the Woolhope Club*, 1952, pp. 24-7: *C. Life*, 15 September 1955.

167. David Green, *Grinling Gibbons*, 1964, pp. 40-1.

168. Geoffrey Beard, *Georgian Craftsmen and their Work*, 1966, pp. 45-7; see also H. Avray Tipping and Christopher Hussey (eds.), *English Homes IV, 2, The Work of Vanbrugh and his School*, 1928; and Laurence Whistler, *The Imagination of Vanbrugh and his Fellow Artists*, 1954.

169. Huntington Library, California, MS., ST.59.

170. Henry-Russell Hitchcock, *Rococo Architecture in Southern Germany*, 1968.

171. Geoffrey Beard, *Apollo*, July 1964; *Georgian Craftsmen and their Work*, 1966, p. 162.

172. Oxford County Record Office, Dillon MSS., 1/p/3h.

173. John Rylands Library, Manchester, Lyme MSS., Box 47.

174. Scottish Record Office, Clerk of Penicuik MSS., GD 18, 2114.

175. John Cornforth, 'Trentham Hall, Staffordshire', *C. Life*, 1 February 1968.

176. Quoted in *Victoria County History, Warwickshire*, VI, p. 232.

177. Information from the late Sir Edward and Lady Blount. The house has been saved from almost certain destruction by the action of the Historic Buildings Council and the extensive restorations done for the present owner, Mr A. Galliers-Pratt.

178. B.L.Grandjean, 'L'activité des Stucateurs Italiens, et Tessinois en Danemark, 1670-1770', *Arte e Artisti dei Laghi Lombardi*, II, 1964.

179. Katherine A. Esdaile, 'Charles Stanley and his English Colleagues', *C. Life*, 2 October, 11 December 1937.

180. *C. Life*, 21 January 1965, pp. 108-109. The author is also indebted to Mrs L.Tanner for information on the Okeover MSS., following his examination of them.

181. Blenheim MS., E.47, cited by David Green, *Blenheim Palace*, 1951, p. 311.

182. Kerry Downes, *English Baroque Architecture*, 1966, Plate 283; H.M.Colvin, 'Grimsthorpe Castle, the North Front', in *The Country Seat: Studies presented to Sir John Summerson*, 1970, pp. 91-3.

183. Kerry Downes, 'Hawksmoor's Sale Catalogue', *Burlington Magazine*, October 1953, p. 334, No. 78.

184. Duchy of Cornwall Office, Vouchers II, III, IV, 1731-4. See especially II, p. 288, IV, p. 229 (Mansfield's bill).

185. Duchy of Cornwall Office, Household Accounts, LX(I), 1738-50, pp. 26-8.

186. J.H.Plumb, *Sir Robert Walpole*, II, 1961, pp. 84-5.

187. S.G.Gillam (ed.), *The Building Accounts of The Radcliffe Camera, Oxford*, Oxford Historical Society, XIII, 1953-4.

188. Mark Girouard in *C. Life*, 13, 27 January and 3 February 1966; Desmond Fitz-Gerald 'Chippendale's Place in the English Rococo', *Furniture History*, IV, 1968, pp. 1-9; and article on Gravelot in *Apollo*, August 1969.

189. Leeds Reference Library, Temple Newsam MSS., EA 12/10.

190. Geoffrey Beard, *Georgian Craftsmen and their Work*, 1966.

191. Desmond Fitz-Gerald, 'The Norfolk House Music Room', *Victoria and Albert Museum Bulletin*, Vol. II, No. 1, January 1966, pp. 1-11. This article was revised in the light of the discovery of the accounts and issued in 1973 as a Victoria and Albert Museum monograph.

192. Laurence Whistler, 'Signor Borra at Stowe', *C. Life*, 29 August 1957, pp. 390-3.

193. John Harris, 'Clues to the Frenchness of Woodcote Park', *Connoisseur*, May 1961, pp. 241-50; see also *Apollo*, August 1969.

194. Guildhall Library, London, MS 6126.

195. James Lees-Milne, *Earls of Creation*, 1962, pp. 221-63.

196. Published in an account of the work of the Franchini brothers by Mr John Cornforth in *C. Life*, 12 March 1970. See also *ibid.*, 19 September 1974, p. 766.

197. C.P.Curran, *Dublin Decorative Plasterwork of the Seventeenth and Eighteenth Centuries*, 1967, p. 27.

198. Leeds Reference Library, Studley Royal MSS., Parcel 286.

199. Gilling-Fairfax papers in the possession of Captain and Mrs V.M.Wombwell, Newburgh Priory, Yorks.

200. John Fleming, *Robert Adam and his Circle*, 1962, pp. 368-9.

201. Kedleston Archives, 'Bills 1759' Parcel.

202. *Apollo*, July 1964, p. 56.

203. British Museum, Add. MSS., 35351, f.406, 21, 28 August 1763.

204. Cambridge University Library, MSS. 6294, firstly noted by Christopher Wall in his research for the National Trust guide-book for Shugborough.

205. *C. Life*, 27 November 1937, p. 554.

206. *Philosophical Transactions of the Royal Society*, Vol. 37, 1731-2, p. 231.
207. *Deputy Keeper of the Public Records, 6th Report*, Appendix II, p. 121.
208. Geoffrey Webb, *Works of Sir John Vanbrugh: The Letters*, IV, 1928.
209. The 1711 Journal is in the Victoria and Albert Museum Library. It is being edited for publication by Dr Katharine Fremantle under the auspices of the Art History Institute of Utrecht University.
210. Geoffrey Beard, *Georgian Craftsmen and their Work*, 1966, pp. 72-4.
211. Sidney C. Hutchison, 'The Royal Academy Schools, 1768-1830', Walpole Society, XXXVIII, 1960-2, pp. 123-91.
212. Beard, *op. cit.*, Ch. 3.
213. Nostell Priory MSS., C3/1/5/16.
214. RIBA Library and P.R.O., AO3/1244.
215. H. Martienssen, 'Chambers as a Professional Man', *Architectural Review*, April 1964, p. 277.
216. John Harris, 'Pritchard redivivus', *Architectural History*, 11, 1968, pp. 17-24.
217. R. B. Wragg, 'The History of Scagliola', *C. Life*, 10 October 1957, pp. 718-21. See also *The Builder*, 1863, p. 840.
218. John E. Ruch, 'Regency Coade; a study of the Coade record books, 1813-21', *Architectural History*, 11, 1968, pp. 34-56.
219. Guildhall Library, London, MS., 6125.
220. Peter Nicholson, *An Architectural Dictionary*, 1819, Vol. 2, p. 554.
221. Isaac Ware, *A Complete Body of Architecture*, 1767 ed., p. 458.
222. C. W. Pasley, *On Limes, Calcareous Cements, Mortars, Stuccoes* etc., 1838 (enlarged 1875); Architectural Publication Society, *Dictionary*, 8 vols, 1848-52.
223. A. P. Thurston, 'Parker's Roman Cement,' *Transactions of the Newcomen Society*, XIX, 1938, pp. 193-206.
224. An excellent start has been made by J. M. Crook, *The Greek Revival . . . 1760-1870*, 1972, and the exact documentation for the Office of Works and the Houses of Parliament is set out in J. M. Crook and M. H. Port, *History of the King's Works*, Vol. VI, 1974.
225. John G. Dunbar, *The Historic Architecture of Scotland*, 1966, Ch. I & II.
226. M. R. Apted, *The Painted Ceilings of Scotland, 1550-1650*, 1966.
227. Scottish Record Office, Bruce of Kinross MSS., GD.29, 1897.
228. Quoted by R. S. Mylne, *The Master Masons to the Crown of Scotland and their Works*, 1893, pp. 195-201. The MSS. are now in the Scottish Record Office (1974).
229. Dunbar, *op. cit.*, p. 96.
230. Ralph Edwards, *Ham House: A Guide* 1950, p. 10.
231. *Times Literary Supplement*, 6 July 1967, p. 600.
232. Scottish Record Office, Lothian MSS., GD/40, VIII (58).
233. John Fleming, *Robert Adam and his Circle*, 1962, pp. 35-7, etc. The Smith drawings were included with those by Colin Campbell added to the collections of the RIBA in 1967.
234. Wren Society, X, Plate 13.
235. Fleming, *op. cit.*, p. 43; A. A. Tait, 'William Adam and Sir John Clerk: Arniston and "The Country Seat" ', *Burlington Magazine*, March 1969, pp. 132-40.
236. Fleming, *op. cit.*, pp. 36, 331.
237. Yester House archives, which have since been deposited at the Scottish Record Office. See John Dunbar 'The Building of Yester House', *Transactions East Lothian Antiquarian Society*, XIII, 1972.
238. The London, York, Newcastle and Durham apprenticeship records have been searched for a mention of Clayton without success.
239. At Lennoxlove, Hamilton Section, of MSS., Box. 127. The author is indebted to Mr Andrew Broom for copies of the relevant letters.
240. Stephen Wren, *Parentalia . . .*, 1750, p. 277.
241. The name of the son 'James' was altered in the Hamilton register and is now not clear enough to allow certain identification.
242. David M. Walker, 'Threat to a Ducal Dog Kennel', *C. Life*, 17 December 1964, pp. 1716-17; *ibid.*, 11 February 1965, p. 301.
243. Fleming, *op. cit.*, p. 59.
244. National Library of Scotland, Minto MSS., Box 2.
245. *C. Life*, 4, 11, 18 November 1949; *C. Life*, Christmas Annual, 1969, pp. 28-37; *The Connoisseur* (articles on the furniture by Anthony Coleridge), March, December 1960; April, October 1963; October 1964; April, May 1965; February 1966.
246. The author is indebted to Mr David M. Walker for mentioning the Clyde Street warehouse. See also Andor Gomme and David Walker, *Architecture of Glasgow*, 1968. The church is described

by James Thomson; *History of St Andrew's Parish Church, Glasgow*, 1905, and George Hay, *The Architecture of Scottish Post-Reformation Churches*, 1957, p. 103.

247. John Fleming in *C. Life*, 5, 12 January 1956; and his *Robert Adam and his Circle*, 1962.

248. John Fleming, 'Enigma of a Rococo Artist', *C. Life*, 24 May 1962, pp. 1224-1226; Eileen Harris, 'Enigmatic Artist', *ibid.*, 5 July 1962, p. 33.

249. National Library of Scotland, Saltoun MSS, 347. Repeated in Lord Milton's 'Inveraray Memoir', Saltoun MSS., 455.

250. The Saltoun MSS., quoted above, also contain extensive details in Saltoun 1757, 1758, 1760 and Boxes 418 and 420. The other details of work at Inveraray are in the castle archives in the *Instructions to Chamberlain* volume, the Chamberlain's Accounts, 1781/2, and

in the notes on Robert Mylne's drawings, dated 1795. See also Ian G. Lindsay and Mary Cosh, *Inveraray and the Dukes of Argyll*, Edinburgh University Press, 1973.

251. Damie Stillman, *The Decorative Work of Robert Adam*, 1966.

252. Geoffrey Beard, 'Mellerstain', *Connoisseur Yearbook*, 1957; Mark Girouard, 'Mellerstain', *C. Life*, 28 August, 4 September 1958.

253. Christopher Gotch, 'Inveraray Castle', *C. Life*, 25 June 1953, pp. 2060-3.

254. Stillman, *op. cit.*, Plate 147.

255. R. S. Mylne, *The Master Masons to the Crown of Scotland and their Works*, 1893, p. 277.

256. In compiling this paragraph the author is grateful to David Walker, Schomberg Scott and William Jack.

257. Alistair Rowan, 'Taymouth Castle', *C. Life*, 8 October 1964, p. 913.

Acknowledgments for Illustrations

The author and the publishers wish to express their thanks to the following for their permission to reproduce the illustrations in this book:

By Gracious Permission of Her Majesty the Queen: 4, 133, 134, 136
Ashmolean Museum, Oxford: 19, 51
The late Anthony Ayscough (negatives in possession of the Hon Desmond Guinness): 55, 57, 58, 75, 82, 91, 92
Geoffrey Beard: 36, 50, 64, 78, 79, 80, 106
The Bodleian Library, Oxford: 38
The British Museum: Moxon figure, p. 15
The British Travel Association: 122
Ursula Clark: 90
Country Life: frontispiece, 5, 8, 12-14, 16, 20-3, 25-7, 29-32, 34, 40-4, 46, 68-71, 74, 87-9, 94, 103, 107, 113-14, 118-20, 127, 129-30, 138, 141, 148, 154
Courtauld Institute of Fine Art: 58-60, 95
Dr Kerry Downes: 49
Department of the Environment: 15, 101
The Fitzwilliam Museum, Cambridge: 45
Iveagh Bequest, Kenwood: 112
A. F. Kersting, F.R.P.S.: 9, 28, 67, 98, 111, 153, 155, colour plate II

Metropolitan Museum, New York: 72, 73, 105, 116
National Monuments Record: 7, 10, 11, 17, 24, 33, 35, 47, 48, 52, 54, 61-3, 65, 66, 76, 77, 83-4, 93, 96, 97, 99, 100, 102
National Monuments Record for Scotland: 121, 123, 124-6, 128, 131, 132, 135, 137, 139, 140, 142, 147, 149-51, 152, 156, 157
National Trust: 1, 6
National Trust for Scotland: 124
Nonsuch Palace Excavations Committee: 2, 3
Oxfordshire County Record Office: 53
The Lord St Oswald: 78-80, 106
Royal Institute of British Architects, Drawings Collection: 37, 39
The late Edwin Smith: 18, 81
Sir John Soane's Museum: 104
Victoria and Albert Museum: 85, 86, 108-110, 115, 117

Plates

DECORATIVE PLASTERWORK IN ENGLAND
Plates 1-120

1. *Hardwick Hall, Derbyshire:* Detail of the plaster frieze in the High Great Chamber, *c.* 1595

2-3. *Nonsuch Palace:* Fragments of the stucco-duro decorative panels from the Inner Court, *c.* 1544

4. *Hampton Court*, Middlesex: The Wolsey Closet ceiling, *c.* 1520. (After cleaning, 1961)

5. *Loseley*, Surrey: The Drawing Room fireplace, *c.* 1565, possibly copied from one at Nonsuch Palace

6. *Hardwick Hall*, Derbyshire: Detail of a plaster panel in the High Great Chamber, *c.* 1595

7. *Speke Hall*, Lancashire: Detail of the Great Chamber ceiling, *c.* 1600

8. *Clenston Manor*, Dorset: Elizabethan plaster adhering to laths

9. *Knole House*, Kent: The Ballroom fireplace and Richard Dungan's plaster ceiling, *c.* 1607

10. *Deene Park*, Northamptonshire: Detail of the Tapestry Room ceiling with short pendants and strapwork cartouches, *c.* 1630

11. *Blickling Hall*, Norfolk: The north end of the Long Gallery ceiling, *c.* 1625, the decoration of which resembles moulded ceilings at Boston Manor, Brentford (Plates 12, 14, 16). Thirty-one panels are filled with devices, and the centre eleven are based on symbols copied from plates in Henry Peacham's *Minerva Britanna* . . . , 1612

12. Panel of grotesque ornament with a central medallion of Andromeda, from an engraving by Abraham de Bruyn, 1581

13. *Sheriff Hutton Hall*, Yorkshire: The fireplace and ceiling in the Oak Parlour. Plasterer: John Burridge, *c.* 1620

14. *Boston Manor*, Brentford, Middlesex: The fireplace panel based on Abraham de Bruyn's engraving, *c*. 1623 (see Plate 12)

15. *Bolsover Castle*, Derbyshire: Detail of the Star Room ceiling, *c*. 1620. Built for Sir Charles and Sir William Cavendish, Bolsover contains some of the most interesting and individual rooms of their date in England

16. *Boston Manor*, Brentford, Middlesex: *Auditus*, one of the Five Senses panels, 1623, based on an engraving by Nicholas de Bruyn, 1597

17. *Lanhydrock*, Cornwall: Detail of the Long Gallery ceiling, *c.* 1640. This ceiling illustrates events of the Old Testament from the Creation to the burial of Isaac

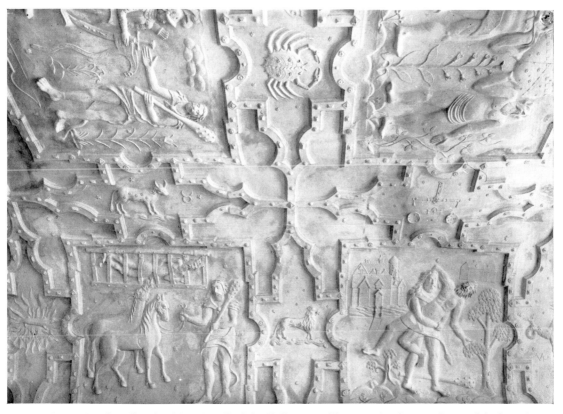

18. *Emral Hall*, Flintshire: Detail of the Ballroom ceiling, *c.* 1647 (now at Portmeirion)

19. *Wilton House*, Wiltshire: Drawing by John Webb inscribed 'for ye vault
of ye Ceelings of ye Roomes East and West end Wilton 1649'.
Ashmolean Museum, Oxford

20. *Wilton House*, Wiltshire: The Little Ante-Room ceiling, *c.* 1650, with Sabbatini's painting
'The Birth of Venus'

21-22. *Forde Abbey*, Dorset: Two details of the Dining Room ceiling, *c.* 1655

23. *Forde Abbey*, Dorset: Detail of the Drawing Room ceiling, *c.* 1655

24. *Coleshill*, Berkshire: The Saloon ceiling, *c.* 1655, destroyed in 1952. Plasterer: probably John Grove

25. Detail of Plate 24

26. *Astley Hall*, Lancashire: The Drawing Room ceiling, *c.* 1666. The plaster enrichments are held by leather and lead strips

27. *Sudbury Hall*, Derbyshire: Plaster decoration under the first-floor landing by Robert Bradbury and James Pettifer, *c.* 1675

28. *Sudbury Hall*, Derbyshire: Looking up at the Staircase ceilings and the central painting by Louis Laguerre (1691) *c.* 1675

29. *Sudbury Hall*, Derbyshire: The Saloon, *c.* 1676. Plasterers: Robert Bradbury and James Pettifer. Central painting 'The Four Seasons' by Louis Laguerre, *c.* 1691

30. *Arbury Hall*, Warwickshire: The Chapel ceiling by Edward Martin, 1678. Martin received £48 for this and another small ceiling

31. *Eye Manor*, Herefordshire: Detail of the Drawing Room ceiling, *c.* 1680

32. *Burghley House*, Northamptonshire: The ceiling of the Marble Hall, *c.* 1682. Plasterer: Edward Martin

33. *St Mary Aldermary*, London: South aisle vault, 1682, in the Gothic style copying earlier work formerly in the church. Plasterer: probably Henry Doogood or Robert Wetherill

34. *Melton Constable Hall*, Norfolk: Detail of the naturalistic plasterwork in the Red Drawing Room, dated 1687

35. *Clarke Hall*, Wakefield, Yorkshire: Detail of the Drawing Room ceiling, *c*. 1680

36. *Castle Bromwich Hall*, Warwickshire: Detail
of the Bridgeman monogram on the Staircase
ceiling, 1689. Plasterer: Edward Goudge

37. Drawing for an unidentified ceiling attributed to Edward Goudge, *c.* 1685. Royal Institute of British
Architects

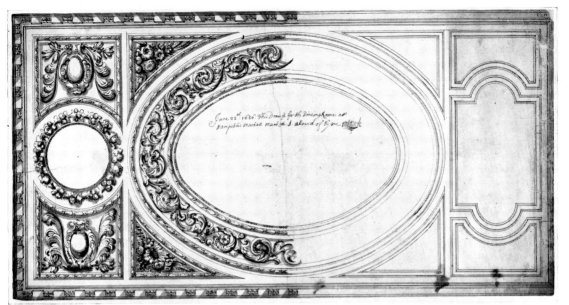

38. *Hamstead Marshall*, Berkshire: Edward Goudge's drawing for the Dining Room ceiling, 1686, inscribed 'June 22th 1686. This Drauft for the Dineing Roome att Hampstead Marshall Marked A. Allowed of by me Will Winde'. Bodleian Library, Oxford

39. *Hampton Court*, Middlesex: A design for a ceiling decoration in paint and plaster by Daniel Marot (1661-1751), probably intended for Hampton Court. The work is not known to have been carried out. Royal Institute of British Architects

40. *Belton House*, Lincolnshire: The Staircase ceiling, *c.* 1688, incorporating the crest of the Brownlow family. Plasterer: Edward Goudge

41. *Belton House*, Lincolnshire: The Chapel ceiling, *c.* 1688. Plasterer:
Edward Goudge

42. *Belton House*, Lincolnshire: Detail of the convincing Victorian copy of Edward Goudge's
work in the Tapestry Room, *c.* 1879

43. *Denham Place*, Buckinghamshire: Detail of the Drawing Room showing the richly plastered frieze, *c.* 1693. Plasterer: William Parker.

44. *Denham Place*, Buckinghamshire: The plaster version of Hollar's engraving 'Fox Hunting', *c.* 1693

45. Hollar's engraving 'Fox Hunting' for Francis Barlow's book *Several Wayes in Hunting*, on which book the *Denham Place* frieze is based

46. *Denham Place*, Buckinghamshire: The Drawing Room ceiling, *c.* 1693. Plasterer: William Parker

47. *Castle Howard*, Yorkshire: Architect: Sir John Vanbrugh.
The Hall, 1709, with Bagutti's and Plura's stucco overmantel

48. *Castle Howard*, Yorkshire: Bagutti's and Plura's overmantel, 1709-10
(see Plate 47)

49. *Blenheim Palace*, Oxfordshire: South dome of the Long Library, 1725. Plasterer: Isaac Mansfield, senior, working under the supervision of the architect Nicholas Hawksmoor

50. *The Mynde*, near Hereford: Stucco decoration attributed to Giovanni Bagutti and Giuseppe Artari, *c.* 1724

51. *Gubbins*, Hertfordshire: Drawing by James Gibbs inscribed 'Ceiling for Mr Sambrooks at Gubbins'. The ceiling was destroyed *c.* 1836. Ashmolean Museum, Oxford; Gibbs Collection, IV, 40

52. *Ditchley House*, Oxfordshire: The Hall, *c.* 1725. The Swiss *stuccatori*, including Artari, worked here for James Gibbs

53. *Ditchley House*, Oxfordshire: 1725. Receipt by Giuseppe Artari for work done, Oxford County Record Office, Dillon MSS

54. *Towneley Hall*, Burnley, Lancashire: Stucco medallion, 1729-30, by Francesco Vassalli.

55. *Mawley Hall*, Shropshire: Stucco medallion, attributed to Francesco Vassalli, *c.* 1730

56. *Mawley Hall*, Shropshire: Stucco figure, *c.* 1730, at the top of the staircase

57. *Moor Park*, Hertfordshire: Life-size stucco figure *c.* 1730, attributed to Giovanni Bagutti

58. *Barnsley Park*, Gloucestershire: The ceiling of the Staircase Hall, described in 1779 as by 'the best Italian masters'

59-60. *Barnsley Park*, Gloucestershire: Two details of the stucco decoration on the wall of the Great Hall

61. *Lumley Castle*, Durham: Stucco medallions in the Garter Room, attributed to Francesco Vassalli, or the Franchini family, *c.* 1730

62. *The Bishop's Palace*, Bishop Auckland, Durham: Detail of stucco-work, *c.* 1730, at the north end of the Charles Room

63. *Music (or Muses?) Pavilion*, Sun Street, Lancaster: Detail of stucco-work *c.* 1729-30, with a similar 'Otho-Imp' medallion to that used at Lumley Castle (see Plate 61)

64. *Music (or Muses?) Pavilion*, Sun Street, Lancaster: Details of stucco-work, *c.* 1729-30, prior to restoration by the Landmark Trust, 1974-5

65. *Lumley Castle*, Durham: Detail of the ceiling of the Garter Room, attributed to Francesco Vassalli, or the Franchini family, *c.* 1730

66. *Wallington*, Northumberland: The Drawing Room ceiling, 1741. Architect: Daniel Garrett. Documented as the work of the Franchini family of *stuccatori*

67. *Clandon Park*, Surrey: The stucco overmantel in the Saloon, *c.* 1730, attributed to Giovanni Bagutti and Giuseppe Artari

68. *Compton Place*, Eastbourne, Sussex: The ceiling of the King's Bedroom, by plasterers working under John Hughes, 1728-9. Although described as 'Germans' in the accounts, one of the plasterers may have been the Anglo-Dane Charles Stanley

69. *Honington Hall*, Warwickshire: The Boudoir ceiling, usually attributed to Charles Stanley, *c.* 1735

70. Colin Campbell (1676-1729): A plaster medallion at *Compton Place*, Eastbourne, probably representing Campbell, who rebuilt the house and employed the Danish Stuccoist Charles Stanley, *c.* 1728

71. *Raynham Hall*, Norfolk: The Hall, *c.* 1730. The centre plaster medallion shows the arms of Charles, 2nd Viscount Townshend. Architect: William Kent. Plasterwork: attributed to Isaac Mansfield

72. *Kirtlington*, Oxfordshire: Drawing for the four walls and ceiling of the Dining Room, *c.* 1748

73. *Kirtlington*, Oxfordshire: Detail of the stucco decoration in the Dining Room, as re-erected at the
Metropolitan Museum of Art, New York, 1955

74. *Okeover Hall*, Staffordshire: Detail of plasterwork by Charles Stanley in a window recess, *c.* 1745

75. *Langley Park*, Norfolk: Centre of the Library ceiling by Charles Stanley, *c.* 1740, representing Diana and Actaeon

76-77. *Temple Newsam House*, Leeds: Two of the thirteen plaster medallion heads on the Long Gallery ceiling, representing King George II and Queen Caroline. Plasterers: Thomas Perritt and Joseph Rose, senior, 1745, charged at 10/6d each medallion

78. *Nostell Priory*, Yorkshire: Detail of the plaster decoration by Thomas Perritt and Joseph Rose, senior, on the North Staircase, *c.* 1740

79. *Nostell Priory*, Yorkshire: One of the four corner decorations on the Dining Room ceiling, *c.* 1740. Plasterers: Thomas Perritt and Joseph Rose, senior

80. *Nostell Priory*, Yorkshire: Drawing by James Paine for the Dining Room ceiling, *c.* 1740. Nostell Archives

81. *Wroxton Abbey*, Oxfordshire: Detail of the Gothic decoration on the Chapel ceiling attributed to Richard Huss and carried out under the supervision of Sanderson Miller, *c.* 1747

82. *Hartwell Church*, Buckinghamshire: Gothic plasterwork done under the supervision of Henry Keene, *c.* 1753-5

83. *Royal Fort*, Bristol: Detail of a rococo plaster overdoor panel, the plaster-work possibly by Thomas Patey and the painting by Michael Edkins, *c.* 1760

84. *Ragley Hall*, Warwickshire: Detail of the ceiling by Giuseppe Artari in the Billiard Room, *c.* 1758

85. *Norfolk House*, London: The Music Room, as re-erected in the Victoria and Albert Museum, London.
Plasterer: Thomas Clark. Woodcarver: John Cuneot, 1755

86. *Norfolk House*, London: Gilded stucco trophy in the Music Room, as re-erected in the Victoria and Albert Museum, London. Rococo decoration of superb quality by Thomas Clark, 1755

87. *Powderham Castle*, Devon: The ceiling of Lady Devon's Sitting Room in the New Tower, *c.* 1765

88. *Lytham Hall*, Lancashire: *c.* 1760. The Staircase Hall. Stucco attributed to Giuseppe Cortese

89. *Lytham Hall*, Lancashire: The Staircase Hall *c.* 1760 using a similar motif to Cortese's documented work at Elemore Hall, Durham (Plate 90)

90. *Elemore Hall*, Durham: Staircase ceiling. Giuseppe Cortese's Neptune panel, 1757

91. *Royal Fort*, Bristol: The centre of the Hall ceiling, *c.* 1760 (see also Plate 83)

92. *Royal Fort*, Bristol: Naturalistic plaster decoration on the Staircase wall depicting a vine, *c.* 1760

93. *Gateley Hall*, Norfolk: Plasterwork overmantel, *c.* 1750. The disposition of the figures, animals and trees in the scene has similarities to the Hollar/Barlow publications (see Plates 43-45)

94. *Powderham Castle*, Devon: Plaster decoration on the Staircase wall, dated 1755. Plasterer: John Jenkins, assisted by William Brown and Stephen Coney

95. *Holkham Hall*, Norfolk: Thomas Clark's ceiling in the Great Hall, 1754

96. *Ragley Hall*, Warwickshire: One of two stucco panels by Giuseppe Artari in the Great Hall, *c.* 1758

97. *Wentworth Woodhouse*, Yorkshire: The Whistlejacket Room, *c.* 1755. Plasterers: Joseph and Jonathan Rose, senior. George Stubbs's painting of 'Whistle-Jacket' at centre

98. *Hagley Hall*, Worcestershire: A stucco trophy by Francesco Vassalli in the Dining Room, *c.* 1758

99. *Shugborough Hall*, Staffordshire: A stucco trophy by Francesco or John Vassalli on the Library ceiling, *c.* 1761

100. *Somerset House*, Halifax, Yorkshire: Decoration above a fireplace, dated 1766 and attributed to Giuseppe Cortese

101. *Audley End*, Essex: A pendant in the neo-Jacobean style, showing the persistence of Gothic amid the all-enveloping neo-Classical mood, *c.* 1785

102. *Burton Constable*, Yorkshire: The seventeenth-century Gothic style simulated on the Long Gallery ceiling and frieze, *c.* 1760

103. *Hatchlands, Surrey*: Part of the Dining (now Drawing) Room ceiling, 1759. Allusion is made in Robert Adam's design to the nautical interests of his client, Admiral Boscawen

Ceiling for the Library at Croome

Janry 1763.

104. *Croome Court*, Worcestershire: Robert Adam's drawing for the Tapestry Room ceiling, January, 1763. Sir John Soane's Museum, London

105. *Croome Court*, Worcestershire: The Tapestry Room ceiling, 1763-4, by Joseph Rose and Co., re-erected at the Metropolitan Museum of Art, New York, the gift of the Kress Foundation, 1958-9. This ceiling was originally designed for the Library at Croome

106. *Nostell Priory*, Yorkshire: Robert Adam design, *c.* 1770, inscribed 'Design of a Cieling for the Saloon at Nostel the Seat of Sir Rowland Wynn Baronet'. Nostell Archives

107. *Sandbeck Park*, Yorkshire: Part of the Ballroom ceiling, *c.* 1766. Plasterer: Joseph Rose & Co.

108. *Osterley Park*, Middlesex: One of Robert Adam's drawings, dated 1767, for the Hall ceiling (see Plate 109 below)

109. *Osterley Park*, Middlesex: The Hall, designed by Robert Adam, 1767-8. Plasterwork attributed to Joseph Rose & Co.

110. *Osterley Park*, Middlesex: The ceiling of the Garden Room exemplifying the precise symmetry of
Neo-Classical plasterwork of the 1770s

111. *Kedleston*, Derbyshire: Plaster panel over the Great Hall fireplace, *c.* 1765.
Plasterer: Joseph Rose & Co.

112. *Kenwood*, Middlesex: Library, *c.* 1768. Detail of Joseph Rose, junior's gilded
plasterwork

113. *Milton Abbey*, Dorset: The Library ceiling, 1775, based on the ceiling of the Temple of the Sun at Palmyra

114. *Drayton House*, Northamptonshire: The Saloon ceiling, 1771, based on Plate XIXB, 'Temple of the Sun', in Robert Wood's *Ruins of Palmyra*, 1753. Plasterer: William Rhodes

Copy of the ceiling for the N. West Tower Bed Room. Milton Abbey

115. *Milton Abbey*, Dorset: James Wyatt's drawing for a ceiling, inscribed 'Copy of the Ceiling for the N. West Tower Bed Room. Milton Abbey', 1775. Victoria and Albert Museum, London

116. Drawing by James Wyatt for the plasterwork of an unidentified ceiling in the Neo-Classical style. Metropolitan Museum of Art, New York

117. *Lee Priory*, Kent: Ceiling of the Strawberry Room by James Wyatt, *c.* 1785, as re-erected at the
Victoria and Albert Museum, London

118. *Kentchurch*, Herefordshire: A frieze in Gothic style, part of the remodelling scheme by John Nash, *c.* 1795

119. *Brockhall*, Northamptonshire: Gothic plaster frieze, *c.* 1790

120. *Harlaxton Manor*, Lincolnshire: The Chapel, *c*. 1837. Unidentified plasterer working for the architect William Burn

DECORATIVE PLASTERWORK IN SCOTLAND
Plates 121-157

121. *Winton House*, East Lothian: The King Charles Room. The union royal arms, *c.* 1635

122. *The Binns*, Linlithgow: The King's Room, with its enriched central pendant and the royal arms over the fireplace, *c.* 1630

123. *Winton House*, East Lothian: Part of the plaster decoration by John White erected *c.* 1635 in honour of King Charles I

124. *The Binns*, Linlithgow: Medallions representing Alexander and David, twelfth-century Kings of Scotland. Plasterer: Alexander White, *c.* 1630

125. *Balcaskie House*, Fife: The ceiling in Sir William Bruce's bedroom, with his initials and those of his first wife Mary Halket, probably by William Lindores, *c.* 1673

126. *Balcaskie House*, Fife: The Library ceiling, *c.* 1670. Building was supervised by Sir William Bruce, who owned the house, from 1665 to 1684

127. *Kinross House*, Kinross-shire: The Staircase ceiling, *c.* 1690. Plasterer: probably Thomas Alborn. The house was built by Sir William Bruce

128. *Thirlestane Castle*, Berwickshire: The Drawing Room ceiling, *c.* 1675, done by John Houlbert and George Dunsterfield probably for the Glasgow plasterer Thomas Alborn

129. *Kellie Castle*, Fife: Heraldic ceiling panel, dated 1676

130. *Kellie Castle*, Fife: The coving of the Vine Room, *c.* 1676

131-132. *Brodie Castle*, Moray: Fantastic figures of mermen adorn this ceiling, one of the most lavish in Scotland, *c.* 1680

133. *The Palace of Holyroodhouse*, Edinburgh: The Grand Staircase ceiling, 1678. Plasterer: John Houlbert

134. Detail of Plate 133

135. *Arbuthnott House*, Kincardineshire: A caryatid figure on the
Drawing Room ceiling, *c.* 1695

136. *The Palace of Holyroodhouse*, Edinburgh: Corner of a second-floor bedroom ceiling, *c.* 1676

137. *Arniston House*, Midlothian: Architect: William Adam. Detail of plasterwork by Joseph Enzer. The house was begun by Adam in 1727 for Lord President Dundas

138. *Arniston House*, Midlothian: The Hall, *c.* 1730

139-140. *Fullarton House*, Ayrshire (demolished 1967): Two details of plasterwork, attributed to Joseph Enzer, *c.* 1730

141. *Yester House*, East Lothian: Staircase ceiling. Rococo plasterwork by Joseph Enzer, *c.* 1736

142. *Drum House*, Edinburgh: The Hall chimneypiece, 1727. Architect: William Adam. Plasterer: Samuel Calderwood

143. *Châtelhêrault*, Hamilton, Lanarkshire (a ruin since 1967):
Plaster medallion, *c*. 1740

144. *Châtelhêrault*, Hamilton, Lanarkshire: Plasterwork panel in the ceiling of the Banqueting Hall, upper
room, *c*. 1740. Plasterer: Thomas Clayton

145. *Blair Castle*, Perthshire: The Dining Room fireplace, 1751, with plaster overmantel by Thomas Clayton. The marble work is by Thomas Carter

146. *Blair Castle*, Perthshire: Detail of stucco-swag in the Dining Room, 1751

147. *Blair Castle*, Perthshire: Detail of the plaster overmantel in the Dining Room (see Plate 145)

148. *Glendoick House*, Perthshire: The Drawing Room ceiling, *c.* 1750. Plasterwork attributed to Thomas Clayton, but also possibly by Alexander Morison

149. *Blair Castle*, Perthshire: Detail of the Large Drawing Room ceiling. Plasterer: Thomas Clayton

150. *Hopetoun House*, West Lothian: Detail of the Red Drawing Room ceiling, *c.* 1754. Plasterwork attributed to Thomas Clayton

151. *Blair Castle*, Perthshire: Detail of the Dining Room ceiling, 1751. Plasterwork by Thomas Clayton surrounding 'Summer', one of the painted roundels of The Seasons by Thomas Bardwell

152. *Inveraray Castle*, Argyll: The Drawing Room ceiling, *c.* 1775. Plasterwork attributed to Thomas Clayton, junior

153. *Mellerstain*, Berwickshire: A detail of the Library ceiling with musical trophies and centre painting
of Minerva

154. *Paxton House*, Berwickshire: The Dining Room chimneypiece,
with an oval medallion depicting 'The Rape of Europa'.
Plasterer: John (?) Morison, *c.* 1772

155. *Mellerstain*, Berwickshire: One of the four sections of a plaster frieze in the Library entitled 'From the
tomb of Emperor Severus at Monte del Grano'

156. *Taymouth Castle*, Perthshire: Gothic plasterwork in the Entrance Hall, *c.* 1810. Plasterer: Francis Bernasconi

157. *Ardkinglas House*, Argyllshire: The convincing 1680s style plasterwork done under the supervision of Sir Robert Lorimer, *c.* 1908

Select List of Plasterers

In the Preface to this book I have noted the factors which needed to be considered before making this a selective rather than a definitive list. It is difficult for one person to include every name, especially as the documentation of plasterwork is sparse. There is, however, a working basis for further attribution in the following list. The literature and documentation on the work of each plasterer is listed after the abbreviation *Lit.*

ABBREVIATIONS

Arch. Rev.	*Architectural Review*, monthly journal.
Baker, *Brydges.*	C.H.C. and M.I. Collins Baker, *The Life and Circumstances of James Brydges, 1st Duke of Chandos*, 1949.
B.M. Add. MSS.	British Museum, Additional Manuscripts.
Colvin.	H.M. Colvin, *A Biographical Dictionary of English Architects, 1660-1840*, 1954.
Croft-Murray.	Edward Croft-Murray, *Decorative Painting in England*, Vol. I, 1962; Vol. II, 1971.
C. Life.	*Country Life*, weekly magazine.
Gibbs.	James Gibbs, *A Book of Architecture*, 1728.
Gunnis.	Rupert Gunnis, *A Dictionary of British Sculptors, 1660-1851*, 1953.
Jourdain, 1926.	Margaret Jourdain, *English Decorative Plasterwork of the Renaissance*, 1926.
Little, *Gibbs.*	Bryan Little, *The Life and Work of James Gibbs*, 1955.
Hussey, E.C.H.: *Early, Mid-Georgian, and Late Georgian*	Christopher Hussey, *English Country Houses: Early Georgian*, 2nd ed. 1965; *English Country Houses: Mid-Georgian*, 1956; *English Country Houses: Late Georgian*, 1958.
P.C.C.	Prerogative Court of Canterbury (wills filed at the Public Record Office).
P.R.O.	Public Record Office.
R.I.B.A.	Royal Institute of British Architects.
V.C.H.	Victoria County History.
Willis & Clark.	R. Willis and J.W. Clark, *Architectural History of the University of Cambridge*, 3 vols., 1886.
Wren Soc.	The Wren Society, 20 vols., 1924-43. Index in Vol. 20.

Abbott, John (1639/40-1727)
Son of Richard Abbott, baptized at Frithelstock, N. Devon, 20 February 1639/40. Worked extensively in Devon and many decorations have been credited to him through the patterns in his sketch-book. Had an apprentice, Lawrence Mabyn. Abbot died on 28 April 1727.
1676 FRITHELSTOCK CHURCH, DEVON
Royal coat-of-arms, etc. Received £13 6s 8d
Lit: Churchwardens' Accounts, cited in *C. Life*, 2 March 1940, p. 222.
1680 CUSTOM HOUSE, EXETER, DEVON
Ceilings. Received £35.
Lit: Accounts, Exeter City Record Office, cited by Kathleen and Cecil French, 'Devonshire Plaster-work', *Devonshire Association, Transactions*, Vol. 89, 1957, pp. 124-44. Abbott's sketch-book and four of his plastering tools are in the Devon County Record Office. See also Margaret Jourdain, 'A Seventeenth Century Plasterer, John Abbott of Barnstaple and his Sketch Book', *C. Life*, 2 March 1940, pp. 222-5.

Addinal, — (*fl.* 1772)
Only recorded in connection with the following commission:
1772 KILNWICK HALL, YORKSHIRE
Worked under Joseph Cortese (q.v.).
Lit: Edward Ingram, *Leaves from a Family Tree*, 1952.

Afflett, W. (*fl.* 1693-1710)
Apprenticed to Henry Doogood (q.v.). Made free of The Worshipful Company of Plaisterers, 21 October 1700.
1708-10 ST PAUL'S CATHEDRAL, LONDON
Worked under Chrysostom Wilkins (q.v.).
Lit: Guildhall Library MS 6122/3; Wren Soc., xv, pp. 169, 196.

Alborn, Thomas (*fl.* 1667-78)
Lived in Glasgow. Took W. Lindores as apprentice in 1667.
1671-4 THIRLESTANE CASTLE, BERWICKSHIRE
Architect: Sir William Bruce.
Received £1,324 14s 4d.
Lit: Thirlestane Castle MSS. Scottish Record Office.
1674-8 HOLYROODHOUSE, EDINBURGH
Worked under George Dunsterfield and John Houlbert (q.v.), but received £1,100 on 25 August 1675, and £659 10s 0d on 9 August 1676, 'for several sorts of Plaister work'.
1675-6 STIRLING (Palace and Castle)
Received £823 6s 6d.
Lit: R. S. Mylne, *The Master Masons to the Crown of Scotland and their Works*, 1893, pp. 195, 201.

1699 CRAIGHALL, FIFE
Lit: Bruce of Arnot MSS, Scottish Record Office. The author is indebted to Mr John Dunbar for this information.
Attributed work:
1673 KINROSS HOUSE, KINROSS-SHIRE
Architect: Sir William Bruce.
Great Staircase.
Lit: Sir William Bruce, 1630-1710 (Scottish Arts Council exhibition catalogue 1970 No. 128).

Allen, Antony (*fl.* 1683)
1683 ST PAUL'S CATHEDRAL, LONDON
Made a model.
Lit: Wren Soc., XIII, p. 168.

Allison, John (*fl.* 1660)
1660 THE TOWER, LONDON
Worked under John Grove I.
Lit: P.R.O. Works, 5/1, November 1660.

Artari
The history of this family, settled at Arogno towards the end of the sixteenth century, is very complex. An extensive literature (summarized in *Dizionario Biografico Degli Italiani*, IV, 1962, pp. 351-2) assumes that Giovanni Battista Artari was born at Arogno, near Lugano, in 1660 and that his son Giuseppe, who worked in England with Bagutti (q.v.), was born there in 1697. Searches in the 'Liber Baptizato' and 'Liber Matrimoni' at Arogno made in 1966-7 in the company of Professor Giuseppe Martinola (Cantonal Historical Commission, Lugano) revealed how the errors arose but have not provided a satisfactory solution. The alternatives are:
1. Giovanni Battista Artari, son of Joseph and Jecomina, was baptized at Arogno on 19 October 1664 (not 1660). He married 'Catherina de Maini' in the same church on 1 March 1688.
2. Giovanni and Catherina had at least two children, Carlo Giuseppe, born 5 September 1692, and Adalbertus, born 7 October 1693. There is no entry for the birth of an Artari in 1697. A problem arises in assuming this Carlo Giuseppe to be the stuccoist who worked in England, since his death is recorded at Arogno on 27 May 1757, 'in the sixty-fifth year of his age', although most sources suggest that Artari died in Cologne in 1769. The entire problem is further complicated by the birth of another Giuseppe Artari, son of Domenico Artari and Bartolomea, née Pianca, at Arogno on 20 September 1700. There was also an Artari family settled at Bissone nearby.

It is therefore clear that the statements about the lives of these two stuccoists in existing literature, my own *Georgian Craftsmen and their Work* (1966) included, need to be viewed in relation to the Artari entries in the Arogno registers. In the absence of a solution they must be listed here under names of convenience.

Artari, Adalbertus (1693-1751)
Born at Arogno. Presumed to be the 'Albert Artari' who assisted Giuseppe Artari at Sutton Scarsdale. Either he or his father Giovanni Battista (see below) could have been one of the 'two Mr Artares' mentioned in the Ditchley archives. He is presumably the Albert Artari who died at Arogno on 22 October 1751.
1724 SUTTON SCARSDALE, DERBYSHIRE
Architect: Francis Smith.
Lit: Text of lead rising-plate formerly at house. House destroyed *c.* 1920 (fragments of stucco remain adhering to ruin). Sale catalogue dated 6 November 1919; text of rising-plate, *C. Life,* 15 February 1919, p. 171.
1725 DITCHLEY, OXFORDSHIRE *Plate 52*
Architect: James Gibbs.
Worked with Giuseppe Artari, Francesco Serena (q.v.) and Francesco Vassalli (q.v.). The accounts record:
   'Ap. 9. 1725 pd the two Mr Artare's in part by my Lord.   10. 10. 0.'

'Joseph' Artari is mentioned elsewhere in the account.
Lit: Oxford County Record Office, Dillon MSS., Dil I/p/3h.

Artari, Giovanni Battista (1664-?)
Born at Arogno. May have worked in England. As some sources (e.g. Benezit, *Dictionnaire . . . des peintres . . .,* 1948) give a third Christian name of 'Alberti' to him he has been confused with his son Adalbertus (see above). In 1707 he was working with Gian Battista Genone at Fulda Cathedral and they were also employed at Rastatt Cathedral, Brühl and Aquisgrana.
   The stuccoist Alfonso Oldelli (1696-*c.*1770), writing to Giovanni Oldelli at Meride on 2 July 1721, mentions the 'Signori Artari' working in England and states that they were doing well and that he had a mind to join them.
Lit: *Dizionario Biografico Degli Italiani,* IV, 1962, p. 351; F. Hermanin, *Gli artisti in Germania,* 1935, II, pp. 35, 42, 44, 64; Nicolas Powell, *From Baroque to Rococo,* 1959, p. 38; Giuseppe Martinola, *Lettere dai paesi Transalpini degli Artisti di Meride,* 1963, p. 117.

Artari, Giuseppe (late seventeenth century-1769)
Born at Arogno in 1692 or 1700 (see introduction above). Stated to have trained with his father and to have worked in Rome, Germany and Holland before coming to England. His association with Giovanni Bagutti is discussed in chapter V. His first recorded employment in England was in 1720. He married, and his wife 'Mary Gertrude' Artari occasionally received payment on his behalf for his work, such as that at the Radcliffe Camera, Oxford (1744-5). He left for Germany some time after 1760 having been called to work for the Elector of Köln. He died there in 1769.
1720 OCTAGON HOUSE, TWICKENHAM, MIDDLESEX
Architect: James Gibbs.
Artari assisted by Giovanni Bagutti.
Lit: Gibbs, p. xix; *C. Life,* XCVI, 15 September 1944; Hussey, *E.C.H: Early Georgian,* 1955, pp. 40-2.
1720-30 AACHEN CATHEDRAL
Octagon of nave (removed 1870-3).
Lit: Dehio and Gall, *Handbuch der Deutschen Kunstdrukmäler, Wordlichen Hessen,* pp. 276, 279; *Die Rheinlande,* p. 108.
1722-6 ST MARTIN-IN-THE-FIELDS, LONDON.
Architect: James Gibbs.
Artari assisted by Giovanni Bagutti.
Lit: Gibbs, p. v: 'the ceiling enrich'd with Fret-work by Signori Artari and Bagutti, the best Fretworkers that ever came into England'; John McMaster, *A Short History of the Royal Parish of St. Martin-in-the-Fields,* 1916; K. A. Esdaile, *St. Martin-in-the-Fields,* 1944; Little, *Gibbs,* p. 91.
1722-30 SENATE HOUSE, CAMBRIDGE
Architect: James Gibbs.
Artari assisted by Giovanni Bagutti.
Lit: Willis & Clark, III, p. 47; Little, *Gibbs,* p. 61.
1723-4 ST PETER'S, VERE STREET, LONDON
(Formerly known as the Oxford or Marylebone Chapel.)
Architect: James Gibbs.
Artari assisted by Giovanni Bagutti.
Lit: Gibbs, p. vii: 'the ceiling is handsomely adorned with Fret-work by Signori Artari and Bagutti'.
1725 DITCHLEY, OXFORDSHIRE *Plate 52*
Architect: James Gibbs.
Artari assisted by Giovanni Artari, Francesco Serena and Francesco Vassalli.
Lit: Oxford County Record Office, Dillon MSS., I/3/p/h.

1726 HOUGHTON HALL, NORFOLK
Architect: Colin Campbell; interior: William Kent;
'the ceiling and the Frieze of Boys are by Artari'
(Horace Walpole, *Anecdotes of Painters*, 1819 ed.,
II, p. 34).
Lit: Isaac Ware, *Plans, Elevations and Sections of
Houghton in Norfolk*, 1735, p. 7; Margaret Jourdain,
William Kent, 1948, p. 63; Hussey, *E.C.H: Early
Georgian*, p. 80.

1729-32 FALKENLUST, BRÜHL (hunting lodge)
Architect: François de Cuvilliés.
Lit: Dizionario Biografico degli Italiani, IV, 1962,
pp. 351-2.

1729 CAVENDISH SQUARE, LONDON
Worked with Francesco Serena (q.v.).
Lit: Baker, *Brydges*, pp. 199, 277.

1730-1 MOULSHAM HALL, ESSEX
Architect: Giacomo Leoni.
Artari assisted by Giovanni Bagutti.
Destroyed 1809. Artari did 'Bustos and Figures'.
He continued to work at Moulsham in later years;
he was engaged on the ceiling of the Great Room in
1746. 24 March 1746: 'Pd. Mrs Artari in part of
£27 due to her husband, £5 5.
Lit: Mildmay Account Books, Hampshire County
Record Office (15M50/31) and Essex County Record
Office (D/DMA5-7).

1736 CASTLE HOWARD, YORKSHIRE
Submitted a drawing to the 3rd Earl of Carlisle
for finishing the Temple of the Four Winds in
stucco. The task was, however, given to Vassalli
(q.v.), and Artari was paid £2 2s for his drawing.
Lit: Castle Howard MSS., 3rd Earl of Carlisle's
Disbursement Book.

1737-8 TRENTHAM, STAFFORDSHIRE
Architect: Francis Smith.
New Library. The accounts also note, 22 March
1737-8, 'Pd. for pipe-clay for moulds for Mr
Artari'. (The author is indebted to Mr John Corn-
forth for this information.)
Lit: Staffordshire County Record Office, Trentham
MSS.; *C. Life*, 25 January 1968, p. 178.

1742 CASTLE HILL, DEVON
Stucco-work; *basso-relievos* in Best Hall. Received
£32 plus travelling expenses. (The author is indebted to Mr Howard Colvin for this information.)
Lit: Castle Hill MSS., Box C.1.

1743-4 PALACE, POPPELSDORF
Worked with Carlo Pietro Morsegno and the
brothers Castelli.
Lit: Dizionario Biografico degli Italiani, IV, 1962,
pp. 351-2.

1743-4 WIMPOLE HALL, CAMBRIDGESHIRE
Received £76 9s.

Lit: B.M. Add. MS., 36228, ff. 170, 180.

1744-5 RADCLIFFE CAMERA, OXFORD
Architect: James Gibbs.
Received £98 16s 8d (Artari's wife Mary Gertrude
received this amount on his behalf).
Lit: 'The Building Accounts of the Radcliffe
Camera, Oxford', *ed.* S.G. Gillam, Oxford His-
torical Society, XIII, 1953-4 (1958); S. Lang, *Arch.
Rev.*, April 1949, pp. 183-90; Little, *Gibbs*, pp.
134-5.

1748-61 SCHLOSS BRÜHL, COLOGNE
Stucco-work started in 1748 in a building erected
to the designs of J.C. Schlaun and, later, François
de Cuvilliés. It continued in 1756-7 in the first-floor
State Room, south wing. All work was completed
by 1761, the date of the death of Clemens August,
the Archbishop and Elector of Cologne.
Lit: Letter from Artari in Düsseldorf Stadtarchiv,
reproduced in Berliner Jahrbuch 100, pp. 101 ff.;
E. Renard and F.G.W. Metternich, *Schloss Brühl*,
1934; Nicolas Powell, *From Baroque to Rococo*, 1959,
pp. 102, 148.

1756-60 RAGLEY HALL, WARWICKSHIRE *Plate* 96
Lit: B.M. Add. MS., 29218: letters of Horace
Walpole to 1st Earl of Hertford, 14 July, 3 August
1759; 1 September, 13 December 1760. Dr Richard
Pococke's record of his visit to the house in
1756.

Attributed works (*Plates* 50, 56, 57, 67):
A considerable amount of careless attribution has
taken place respecting Artari's work. James Gibbs
consistently used his services, in company with
Giovanni Bagutti, and possibly they worked at such
houses as Sudbrook, Kelmarsh, and Fairlawne.
A comparison of details of the ceilings at Moor
Park, Hertfordshire, and Clandon Park, Surrey,
reasonably allows that they worked at Clandon
(Geoffrey Beard, *Georgian Craftsmen and their
Work*, 1966, Plates 37, 38, 50-3). Comparison of
the Hall at Houghton, Norfolk, with the work at
Bedale Hall, Yorkshire, (Beard, *op. cit.*, Plates 57-8)
reveals close connections, but the Bedale ceiling is
too coarse in execution to be by Artari and may be
by Giuseppe Cortese. He may also have provided
the ceiling at 11 Henrietta Place, St Marylebone
(now in the Victoria and Albert Museum, W5-
1960). It is close to Gibbs, *Book of Architecture*
plates in style and the stucco surrounds paintings
by Bellucci.

It is certain that Artari slipped abroad to work
from time to time. In addition to the work cited
he is credited with stucco decoration in Bonn and
Münster (*Dizionario Biografico degli Italiani*, IV,
1962, 351-2).

Artima, Baltassar (*fl.* 1686)
1686 WHITEHALL PALACE, LONDON
'Allowed for one Chimney piece with a frame wrought out of stuccoe . . .' £8.
Lit: Wren Soc., VII, p. 116; P.R.O. Works, 5/54.

Atherton, Charles (*fl.* mid-seventeenth century)
Although he worked for Sir Robert Hooke, Atherton is presumably to be identified with the Serjeant Plumber who did extensive work for the Office of Works.
Lit: Sir Robert Hooke, *Diary*, (1935 ed., p. 311); Wren Soc., XX (references cited).

Audsley, David (*fl.* 1726)
Subscriber to Leoni's *Alberti*, 1726.

Bacon, George (*fl.* 1779-89)
1779-89 OSTERLEY, MIDDLESEX
Retouching and general plastering.
Lit: Osterley Archives, Victoria and Albert Museum (Department of Furniture and Woodwork). (The author is indebted to Dr Damie Stillman for this information.)

Bagnall, John (*fl.* 1710-46)
Resident at York and Richmond (1746).
1712 (and after) CASTLE HOWARD, YORKSHIRE
Architect: Sir John Vanbrugh.
Plain plastering.
Lit: Castle Howard Archives, Building Books.
1726 TEMPLE NEWSAM HOUSE, LEEDS
Plain plastering £3 4s od.
Lit: Leeds Reference Library, EA 12/10, September, 1726.
1731-4 ASSEMBLY ROOMS, YORK
Architect: Lord Burlington.
Entablature capitals, and 'all the plaister work of the Great Room'. Paid £400, an extra £20 at the recommendation of Lord Burlington, and 4 guineas for doing festoons in the Great Room.
Lit: Minute Book, York Reference Library. Entries dated as follows: 22 January 1731, 18 January, 13 April, 23 June 1732; 22 January, 22 August 1733; 22 August, 29 August 1734.
In 1746 Bagnall submitted an estimate for work at Minto House, Scotland.
Lit: National Library of Scotland, Minto Papers, Box 2. (The author is indebted to Mr Howard Colvin for this information.)

Bagutti, Giovanni (1681-after 1730)
Born on 14 October 1681, at Rovio, near Lugano, Switzerland. Son of Bernard Bagutti and Angela Maria (née Falconi). He married Caterina Bagutti, presumably his cousin, on 22 March 1713. He was in England by 1709, but it is doubtful if he came from Italy with James Gibbs as sometimes suggested (see chapter V). Must be regarded as the senior partner to Giuseppe Artari. Daniel Defoe called him 'the finest artist in those particular works now in England'. Subscribed to Leoni's *Alberti*, 1726, and to James Gibbs's *A Book of Architecture*, 1728.
His name occurs in a list of the family and other people assembled in the house of the Duke of Chandos at Cannons, Middlesex, on New Year's Day, 1722—'Mr Bagutti, his partner Mr Artree [Artari]'. Lord Chandos's 'smith', Walter Husbands, was also there to help and was probably employed on the metal frameworks for the stucco figures which are a feature of his work. Bagutti should not be confused with a painter Abbondio Bagutti, nor Pietro Martire Bagutti of Bologna.
1710 CASTLE HOWARD, YORKSHIRE *Plates* 47, 48
Architect: Sir John Vanbrugh.
Bagutti did the stucco chimneypiece and facing scagliola niche in the Great Hall, assisted by Plura.
Lit: Castle Howard MSS., Building Books:
'1710. Feb. 10 Mr. Bargotee, Italian, given him

Upon Acct. of work		25	0	0
June Pd. Mr. Bargotee		20	0	0
Given Mr. Bargotee		10	15	0
Given Mr. Bagutti		10	15	0
Given Mr. Bagutti		10	0	0'

Before 1720 CANNONS, MIDDLESEX
Architects: John James and James Gibbs.
Chapel ceiling (surrounding Antonio Bellucci's paintings, some of which are now at Great Witley church, Worcestershire). Received £210. The chapel was dedicated in August 1720. In 1722 Bagutti was assisted at Cannons by Artari.
Lit: Cannons Inventory—'frettwork ceiling by Mr. Burgooty'; J. Macky, *Journey Through England*, 1722—'gilded by Pargotti' [sic]; Daniel Defoe, *Tour Through the Whole Island of Great Britain . . .*, 1725 —'by Pargotti'; Baker, *Brydges*, p. 149; F.J.B. Watson, *Arte Veneta*, 1954, p. 209.
1720 OCTAGON HOUSE, TWICKENHAM, MIDDLESEX
Architect: James Gibbs.
Bagutti assisted by Giuseppe Artari.
Lit: Gibbs, p. xix; *C. Life*, XCVI, 15 September 1944;
1722-5 MEREWORTH, KENT *Frontispiece*
Architect: Colin Campbell.
Lit: Colin Campbell, *Vitruvius Britannicus*, 1725, III, p. 3—'the ornaments are executed by Signor Bagutti, a most ingenious artist'; Hussey, *E.C.H.: Early Georgian*, p. 58.

1722-6 ST MARTIN-IN-THE-FIELDS, LONDON
Architect: James Gibbs.
Received £419 6s. Bagutti presumably divided the money with Artari, who is not mentioned in the accounts.
Lit: Gibbs, p. v: 'the ceiling enrich'd with Fretwork by Signori Artari and Bagutti, the best Fretworkers that ever came into England'; John McMaster, *A Short History of the Royal Parish of St. Martin-in-the-Fields*, 1916; K. A. Esdaile, *St. Martin-in-the-Fields*, 1944.

1723-4 ST PETER'S, VERE STREET, LONDON
Formerly known as the Oxford or Marylebone Chapel.
Architect: James Gibbs.
Lit: Gibbs, p. vii—'the ceiling is handsomely adorned with Fret-work by Signori Artari and Bagutti'; Colvin, pp. 231-2.

1725-6 SENATE HOUSE, CAMBRIDGE
Architect: James Gibbs.
Bagutti assisted by Giuseppe Artari.
Plain plasterwork by Isaac Mansfield. Bagutti received £310.
Lit: University Registry, XLVI, 5 October 1725; Vice-Chancellor's Receipts, 31 March 1726: 'Receiv'd then of the Reverend Dr Davies Vice-chancellr of the University of Cambridge one hundred and fifty pounds in part for the ornaments of the ceiling of the New Senate House by me John Bagutti'. Similar receipt on 8 September 1726, for the balance of £160. Willis & Clark III, p. 47; Little, *Gibbs*, p. 61. An alternative design by Bagutti is in the Ashmolean Museum, Oxford, Gibbs Collection, II, 63-4.

1730-1 MOULSHAM HALL, ESSEX
Architect: Giacomo Leoni.
Lit: Mildmay Account Books, Hampshire County Record Office (15M50/31), and Mildmay Account Books, Essex County Record Office, (D/DMA5-7).
The Hampshire entries read:
'1730. Decr. 7. Pd. Mr. Bagutti, the Italian stuccatori for work by agreemt. he and Mr. Altari did at Moulsham Hall for wch. [he] is to have £150 having pd. him before. £10.10.0. Pd. this day £100.0.0. . . . £100.0.0.
1731. Febry. 13th. having [paid] Mr. Bagutti the Italian stuccatori for his work done in my Hall and dining-room at Moulsham—

	£		
	115	15	0
I have this day also pd. him	45	13	0
Wch in the whole amts to	161	8	0

in full for all the work Mr. Altari and he have done for me to this day, my agreemt. was only with Mr. Bagutti & Mr. Altari who did the Bustos & Figures assisted him.'

c. 1732 MOOR PARK, HERTFORDSHIRE *Plate 57*
Lit: Drawing in the Ashmolean Museum, Oxford, Gibbs Collection, IV, 24. *Burlington Magazine*, Nov. 1971, p. 659. This drawing for the four walls and cove of a minor room at Down Hall or Stowe is inscribed 'For Mr. Baguti att More Parke near Rikmonsworth in Hertfordshire'. This suggests that Bagutti did work at Moor Park and was responsible for the plasterwork surrounding the paintings by Francesco Sleter.
Date uncertain CASSIOBURY PARK, HERTFORDSHIRE
Horace Walpole, *Anecdotes of Painting*, 1797, III, p. 397; The Walpole Society, XXIV, 1935, Vertue IV, 7—'a ceiling for Lord Essex representing Flora and other figures and boys in alto-relievo by Bagotti'.
Attributed works:
1724 THE MYNDE, near HEREFORD *Plate 50*
The 1st Duke of Chandos acquired this house in 1715. He did some building there in 1724, hoping to go into residence the following year. However, by 1726 he was negotiating its sale. There is good plasterwork attributable to Bagutti and Artari.
Lit: Baker, *Brydges*, p. 272, fn.
1731-5 CLANDON PARK, SURREY *Plate 67*
Architect: Giacomo Leoni.
The architect of Clandon, Leoni, engaged Bagutti and Artari to work at Moulsham Hall, Essex, in 1730-1, and it seems very likely that the Clandon work is due to them, the figurework being by Artari. A comparison of the Moor Park ceilings, which are thought to be Bagutti's work, with those at Clandon supports this attribution.
Lit: Geoffrey Beard, *Connoisseur*, CXXXVIII, No. 556, October 1956.

Baily, John (*fl.* 1821-5).
Master Plasterer to Sir John Soane. Possibly the John Bayley (q.v.) who worked at Ditchley. His bust is at Sir John Soane's Museum, London, together with some of his models of Soane buildings, *c.* 1825.
1821-3 WOTTON HOUSE, AYLESBURY, BUCKINGHAMSHIRE
Sir John Soane employed John and Joseph Baily here.
Lit: C. *Life*, 15 July 1949; *Architectural History*, 12, 1969, p. 25.

Baker, Thomas (*fl.* 1775)
Mentioned in Sketchley's 1775 Bristol Directory as a 'tiler and plasterer'.

Barnes, James (*fl.* 1775)
Mentioned in Sketchley's 1775 Bristol Directory as a 'tiler and plasterer'.

Bates, W. (*fl.* 1710)
1710 ST PAUL'S CATHEDRAL, LONDON
Worked under Chrysostom Wilkins.
Lit: Wren Soc., XV, p. 196.

Baxter, John (*fl.* 1689)
1689 HAMPTON COURT, MIDDLESEX
Worked under John Grove (q.v.).
Lit: P.R.O., Works, 5/55, May 1689.

Bayley, John (*fl.* 1769)
Possibly the same as Soane's plasterer, John Baily
(Bailey) (q.v.).
1769 DITCHLEY, OXFORDSHIRE
Plain plastering at a temple in the park, and one
room in the house.
Lit: Oxford County Record Office, MSS., Dil/I/
p/3r.

Bayly, Abraham (*fl.* 1775)
Mentioned in Sketchley's 1775 Bristol Directory as
a 'tiler and plasterer'.

Beale, Henry (*fl.* 1716-17)
Official of the Worshipful Company of Plasterers.
1716 Upper Warden.
1717 Master.
Lit: London, Guildhall Library, MS., 6122/3.

Beddington, Edward (*fl.* 1775)
Mentioned in Sketchley's 1775 Bristol Directory
as a 'tiler and plasterer'.

Bedwell, Charles (*fl.* 1690)
1690 KENSINGTON PALACE, LONDON
Worked under Henry Margetts (q.v.).
Lit: P.R.O., Works, 19,48/1.f.108.

Bennett, Richard (*fl.* 1660)
1660 THE TOWER, LONDON
Worked under John Grove I.
Lit: P.R.O., Works, 5/1, 16 November 1660.

Bernasconi, Bernato (*fl.* 1770-1820?)
Presumably of the family of stuccoists of this name
who settled at Riva St Vitale, birthplace of Vassalli
(q.v.) near to Lugano.
C.R. Cockerell told the *Select Committee on Arts
and their connection with Manufactures* (27 July 1835,
to 13 August 1836) on 28 August 1835, that 'a few
artists still survived in Ireland and there remained
in England a Mr Bernasconi till 1820 . . .'. (The
author is indebted to Mr Edward Croft-Murray
for this information.)

1770-84 CLAYDON, BUCKINGHAMSHIRE
Plasterwork in Hall and Ballroom. Money became
short, and in 1782 Bernasconi complained of the
accommodation provided for him—a cottage in East
Claydon—and noted he was 'a poor man with a
large fameley in the town of Buckingham'.
Lit: C. Life, 7 November 1952, pp. 1483-4; Gunnis,
p. 51.

Bernasconi, Francis (1762-1841)
Said to have been the son of Bartholomew Bernasconi (d. 1786). As well as being 'the most fashionable purveyor of Regency Gothic stucco' Francis
was largely employed on scagliola work, and there
is no doubt that the following list only represents
a fraction of his work.
Lit: Hussey, *E.C.H.: Late Georgian,* p. 25.
1800-9 COBHAM HALL, KENT
Received £1,556 for plasterwork, Gothic mouldings,
etc.
Lit: Earl of Darnley's Archives; Gunnis, p. 51.
1803 WESTMINSTER ABBEY, LONDON
Received £826 for plasterwork in the Great Tower.
Lit: Westminster Abbey Archives; Gunnis, p. 51.
1803 SHUGBOROUGH, STAFFORDSHIRE
Work in Saloon.
Lit: Hussey, *E.C.H.: Mid-Georgian,* p. 85.
1803-5 YORK MINSTER
Work in south transept: stucco birds, finial on
canopy of Archbishop de Grey monument.
Lit: York Minster Library E3, E4a, Fabric Rolls
and Bills.
1804 CARLTON HOUSE, LONDON
Lit: P.R.O., Works, 5/94 cited in J.M. Crook and
M.H. Port, *The History of the King's Works 1782-
1851,* 1974, p. 313.
1805 WINDSOR CASTLE
Architect: Sir Jeffry Wyatville.
Gothic compo mouldings, enriched spandrels, etc.
Lit: P.R.O., Works, 5/93; Gunnis, p. 51; W. St John
Hope, *Windsor Castle,* 1913, pp. 350, 352, 366-7,
369, 557.
He also worked there in 1824.
1805 SHUGBOROUGH, STAFFORDSHIRE
Supplied twelve capitals to scagliola columns worked
by Joseph Alcott.
Lit: C. Life, 11 March 1954, p. 678
1806- ? COMPTON PLACE, EASTBOURNE, SUSSEX
Outside compo, stucco, colouring and inside works.
Received £1,754 18s 5¾d.
Lit: Compton Place Archives, Box Q.
1807 GROSVENOR HOUSE, LONDON
Received £2,097 for plasterwork.
Lit: Grosvenor Archives, Eaton Hall, Cheshire.

(The author is indebted to Mr Rupert Gunnis for this reference.)

c. 1810 DODINGTON PARK, GLOUCESTERSHIRE
Architect: James Wyatt.
Lit: C. Life, 29 November 1956, p. 1232.

1810-11 LOWTHER CASTLE, CUMBERLAND
Architect: Sir Robert Smirke; house survives as a ruin.
Received £852.
Lit: County Record Office, Carlisle, Lowther MSS.

c. 1810 LONGLEAT, WILTS.
Architect, Sir Jeffry Wyatville. Bernasconi was then resident at Alfred Place, Bedford Square, London.
Lit: D. Linstrum, *Sir Jeffry Wyatville*, 1972, p. 244.

1811 BADMINTON, GLOUCESTERSHIRE
Library.
The author is indebted to Mr H. M. Colvin for this information.

c. 1812 EATON HALL, CHESHIRE
Architect: William Porden.
Lit: C. Life, 18 February 1971, p. 361.

1813-15 ASHRIDGE PARK, HERTFORDSHIRE
Received £879.
Lit: Brownlow Archives, Belton; Gunnis, p. 51.

1813-19 ASHBURNHAM PLACE, SUSSEX
Worked under George Dance and S. W. Reynolds, and refaced the house in stucco. Bernasconi at this time was living at Alfred Place, Bedford Square, London.
Lit: Ashburnham Archives, East Sussex Record Office, 2809, 2834-41, 2847-8; *C. Life*, 30 April 1953, p. 1336.

1816 EASTNOR CASTLE, HEREFORDSHIRE
Architect: Sir Robert Smirke.
Received £961 16s 8d.
Lit: Eastnor Castle Building Books, 1812-20.

1816 CHICKSANDS PRIORY, BEDFORDSHIRE
Lit: Hussey, *E.C.H.: Late Georgian*, p. 25.

1819-21 GARNONS, HEREFORDSHIRE
Lit: Herefordshire County Records, Cotterell MSS.

1820- ? CHATSWORTH, DERBYSHIRE
Extensive work including Cabinet Library as late as 1830.
Lit: Linstrum *op. cit.*, pp. 141-62.

1822 BLITHFIELD, STAFFORDSHIRE
The Great Hall in Gothic style, of which the patron Lord Bagot said that it was 'as perfect a specimen ... as has ever been executed in modern times'. Bernasconi was at work at Blithfield for most of the first quarter of the nineteenth century.
Lit: C. Life, 4 November 1954, p. 1577. Staffs County Record Office, Dyott MSS.

c. 1824 LILLESHALL HALL, SHROPSHIRE
Received £1,456 5s 10d.

Lit: Linstrum *op. cit.*, p. 240.

1827-8 STAFFORD HOUSE, LONDON
Received £6,696.
Lit: Architectural History, Vol. x, 1967: *C. Life*, 14 November 1968.

1833 KENSINGTON PALACE
As 'Bernasconi & Son'.
Lit: Linstrum, *op. cit.*, p. 242.

1833 ST JAMES'S SQUARE, LONDON
House for Earl de Grey.
Lit: C. Life, 2 July 1970, p. 20.
Other work:
A design by Thomas Stothard (1755-1834) for Bernasconi's work at Buckingham Palace is reproduced by A. P. Oppé, *English Drawings at Windsor*, 1950, p. 93. He is also known to have worked in Wales and Scotland, *c.* 1810, at Taymouth Castle, Perthshire (Plate 156). He probably did the work at Penrhyn Castle, Caernarvonshire.
Lit: Hussey, *E.C.H.: Late Georgian*, p. 191.
He may have done the French style work at Wrest Park, Bedfordshire.
Lit: C. Life, 2 July 1970, p. 20.

Berrill, Jeremiah (*fl.* 1668-9)
1668 WHITEHALL PALACE, LONDON
Worked under John Grove I.
Lit: P.R.O., Works 5/12.

Betley, Arthur (*fl.* 1745)
c. 1745 COPPED HALL, ESSEX
Destroyed 1917.
Lit: Essex County Record Office, Copped Hall MSS., 'An Estimate of Plaisters Work proposed to be done for Esqr Conyers by Order of Mr Sanderson Including Labour only by Arthur Betley', no date.

Betson, Thomas (*fl.* 1730-45)
1730-3 COMPTON PLACE, EASTBOURNE, SUSSEX
Various works other than the decorative plasterwork.
Lit: Compton Place Estate Office (Box P, File 2, 6 July 1730; Lord Wilmington's account-book, 1 August 1733, etc.).
1745 WIMPOLE HALL, CAMBRIDGESHIRE
Received £56 11s 6d. Decorative plasterwork by Giuseppe Artari.
Lit: B.M. Add. MS., 36228, f. 190.

Bettington, Joseph (*fl.* 1775)
Mentioned in Sketchley's 1775 Bristol Directory as a 'tiler and plasterer'.

Bever, — (*fl. c.* 1770)
Plasterwork at the *Repository*, St Martin's Lane, London.

Took as his 'clerk' Charles Clarke (q.v.).
Lit: Charles Clarke, *The Plaisterer's Bill for Works done at the New Building Somerset House . . .*, 1783.

Birch, John (*fl.* 1720)
1720 PURLEY HALL, BERKSHIRE
Received £1 6s 0d for plainwork at the house of Francis Hawes.
Lit: The Particulars and Inventories of the Late Directors of the South Sea Company, 1721, Vol. 2.

Blackley, S. (*fl.* 1708-10)
1708-10 ST PAUL'S CATHEDRAL, LONDON
Worked under Chrysostom Wilkins.
Lit: Wren Soc., XV, pp. 169 and 196.

Blincoe, Christopher (*fl.* 1719-20)
1719-20 CARSHALTON, SURREY
Received £39 for work at the house of Sir John Fellowes.
Lit: The Particulars and Inventories of the Late Directors of the South Sea Company, 1721, Vol. I, p. 10.

Blincoe, John (*fl.* 1719-20)
1719-20 CARSHALTON, SURREY
Assisted Christopher Blincoe (see above).
1720 WIMBLEDON, SURREY
Received £40 for work at the house of Sir Theodore Janssen, Bt.
Lit: The Particulars and Inventories of the Late Directors of the South Sea Company, 1721, Vol. 2.

Blount, — (*fl.* 1688-9)
1688-9 ST SEPULCHRE'S, HOLBORN, LONDON
'To be employed for performing the Plasterer's work for the Church and Vestry.'
Lit: Wren Soc., XIX, p. 51, citing the Vestry Minutes (Guildhall Library) of 2 March 1689.

Boyse, William (*fl.* 1723-4)
1723-4 NEWBY PARK, YORKSHIRE
Architect: Colin Campbell.
Lit: Leeds Reference Library, Vyner letters, 13595. The author is indebted for this reference to Dr L.O.J. Boynton.

Bradbury, Robert (*fl.* 1675-6)
1675-6 SUDBURY HALL, DERBYSHIRE *Plates 27-29*
Worked with James Pettifer (q.v.) and charged at the rate of 6s a yard. Six ceilings: Drawing Room, Parlour, Staircase Hall, Staircase Landing, Queen's Bedroom, Long Gallery. Payments of £64 (Staircase and Parlour) were made in 1675 and £101 in 1676. All payments were made to Bradbury.
Lit: Vernon Archives, cited in *C. Life*, 22-9 June 1935; 10 June 1971; *Connoisseur Yearbook*, 1953.

Brice, Robert (*fl.* 1660)
1660 THE TOWER, LONDON
Worked under John Grove I.
Lit: P.R.O., Works, 5/1, November 1660.

Brockway, R. (*fl.* 1639-47)
c. 1639 EAST KNOYLE CHURCH, WILTSHIRE
He deposed in 1647 that in the chancel of East Knoyle Church he had put up for the Rev Christopher Wren pictures 'in frett work' of Evangelists, the Ascension, the Trinity and Jacob's Ladder.
Lit: A.G. Matthews, *Walker Revised*, 1948, p. 382. (The author is indebted to Mr Howard Colvin for this information.)

Bromfield, Joseph (*fl.* 1771-95)
Of Shrewsbury. Subscribed to George Richardson's *A Book of Ceilings composed in the Style of the Antique Grotesque*, 1776. He also worked as a builder and architect.
1771 WYNNSTAY, DENBIGHSHIRE
Theatre in grounds.
Lit: C. Life, 6 April 1972, p. 851.
1782 HARTLEBURY CASTLE, WORCESTERSHIRE
Library ceiling, and the ceiling and walls of the Saloon.
Lit: E.H. Pearce, *Hartlebury Castle*, 1926, p. 287.
1784 OAKLY PARK, SHROPSHIRE
Lit: Hussey, *E.C.H.: Late Georgian*, p. 153.
1794-5 ST ALKMUND'S CHURCH, SHREWSBURY
Lit: D.H.S. Cranage, *The Churches of Shropshire*, Vol. 2, p. 895, citing *The Shrewsbury Chronicle* of 7 November 1794, and 30 October 1795.
Attributed work:
c. 1790 LION INN, SHREWSBURY
Assembly Room at rear.
Lit: Sacheverell Sitwell, *British Architects and Craftsmen*, 1945, pp. 172-3, Pl. 177.

Brown, William (*fl.* 1755)
c. 1755 POWDERHAM CASTLE, DEVON *Plate 94*
Staircase (assisted John Jenkins). His signature on a mould used at the Castle.

Browne, Thomas (*fl.* 1562-70)
Attributed work:
1562-70 LOSELEY, SURREY *Plate 5*
The Loseley MSS. contain a petition from Browne

(N.R.A. list 9475) which might indicate he was employed at the house.
Lit: C. Life., 9 October 1969, p. 894.

Brownrig, G. (*fl.* 1710)
1710 ST PAUL'S CATHEDRAL, LONDON
Worked under Chrysostom Wilkins.
Lit: Wren Soc., XV, p. 196.

Bunce, John (*fl.* 1717-78)
Official of the Worshipful Company of Plaisterers.
1717 Upper Warden.
1718 Master.
Lit: London, Guildhall Library MS., 6122/3.

Burnett, John (*fl.* 1726)
Assistant to John Hughes (q.v.).
1726-7 COMPTON PLACE, EASTBOURNE, SUSSEX
Architect: Colin Campbell.
19 November 1727:
'John Burnett, Hewes's man.   8.14.8
When he came with Mr. Campbell.   1. 1.0'
Lit: Compton Place Archives, Box P, File 5.

Buchan, Robert (*fl.* 1795)
1795 INVERARAY CASTLE, ARGYLLSHIRE
Received £18 1s 11½d.
Lit: Inveraray MSS., Chamberlain's Accounts, 1795. (The author is indebted to Miss Mary Cosh for this information.)

Burnop, William (*fl.* 1799)
1799 HESLEYSIDE, BELLINGHAM, NORTHUMBERLAND
Plastering, and supplying eight capitals of the Corinthian order.
Lit: History of Northumberland, 1940, XV, p. 253.

Burridge, John (*fl. c.* 1620)
c. 1620 SHERIFF HUTTON HALL, YORKSHIRE *Plate 13*
Bird and Baby Room ceiling; ceiling and fireplace in the Oak Parlour.
Lit: Christopher Gilbert, guidebook to house quoting archives, 1965.
c. 1620 YORK, Sir Arthur Ingram's house.
Lit: Leeds Arts Calendar, No. 71, 1972, p. 62.

Burton, Thomas (*fl.* 1676-89)
A 'Thomas Burton', possibly a son, was one of five contestants for the job of Plaisterer to Christ's Hospital, London, in 1698, ten years after Burton's death. Burton's will is P.C.C., 1689, fol. 1.
1678-9 ST STEPHEN, COLEMAN STREET, LONDON
Worked with Robert Horton (q.v.).
'Plastered Vestry, Walls, Ceiling and Cornice in

the Vestry Room and Stairs and the room over it, excepting the Ceiling. Rendering the Brickwork in the Upper Room for £15. 14 August 1676.' The total bill submitted by Burton and Horton was £136.
Lit: Wren Soc., X, pp. 53, 124; XII, p. 53. XIX, p. 53.

Calderwood, Samuel (*c.* 1687-after 1734)
Born in London and apprenticed to Robert Dyer in 1701.
1726-7 MAVISBANK HOUSE, MIDLOTHIAN
Architect: William Adam.
Lit: John Fleming, *Robert Adam and his Circle . . .* 1962, p. 42; Edinburgh Register House, GD 18/1765-1774 (accounts); 18/4719-4736 (letters).
1727 DRUM HOUSE, MIDLOTHIAN *Plate 142*
Lit: Fleming, *op. cit.*, p. 43, Pl. 14.
1734 WHIM, PEEBLESSHIRE
Lit: National Library of Scotland, Saltoun MSS., Box 423; Royal Commission, *Peeblesshire*, Vol. II, 1967, p. 327. (The author is indebted to Mr John G. Dunbar for this information.) Calderwood's work is to be suspected at many William Adam houses and certainly at New Hailes (Fleming, *op. cit.*, p. 43). Calderwood may also have worked for the Scottish architect James Smith (*c.* 1646-1731).

Campelman, Ralph (*fl.* 1735-6)
1735-6 CASTLE HOWARD, YORKSHIRE
Plain plastering.
Lit: Castle Howard Archives (the author is indebted to Miss Mary Lawson-Tancred for this information).

Carabellas, — (*fl. c.* 1798)
c. 1798 ICKWORTH HOUSE, SUFFOLK
In 1813 the architect Fulcher stated in his *Hints to Noblemen and Gentlemen of Landed Property . . .*, that he had invented a stucco, it being the same as that used by the Signor Carabellas, two Italian Artists, at the Right Honourable the Earl of Bristol's Palace at Ickworth . . . which has stood fifteen years, in ornamental Pannels, at a height of eighty feet from the Ground'.
Lit: Colvin, p. 218.

Carlile, Charles (*fl.* 1713)
Apprenticed to Isaac Mansfield (q.v.) of York.
Lit: London, Guildhall Library, Boyd's Index to Apprenticeship Registers.

Carmichall, James (*fl.* 1745)
An Edinburgh Plasterer who submitted an estimate (with Thomas Clayton and John Bagnall) for work at Minto House, Roxburghshire.

Lit: National Library of Scotland, Minto Papers, Box 2.

Casell, R. (*fl.* 1710)
1710 ST PAUL'S CATHEDRAL, LONDON
Worked under Chrysostom Wilkins.
Lit: Wren Soc., XV, p. 196.

Cheek, Thomas (*fl.* 1760-80)
Official of the Worshipful Company of Plaisterers.
c. 1760-80 Mentioned in the Minutes of the Company. Acted as Master in 1760.
Lit: London, Guildhall Library, MS., 6122/4; 6126.

Chillingworth, William (*fl. c.* 1803)
c. 1803 AYNHOE PARK, NORTHAMPTONSHIRE
Worked under the architect, Sir John Soane.
Lit: C. *Life,* 16 July 1953, p. 205.

Chippine, Henry (*fl.* 1652)
Official of the Worshipful Company of Plaisterers.
1652 Master.
Lit: London, Guildhall Library, MS., 6122/2.

Chislo, — (*fl.* 1730)
1730 SHAW HALL, BERKSHIRE
Received £20 for work for James Brydges, 1st Duke of Chandos, presumably at this house.
Lit: Baker, *Brydges,* p. 370, fn. 2.

Clark, Thomas (*fl.* 1742-82)
Clark was one of the most successful plasterers of the later eighteenth century. Based at Westminster he was Master Plasterer to the Office of Works from 1752 until his death in 1782. From about 1770 he had Charles Clarke (q.v.) as his partner. Despite his eminence he was fined in 1742 by the Worshipful Company of Plaisterers for bad work at St James's Palace. He subscribed in 1767 to the first volume of *James Paine's Plans . . . of Noblemen and Gentlemen's Houses.* His will does not seem to survive in P.C.C.
1745-60 HOLKHAM HALL, NORFOLK *Plate 95*
Various rooms, Clark was working on the Saloon in 1753 and the Hall after 1759.
Lit: Earl of Leicester's archives. (The author is indebted to Dr W.O.Hassall and Mr John Hardy for information about the building sequence at Holkham.)
1750 MILTON HOUSE, NORTHAMPTONSHIRE
Received £542 11s 0d.
Lit: Northants County Record Office, Fitzwilliam Archives, Misc., Vol. 156.

1753 HORSE GUARDS, WHITEHALL, LONDON
Designed by William Kent, executed after his death.
Lit: RIBA, Library, Building Accounts; Jourdain, 1926, p. ix, fn.
1755 NORFOLK HOUSE, LONDON
Received £225 7s 8d.
Lit: Duke of Norfolk's Archives (West Sussex County Record Office, uncatalogued), Victoria and Albert Museum, *Bulletin,* January 1966, pp. 1-11; D.Fitz-Gerald, *The Norfolk House Music Room,* Victoria and Albert Museum publication, 1973, pp. 9-10.
1758 OLD UNIVERSITY LIBRARY, CAMBRIDGE
Received £532 15s 0d.
Lit: University Registry Audit Book, 1759, Vice Chancellor's Vouchers, 16 May 1759.
1760 ASHBURNHAM PLACE, SUSSEX
Lit: C. *Life,* 23 April 1953.
c. 1765 BURLINGTON STREET, LONDON
House for Sir Richard Lyttelton, rebuilt 1761-7 by Matthew Brettingham, senior and junior.
Lit: Herts County Record Office, Ashridge Deeds.
c. 1782 SOMERSET HOUSE, LONDON
Architect: Sir William Chambers.
Received £1,176 8s 6d (see Charles Clarke, below).
Lit: Somerset House Accounts, RIBA, Library; P.R.O., AO3/1244 (information from Mr Howard Colvin).

Clarke, Charles (*fl.* 1770-83)
1783 SOMERSET HOUSE, LONDON
Architect: Sir William Chambers.
Worked with Thomas Clark (see above). Charged £1,352 11s 3d, but his bill was disputed and the architect James Paine suggested a reduction in the cost. In reply Clarke, indignant at the treatment of the matter by Sir William Chambers, published in 1783 *The Plaisterers' Bill for works done at the New Building Somerset House in the Strand By the late Mr Thomas Clark and his surviving partner Charles Clarke, Plaisterer.* In this he indicates that he started his career with Thomas Clark, left him for a time to go to a Mr Bever, and returned in about 1770, at Thomas Clark's suggestion, as his partner.
Clarke finally received £1,170 19s 6¾d.
Lit: Pamphlet cited (copy in RIBA, Library).

Clarke, Robert (*fl.* 1685)
1685 WHITEHALL PALACE, LONDON
Worked under John Grove I.
Lit: P.R.O., Works, 5/39, January 1685.

Clarke, Samuel (*fl.* 1683)
1683 ST PAUL'S CATHEDRAL, LONDON
Made a model.
Lit: Wren Soc., XIII, p. 168.

Clayton, Thomas (and Thomas Clayton junior)
Clayton's birthplace is unrecorded, but it was probably in London. No record of his apprenticeship there has, however, been traced. As far as is known he worked entirely in Scotland from about 1740 for at least twenty years. His son Thomas Varsallis Clayton, born in 1743, seems to have been responsible for work at Inveraray Castle (Plate 152) and the Edinburgh Register House in the 1780s, and possibly at Mellerstain. It has not yet proved possible to establish the exact connections of this Thomas Clayton, but it seems useful to give a conjectural pedigree. This owes much to the researches of Miss C. H. Cruft, who has recorded the evidence in files at The Scottish National Monuments Record, Edinburgh. A full description of Clayton's activities is given in chapter VII.

Thomas Clayton, senior = Elizabeth Wilson
fl. 1710-60; married
c. 1735; lived mostly
at Hamilton)

Thomas Varsallis = ?   Archibald   James (?)
(b at Hamilton,   (b at Hamilton, (b. at Hamilton,
8 March 1743;   25 December   April 1747)
died October   1745)
1793)

Isabella = Reverend John Reston
(married   (ordained 1783; some-
3 Septem- time minister at Alnwick,
ber 1788) Biggar, Kilsyth and
           Bridgeton, Glasgow. See
           William Hunter, *Biggar
           and the House of Fleming*,
           1867)

If Thomas Varsallis Clayton is the same person as the 'Thomas Clayton, plasterer, Edinburgh', father of Isabella Clayton, then account needs to be taken of Thomas's brother, Francis, a merchant in North and South Carolina. Research may eventually prove that, as with the Rose family, there were several relatives, all plasterers, and all bearing the same Christian name.

1740 THE DRUM, EDINBURGH
Architect: William Adam.
Probably the Drawing Room.
Lit: Lennoxlove, Hamilton Archives (Hamilton section Box 127). Letters from William Adam, quoted in chapter VII.

1740 HOLYROODHOUSE, EDINBURGH
Decoration of the Hamilton apartments under the supervision of William Adam.
Lit: Lennoxlove, Hamilton Archives, *op. cit.*

c. 1742-6 HAMILTON PALACE, LANARKSHIRE
Plasterwork in various rooms, and in 1743 at Châtelhêrault, the garden pavilion at Hamilton Palace, *Plates 143, 144.*
Lit: Letter of 7 April 1742, and bill for materials. Lennoxlove, Hamilton Archives, *op. cit.* Hamilton Baptismal Registers, April 1743.

1747-57 BLAIR CASTLE, PERTHSHIRE *Plates 145-147, 149, 151*
Received £1,840 12s 8d.
Lit: Blair Castle Archives, 40 II D(4) 31-39, 40 III, 39-40 (letters).

1753-4 ST ANDREW'S CHURCH, GLASGOW
To be finished by January 1754. Clayton to 'find stucco, lime, sand, hair, carriages and all other materialls necessary' for £487.
Lit: Glasgow, City Minute Book, 9 March 1753; James Thomson, *History of St Andrew's Parish Church, Glasgow*, 1905.

Attributed works:
c. 1750 GLENDOICK, PERTHSHIRE *Plate 148*
Drawing Room ceiling; staircase.
Lit: David Walker 'Glendoick', *C. Life*, 30 March 1967, pp. 706-12.

c. 1752 130 CLYDE STREET, GLASGOW
(Information from Mr David Walker.)

c. 1754 HOPETOUN HOUSE, WEST LOTHIAN *Plate 150*
Architect: William Adam and his sons.
Yellow and Red Drawing Rooms.
Lit: John Fleming, *Robert Adam and his Circle . . .*, 1960, p. 332; *C. Life*, 12 January 1956.
Note should also be taken of the stuccoist John Dawson (q.v.) who was working at Hopetoun House in 1757.
Lit: Hopetoun House, Building accounts, 1757. (The author is indebted to Mr John Dunbar for this information.)

c. 1756 DUMFRIES HOUSE, AYRSHIRE
Architects: John and Robert Adam.
Lit: Sir John Stirling Maxwell, *Shrines and Homes of Scotland*, 1938, pp. 193-4.

c. 1760 YESTER HOUSE, EAST LOTHIAN, *Plate 141*
Architect: Robert Adam.
Saloon. Noted by Dr Richard Pococke in 1760 as

having unfinished ornamentation. The painted panels by William Delacour are dated 1761.

Lit: Pococke, cited by John Swarbrick, *Robert Adam and his Brothers*, 1915, p. 220.

1771-2 36 ST ANDREW SQUARE, EDINBURGH
Architect: Sir William Chambers.
House for Sir Lawrence Dundas.
Worked with Coney (q.v.).

Lit: B.M. Add. MS., 41133, f. 53; George Richardson, *Book of Ceilings . . .*, 1776, p. 4.

Clayton or his descendants probably also worked at Pollok House, Glasgow; Touch, Stirlingshire; and Oxenfoord (Fleming *op. cit.*, p. 333). In 1745-6 he submitted an estimate for work at Minto House (National Library of Scotland, Minto Papers, Box 2). This gives the prices charged for various kinds of work.

Cobbe, John (*fl.* 1601)
1601 ST JOHN'S COLLEGE, CAMBRIDGE
Cobbe was responsible for the 'frettishing of the ceiling of the great chamber and long gallery'.

Lit: Jourdain, 1926, pp. 22-3.

Cole, J. (*fl.* 1708-10)
1708-10 ST PAUL'S CATHEDRAL, LONDON
Worked under Chrysostom Wilkins.

Lit: Wren Soc., xv, pp. 169, 196.

Collins, Thomas (1735-1830)
Apprenticed in 1750 to William Wilton (q.v.). Married 17 November 1761, Henrietta Patterson at St Mary le Bone, Middlesex. Had a bank account (Drummonds) with Sir William Chambers, and also developed various properties while his partner. In 1796 he was appointed an executor and trustee at the death of Sir William Chambers. Portraits of Collins by von Breda, the Swedish artist, and Beechey exist in the Dr J. Gurney Salter Collection and at Marylebone Town Hall. He died on 3 May 1830.

Lit: A detailed account of Collins's long career was prepared, 1965-6, by Colonel J. H. Busby (copy RIBA, Library).

1765 WALCOT, SHROPSHIRE
Worked with William Wilton.

Lit: Bills at house.

1765-6 45 BERKELEY SQUARE, LONDON
Lit: India Office Library, Clive Papers.

1771 MILTON HOUSE, NORTHAMPTONSHIRE
Work under Sir William Chambers for Lord Fitzwilliam.
Received £301 18s 6d.

Lit: B.M. Add. MS., 41133, 9 November 1771.

1773 MELBOURNE HOUSE, PICCADILLY, LONDON
Architect: Sir William Chambers.

Lit: B.M. Add. MS., 41133, 14 August 1773.

1773 STRATTON STREET, LONDON
Received £764 1s 2¾d for work at Lord Fitzwilliam's house.

Lit: Northants County Record Office, Milton Archives, Vouchers, 114, and letter from Collins.

1774 DRAPERS' COMPANY HALL, LONDON
Worked with Joseph Rose. Cost of work £1,384 6s 7d.

Lit: Bill preserved at the Worshipful Company of Drapers.

1777 PEPER HAROW, SURREY
Architect: Sir William Chambers.

Lit: Bill of June, 1777; *C. Life*, 26 December 1925.

1780 SOMERSET HOUSE, LONDON
Architect: Sir William Chambers.
Work divided between Collins and Thomas Clark (q.v.) with Collins doing the modelling 'under the pretence of his being more used to Sir William's manner'. Collins was paid £1,990 2s 0d and, from 1784, in company with John Papworth (q.v.), £7,915 2s 8d.

Lit: Accounts, RIBA, Library; P.R.O. A.O.3/1244.
Other work:
Collins was also listed in the Somerset House accounts for ceilings at the Royal Academy (1780), the Royal Society Meeting Rooms (1783) and for other work jointly with Papworth.

Collins, William (1721-93)
For details of Collins's career as a sculptor see Gunnis, p. 111. A pupil of Sir Henry Cheere, he was much employed in providing Classical statues and bas-reliefs. There is little doubt that many of the features in houses designed by Robert Adam were from his hand, and are documented as such at Kedleston. Collins, who died on 24 May 1793, is buried in the old cemetery at King's Road, Chelsea. Subscriber to James Paine's *Plans . . . of Noblemen and Gentlemen's Houses*, 1767, Vol. 1.

1756 MAGDALENE COLLEGE, CAMBRIDGE
Chapel: Altarpiece in plaster of Paris, now in the College Library. Subject: The Three Marys by the Holy Sepulchre.

Lit: Cambridge Depicta, 1764, p. 77; Gunnis, p. 111; N. B. Pevsner, *Cambridgeshire*, 1954, p. 96, repr. Pl. 40.

1760 HAREWOOD HOUSE, YORKSHIRE
Architect: Robert Adam.
Various medallions including figures of *Mars* and *Neptune* for the Great Hall.

Lit: Hargrave, *History of Knaresborough*, p. 157; Richard Buckle, *Guidebook to Harewood House*, 1959; Mary Mauchline, *Harewood House*, 1974.

1763 KEDLESTON, DERBYSHIRE
Architect: Robert Adam.
Statues in the Great Hall and medallions.
Lit: Curzon Archives, Kedleston; James Lees-Milne, *The Age of Adam*, 1947, p. 122; Geoffrey Beard, *Connoisseur Yearbook*, 1958, p. 26.

1769 BURTON CONSTABLE, YORKSHIRE
Medallions in the Dining Room, one depicting *Pan and the Graces*. The stucco frame is the work of Giuseppe Cortese (q.v.).
Lit: Georgian Soc., East Yorkshire, IV, Pt. 1 (1953-1955), p. 45; *C. Life*, 3 September 1932; 10 September 1959, *repr.* p. 256; Collins's bill of 10 September 1769 (£21 plus half the cost of travelling from London: £3 3s od) is cited by Dr Ivan Hall in *William Constable as Patron*, Hull Art Gallery Exhibition Catalogue, 1970, No. 46. See also T.F. Friedman, *Sculpture by John Cheere* Temple Newsam House, Leeds, Exhibition Catalogue, Summer 1974.

Colombani, Placido (*fl.* 1744-80)
1775 DOWNHILL, CO. ANTRIM, N. IRELAND
Lit: C. Life, 6 January 1950
c. 1780 MOUNT CLARE, SURREY.
Lit: Hussey, *E.C.H.: Mid-Georgian*, p. 240.
c. 1797 ICKWORTH, SUFFOLK
Lit: C. Life, 7 November 1925; Hussey, *op. cit.*, p. 240.

Combes, John (*fl.* 1681-1709)
Official of the Worshipful Company of Plaisterers.
1701 Master (succeeded Henry Doogood).
1709 One of the Company Auditors.
Lit: London, Guildhall, Library, MS., 6122/3 (29 September).
1681-7 ST AUGUSTINE, WATLING STREET, LONDON
Worked with Henry Doogood (q.v.)
He received £98.
Lit: Wren Soc., XII, p. 44.

Combes, Thomas (*fl.* 1695-1719)
Apprentice of John Combes (q.v.). Free of the Worshipful Company of Plaisterers by 25 July 1702. In 1718 he was Upper Warden and in 1719 Master of the Company. In 1709 some £50 was still owed to him for unspecified work for the Duke of Montagu.
Lit: London, Guildhall Library, MS., 6122/3; Boughton House (Northants), Executors' Accounts, of the estate of Ralph, Duke of Montagu.

Coombs, — (*fl.* early eighteenth century)
Paid £13 by James Brydges, 1st Duke of Chandos for unspecified work, presumably at Cannons. Possibly 'Coombs' was John or Thomas Combes (q.v.).
Lit: Baker, *Brydges*, p. 199.

Coney, — (*fl.* 1771-83)
A Stephen Coney worked at Powderham, Devon, *c.* 1765 (Plate 94).
Lit: C. Life, 11 July 1963, p. 83.
1771-2 36 ST ANDREW SQUARE, EDINBURGH
Architect: Sir William Chambers.
House for Sir Lawrence Dundas.
Worked with Thomas Varsallis Clayton (q.v.).
Lit: B.M. Add. MS., 41133, f. 53; George Richardson, *Book of Ceilings*, 1776, p. 4.
1783 SOMERSET HOUSE, LONDON
Architect: Sir William Chambers.
Worked under Charles Clarke (q.v.).
Lit: Charles Clarke, *The Plaisterers' Bill for Works done at . . . Somerset House . . .*, 1783.

Consiglio, Francesco (*fl.* 1734-9)
1734 LYME PARK, CHESHIRE
Architect: Giacomo Leoni.
Staircase Hall.
Lit: C. Life, 26 December 1974.
1739 EUXTON HALL, LANCASHIRE
Lit: C. Life, 6 February 1975.

Cook, John (*fl.* 1748-63)
In 1763 Cook was apprenticed, presumably at the age of fourteen, to George Fewkes (q.v.).
Lit: London, Guildhall Library, MS., 6122/4.

Cooper, Charles (*fl.* 1683)
In 1683 Cooper signed a receipt on behalf of John Grove (q.v.).
Lit: Wren Soc., XIII, p. 176.

Cordey, John (*fl.* 1710-11)
Official of the Worshipful Company of Plaisterers.
1710 Upper Warden.
1711 Master.
Lit: London, Guildhall Library, MS., 6122/3.

Corlett, Richard (*fl.* 1804-13)
Worked on two recorded occasions for Lord Grosvenor:
1804-12 EATON HALL, CHESHIRE
Architect: William Porden.
1809-13 ECCLESTON CHURCH, CHESHIRE
Lit: Grosvenor Archives, Eaton Hall, Cheshire.

(The author is indebted to Mr Howard Colvin for this information.)

Cortese, Giuseppe (*fl. c.* 1725-78)
Presumably of the family of stuccoists long-settled at Mendrisio, near Lugano. The first mention of his name seems to be 'For Mr Cortesy' on a plan in the Colin Campbell collection, RIBA, Library, perhaps by William Wakefield and intended for Gilling Castle, Yorkshire, *c.* 1725. Cortese lived for a time at Whitby, had an assistant named Taddei (possibly the Michel Angelo or Francesco Taddei who worked later at Augustenborg in Denmark), and had an extensive practice in the north working mainly for the architect John Carr. He died at York in 1778, his executors being the Wakefield cabinet-maker Edward Elwick and the York plasterer James Henderson (q.v.).
Lit: York Courant, cited in 'York Georgian Society Report', 1955-6, p. 58.
1739 NEWBURGH PRIORY, YORKSHIRE
Cortese's name first appears in the accounts in July 1739. He did other work in 1743, 1744, 1745, and later in 1764-67.
Lit: Archives at house; Geoffrey Beard, *Georgian Craftsmen and their work*, 1966, Pl. 109; *C. Life*, 7 March 1974, p. 484.
1745-52 STUDLEY ROYAL, RIPON, YORKSHIRE
Destroyed by fire in 1945.
Main rooms of the house for William Aislabie. Received, in all, £409. His measurement of 28 December 1751, and several bills survive. His work in the Temple also survives.
Lit: Studley Royal Archives, Parcel 286; *C. Life*, 25 July, 1 and 8 August 1931; 10 September 1959.
1747-9 BRANDSBY HALL, YORKSHIRE
Worked for Francis Cholmely. House attributed to John Carr.
Received £328.
Lit: Archives at house, cited by John Cornforth in *C. Life*, 2-9 January 1969.
c. 1750 GILLING CASTLE, YORKSHIRE
Plasterwork of the Great Hall, etc. Cortese also worked for the Fairfax family at Newburgh Priory, Coxwold (below) as early as December 1744, when he was paid for drawing-paper, and in 1765.
Lit: Leeds, Yorkshire Archaeological Society, Library, Newburgh Archives; Thorold Rogers, *History of Agricultural Prices*, VII, p. 452—'Dec. 1744, Coxwold. 2 sheets of drawing paper for Mr. Cortese, 1s.'
1752 and 1757 ELEMORE HALL, DURHAM *Plate 90*
Various ceilings; one uses the same Neptune motif as the ceiling at Lytham Hall, Lancs. (Plates 88, 89)

Lit: Durham C.R.O. Baker-Baker papers. (The author is indebted to Mr Neville Whittaker for this information.)
1757 HARDWICK PARK, DURHAM
Architect: James Paine, Garden Temple
Lit: As for Elemore Hall, above. Cortese's 1757 letters to George Baker of Elemore were written while working at Hardwick. This work under Paine's supervision may imply that Cortese also worked at St Helen's Hall, St Helen Auckland, Durham, although Thomas Perritt (q.v.) and Joseph Rose senior are other possible contenders. The work is however not close to the style of either and it is necessary to remember work by the Franchini family of *stuccatori* for the architect Daniel Garrett (cf. *C. Life*, 12 March 1970; 19 September 1974).
1762 GUILDHALL, BEVERLEY
Cortese's work in the Court Room is recorded:
15 November 1762: 'Ordered that the sum of Forty Guineas be laid out in Ornamenting the Town's Hall, lately Rebuilt, by Erecting on The Inside thereof the King's Arms in Plaister or Stukoe for which the Corporation have this day agreed with Mr Courtezie to be by him finished for the above sum'.
24 October 1763: 'Ordered that Mr Cortese's bill of twenty-five pounds and five shillings as a present be paid by the Town's Receiver'.
Lit: Beverley Corporation Minute Books (Yorks. Arch. Soc. Record Series, CXXII, *ed.* K.A. Macmahon, 1958, pp. 42-3 (extracts quoted above); R.H. Whiteing, *Trans., East Yorks., Georgian Soc.*, ii (Pt. 4), 1950, p. 62; *C. Life*, 19 April 1956, p. 808.
1769 BURTON CONSTABLE, YORKSHIRE
The stucco frame to the panel of the Three Graces by William Collins (q.v.) in the Dining Room.
Lit: William Constable as Patron, Hull Art Gallery Exhibition Catalogue, 1970, No. 46.
1772 KILNWICK HALL, YORKSHIRE
Architect: John Carr.
Worked with Addinal, and for Colonel Condon.
Lit: Edward Ingram, *Leaves from a Family Tree*, 1952.
Attributed work:
Arncliffe Hall, Yorkshire, *c.* 1753-4; Escrick, Yorkshire; Bedale Hall, Yorkshire; Rievaulx Temple, Duncombe Park, Yorkshire; Somerset House, George Street, Halifax (Plate 100); Lytham Hall, Lancashire, same motif as Elemore.

Crabtree, Ely (*fl.* 1760-1803)
Of York, where he lived for a time in Lendal. Worked in liaison with John Carr for many years. In 1803 he did the apsidal staircase at Wentworth Woodhouse to Carr's design. He had already worked

there in 1783 with Thomas Henderson (q.v.) at the Mausoleum.

Lit: R.B.Wragg, York Georgian Society, Report, 1955-6, p. 60; *C. Life,* 19 October 1957, p. 719.

The York firm of Crabtree worked at Everingham Roman Catholic Church, Yorkshire.

Lit: Arch. Rev., September 1957, pp. 198-200.

Crisp, William (*fl.* 1719-20)

1719-20 PURLEY HALL, BERKSHIRE

Received £4 9s 0d from Francis Hawes for work at this house.

Lit: Particulars and Inventories of the Late Directors of the South Sea Company, 1721, Vol. 2.

Cromwell, Henry (*fl.* 1698)

Official of the Worshipful Company of Plaisterers. 1698 Master.

Lit: London Guildhall Library, MS., 6122/3.

Crouch, John (*fl.* late seventeenth century-1715)

Official of the Worshipful Company of Plaisterers. 1714 Upper Warden.

1715 Master.

Lit: London Guildhall Library, MS., 6122/3.

1714 ST STEPHEN, WALBROOK, LONDON

Unspecified work.

Lit: Wren Soc., X, pp. 115 and 124.

Cryer, Clement (*fl. c.* 1769-1800)

The Christie's sale catalogue of Joseph Rose junior's effects, 1st day, 10 April 1799, states: 'Clement Cryer, Plasterer Humbly solicits the Favours of the Employers of Mr Joseph Rose of Queen Anne Street East . . . as he has permission of the Executor to make this Application and flatters himself that a servitude of near thirty years as Apprentice and Assistant, under the inspection of his late Ingenious Master . . . He has engaged part of the premises in which the trade was carried on. Orders for present to 18 Edward St, Queen Anne Street East.'

He presumably worked on most Rose junior's commissions and is specifically mentioned at Packington Hall, Warwickshire, 1785-6.

Lit: C. Life, 16 July 1970, p. 229.

Curryer, Thomas (*fl.* 1730-2)

1730-2 ST BARTHOLOMEW'S HOSPITAL, LONDON

Lit: Hospital Archives, Ha 19/5/2-3.

Daves, Charles (*fl.* 1655)

Official of the Worshipful Company of Plaisterers. 1653 Master.

Lit: London Guildhall Library, MS., 6122/2.

Dawson, John (*fl.* 1750-65)

Apprenticed in 1738 to Charles Stanley (q.v.) but most of the recorded mentions of him depict him as a wood-carver. However when John Adam was preparing designs at Yester House, East Lothian in 1751 he told Lord Tweeddale that he was proposing to employ as stuccoist 'the person who did the two glass frames for my Lady Marchioness, who works also in stucco. He is a Scotch lad, but served his time in London.' He has been identified fairly positively as the 'Mr Dawson' who was employed as a carver by the Adam brothers at Lord Tweeddale's Edinburgh home in the early 1750s. He also worked at Inveraray Castle, Argyll, and in 1757 at Hopetoun House. A 'John Dawson, plasterer' was also married in Edinburgh in 1773.

Lit: Information from Mr John Dunbar; Geoffrey Beard, *Georgian Craftsmen and their work,* 1966, p. 175; Mary Cosh, *Inveraray,* 1973; John Dunbar, 'The Building of Yester House' Transactions, *East Lothian Antiquarian Society,* XIII, 1972, p. 41 fn. 72.

Dawson, Robert (*fl.* 1742-51)

1742-51 17 ARLINGTON STREET, LONDON

Architect: William Kent.

Received £779 13s 4½d for work at the house of the Rt Hon Henry Pelham. Also worked on the 'New Building next the Park att Mr Pelham's House in Arlington Street', received £253 16s 7d.

Lit: London, RIBA, Library, MSS., 728.3(42.13)A

It was presumably Robert Dawson who was foreman to Isaac Mansfield (q.v.). He was described as such and made 'Master Plaisterer to his Majesty's Palaces in the room of his said deceas'd Master'.

Lit: London Daily Post and General Advertiser, Monday, 21 January 1739-40, No. 1635.

1743 44 BERKELEY SQUARE, LONDON

Architect: William Kent.

Lit: Sir John Soane's Museum, accounts; Margaret Jourdain, *The work of William Kent,* 1948, p. 55.

Denis, Thomas (*fl.* late eighteenth century)

Son of John Denis of Bristol, tiler.

c. 1780 Made apprentice to Thomas Stocking, senior (q.v.).

Lit: Bristol City Archives, Apprentices' Book, 1777-1786, p. 369.

Denston (Denstone), family of (*fl.* eighteenth century)

Joseph Denston, a plasterer of Derby was buried at All Saints Church there is 1728. His son Abraham was a plasterer and his grandson, also named Abraham, worked extensively at Kedleston for

Robert Adam. This Abraham had a son, James, and at least two brothers, Thomas, a plasterer like himself, and James, a masonry contractor who sometimes styled himself architect. Thomas tendered for the plasterwork at Yoxall Lodge, Derbyshire, but little else. Abraham died at his home in St Mary's Gate, Derby on 24 March 1779. He was buried on 27 March in All Saints Churchyard. W. Millar, *Plastering Plain and Decorative*, 1897, p. 20, states that Denston 'a Derbyshire plasterer' assisted Artari and Bagutti. This must have been in 1725-6 on The Senate House, Cambridge; architect: James Gibbs.

1759-64 KEDLESTON, DERBYSHIRE
Plain plastering, the main decorative work being by Joseph Rose (q.v.).
Received £412 5s 9¼d.
Lit: Kedleston, Curzon Archives, Book 3R, pp. 60-63; Bills, 1759.
1773-4 THE ASSEMBLY ROOMS, DERBY (demolished)
Lit: Kedleston archives, letters from James Adam to Lord Scarsdale; photographs, Derby Borough Library; will of Abraham Denstone, 1779 (filed at Lichfield). The author is indebted to Mr Edward Saunders for information about the Denston family.

Dew, John (*fl.* 1664-80)
1664 SHELDONIAN THEATRE, OXFORD
Lit: V.C.H.: Oxfordshire, III, p. 51.
1680 OLD ASHMOLEAN MUSEUM, OXFORD
Lit: Ibid., p. 48.

Dewick, Petty (*fl.* 1697)
1697 SIR JOHN MOORE'S SCHOOL, APPLEBY, LEICESTERSHIRE
Architects: Sir Christopher Wren; Sir William Wilson.
Received £23 15s 6d.
Lit: Wren Soc., XI, p. 100.

Dibbins, Edward (*fl.* 1775)
Listed in Sketchley's 1775 Bristol Directory as living at 14 Tower Street, Bristol.

Dodgson, John (*fl.* 1762-69)
1762-67 HAREWOOD HOUSE, YORKSHIRE
Bricklaying and plain plastering.
Lit. Mary Mauchline, *Harewood House*, 1974, p. 48.

Doegood, Joseph (?-1692)
1692 His Will is P.C.C., 1692, fol. 165.

Doogood, Henry (*fl.* 1663-1707)
Doogood, with John Grove II, was employed very extensively by Sir Christopher Wren and worked at thirty-two City churches. In 1700 he was made Master of the Worshipful Company of Plaisterers (London Guildhall Library, MS., 6122/3). He died in 1707.

1663 PEMBROKE COLLEGE CHAPEL, CAMBRIDGE
Lit: Willis & Clark, I, p. 147; Wren Soc., VI, pp. 27-9, pl. xi; N.B. Pevsner, *Cambridgeshire*, 1954, p. 27, Pl. 58.
c. 1681 ST MARY ALDERMARY, LONDON *Plate 33*
Architect: Sir Christopher Wren.
Lit: Wren Soc., X, p. 13; A.E. Daniell, *London City Churches*, 1896, p. 233.
1670-94 CITY CHURCHES, LONDON
Architect: Sir Christopher Wren.
The following alphabetical list is based on Wren Soc., Vol. XII. A useful summary with further information is given by Colvin, pp. 709-15.

ST ALBAN, WOOD STREET, 1682-5. With John Grove. Destroyed 1940.
ALL HALLOWS, LOMBARD STREET, 1686-94. Demolished 1939.
ALL HALLOWS THE GREAT, UPPER THAMES STREET, 1677-83. With John Grove and Thos. Sherwood. Demolished 1893-4.
ALL HALLOWS, WATLING STREET, 1677-84. With John Grove. Demolished 1876-7.
ST ANDREW BY THE WARDROBE, 1685-93. Destroyed 1940.
ST ANTHOLIN, WATLING STREET, 1678-82. Demolished 1875.
ST AUGUSTINE, WATLING STREET, 1680-83. With John Combes. Partly destroyed 1941.
ST BARTHOLOMEW EXCHANGE, 1674-9. With John Grove. Demolished 1840-1.
ST BENET, GRACECHURCH STREET, 1681-6. With John Grove. Demolished 1867-8.
ST BENET, PAUL'S WHARF (now the Welsh Church), 1677-83.
CHRIST CHURCH, NEWGATE STREET, 1677-87. Destroyed 1940.
ST CLEMENT, EASTCHEAP, 1683-7. With John Grove.
ST DIONIS BACKCHURCH, FENCHURCH STREET, 1670-1674. With John Grove. Demolished 1878-9.
ST GEORGE, BOTOLPH LANE, 1671-4. With John Grove. Demolished 1903-4.
ST JAMES, GARLICK HILL, 1676-83. With John Grove.
ST MAGNUS, MARTYR, LOWER CHURCH STREET, 1671-1676. With John Grove.
ST MARGARET, LOTHBURY, 1686-90.
ST MARGARET, PATTENS, 1684-7. With John Grove.
ST MARTIN, LUDGATE, 1677-84. With John Grove.
ST MARY ABCHURCH, 1681-6. With John Grove. Damaged 1940.

ST MARY AT HILL, 1670-6. Doogood whitewashed the church for £18, Wren Soc., XIX, p. 32.

ST MARY MAGDALEN, OLD FISH STREET, 1683-5. Demolished 1887.

ST MARY SOMERSET, THAMES STREET, 1686-95.

ST MARY LE BOW, CHEAPSIDE, 1670-3. With John Grove. Damaged 1941.

ST MATTHEW, FRIDAY STREET, 1681-5. With John Grove. Demolished 1881.

ST MICHAEL, CROOKED LANE, 1684-8. With John Grove. Demolished 1831.

ST MICHAEL, PATERNOSTER ROYAL, COLLEGE HILL, 1686-94.

ST MICHAEL, QUEENHITHE, 1676-87. With John Grove. Demolished 1876.

ST MILDRED, BREAD STREET, 1677-83. With John Grove. Destroyed 1941.

ST MILDRED, POULTRY, 1670-6. With John Grove. Demolished 1872.

ST PETER, CORNHILL, 1677-81. With John Grove.

ST STEPHEN, WALBROOK, 1672-9. With John Grove.

ST SWITHIN, CANNON STREET, 1677-85. Destroyed 1941.

1681 WESTMINSTER ABBEY CLOISTERS, LONDON
House of Dr Richard Busby. Received £43 15s od for 'fretwork, plastering, &c.'.
Lit: Wren Soc., X, p. 22.

1682 and 1690 ST CHARLES THE MARTYR, TUNBRIDGE WELLS, KENT
Dated ceilings by Doogood. Received £190.
Lit: Marcus Whiffen, *Stuart and Georgian Churches,* 1947, p. 97.

1686-7 TRINITY COLLEGE, CAMBRIDGE
See entry for John Grove.

1689 BISHOP'S PALACE, LICHFIELD, STAFFORDSHIRE
Architect: Edward Pearce.
Doogood's work no longer survives.
Lit: H. M. Colvin and Arthur Oswald, *C. Life,* 30 December 1954, citing Church Commissioners MS., 123828.

1689 MONTAGU HOUSE, LONDON
Received £826 in 1689-90.
Doogood also worked on the New Chapel in Whitehall, at Boughton House, Northants (1694-6 and 1701), Geddington, Weekley Church, and Ditton Park. The total of his bills submitted to the executors of the Duke of Montagu was £2,027.
Lit: Boughton House, Duke of Montagu's Executors' Accounts, Vol. 2, ff. 609-24. (The author is indebted for information to Mr Patrick King, Mr John Cornforth and Sir David Scott.)

1695 CHRIST'S HOSPITAL, LONDON
Received £33 18s 6d.
Lit: Wren Soc., XI, p. 75. In 1698 Doogood was one of five contestants for the job of Plaisterer to Christ's Hospital (Wren Soc., XI, p. 70). The others were Thomas Burton, John Eales, Jerome Hall and William Smith.
Attributed work:

1688 5 MARKET HILL, CAMBRIDGE
Ceiling dated 1688.
Lit: Sir Alfred Clapham, *Cambridge Antiquarian Society,* 1943-7, XLI, pp. 56-9.

Doogood, Ralph (*fl.* 1708-10)
1708-10 ST PAUL'S CATHEDRAL, LONDON
Worked under Chrysostom Wilkins.
Lit: Wren Soc., XV, pp. 169, 196.

Dugdale, James (*fl.* 1675)
c. 1675 CLIFTON HALL, NOTTINGHAMSHIRE
Lit: C. Life, 25 August 1923.

Duking, Francis (*fl.* 1697)
1697 SIR JOHN MOORE'S SCHOOL, APPLEBY, LEICESTERSHIRE
Architects: Sir Christopher Wren; Sir William Wilson.
Supplied plaster.
Lit: Wren Soc., XI, p. 99.

Dungan, Richard (*fl.* 1605-9)
1605-7 KNOLE, KENT *Plate 9*
Dungan's work at Knole is recorded in the accounts:

'August 5. Paid to Richard Dungan the H. Plaisterer the some of One hundred and fortie poundes in part paiement of a bill of—*cciiii xviii iii* for ffresse and plaistering work paid to him upon yo͏ʳ lo; warrant dated 4 August 1607, being performed by him at yo͏ʳ lo: house at Knoll

September 10. Paid to Mr Richard Dungan plaisterer for half a form of plaister of Paris sent to Knoll and for the charges of water carriage in all

December 8. Paid to Richard Dungan Plaisterer in discharge of ii bills for work done for yo͏ʳ lo: between the monthes of March 1605 and 1 July 1607 the some of ciiii xix vj viz in full discharge of a bill of cxl xiiii vi in full for fretts & other worke done at Knoll and for worke done about m͏ʳ Thoms Sackville stable in all'

Lit: Kent County Record Office, MS. no. U 269 A 1/1, 'A Booke of severall Accompts of Tho: Earle

of Dorsett Ld High Treasurer of England', 1607, No. 22. (The author is indebted to Mr Edward Croft-Murray for this reference.)
1606-9 WHITEHALL PALACE, LONDON
Received £303 6s 0d for plastering the ceiling of the old Banqueting House.
Lit: Archaeological Journal, CX, 1953, p. 151.

Dunn, Richard (*fl.* 1775)
Mentioned as a tiler and plasterer in Sketchley's 1775 Bristol Directory.

Dunsterfield, George (*fl.* 1660-75)
Possibly to be identified with 'George Dunstervile' who worked at Whitehall in November 1660.
Lit: P.R.O., Works, 5/1, September 1660. 'George Dunstervile xxii dayes, 1s . . .'.
In 1674 he was sent north with John Houlbert by the Earl of Lauderdale to work for Sir William Bruce at Balcaskie, at Thirlestane and Holyroodhouse.
1673-4 BALCASKIE HOUSE, FIFE *Plates 125, 126*
Architect: Sir William Bruce. Worked in most of the rooms of the house. He was paid at the daily rate of 3s 6d. Probably assisted by William Lindores (q.v.).
Lit: Scottish Record Office, Kinross House MSS., cited in *Sir William Bruce, 1630-1710*, Scottish Arts Council exhibition catalogue, 1970. No. 77.
1674-6 THIRLESTANE CASTLE, BERWICKSHIRE *Plate 128*
Signed receipts 10 July 1674, and 6 March 1676, for plastering.
Lit: Thirlestane Castle MSS., Scottish Record Office.
1674-9 HOLYROODHOUSE, EDINBURGH *Plates 133, 134*
Assisted John Houlbert (q.v.).
Lit: R.S. Mylne, *The Master Masons to the Crown of Scotland*, 1893, p. 197.

Eales, John (*fl.* 1698)
1698 One of five contestants for the job of Plaisterer to Christ's Hospital, London.
Lit: Wren Soc., XI, p. 70.

Earl, James (*fl.* 1791-2)
A 'James Earle' plasterer, appears in 1789 in the York Freeman's Roll.
1791 Living at Trinity House Lane, Kingston-upon-Hull. There is a counterpart of a lease in the Civic Records of a messuage in High Street, at the south end of the town.
1792 Living at 'Southend', Kingston-upon-Hull.
Lit: Kingston-upon-Hull, Civic Records M843; 1791 Directory.

Eastbourne, Martyn (*fl.* 1650-2)
Official of the Worshipful Company of Plaisterers.
1650-2 Master.
Lit: London Guildhall Library, MS. 6122/2.

Eaton, — (*fl.* 1615)
1615 CHANTMARLE, DORSET
Chapel ceiling. Finished 2 December 1615.
Received £6 16s 0d for his work and £5 0s 0d for materials.
Lit: Dorset County Record Office, Sir John Strode's notebook; Hutchins, *History of Dorset*, 3rd ed., 1873. Vol. IV, p. 5. (The author is indebted to Mr Howard Colvin and Mr Arthur Oswald for this information.)

Edisbury, Kenridge (*fl.* 1685)
1685 ST PAUL'S CATHEDRAL, LONDON
Glacis paving.
Lit: Wren Soc., XIII, p. 201; XVI, pp. 20-1.

Edmonson, John (*fl.* 1694-1704)
Master of Worshipful Company of Plaisterers, 1704.
1694-5 ST SWITHIN, CANNON STREET, LONDON
Received £20.
Lit: Wren Soc., XIX, p. 56, citing the churchwardens' accounts at the Guildhall Library.

Edwin, Francis (*fl.* 1760)
1760 Fined 40s for bad materials used in a 'new house in New London Street, Crutched Fryers, London'.
Lit: Guildhall Library, London, MS., 6126, 7 August 1760.

Elliot, Charles (*fl.* 1689)
1689 HAMPTON COURT, MIDDLESEX
Worked under John Grove (q.v.).
Lit: P.R.O., Works, 5/55, April 1689.

Ellis, James (*fl.* 1703-58)
Of 'Watling Street in Parish of St Antholin, London'. In partnership with James Hands (q.v.). Dismissed from the 'Livery' of the Plaisterers' Company in 1711 for 'disturbing the good order and government of the said Company'. He did, however, get readmitted to office in 1715 and 1719 and at his death in 1758 left a gift of money to the Company to distribute '40 Bushells of Coal at the discretion of the Company's Renter-Warden'. He took an apprentice, John Wright of Southwark, in 1703.
Lit: Guildhall Library, London, MS., 6122/3.
1712-14 ST ALPHEGE, GREENWICH, LONDON
Architect: Nicholas Hawksmoor.

Lit: Colvin, p. 43; *Arch. Rev.*, March 1950.

c. 1715 ST PAUL, DEPTFORD, LONDON
Architect: Thomas Archer.
Worked with his partner James Hands (q.v.). The church was under construction from 1712 to 1730.
Lit: Colvin, p. 43; *Arch. Rev.*, March 1950.

Elsey, Richard (*fl.* 1707-8)
Official of the Worshipful Company of Plaisterers.
1707 Upper Warden.
1708 Master.
Lit: London Guildhall Library, MS., 6122/3.

Elson, James (*fl. c.* 1765)
c. 1765 POWDERHAM, DEVON
Lit: C. Life, 11 July 1963, p. 83.

Engleheart, Francis (1713-73)
Born in Germany in 1713 and is traditionally supposed to have to come to England about 1721-2. He settled in Kew and married Ann, the daughter of the parish clerk of Kew in 1734. Either he or his wife was a nephew or niece of John Dillman, also a German, who worked at Kew Gardens for Frederick, Prince of Wales. He had ten sons, five of whom survived infancy. The two elder, John Dillman Engleheart (1735-1810) and Paul Engleheart (d 1774) were also plasterers. In his will of 1772 he left his 'moulds and scaffolding' to these two eldest sons.

Francis Engleheart is mentioned from time to time in Sir William Chambers's letters and in James Paine's bank account. He worked consistently at Kew in the employment of the Princess Dowager and was said by his grandson, Nathaniel, writing about 1850, to have 'with his own hands fabricated some of the admirably ornamental ceilings at Hampton Court, and some other Royal Palaces . . .'.

John Dillman Engleheart seems to have been the plasterer at 356 and 358 Kew Road, houses he built and owned in 1776. No. 21 Kew Green and 352 Kew Road also have good ceilings.
Lit: Letter Books of Sir William Chambers, B.M. Add. MS., 41133 (13 May 1770; 12 March 1772); Paine's Bank Account (Messrs Coutts & Company); Duchy of Cornwall Office, Vouchers XLI, 1757, p. 63; information kindly communicated by Mrs J. Wilners and Mr John Harris and particularly by his descendant H. F. A. Engleheart of Stoke by Nayland, Suffolk.

Enzer (Enzier), Joseph (*fl. c.* 1725-43)
Known for his work at Arniston and Yester, Enzer is said to have been Dutch. He married 'Helen

Arskin' (Erskine) on 22 July 1738, at Edinburgh, and on 18 May 1739 a daughter Susan was born. Enzer was then described as 'plaisterer at Yester', and 'John Adams son to Wm Adams (sic) architect' was one of the two witnesses. William, John and Robert Adam had known Enzer, and William, in a letter of 5 July 1743, informed the Marquess of Tweeddale, their patron at Yester House, East Lothian, that 'poor Joseph Enzer died last week'. The testaments made at the time of Enzer's death were not proved until 1745.
Lit: Edinburgh, Register of Marriages, Canongate (Scottish Record Society, 1915); Commissariat of Edinburgh, printed lists, 30 April 1745 (copy Scottish Record Office); information from Miss C. H. Cruft (National Monuments Record of Scotland).

c. 1730 ARNISTON HOUSE, MIDLOTHIAN *Plates* 137, 138
Architect: William Adam.
Lit: Jourdain, 1926, p. x; *C. Life*, 9 October 1915; *Burlington Magazine*, March 1969, pp. 132-140.

1736-9 YESTER HOUSE, EAST LOTHIAN *Plate 141*
Architect: William Adam.
Great Staircase and Dining Room. Assisted by Philip Robertson, Francis Nicols, Daniel Ross and Abraham Lester.
Lit: Enzer's account-book, Yester House archives, National Library of Scotland; John Dunbar, *Transactions, East Lothian Antiquarian Society*, XIII, 1972, p. 28; *C. Life*, 16 August 1973, p. 432.

c. 1740 ROYAL INFIRMARY, EDINBURGH
Architect: William Adam.
In the Testament made at the time of Enzer's death in 1743 a sum of £230 was due 'as part of a greater sum for work done by the defunct upon the sd. Infirmary'.

Other work:
There is little doubt that with Samuel Calderwood (q.v.) Enzer shared the task of providing plasterwork at William Adam houses. These are discussed by Fleming, *Robert Adam and his Circle* . . ., 1962, and may have included Dun House, Montrose; Duff House, Banffshire; Lawers, Perthshire, *c.* 1725; and Fullarton House, Troon (Plates 139, 140). The emblematic heads in the cove of the Old Library ceiling at Touch, Stirlingshire (*C. Life*, 2 September 1965, Figs. 2-3) are similar in treatment to work at Dun House. His work at Yester House, East Lothian, being documented, provides a reliable point for future comparisons. The Yester accounts show that Enzer's apprentices, Philip Robertson and Daniel Ross went 'on to Leslie' which may imply work at Leslie Castle, Aberdeenshire, or elsewhere.

Fewkes, George (*fl. c.* 1750-63)
1760 Appointed by Worshipful Company of Plaisterers as one of the assessors for bad work.
1763 Takes an apprentice, John Cook.
Lit: London Guildhall Library, MS., 6122/4; 5126.
c. 1750 MANSION HOUSE, LONDON
Architect: George Dance, senior.
Worked with Humphrey Wilmott.
First floor: received £905.
Second floor and attic: received (with Wilmott) £750.
Egyptian Hall: Wilmot received £600.
Total of £2,255.
Lit: N.B. Pevsner, *Buildings of England, London Pt. 1*, 1957 p. 176, Pl. 68b.

Fifield, David (*fl.* 1690)
1690 Makes oath that Henry Margetts (q.v.) was to do work for Sir George Downing, then deceased, at East Hattley, Cambridgeshire, 1684.
Lit: Castle Howard Archives, Executors' accounts, Sir George Downing.
1712 CLARENDON BUILDING, OXFORD
Lit: V.C.H., *Oxfordshire*, III, pp. 55n, 140.

Fludyer, William (*fl.* 1691)
1691 His will is P.C.C., 1691, fol. 5.

Fly, J. (*fl.* 1710)
1710 ST PAUL'S CATHEDRAL, LONDON
Worked under Chrysostom Wilkins.
Lit: Wren Soc., XV, p. 196.

Foote, Edmond (*fl.* 1660)
1660 THE TOWER, LONDON
Worked under John Grove I.
Lit: P.R.O., Works, 5/1.

Foster, — (*fl.* 1737)
1737 CAVENDISH SQUARE, LONDON
Architect: Edward Shepherd.
End house, north side. Staircase for James Brydges, 1st Duke of Chandos. Received £70.
Lit: Baker, *Brydges*, pp. 199 and 285; Colvin, p. 539.

Franceys, Samuel (*fl.* 1760)
Possibly of Liverpool and connected with the statuaries of this name.
1760 MELBOURNE HALL, DERBYSHIRE
Decorative work.
Lit: Melbourne Archives, cited by Gunnis, p. 156.

Franchini (Francini), Paul and Philip (*fl.* 1730-60)
As with all the Italian-speaking Swiss *stuccatori* working in England, exact identification is not possible. It has been suggested that they came from Modena but in view of the births of those *stuccatori* working in England being recorded in the vicinity of Lake Lugano the village of Mendrisio near there appears most likely. The parish archives there record the baptism on 3 May 1694 of 'Jacobus Philipus', son of Filippo Franchini and Anna Maria. One of the godparents was the well-known *stuccatore* Giovanni Battista Clerici. No trace has been found of Paul Franchini's birth. There may well have been two or even three of the family at work in England and particularly Ireland.
Their work in both these countries is obscure, with little documentation. Two payments in James Gibbs's bank account at Drummonds show he had some association with one of them.
1731 December 20   Paid la Franchino £10.10.—.
1736 August 4   To ditto paid Mr La Franchino £95.
While their work in Ireland is beyond the scope of this book I have had the opportunity of discussing their activities with Dr C.P. Curran (see his *Dublin Decorative Plasterwork of the 17th & 18th Centuries*, London, Tiranti, 1967) and with Mr Edward Murphy, who is (1974-6) writing a thesis on their work. Mr Peter Leach has also noted their connections with the northern architect, Daniel Garrett, and Professor Giuseppe Martinola of Lugano has discussed their origins with me and in his various publications on Mendrisio and the *stuccatori* of the Ticino. It should be noted that he refers to the births of four members of the family: Cosimo, Pietro Antonio, Giovanni Battista and Giuseppe in addition to Paul and Philip (see G. Martinola *Le Maestranze d'Arte del Mendrisiotto in Italia nei Secoli XVI-XVIII*, 1964, p. 62).
1740-1 WALLINGTON, NORTHUMBERLAND *Plate 66*
Dining Room. Received £23 19s 6d.
Saloon. Received £44 19s 4d.
The Dining Room chimneypiece has affinities with that in the Garter Room, Lumley Castle, Durham (below).
Lit: House archives, Wallington; Countess of Northumberland's Diary, Alnwick Castle MSS., cited in *C. Life*, 12 March 1970; 23 April 1970; 19 September 1974.
1748 FENHAM HALL, NORTHUMBERLAND
Received £60.
Lit: C. Life, 19 September 1974, p. 767.
1750 LONDON, House for Duke of Cleveland
Received £31 10s.

Lit: C. Life, above.

1750-4 LONDON, NORTHUMBERLAND HOUSE (demolished 1874)
Received £830 in several payments.
Lit: C. Life, 12 March 1970, p. 635.
Work attributed:
Work in Bath (15 Queen Square) and at St Mary's Chapel, Queen Square (demolished *c.* 1875) has in my opinion been erroneously attributed to the Franchinis by G. N. Wright who did *Guides* to both Bath and Dublin in the 1820s. In the Dublin one he makes attributions to them which are very doubtful. The Franchinis obviously became his favourite citation. John Wood in his *Description of Bath*, 1743 makes no reference to them. A panel at Fairfax House, Castlegate, York is identical with one in the President's House, Phoenix Park, Dublin, taken as a cast from one formerly at Riverstown House where the brothers worked. There is however no need to credit the York panel to them.

The most likely further attribution is work in the Garter Room, Lumley Castle, Durham (Plate 61). It compares well with their work in Ireland (particularly Castletown, Co. Kildare). There is use of an identical medallion at Lumley and the Music or Muses Room, Lancaster (Plates 63, 64). As noted above they had association with the architects James Gibbs and Daniel Garrett. As knowledge of the work of both, and particularly the latter, emerges it seems likely more commissions will be recorded for these talented *stuccatori*.

Frith, Robert (*fl.* 1719-21)
1719-21 LEICESTER HOUSE, LONDON
Lit: Windsor, Royal Household Accounts, Establishment Book, 1719-21, p. 5.

Fry, Alexander (*fl.* 1775)
Mentioned as a 'tiler and plasterer' in Sketchley's 1775 Bristol Directory.

Gard, Philip (*fl.* 1730-2)
1730-2 CHILSTON HOUSE, DEVON
Lit: Exeter City Library, Mallock MSS., 2085-90.

Garrard, George (1760-1826)
Born 31 May 1750. Studied as a boy under Sawrey Gilpin. After attending the Royal Academy Schools, 1778-*c.* 1795 he deserted painting for sculpture. 'He became well known for his reliefs and accurate small-scale models of animals in *plaster* and bronze.'
Lit: Gunnis, pp. 163-4 for a full biography; Dorothy

Stroud, *Henry Holland*, 1950, pp. 37, 49 and frontis.

Gering, Giles (*fl.* 1541-4)
Worked with William Kendall at Nonsuch Palace.
Lit: John Dent, *The Quest for Nonsuch*, 1962, p. 49.

Gill, E. (*fl.* 1697)
1696-7 PETWORTH, SUSSEX
Received £10 in 1696, £89 15s 0d in 1697.
Lit: Petworth Archives, William Miller's Account Rolls, 1696-7
See also Edward Goudge *and* David Lance.

Gill, Robert (*fl.* 1718-29)
Presumably of Liverpool.
1718-29 KNOWSLEY, LANCASHIRE
Lit: Lancs. County Record Office, Derby (Knowsley) Archives. (The author is indebted to Mr S. A. Harris for this information.)

Ginks, C. (*fl.* 1708)
1708 ST PAUL'S CATHEDRAL, LONDON
Worked under Chrysostom Wilkins.
Lit: Wren Soc., XV, p. 169.

Ginks, T. (*fl.* 1710)
1710 ST PAUL'S CATHEDRAL, LONDON
Worked with C. Ginks under Chrysostom Wilkins.
Lit: Wren Soc., XV, p. 169.

Glynn, — (*fl.* 1707)
1707 ST JAMES, GARLICK HILL, LONDON
Small payment made to Glynn.
Lit: Wren Soc., X, p. 124; XIX, p. 22.

Godfrey, T. (*fl.* 1710)
1710 ST PAUL'S CATHEDRAL, LONDON
Worked under Chrysostom Wilkins.
Lit: Wren Soc., XV, p. 196.

Godwin, James (*fl.* 1775)
Mentioned as a 'tiler and plasterer' in Sketchley's 1775 Bristol Directory.

Good, William (*fl.* 1720-1)
1720-1 PURLEY HALL, BERWICKSHIRE
Received £1 4s 10d.
Lit: Typewritten sheet of *Building Accounts* of 1720-1721 (source unspecified) preserved at Purley Hall. (The author is indebted to Dr Peter Willis for this reference.) The source may be *The Particulars and Inventories of the . . . Late Directors of the South Sea Company*, 1721.

Goodenough, Edward (*fl.* 1656)
Official of the Worshipful Company of Plaisterers.
1656 Master.
Lit: London, Guildhall Library, MS., 6122/2.

Goudge (Gouge), Edward (*fl.* late seventeenth-
early eighteenth centuries)
One of the most talented of 'late Renaissance'
plasterers, Goudge seems to have had an early
connection with Hawksmoor. Vertue says that
Goudge did 'some frettwork ceilings' at Justice
Mellust's house in Yorkshire. This was probably
Samuel Mellish of Doncaster, Deputy Lieutenant
for Yorkshire, who died in 1707 (Colvin, p. 272).
Vertue says that Hawksmoor was 'Clerk to Justice
Mellust', and it seems probable that Goudge intro-
duced him to London circles.

It is, however, with the architect Captain William
Winde that Goudge's name is generally connected,
and we owe it to Winde's letters on occasion to
indicate works by Goudge. Writing on 8 February
1690, to Lady Mary Bridgeman, Winde says that
'Mr Goudge will undoughtedly have a goode deall
of worke for hee is now looked on as ye beste
master in England in his profession as his worke
att Combe, Hampstead, & Sʳ John Brownlowe's will
Evidence'. It is this statement which not only
suggests that Goudge was the plasterer at Belton
but that Winde may have been the architect. The
mason contractor was William Stanton. Goudge
also worked for Thomas Coke at his London house
and was also engaged to work at Hampton Court.
It is not known whether he was the 'Mr Edward
Goudge' granted a pass to go to Harwich and
Holland in 1693. (Calendar, State Papers, Domestic.
[1693] p. 37.) See chapter IV for a further discussion
of his career.
1682-3 COMBE ABBEY, WARWICKSHIRE
Architect: William Winde.
Lit: Bodleian Library, MS., Gough Warwickshire,
I. 5 February 1682-3; 1 October 1683.
1684-8 SESSIONS HOUSE, NORTHAMPTON
Received £150 and £5 as a gratuity.
Lit: Arch. Jnl., CX, 1953, p. 181.
c. 1688 HAMPSTEAD MARSHALL, BERKSHIRE *Plate 38*
Architect: William Winde.
House completed for Lord Craven by Winde.
Goudge was also said by Winde (18 August 1688)
to have worked 'in a late building att Drury House'.
This Drury House was also owned, as was Combe
Abbey (below), by Lord Craven.
Lit: Weston Hall, Staffordshire, Earl of Bradford's
Archives, Winde letters, Box 18/4; Geoffrey Beard,
C. Life, 9 May 1952.

1688 BELTON, LINCOLNSHIRE *Plates 40-2*
Architect: William Winde.
Goudge's work at Belton is referred to in Winde's
words: '. . . as his worke at . . . Sr John Brown-
lowe's will Evidence.'
Lit: See notes above, and letters of William Winde
to Lady Bridgeman, Earl of Bradford's Archives;
Geoffrey Beard, *C. Life,* 12 October 1951, p. 1157.
1688-90 CASTLE BROMWICH, WARWICKSHIRE *Plate
36*
Architect: William Winde.
Lit: Geoffrey Beard, *C. Life,* 9 May 1952, citing
Winde and Goudge letters in Earl of Bradford's
Archives.
1690-1 SWALLOWFIELD, BERKSHIRE
Architect: William Talman.
Winde's letter to Lady Bridgeman 8 February 1690,
states: 'Mr Goudge is employed by ye Earle of
Clarendone att his house at Swallowfield where I
believe hee will have above a 12 monthes worke'.
Lit: Earl of Bradford's Archives, as above.
1691-2 PETWORTH, SUSSEX
Chapel ceiling and Hall of State. Received £49. His
assistant David Lance was also there.
Lit: Petworth Archives, Richard Stiles's Account
Rolls, 1691-2 (The author is indebted to Miss
G. M. A. Beck, and Mr G. H. Kenyon for much
assistance at Petworth.)
1696-7 CHATSWORTH, DERBYSHIRE
Gallery ceiling. Received £155 in four payments.
Lit: Chatsworth, Devonshire Archives. James
Whildon's Account 1685-99, pp. 121, 123, 125,
135; Francis Thompson, *History of Chatsworth,*
1949, pp. 56, 166-8.

Grainger, Ambrose (*fl.* 1688)
1688 His will is P.C.C., 1688, f. 15.

Green, Charles (*fl.* 1723)
1723 GUILDHALL, WORCESTER
Architect: Thomas White.
'Agreed with Charles Green and Samuel Robinson
to plaster all Worcester Guildhall including all the
mouldings with the ornaments belonging to the
same and to find all materials for £180 allowing
them the thirty barrells of lime, eighty strikes of
haire, six cords of sand and 3000 of lath nails and
the white hare already used. And they doe hereby
promise to doe all the said work with the best
sand, lime, lath nails, haire and white haire for the
second coate, and to be done in the best workmanship like manner.'
Lit: Worcester City Archives, Guildhall Building
Accounts, 29 April 1723.

Greenhough, William (*fl.* 1768-70)
1768-70 BOYNTON CHURCH, YORKSHIRE
Architect: attributed to John Carr.
Lit: C. Life, 22 July 1954, p. 283; Colvin, p. 125.

Greenough, James (*fl.* 1791)
Living in 1791 at Eastgate, Beverley, Yorks.
Lit: Battle, *Hull and Beverley* Directory, 1791.

Griffin, John (*fl.* 1742)
1742 EXCHANGE, BRISTOL
Architect: John Wood the elder.
Ornamental plasterer.
Lit: Bristol City Archives, Exchange Building Book;
John Wood, *A Description of the Exchange of Bristol,* 1743 (list of subscribers).

Griffin, William (*fl.* 1690)
1690 KENSINGTON PALACE, LONDON
Worked under Henry Margetts (q.v.).
Lit: P.R.O., Works, 19, 48/1, f. 108.

Grilten, R. (*fl.* 1710)
1710 ST PAUL'S CATHEDRAL, LONDON
Worked under Chrysostom Wilkins.
Lit: Wren Soc., XV, p. 196.

Grinsell, John (*fl.* 1712-13)
Official of the Worshipful Company of Plaisterers.
1712 Upper Warden.
1713 Master.
Lit: London, Guildhall Library, MS., 6122/3.

Grivens, R. (*fl.* 1708)
1708 ST PAUL'S CATHEDRAL, LONDON
Worked under Chrysostom Wilkins.
Lit: Wren Soc., XV, pp. 169, 196.

Groome, Richard (*fl.* 1780)
1780- ? SOMERSET HOUSE, LONDON
Architect: Sir William Chambers.
Ornamental plasterer working under Charles Clarke (q.v.).
Lit: Charles Clarke, *The Plaisterers' Bill for Works done . . . Somerset House,* 1783.

Grove, John I (?-1676) John II (?-1708)
During their careers both John Grove and his son became Master Plasterers to the Office of Works, John II succeeding his father in 1676. John I's will, proved P.C.C., 29 March 1676, shows that his mother had remarried, her second husband being a member of the Tucke family of plasterers, possibly Anthony. His daughter Patience was

married to the master carpenter Matthew Bankes. John I left to Bankes his 'modell or Draught of St Pauls Church together with all the drawings & draughts hereunto belonging'. He left to his sons John II and James (another Master carpenter) his library of books and in addition to John II his 'Scaffolding Boards & poles'.

In 1657 Grove, senior, was Renter Warden of the Worshipful Company of Plaisterers. His son John II frequently worked with Henry Doogood, and a list of their joint work on the City churches is given in the entry on Doogood. The work prior to 1676 in the following list is by Grove, senior, possibly assisted by his son. John Grove II's will is P.C.C., Barrett, 39. He left property to his wife and his brother James. The overseers were James and the 'Queen's Carpenter', John Churchill.
1661 QUEEN'S HOUSE, GREENWICH
Ceiling, East Bridge Room, under the superintendence of John Webb.
Lit: Survey of London, XIV, pp. 72, 74, *repr.* pl. 65-7.
1662 Worked in 'the Queen's Privy Chamber, Secretary Bennett's Lodgings &c'.
Received £67 18s 0d.
Lit: P.R.O. E351/3276.
1664-7 CLARENDON HOUSE, PICCADILLY, LONDON (demolished 1683)
Architect: Sir Roger Pratt.
Received £2,082 14s 0d 'whereof the fret ceilings came to about £820 besides "bracketting" which I conceive came almost to as much more'.
Lit: R. T. Gunther, *The Architecture of Sir Roger Pratt,* 1928.
1675 EMMANUEL COLLEGE CHAPEL, CAMBRIDGE
Architect: Sir Christopher Wren.
Lit: Willis & Clark, II, pp. 703-9; Wren Soc., V, pp. 29-31; N. B. Pevsner, *Cambridgeshire,* 1943, p. 27.
c. 1678 ROYAL COLLEGE OF PHYSICIANS, LONDON (demolished 1879)
Architect: Sir Robert Hooke.
Dining Room.
Lit: H. W. Robinson & W. Adams, *The Diary of Robert Hooke,* 1935.
c. 1681 and 1687 WINDSOR CASTLE
Minor works. Paid £18 11s 4d in 1681 and £31 9s 6d in 1687.
Lit: W. St John Hope, *Windsor Castle,* pp. 321 and 329.
1682-3 BADMINTON HOUSE, GLOUCESTERSHIRE
7 March. 'Paid Mr Groves, Plasterer, £115.'
Lit: Child's Bank (Glyn Mills). Account of the 1st Marquess of Worcester.

1685-7 WHITEHALL PALACE, LONDON
Chapel, Privy Gallery, etc.
Lit: P.R.O., Works, 5/54.

1686-7 TRINITY COLLEGE, CAMBRIDGE
Staircase to Library.
Lit: Willis & Clark, II, pp. 533-51, esp. p. 540;
Wren Soc., v, pp. 32-44.
Attributed work:
c. 1660 COLESHILL, BERKSHIRE *Plate 24*
1664 CORNBURY PARK, OXFORDSHIRE
Architect: Hugh May.
Chapel for the Earl of Clarendon.
c. 1690 EASTON NESTON, NORTHAMPTONSHIRE
Grove's relative, the Master Carpenter James
Grove, worked at the house. It may be assumed,
therefore that work was kept in the family.
Lit: B.M. Add. MS., 30092. The author is indebted
to Mr H.M.Colvin for this reference. *C. Life*, 15
October 1970, p. 969.

Gum, Richard (*fl.* 1670-1)
1670-1 WHITEHALL PALACE, LONDON
Worked under John Grove.
Lit: P.R.O., Works, 5/15, June 1670.

Hale, Joseph (*fl.* 1775)
Mentioned as a 'tiler and plasterer' in Sketchley's
1775 Bristol Directory.

Hall, Jerome (*fl.* 1698)
1698 One of five contestants for the job of Plaisterer
to Christ's Hospital, London.
Lit: Wren Soc., XI, p. 70.

Handley, Francis (*fl.* 1708-9)
Official of the Worshipful Company of Plaisterers.
1708 Upper Warden.
1709 Master.
Lit: London, Guildhall Library, MS., 6122/3.

Hands, James (*fl.* 1712-18)
Of 'Wild Street'. Partner to James Ellis (q.v.).
Was described as 'late' in the minutes of the
Worshipful Company of Plaisterers, 25 July 1718.
(London, Guildhall Library, MS., 6122/3.)
1694 QUEEN'S COLLEGE, OXFORD
Library ceiling. Altered in 1756 by Thomas Roberts
(q.v.).
Lit: V.C.H. Oxfordshire, III, p. 138.
1712-14 ST ALPHEGE, GREENWICH, LONDON
Architect: Nicholas Hawksmoor.
Lit: Colvin, p. 43; *Arch. Rev.*, March 1950.
c. 1715 ST PAUL, DEPTFORD, LONDON
Architect: Thomas Archer.

The Church was under reconstruction from 1712
to 1730.
Lit: Colvin, p. 43; *Arch. Rev.*, March 1950.

Hanwell, W. (*fl.* 1780-90)
1786 ARBURY HALL, WARWICKSHIRE *Colour Plate 11*
Saloon, based on Henry VII Chapel, Westminster
Abbey.
Assisted by G.Higham and Robert Hodgson.
Lit: Warwicks. County Record Office, Newdigate
Archives; Hussey, *E.C.H.: Mid-Georgian*, p. 47;
C. Life, 29 October 1953, p. 1415.

Harrod, Robert (*fl.* 1670-80)
1670-80 WIMBLEDON, SURREY
Worked for the Marquis of Carmarthen.
Lit: B.M. Add. MS., 28094, f. 139.

Hawkins, James (*fl.* 1775)
Mentioned as a 'tiler and plasterer' in Sketchley's
1775 Bristol Directory.

Hayes, William (*fl.* 1713-14)
Official of the Worshipful Company of Plaisterers.
1713 Upper Warden.
1714 Master.
Lit: London, Guildhall Library, MS., 6122/3.

Hebberd, — (*fl. c.* 1780)
1780- ? SOMERSET HOUSE, LONDON
Architect: Sir William Chambers.
Worked under Charles Clarke (q.v.).
Lit: Charles Clarke, *The Plaisterers' Bill for Works
done . . . Somerset House*, 1783.

Hefford, Thomas (*fl. c.* 1760)
Presumably the plasterer 'Heafford' who was paid
for work at Northumberland House, London, in
1752-3 (Alnwick Castle MSS., U-1-25). One of
thirteen figures in a picture by Robert Pyle, 1760,
which was destroyed by fire in 1940.
Lit: C. Life, 30 March 1945, *repr.* p. 556; Colvin,
p. 334.

Henderson, James (*fl. c.* 1755-87)
This York plasterer is best known for his association
with the architect John Carr. Mr R.B.Wragg has
suggested that he probably did not come of a York
family because, when taking up the Freedom of
York in 1764, Henderson paid the levy of £25
rather than claiming free entry by patrimony. He
was established near Bootham Bar in York and in
1755 advertised in the *York Courant* for an apprentice.

In 1765 he took William Holliday of Byland as an apprentice 'to be taught, learned and informed in the five orders of the Inrichment of Architecture & whatever mouldings may occur'. A year later he took Thomas Nicholson of Richmond 'to learn the art, trade or mystery of a Plaisterer as to Mouldings in general'. His own son, Thomas, was apprenticed to him in 1764. Henderson was then living at Gillygate, York. Wragg assumes that Henderson was the plasterer at most of Carr's ventures, and the liaison may be compared to that between Robert Adam and Joseph Rose (q.v.). There was a strong connection between Henderson and Cortese, and Henderson was executor at Cortese's death in 1778.

Lit: R.B.Wragg, *York Georgian Society Report*, 1955-6; York Reference Library, *Register of Apprentice Indentures*, D14, 1766, f. 93.

1762 FAIRFAX HOUSE, CASTLEGATE, YORK
Lit: Leeds, Yorkshire Archaeological Society Library, Newburgh Archives.

1765 HAREWOOD HOUSE, YORKSHIRE
Plastering other than State Rooms (Joseph Rose, q.v.) with a partner, Rothwell (q.v.).

1766-7 CANNON HALL, BARNSLEY, YORKSHIRE
John Carr wrote to his client Spencer Stanhope: 'I am at a loss how to advise you as to the Execution of it [the Dining Room ceiling], as I assure you we have no person in the county that can execute it but Henderson and if you do not chuse to have him Imploy'd some person must be sent from London.'
Henderson did the Library ceiling in 1766 and the Drawing Room ceiling in 1767. The latter was destroyed c. 1956.
Lit: R.B.Wragg, *York Georgian Society Report*, 1955-6, p. 59; Geoffrey Beard, Cannon Hall *Guidebook*, 1966.

1767 KIRKLEATHAM HALL, near REDCAR, YORKSHIRE
Lit: R. B. Wragg, *op. cit.*
Saloon, coved ceiling.

1771 TEMPLE NEWSAM HOUSE, LEEDS, YORKSHIRE
Minor alterations.
Lit: R.B.Wragg, *op. cit.*

1771 GILLING CASTLE, YORKSHIRE
Minor alterations to the 'Gothic Temple'.
Lit: R.B.Wragg, *op. cit.*

1773 THIRSK HALL, YORKSHIRE
Architect: John Carr.
Lit: Bills at the County Record Office, Northallerton.

Henderson, Thomas (*fl. c.* 1749-*c.* 1790)
Son of James Henderson above. Apprenticed to his father for seven years on 13 June 1764. He took over the business in Blake Street, York, in about 1785, and 'continued the relationship with Carr at Wentworth Woodhouse, particularly on the Mausoleum, in company with Ely Crabtree' (q.v.). Submitted a specification for a mathematic instrument in January 1787, when he was described as a 'Stucco Plaisterer'.
Lit: R.B.Wragg, *York Georgian Society Report*, 1955-6, p. 60; York Reference Library, *Register of Apprentice Indentures*, D14, 1764, f. 73; Deputy Keeper of the Public Records, 6th Report, Appendix 11, p. 177.

Higginson, — (*fl.* 1771-2)
1771-2 SOHO WAREHOUSE, BIRMINGHAM
Work for Matthew Boulton.
Lit: Birmingham Assay Office, John Scale Box 9. The author is indebted to Mr Nicholas Goodison for this information.

Higham, G. (*fl.* 1779)
ARBURY HALL, WARWICKSHIRE
Dining Room. Worked with Robert Hodgson.
Lit: Hussey, *E.C.H.: Mid-Georgian*, p. 44.

Hill, Richard (*fl.* 1775)
Mentioned as a 'tiler and plasterer' in Sketchley's 1775 Bristol Directory.

Hillam, James and John (*fl. c.* 1780)
1780- ? SOMERSET HOUSE, LONDON
Architect: Sir William Chambers.
Ornamental plasterers working under Charles Clarke (q.v.).
Lit: Charles Clarke, *The Plaisterer's Bill for Works done . . . Somerset House*, 1783.

Hindle, James (*fl.* 1587-8)
1587-8 HARDWICK HALL, DERBYSHIRE
Various works in the Great Chamber and the rooms under the Gallery.
Lit: Basil Stallybrass, 'Bess of Hardwick's Buildings and Building Accounts', *Archaeologia*, LXIV, 1913, pp. 364-97.

Hodgson, Robert (*fl.* 1780-90)
1780-90 ARBURY HALL, WARWICKSHIRE
Worked with G.Higham and W.Hanwell.
Lit: C. Life, 29 October 1953, p. 1415.

Holliday, William (*fl.* 1750-78)
Of Byland, Yorks. Apprenticed for seven years in 1765 to James Henderson of York (q.v.). Admitted as a Freeman of York in 1778.

Lit: York Reference Library, *Register of Apprentice Indentures*, D14, 1766, f. 93.

Hollingshead, William (*fl.* 1683)
His will is P.C.C., 1687, f. 49.

Hollins, William (*fl.* 1660)
Official of the Worshipful Company of Plaisterers. 1660 Master.
Lit: London, Guildhall Library, MS., 6122/2.

Hooper, William (*fl.* 1775)
Mentioned as a 'tiler and plasterer' in Sketchley's 1775 Bristol Directory.

Horton, Robert (*fl.* 1672-9)
1672-9 ST STEPHEN, COLEMAN STREET, LONDON
Architect: Sir Christopher Wren.
Worked with Thomas Burton (q.v.). Their bill totalled £136.
Lit: Wren Soc., X, pp. 53, 124; XII, p. 53; XIX, p. 53.

Houlbert (Hulbert), John (*fl.* 1674-9)
A London plasterer, known for his work for the Earl of Lauderdale and for the Crown in Scotland.
1674-7 THIRLESTANE CASTLE, BERWICKSHIRE *Plate 128*
Signed receipts on 15 November 1674, and 31 August 1677.
Lit: Thirlestane Castle MSS., Scottish Record Office.
1675-8 HOLYROODHOUSE, EDINBURGH *Plates 133, 134, 136*
Worked with George Dunsterfield (q.v.).
Received £1,564 2s 6d (1675); £2,406 9s 9d (1677); £1,996 2s 0d (1679).
Lit: R. S. Mylne, *The Master Masons to the Crown of Scotland*, 1893, p. 197.

Hughes, John (*fl.* 1718-29)
1718 THE ROLLS HOUSE, CHANCERY LANE, LONDON
Architect: Colin Campbell.
Lit: P.R.O., A.O.1/2494/407.
1719-21 BURLINGTON HOUSE, PICCADILLY, LONDON
Architect: Lord Burlington.
Worked with Isaac Mansfield (q.v.).
Received £230 in six instalments between 24 September 1719, and 26 January 1721.
Lit: Chatsworth, Burlington account-book (the author is indebted to Mr John Harris for this reference).
1729 COMPTON PLACE, EASTBOURNE, SUSSEX
Presumably the 'Mr Hewes/Hughes' who died in November 1729, and who employed three 'German'

plasterers to do decorative work. For a full discussion of this matter see chapter V.

Huish, John (*fl.* 1775)
Mentioned as a 'tiler and plasterer' in Sketchley's 1775 Bristol Directory.

Hurst, — (*fl.* early eighteenth century)
Worked at Greenwich Hospital, and corresponded with Sir James Thornhill. Provided Derbyshire lime for plasterwork.
Lit: Wren Soc., vi, pp. 67-8.

Huss, Richard (*fl.* 1710-20)
1710 ST PHILIP'S CHURCH, BIRMINGHAM
Architect: Thomas Archer.
Lit: Marcus Whiffen, *Thomas Archer*, 1950, p. 15.
1720 WENTWORTH CASTLE, YORKSHIRE
Unspecified work.
Lit: B.M. Add. MS., 22241.

Hutchison, James (*fl.* 1782)
1782 INVERARAY CASTLE, ARGYLLSHIRE
Unspecified work. Received £7 10s 0d.
Lit: Inveraray MSS., Chamberlain's Accounts, 1781/2.

Jackson, Amos (*fl.* 1660)
1660 THE TOWER, LONDON
Worked under John Grove I.
Lit: P.R.O., Works, 5/1, November 1660.

Jackson, George (1756-1840)
When George Jackson & Sons, Ltd., the firm of plasterers and modellers, advertised in the RIBA Exhibition Catalogue 'One Hundred Years of British Architecture 1851-1951', they proudly stated that 'When Robert Adam bought the famous recipe for composition from John Liardet, George Jackson made reverse moulds in boxwood and pressed out the ornament in this material. This laid the foundation in 1780 at 49 Rathbone Place, London, of the present firm of G. Jackson & Sons Ltd. Their collection of moulds is now unrivalled and numbers many thousands'.
 George Jackson's son, John, brought the Carton-Pierre process from France, and his son introduced 'fibrous plaster'.

Jemmett, Thomas (*fl.* 1689-1710)
1689 HAMPTON COURT, MIDDLESEX
Worked under John Grove (q.v.).
Lit: P.R.O., Works, 5/55, May 1689.
1710 ST PAUL'S CATHEDRAL, LONDON

Worked under Chrysostom Wilkins.
Lit: Wren Soc., XV, p. 196.

Jenkins, John (*fl.* 1755)
c. 1755 POWDERHAM CASTLE, DEVON *Plate 94*
Staircase (assisted by William Brown).
Lit: C. Life, 11 July 1963, p. 80.

Jenset, T. (*fl.* 1708)
1708 ST PAUL'S CATHEDRAL, LONDON
Worked under Chrysostom Wilkins.
Lit: Wren Soc., XV, p. 169.

Johnstoun (Johnston ?), John (*fl.* 1617)
Travelled from York, his home town, to work in Scotland.
1617 EDINBURGH CASTLE
'Item. to Johne Johnstoun and his man plaisteris in consideratioun of his paynes in comeing fra york to his work, xlib.'
Lit: Accounts, Masters of Works, Edinburgh Castle, Vol. 2, p. 79 (kindly shown to the author in page-proof by Mr John G. Dunbar in 1967). There is reason to think that Johnston worked at Kellie Castle as some of the moulds employed at Edinburgh were brought from Kellie (*ibid.*, 9 June 1617). A John Johnston worked at Inveraray Castle, Argyllshire (kitchen etc.) in 1757 (information from Miss Mary Cosh).

Kendall, Robert (*fl.* 1660)
Possibly a grandson of William (see below).
1660 THE TOWER, LONDON
Worked under John Grove I in November.
Lit: P.R.O., Works, 5/1.

Kendall, William (*fl.* 1541)
1541 NONSUCH PALACE, SURREY *Plates 2, 3*
Lit: John Dent, *The Quest for Nonsuch*, 1962, p. 49.

Kibblewhite, — (*fl.* 1774-7)
1774-7 REDBOURNE HALL, LINCOLNSHIRE
'1774, 14 June. To the Plaisterers 5s.
    20 Oct. Kibblewhite, Plasterer in full of
      £39.3.0.
      £19.3.0.
1775,   Nov. Kibblewhite, Plaisterer. £15.16.0.
1776,   Dec. Kibblewhite, Plaisterer. £44.1.0.
1777, 16 July. Kibblewhite, Stuccoing chancel
      aisles. £14.3.0'
Lit: Lincolnshire County Record Office, Red. 3/1/4/6/2, pp. 34, 36, 44, 51. (The author is indebted to Mrs Joan Varley for this information.)

Kidgell, Henry (*fl.* 1686)
His will is P.C.C., 1686, f. 32.

Kilminster, — (*fl.* 1772)
1772 CHIRK CASTLE, DENBIGHSHIRE
Saloon ceiling.
Lit: C. Life, 12 October 1951.

Kinsman, Joseph (*fl.* 1637-55)
Official of the Worshipful Company of Plaisterers. Fined for bad work 9 October 1655, the year he was appointed Master of the Company.
Lit: London, Guildhall Library, MS., 6122/2; 6126.
1637-8 HAM HOUSE, SURREY
Staircase (£38 17s 0d); North Drawing Room (£35 4s 0d); Hall.
Lit: Ralph Edwards, Victoria & Albert Museum *Guide to Ham House*, 1950, p. 36.

Kipling, John (*fl.* 1761)
1761 Freeman of York.
Lit: Surtees Society, Vol. 102.

Lamb, William (*fl.* 1775)
Mentioned as a 'tiler and plasterer' in Sketchley's 1775 Bristol Directory.

Lance, David (*fl.* 1691-1724)
Lance may have been a son of Nicholas Lance, a plasterer who worked under John Grove at Whitehall in June 1670 (P.R.O., Works, 5/15).
In the late seventeenth century he worked for Edward Goudge. Captain William Winde, writing to his cousin Lady Mary Bridgeman on 27 April 1691, indicated that 'Mr Lance is at the Duke of Summersetts at Pettworth in Sussex'. Lance was presumably present on most of the commissions in which Edward Goudge was involved.
He was appointed Master Plasterer to the Office of Works in succession to John Grove II (q.v.) on 27 May 1708 (P.R.O., Works, 6/14, f171). His appointment was reconfirmed by George I, 27 May 1715 (Works, 6/11, f41).
In his capacity as Master Plasterer Lance submitted many proposals for work. With Robert Wetherill he shared certain work at Hampton Court in 1716 (P.R.O., Works, 4/1, 6 March 1716).
Lit: P.R.O., Works, as cited; *Post Boy*, 27 December 1712 cited by David Green, *Blenheim*, 1951, p. 305; Wren Soc., VI, pp. 58, 62, 63; VII, pp. 201-2, 214, 222-4, 228; *Calendar of Treasury Papers*, XXIX, Pt. 2, p. 102.

Langley, Thomas (*fl.* 1660)
1660 THE TOWER, LONDON
Worked under John Grove.
Lit: P.R.O., Works, 5/1, November 1660.

Lee, Francis (?-1638/9)
Lit: Yorks. Arch. Soc., *Journal*, XXVI, p. 144.

Lee, James (*fl. c.* 1611)
c. 1611 HATFIELD HOUSE, HERTFORDSHIRE
Unspecified plastering.
Lit: Lawrence Stone, *Arch Jnl.*, CXII, 1955, p. 121.

Lindores, William (*fl.* 1667-72)
1667 Apprenticed to Thomas Alborn of Glasgow (q.v.)
1672 WEMYSS CASTLE, FIFE
Worked with John Nicoll (q.v.).
Lit: C. Life, 6 January 1966, p. 23.

Lock, — (*fl. c.* 1770-80)
Worked for Sir William Chambers.
Lit: Laurence Turner, *Decorative Plasterwork in Great Britain*, 1927, p. 249.

Louder, James (*fl.* 1715)
Worked at Whitehall Palace, London.
Lit: P.R.O., Works, 4/1, f60.

Lovell, James (*fl.* 1750-80)
Worked at Norfolk House, London in the 1750s; also at Waldershare, Kent, Wroxton Abbey, Oxford-shire and at Stowe, Buckinghamshire, 1754-77, in plaster and papier-mâché. He was also a sculptor and worked extensively for the Lyttelton circle at Hagley and elsewhere.
Lit: D. Fitz-Gerald, *The Norfolk House Music Room* (Victoria & Albert Museum publication, 1973).

Lundy, William (*fl.* 1731)
Brought up by Lord and Lady Lundy and recom-mended by Lady Lundy and William Adam to Sir John Clerk.
1731 MAVISBANK, MIDLOTHIAN
Dining Room and Summer-house; other work by Samuel Calderwood (q.v.).
Lit: John Fleming, *Robert Adam and his Circle . . .*, 1962, p. 332; Roxburghe Club, 1895, *Memoirs of Sir John Clerk.*

Lycense, Thomas (*fl.* 1659)
Official of the Worshipful Company of Plaisterers.

1659 Master.
Lit: London, Guildhall Library, MS., 6122/2.

Mabbs, Robert (*fl.* 1715-16)
Official of the Worshipful Company of Plaisterers.
1715 Upper Warden.
1716 Master.
Lit: London, Guildhall Library, MS., 6122/3.

Mabyn, Lawrence (*fl.* late seventeenth century)
Apprentice to John Abbott (q.v.).
Lit: C. Life, 2 March 1950, p. 222.

MacClure, John (*fl. c.* 1777)
After 1777 CULZEAN CASTLE, AYRSHIRE
Architect: Robert Adam.

MacGlashan, — (*fl.* 1770-80)
c. 1770-80 worked for Sir William Chambers.
Lit: Charles Clarke, *The Plaisterers' Bill for Work done . . . Somerset House*, 1783.

McQueen, Alexander (*fl.* 1820-40)
1823- ? MILLEARNE, PERTHSHIRE
Lit: C. Life, 2 March 1972, p. 429.

Mahatloe, Richard (*fl.* 1669)
1669 CONVOCATION HOUSE YARD
Work in one room.
Lit: Wren Soc., XIII, p. 58.

Malings, Thomas (*fl.* 1634)
1634 UNIVERSITY COLLEGE
West range.
Lit: V.C.H., Oxfordshire, III, p. 75, n. 31.

Mansfield, Isaac (*fl.* before 1697-1739)
Isaac Mansfield may have been born at Derby. His father Samuel (q.v.) was a plasterer and was living at Derby at the time of his death. We first hear of Isaac when on 4 October 1704, 'Isaac Mansfield of London' was admitted a Freeman of York on payment of £25. He seems to have alternated between York and London, being described as 'of York' in 1713 when he took an apprentice Charles Carlile, and of 'St. James, Westminster' in 1724, when he took Samuel Smith. Mr Derek Sherborn points out that Mansfield had a house in Henrietta Street, a few doors away from Gibbs.

Mansfield was Sheriff of York in 1728-9. He subscribed to the 3rd volume of *Vitruvius Britan-nicus*, 1725, and together with Isaac Mansfield, junior, to Gibbs's *Book of Architecture*, 1728. He did unspecified work (£68) for James Brydges, 1st

Duke of Chandos. At the end of his life he became bankrupt (see chapter V).

Lit: Surtees Society, Vol. 102, p. 186, York Reference Library, Sessions Book, 1728-44; Baker, *Brydges*, p. 199. His death is recorded in *The Daily Post* 4 January 1739-40, No. 6341 and *The London Daily Post and General Advertiser*, 5 January 1739-1740, No. 1621—'Yesterday Morning died at his Lodgings at Charing Cross, Isaac Mansfield, Joint-Plaisterer with Geo. Worrall to his Majesties Palaces, and likewise Plaisterer to his Royal Highness the Prince of Wales'.

1710 CASTLE HOWARD, YORKSHIRE

Architect: Sir John Vanbrugh.

Assisted Bagutti and Plura and did the following: '1710 June. Pd. Is. Mansfield for wh^a he did & pd upon Acct £2 13s od.'

He worked in the Library (£3 1s 11d); My Lady's Closett (£1 5s 3d); My Lady's Dressing Room (£1 4s 5d); in the Bedchamber (£3 1s 10d and £2 16s 6d); Withdrawing roome (two payments of £1 11s 6d); lath work (£9 10s od); in all he received £105 2s 6d.

Lit: Castle Howard Archives, Building Books.

LONDON CHURCHES

1723-9 CHRISTCHURCH, SPITALFIELDS

For Nicholas Hawksmoor.

1712-24 ST GEORGE, HANOVER SQUARE

For John James.

1714-28 ST JOHN, WESTMINSTER

For Thomas Archer.

1727-33 ST LUKE, OLD STREET

For Wren and Hawksmoor.

1720-30 ST GEORGE, BLOOMSBURY

For Hawksmoor.

Lit: H. M. Colvin, *Arch .Rev.*, March 1950.

1720-1 BURLINGTON HOUSE

Architect: Lord Burlington.

Worked with John Hughes (q.v.).

Received £220 in seven instalments between 4 July 1720, and 23 January 1721.

Lit: Chatsworth, Burlington account-book. (The author is indebted to Mr John Harris for this information.)

c. 1720-1 CHICHELEY HALL, BUCKINGHAMSHIRE

Hall and Staircase. Received £108

Lit: C. Life, 20 February 1975, p. 437

1721 LANGLEYS, ESSEX

Received £85 on 14 June 1721 for plastering the Hall.

Lit: Essex County Record Office, Samuel Tufnell's accounts. *Connoisseur*, December 1957, p. 211.

1725 BLENHEIM PALACE, OXFORDSHIRE *Plate 49*

Architect: Nicholas Hawksmoor.

Long Library; Chapel.

'I presume Mr Mansfield has near upon finnished great part of the Gallery by this time and I hope to your satisfaction . . . I suppose the Chapel will not be taken in hand till the Gallery is quite done . . .'.

Lit: Blenheim MS., E47, Hawksmoor to Sarah, Duchess of Marlborough, 23 December 1725, cited by David Green, *Blenheim Palace*, 1951, pp. 310-1.

1725 SENATE HOUSE, CAMBRIDGE

Architect: James Gibbs.

Plain plasterwork (decorative work by Bagutti and Artari). Received £315.

Lit: Little, *Gibbs*, 1955, pp. 60-1.

1730 KEW PALACE, SURREY

Architect: William Kent.

Work for Frederick, Prince of Wales. Received £625 8s 9½d (see chapter V).

Lit: Duchy of Cornwall Office, Vouchers, IV, p. 229.

Attributed work:

c. 1730 RAYNHAM HALL, NORFOLK *Plate 71*

Lit: M. Jourdain, *The Work of William Kent*, 1948, p. 65.

Mansfield, Samuel (*fl.* 1672-97)

Father of Isaac Mansfield (q.v.). Samuel lived at Derby. His will (at Lichfield) is dated 20 April 1697, and was proved on 8 October 1697. In it he leaves to his wife Hannah his cottages 'near to St Mary's Gate in Derby for life and then the same to my six daughters, Elizabeth, Anne, Mary, Sarah, Hannah and Rebecca' and to his son 'Isaac Mansfield, one shilling'. He left the residue to his wife, who was appointed as executrix.

1672-5 SUDBURY HALL, DERBYSHIRE

Mansfield agreed with George Vernon in 1672 to 'fretworke my roome wth archa: frieze & cornishe', and did the plain plastering throughout the house.

In 1675 he agreed to 'frettworke the great staire heade chamber, £20'. This refers to the Queen's Room.

Lit: C. Life, 22-9 June 1935.

Mantle, William (*fl.* 1726-9)

1726 Subscriber to Leoni's *Alberti*. Noted in Vol. 3. He is presumably the 'Mantle' who worked further for Leoni at Moulsham.

Mantle, — (*fl.* 1729)

1729 MOULSHAM HALL, ESSEX

Architect: Giacomo Leoni.

Interior work on south range. Received £74 15s od. Decorative plasterwork by Artari and Bagutti.

Lit: Essex County Record Office, D/DM A5. (The

author is indebted to Mr Arthur C. Edwards for this information.)

Margetts, Henry (*fl.* 1684-1704)
Worked on Office of Works Contracts under John Grove II.
1684 EAST HATTLEY, CAMBRIDGESHIRE
Work with two labourers at Sir George Downing's. Received £12 14s 7d, paid in 1690 by Sir George's executor, the 2nd Earl of Carlisle.
Lit: Castle Howard Archives, Executor's Accounts, Sir George Downing.
1690 KENSINGTON PALACE, LONDON
Outworks, stables, etc., received about £40. Also worked in Palace.
Lit: P.R.O., Works, 19/48/1. f.108.
?-1695 CHATSWORTH, DERBYSHIRE
As Master Plasterer.
Lit: Francis Thompson, *Chatsworth*, 1949, pp. 36, 59, 67.
c. 1700 KIVETON, YORKSHIRE.
Architect: William Talman.
Received £372 16s 0d.
The house was under construction 1694-1704.
Lit: Yorkshire Archaeological Society, Leeds, Duke of Leeds Archives, Box 33.

Marker, John (*fl.* 1595)
1595 HARDWICK HALL, DERBYSHIRE
Employed for work at both the old and the new Hall, generally on plain work, but he did the ceiling and cornice in the Long Gallery of the new Hall, May 1595. His daily rate was 6d.
Lit: Basil Stallybrass, 'Bess of Hardwick's Buildings and Building Accounts', *Archaeologia*, LXIV, 1913, pp. 381, 397.

Martin (Martyn), Edward (*fl.* 1648-99)
Son of John Martin (see below). Made free of the Worshipful Company of Plaisterers, 21 September 1655. Fined for arrears, 25 January 1657. Beadle of the Company, 1660, and Master, 1699. Fined for bad work in 1671 and 1685. His name appears in the 1668-1724 Contracts Book of the Office of Works (P.R.O., Works, 5/145, f.13) for work at 'The great foott Guard in Scotland Yard'. Both Edward and John worked at The Tower, November, 1660.
Lit: Guildhall Library, London, MS., 6122/2; MS., 6126 (12 May 1671; 27 April 1685). P.R.O., Works 5/1.
1671 31 ST JAMES'S SQUARE, LONDON
This work has since been destroyed. Martin was fined for bad work at the house.
Lit: As above, entry of 2 May 1671; *Survey of London*, XXIX, 1960, p. 198, for description of house

in 1671 when owned by Thomas Belasyse (Lord Fauconberg).
1671-81 ST NICHOLAS COLE ABBEY, QUEENHITHE, LONDON
Worked with John Sherwood (q.v.).
Lit: Wren Soc., X, p. 73.
1678 ARBURY, WARWICKSHIRE *Plate 30*
Chapel ceiling. The agreement also mentions doing 'my wife's closet fretworke, hee is to have £48 besides comeing and going and goate's haire'.
Lit: Warwicks. County Record Office, Newdigate Archives; Wren Soc., X, p. 22; L. Turner, *Decorative Plasterwork in Great Britain*, 1927, p. 142.
1682 BURGHLEY HOUSE, NORTHAMPTONSHIRE *Plate 32*
Received £150, but this probably represents only a portion of his full bill.
Lit: Exeter Bank Account, Child's (Glyn Mills). Entries dated 1 July 1682, 14 February 1682/3.
1682 NORTHUMBERLAND HOUSE, LONDON
Received £21 10s 0d for 'whiteing'.
Lit: Alnwick Castle MSS., U-1-17, 18 December, 1682.

Martin, John (*fl.* 1660-82)
1660 WHITEHALL and THE TOWER, LONDON
Worked under John Grove I.
Lit: P.R.O., Works, 5/1, September, November 1660.
1676-82 WINDSOR CASTLE
Lit: W. H. St John Hope, *Windsor Castle*, Vol. I, 1911, pp. 314, 321, 485.

Masters, John (*fl.* late seventeenth century)
1680 ST CLEMENT DANES, OLD CHURCH, LONDON
Lit: Wren Soc., X, p. 109.

Mathews, John (*fl.* 1689-1710)
1689 HAMPTON COURT, MIDDLESEX
One of the plasterers working under John Grove II (q.v.).
Lit: P.R.O., Works, 5/55, April 1689.
1710 ST PAUL'S CATHEDRAL, LONDON
Worked under Chrysostom Wilkins.
Lit: Wren Soc., XV, p. 196.

Meade, Thomas (*fl.* late seventeenth century)
Mentioned in Robert Hooke's *Diary*, 1935 ed., p. 60.
1678 ST LAWRENCE JEWRY, LONDON
Architect: Sir Christopher Wren.
Meade agreed to do the ceiling for the Vestry Room to Wren's design. Received £26, on 1 October 1678.
Lit: Wren Soc., XIX, pp. 24-6.

1685 ST MARY ABCHURCH, LONDON
Lit: Wren Soc., X, p. 124.

Medcalfe, — (*fl.* 1613)
1613 WADHAM COLLEGE, OXFORD
For work in the Hall, Medcalfe received £216 15s 0d.
Lit: V.C.H., *Oxfordshire,* III, p. 284.

Mines, John (*fl.* 1726-30)
1726 WESTMINSTER SCHOOL, LONDON
New Dormitory. Charged £220 13s 0d. Received
£186 in November 1726.
Lit: Westminster Abbey Archives, MS. 35394;
Wren Soc., XI, p. 45.
1730 WOLTERTON, NORFOLK
Worked for Sir Robert Walpole.
Lit: C. Life, 25 July 1957, p. 168.

Moor (Moore), Robert (*fl.* 1754-70)
c. 1745 RADWAY, WARWICKSHIRE
Architect: Sanderson Miller.
In Sanderson Miller's account-books (Warwickshire County Record Office) there are occasional
payments to 'Mr Moor', which may indicate the
employment of Robert Moor at the ruinated castle
Miller built at Radway. It is just possible that Moor
came from Banbury, as Miller refers on occasion
to 'the Banbury plasterer and his man'.
1750-2 ALSCOT, WARWICKSHIRE
Staircase (1750-2); Great Hall ceiling (*c.* 1763).
'I have not seen Mr. Moore for some time but his
man has finished the first coat on the Great Hall
ceiling'.
Lit: C. Life, 22 May 1958, p. 1126, citing a letter
at Alscot from the steward Mr Allen to his master
James West, M.P.
1755 ARBURY, WARWICKSHIRE
Library.
Lit: Warwicks. County Record Office, Newdigate
Archives cited in Hussey, *E.C.H.: Mid-Georgian,*
p. 43.
c. 1760 STONELEIGH, WARWICKSHIRE
Received £75.
Lit: Shakespeare's Birthplace Trust, Stratford-
upon-Avon, Leigh Archives.

Moore, Edward (*fl.* 1660)
1660 THE TOWER, LONDON
Worked under John Grove.
Lit: P.R.O., Works, 5/1, November 1660.

More, T. (*fl.* 1708)
1708 ST PAUL'S CATHEDRAL, LONDON
Worked under Chrysostom Wilkins.
Lit: Wren Soc., XV, p. 169.

Morison, Alexander (*fl.* 1757-62)
1757-8 PIRN HOUSE, PEEBLESSHIRE
Received £25 12s 8d.
Lit: Hist. Monumts. Comm. *Peeblesshire,* II, 1967,
pp. 303-5.
Morison was also working at Pirn in 1761-2. (The
author is indebted to Mr John G. Dunbar for information on the Morison family.)

Morison, John (*fl.* 1761)
1761 RUCHLAW, LANARKSHIRE
Lit: H.M. Register House, Edinburgh, Misc.
Papers, Room 12, Bundle 201.
Either Alexander or John worked *c.* 1761 at Paxton
House, Berwickshire (Plate 154).
Lit: C. Life, 17 August 1967, p. 367.

Morison, Thomas (*fl.* 1734-48)
Probably the father of Alexander and John Morison.
He died in Edinburgh on 4 February 1748.
Lit: Register of Testaments, III, 1701-1800 (Scottish
Record Society, 1899).
1734 DONIBRISTLE HOUSE, FIFE
Architect: Alexander Macgill.
Lit: Darnaway Castle, Murray MSS., Vols 4-6.

Morris, Daniel (d 1697/8)
Plaisterer to Christ's Hospital, Newgate Street.
Succeeded by James Pettifer after his death on 10
December 1697/8.
Lit: Wren Soc., XI, p. 70.
1675 ST EDMUND THE KING, LOMBARD STREET,
LONDON
Worked with John Sherwood. Received £85.
Lit: Wren Soc., XII, p. 44.
ST MICHAEL, WOOD STREET, LONDON
Worked with John Sherwood. Received £81.
Lit: Wren Soc., XII, p. 44.

Moss, T. (*fl.* 1710)
1710 ST PAUL'S CATHEDRAL, LONDON
Worked under Chrysostom Wilkins.
Lit: Wren Soc., XV, p. 196.

Mott, Richard (*fl.* 1752-99)
Came from Martin, Lincolnshire. Apprenticed in
1752 to Joseph Rose, senior. He worked for the
Rose firm and is mentioned in Rose's will in 1780.
In 1799 he bought items at Joseph Rose junior's sale
(Christie's, 10, 12 April 1799). He must have worked
at most of Rose's commissions and certainly at
Kedleston in 1775, where he did the Hall frieze.
Lit: Rose sketchbook; Guildhall Library, London,
Boyd's Index to Apprenticeship Registers.

Nadue, — (*fl.* late seventeenth century)
1698 HAMPTON COURT, MIDDLESEX
Lit: Wren Soc., IV, p. 25, where Nadue is erroneously listed under the name 'Medoe'. He appears
as 'Nadue' in the account-books of the Office of
Works.

Needham, Joshua (*fl.* 1725-5)
c. 1720 CHICHELEY HALL, BUCKINGHAMSHIRE
Lit: C. *Life,* 27 February 1975, p. 499
1724 SUTTON SCARSDALE, DERBYSHIRE
Architect: Francis Smith.
Name appears on lead rising-plate (now lost) for-
merly at house.
Lit: C. *Life,* 15 February 1919.
1724 DITCHLEY, OXFORDSHIRE
Architect: Francis Smith; built by James Gibbs.
Plain work: see p. 201 for work by Artari and others.
Lit: Oxford County Record Office, Dillon papers.
1725 GUILDHALL, WORCESTER
Architect: Thomas White.
Received £77 2s od; 'Needham the Plasterer at
several times as pr. Receipts.'
Lit: Worcester Guildhall, Building Accounts, 20
April 1725.

Nelthorpe, Richard (*fl.* 1724-31)
1724 NEWBY PARK, YORKSHIRE
Architect: Colin Campbell.
Lit: Leeds Reference Library, Vyner letters, 13595.
1731 YORK MANSION HOUSE, SALOON

Nicholson, Thomas (*fl.* 1754-74)
Of Richmond, Yorkshire. Apprenticed on 24 February 1766, at York to James Henderson (q.v.)
for seven years 'to learn the art, trade or Mystery
of a Plaisterer as to Mouldings in general'. In 1774
became a Freeman of York.
Lit: York Reference Library, Apprenticeship Register 1756-86; Surtees Society, Vol. 102.

Nicoll, John (*fl.* 1672-3)
Said to be Danish.
1672-3 WEMYSS CASTLE, FIFE
Lit: David, Earl of Wemyss Minute Book, Wemyss
Castle (the author is indebted to Mr John Hunt for
this information).

Nicols, Francis (*fl.* 1736-9)
1736-9 YESTER HOUSE, EAST LOTHIAN
Worked at the house for 611 days, 1736-9, as
apprentice to Joseph Enzer (q.v.).
Lit: Enzer's account-book, Yester House archives,
Scottish Record Office.

Noble, Henry (*fl.* 1668-9)
Worked under John Grove II at Whitehall.
Lit: P.R.O., Works, 5/12.

Nollekens, Joseph (1737-1823)
Well-known sculptor (cf. *Gunnis*). George Richardson in his *Book of Ceilings,* 1776, p. 3, records that
the bas-reliefs of the two ceilings in the Drapers'
Company, London, are said to have been 'ex-
cellently modelled by the ingenious Joseph Nollekens'. Work for this Company was also done by
Joseph Rose, junior, and Thomas Collins (q.v.).

Oliver, Thomas (?-1776)
Of Warrington. His will, of 1776, is filed at Chester.
1762-7 TABLEY HOUSE, CHESHIRE
Dining Room and other rooms.
Lit: Hussey, *E.C.H.: Mid-Georgian,* p. 58.
1763 CHIRK CASTLE, DENBIGHSHIRE
New Drawing Room.
Lit: C. *Life,* 12 October 1951.

Oram, William (*fl.* 1713)
1713 Worked at Royal Palaces.
Lit: Wren Soc., XVIII, p. 164.

Page, Joseph (?-1775)
Born in Lincolnshire, Page completed his apprenticeship at Hull in 1740 and worked extensively
with the bricklayer-plasterers, Aaron Pycock,
Thomas Scott and Charles Mountain the elder (*c.*
1743-1805). In 1743 he was designing the Maister's
house in Hull. His proposals were scrutinized by
Lord Burlington. The gallery was plastered in
1744. In about 1750 Henry Maister the younger
wrote to John Grimston: 'Page the Man who was
employed to do the stucco in my house will be
with you today'—presumably a reference to work
for Grimston at Kilnwick. He may have done the
work *c.* 1760 at No. 6 High Street, Hull.
Lit: Edward Ingram, *Leaves from a Family Tree,*
1952, p. 177; Georgian Soc., E. Yorks, *Trans.,*
1952-3, Vol. 3, Pt 3, pp. 56-7; *V.C.H.,* East Riding,
1969, pp. 445-6; information from Dr Ivan Hall.

Papworth, John (1750-99)
Of Italian origin. Apprenticed to Joseph Rose & Co
and became a leading stuccoist in the second half
of the eighteenth century. Employed many times
by Sir William Chambers. He married Catherine
Searle, daughter of the potter, Robert Searle and
had at least two sons, Thomas (below) and John
Buonarotti Papworth (1775-1847), an architect and
friend of James and Matthew Cotes Wyatt. He

worked at Greenwich Hospital Chapel, the Royal Academy of Arts and Somerset House. Here he collaborated (1784) with Thomas Collins (q.v.) whose business he may have carried on. They received jointly £7,915 2s 8d. At Inveraray Castle, Argyllshire, he worked under the architect Robert Mylne (1781-2). His account reads: 'Plaster work in casts, models and moulds for ornamented ceilings and walls of hall and the dining-room by Mr Papworth £150 0s 6d.'

Papworth was rated for a house in Wells Street, Marylebone, 1778-91. At his death his business was carried on by his eldest son Thomas.
Lit: R.S.Mylne, *The Master Masons to the Crown of Scotland*, 1893, p. 277; Wyatt Papworth, *John B. Papworth*, 1879, pp. 4-5; RIBA, Library, Somerset House Accounts; *C. Life*, 25 June 1953, p. 2061; Jourdain, 1926, p. xii; information from Colonel J.H.Busby and Miss Mary Cosh.

Papworth, Thomas (1773-1814)
Son of John Papworth (see above). Owner of the last stucco and plastering business (Jackson's apart) carried on in London on a large scale. Plasterer to the Office of Works. Subscribed to George Richardson's *Vitruvius Britannicus*, 1802.
Lit: Wyatt Papworth, *John B.Papworth*, 1893, p. 3; J.M.Cook and M.H.Port, *History of the King's Works*, Vol. VI, 1782-1851, 1974.

Parker, William (*fl.* 1677-96)
Mentioned in the records of the Worshipful Company of Plaisterers (London, Guildhall Library).
1691-5 DENHAM PLACE, BUCKINGHAMSHIRE *Plates 43-46*
Chapel (1692); Tapestry Room (1693) etc. Received £274 11s 0d.
Lit: Archives at house (the author is indebted to Mr John Harris for this information).
A William Parker worked in 1764-7 at Shardeloes, Buckinghamshire and in the 1770s at West Wycombe Park, Buckingham.
Lit: Tyrwhitt-Drake MSS., Bucks County Record Office, Hussey, *E.C.H.: Early Georgian*, p. 239.

Parkin, Robert (*fl.* 1791)
In 1791 Parkin was living at Kelgate, Beverley, Yorks.
Lit: Battle, Hull and Beverley Directory, 1791.

Patroli (*fl.* late eighteenth century)
'An Italian artist of great ingenuity' long employed at Claydon, Buckinghamshire, late eighteenth century. He would work here to the supervision of the Rose firm and is perhaps to be identified with the 'Signor Pedrola' who worked with Joseph Rose, senior, at Ormsby Hall, Lincolnshire, c. 1755.
Lit: Lipscombe, Buckinghamshire, I, p. 186; N. Pevsner and John Harris, *Buildings of England: Lincolnshire*, 1964, p. 370.

Pearce (Pierce), Edward (*c.* 1635-95)
Talented carver in wood and stone. It is suggested in Wren Soc., X, p. 93, that 'he may also have been a modeller in plaster, if the profuse ornamentation of St Clement Danes is due to his large share in that work'. Pearce's father, also named Edward (*fl.* 1630-58), issued a *Book of Freeze work* in 1640 (reissued in a second edition) which may have been used by plasterers.
Lit: Wren Soc., as cited; Croft-Murray, 1962, p. 206, *Guildhall Miscellany*, I, 1952, pp. 10-18 (article on Pearce by June Seymour).

Pearce, William (*fl.* 1762-72)
In Sir John Soane's Museum is a quarto notebook with the name 'R.Pearce' on the first page. It contains accounts for plasterwork by William Pearce, many of the projects being for the architect Henry Holland.
1762-76 BOWOOD, WILTSHIRE
Architect: Robert Adam.
Pearce worked with Joseph Rose and William Snow (q.v.).
Lit: Bowood, Lansdowne Archives. (The author is indebted to Mr J.R.Hickish, the Bowood agent, for this information.)
1772 CLAREMONT, SURREY
Lit: Hussey, *E.C.H.: Mid-Georgian*, p. 135.
Attributed work:
BERRINGTON HALL, HEREFORDSHIRE
May have worked here under Henry Holland.

Peart, Charles (1759-98)
1790 STOWE, BUCKINGHAMSHIRE
Queen's Temple.
Three panels, signed and dated 1790.
Lit: Gunnis; *C. Life*, 9 January 1969, p. 79.

Perritt, Thomas (1710-59)
When Perritt's father, Jonathan, a well-known York bricklayer, died in 1741, he left three sons, William, John and Thomas, the subject of this note. Trained by his father, Perritt dominated plastering in Yorkshire until his death in 1759. He was made a Freeman of York (1737-8) and took his first apprentice, Joseph Rose, senior, in 1738. He married twice—firstly Ann Etty (presumably a daughter of William

Etty, the York joiner) at the Minster on 8 December 1739, and secondly Grace Perritt of York at Hampsthwaite, on 8 July 1749. In 1742 he took another apprentice, William Whatson.

Perritt lived in York in the Mint Yard and at his death was stated to be of 'Bederns in the City of York'. He died intestate and the letters of administration were granted to the guardians of Anne and Dorothy Perritt, minors. Anne had been baptized at St Michael-le-Belfrey, York, on 3 March 1741-1742. Perritt was made Chamberlain of York in 1753.

Lit: Skaife MSS., York Reference Library; Yorks. Parish Register Society Vol. II, p. 196; Surtees Society, Vol. 102, p. 246; Borthwick Institute, York, Wills and Administrations, 13 December 1759.

1738-53 RABY CASTLE, DURHAM
Architect: James Paine.
Various work, some in company with Joseph Rose, senior (q.v.).
Lit: C. Life, 1 January 1970, pp. 20-1.

1741-7 TEMPLE NEWSAM HOUSE, LEEDS *Plates 76, 77*
Long Gallery (£190 10s 9d), Library (£130), and other principal rooms. Received a total sum of £419 16s 1d.
Lit: Leeds Reference Library, Temple Newsam Archives, EA 12/10. Jacob Simon in *Leeds Arts Calendar,* No. 74, 1974, identifies the thirteen medallions as George I, George II, his Queen, children and children-in-law.

1744 ASSEMBLY ROOMS, YORK
'June 16, 1744. 'Ordered that Mr Thos Perritt do clean the weekly Assembly Room, the Cube Room and the Circular Room, and Colour the Stucco with a good Stone Colour sized, and white wash the Ceilings before the next Assizes . . .'
October 17, 1744. 'To Mr Thos Perritt. £8.5.0.'
Lit: York Reference Library, York Assembly Room Minute Book, entries as above, and similar ones for 5 June 1751, 12 July 1753.

1745 MANSION HOUSE, DONCASTER
Architect: James Paine.
Lit: J. Paine, *Plans, Elevations, Sections and other Ornaments of the Mansion House at Doncaster,* 1751.

1749 KILNWICK HALL, YORKSHIRE
Received £53 18s 11¾d.
Lit: Edward Ingram, *Leaves from a Family Tree,* 1952.
Attributed work:
c. 1740 NOSTELL PRIORY, YORKSHIRE *Plates 78-80*
Architect: James Paine.
Dining Room; Music Room; North and South

Staircase; medallions similar to those at Temple Newsam (see above).
Lit: C. Life, 23 May 1952, pp. 1573-4.

Perritt, William (*fl.* 1724-*c.* 1770)
Presumably William was a son of Jonathan Perritt of York, and elder brother of Thomas Perritt (see above).

1724-8 BALDERSBY, NEWBY PARK, YORKSHIRE
Lit: Leeds Reference Library, Newby Archives; L. O. J. Boynton, 'Newby Park, the first Palladian Villa in England' in *The Country Seat: Studies presented to Sir John Summerson,* 1970, pp. 97-105, where Perritt is referred to in the archives quoted as 'Jon Perrott and young Perrott'.

1728 STUDLEY ROYAL, YORKSHIRE
'Oct ye 15, 1728. A Mesurement of ye Plastering Woork don for John Aislabie by Wm Perritt.'
Received £22 5s 8d. John Aislabie of Studley Royal was related to Sir William Robinson, who employed Perritt at Baldersby.
Lit: Studley Royal Archives, Parcel 286.

1741-2 RANELAGH AMPHITHEATRE, CHELSEA, LONDON
Lit: P.R.O., C/105/37/32.

1750 FARNBOROUGH, WARWICKSHIRE
Received £434 4s 4d. Work measured by James Morris.
Lit: C. Life, 18 February 1954; Bill at house.

1755 BLAIR CASTLE, PERTHSHIRE
Estimate for work done in various rooms—'to be done like that at the Duke of Argyle's at Whitton', presumably work by Perritt.
Lit: Blair Castle MSS., Box 40 (iv), 91.

1761-3 GROSVENOR SQUARE, LONDON
Received £98 0s 8¼d.
Lit: Compton Place, Eastbourne, Northampton Archives, Box Q.

1761-68 GLYNDE CHURCH, SUSSEX
Architect: Sir Thomas Robinson.
Coved ceiling. Joseph Rose, senior (?), was paid 4 guineas 'for fruitless designs'.
Lit: Sussex Arch. Soc., *Collections,* Vol. 20; *C. Life,* 28 April 1955.

Perwick, Edmund (*fl.* 1661-2)
1661-2 Master, Worshipful Company of Plaisterers.
Lit: Guildhall Library, London, MS., 6122/2.

Petiver, James (*fl.* 1658-89)
Son of William Petiver, a Northamptonshire yeoman. Apprenticed to Arthur Toogood (q.v.) on 23 April 1658, for seven years. His will is filed in P.C.C. (1689, folio 85).
Lit: Guildhall Library, London, MS., 6122/2.

Pettifer, James (*fl.* 1685-98)
Fined in 1685 for bad work at two houses in Red Lion Fields, London. He succeeded Daniel Morris as Plasterer to Christ's Hospital, Newgate Street, London, in 1698.
Lit: Guildhall Library, London, MS., 6216, 27 April, 1685; Wren Soc. XI, p. 70.
1675-6 SUDBURY, DERBYSHIRE *Plates 27-9*
Worked with Robert Bradbury (q.v.).
Lit: C. Life, 22-9 June 1935.
1702 ST BRIDE'S, FLEET STREET, LONDON
Received £2 18s 6d.
Lit: Wren Soc., XIX, p. 14.
1702 ST JAMES, PICCADILLY, LONDON
Lit: Wren Soc., X, p. 124.

Piggott, — (*fl.* 1665)
1665 COBHAM HALL, KENT
Architect: Peter Mills.
Several ceilings.
Lit: P.R.O., C 108/53, cited by H.M.Colvin in 'Peter Mills and Cobham Hall, Kent' in *The Country Seat: Studies presented to Sir John Summerson*, 1970, p. 45.

Plura (*fl.* 1711-12)
Possibly connected with J.Plura, who died in 1756 (Gunnis). See also John Fleming in *The Connoisseur*, November 1956, writing of the Plura family of Turin and Bath.
1710-12 CASTLE HOWARD, YORKSHIRE *Plate 71*
Assisted Giovanni Bagutti (q.v.) with the stucco fireplace and scagliola niche in the Great Hall.

'1710 June.	Given Mr Plewra	34. 8. 0.
March 1711	Given Mr Plewra when went to London	10.15. 0.
	Given Mr Plura	34.11. 6.
Aug. 1712.	Pd Mr Plura & Bargote in full of all work done to this day	156. 0. 0.'

With Bagutti's work the full bill came to £321 17s 0d
Lit: Castle Howard Archives, Building Books.

Pope, William (*fl.* 1719-20)
1719-20 Upper Warden and Master, Worshipful Company of Plaisterers.
Lit: Guildhall Library, London, MS., 6122/3.

Porter, Thomas (*fl.* 1683-1703)
A London plasterer.
1683 ST PAUL'S CATHEDRAL, LONDON
Paid for a model.
Lit: Wren Soc., XIII, p. 168.

1694 DYRHAM, GLOUCESTERSHIRE
Architects: William Talman and Samuel (?) Hauduroy.
Great Hall, Staircase, etc.
Lit: Dyrham Archives, B13/2; B/15/5; *C. Life*, 15 February 1962, p. 338.

Powell, Robert (*fl.* 1680-1706)
Master of the Worshipful Company of Plaisterers, 1706.
1680-8 ST CLEMENT DANES, LONDON
Received £450.
Lit: Wren Soc., X, p. 111; Guildhall Library, London, MS., 6122/3.

Powell, Thomas (*fl.* 1668-9)
Worked under John Grove II at Whitehall.
Lit: P.R.O., Works, 5/12.

Pritchard, William (*fl. c.* 1780)
c. 1780 NORTHUMBERLAND HOUSE, LONDON
Architect: Robert Adam.
Worked with Joseph Rose, junior. Received £62 14s 7¾d.
Lit: Alnwick Castle Archives, U.III.7.

Puttenham, Richard (*fl.* 1749)
1749 BURLINGTON GARDENS, LONDON
'Plaisterers work done for Mr. Robinson att his House in Burlington Gardens. By order of Mr Bradshaw' [William Bradshaw]. Received £4 5s 9d on 26 September 1749.
Lit: Leeds Reference Library, Newby Hall Archives 2277/20/4.

Randal, J. (*fl.* 1710)
ST PAUL'S CATHEDRAL, LONDON
Worked under Chrysostom Wilkins.
Lit: Wren Soc., XV, p. 196.

Rhodes, William (*fl.* 1771-4)
Subscribed to George Richardson's *Book of Ceilings*, 1776.
1771-2 DRAYTON HOUSE, NORTHAMPTONSHIRE *Plate 114*
Dining Room. Charged £304 7s 6d.
Drawing Room £125 13s 10d.
Lit: N. V. Stopford Sackville, *Drayton*, 1939, pp. 33-5; G. W. Whiteman, *Some Famous English Country Homes*, 1951, p. 100.

Richardson, George (*c.* 1736-*c.* 1813)
Accompanied James Adam on the Grand Tour and

was employed as a draughtsman and designer by the Adam brothers. Lived in Great Titchfield Street, London. Important mainly for his published works (Colvin gives a list in his biography of Richardson), which included *A Book of Ornamental Ceilings, in the style of the Antique Grotesque*, 1776, 1781, 1793 and *Iconology, or a collection of Emblematical Figures*, 2 vols., 1779-80. These circulated widely among plasterers (both, for example, were in the possession of Joseph Rose, junior).

Lit: John Fleming, *Robert Adam and his Circle . . .*, 1962, pp. 368-9.

1759 KEDLESTON, DERBYSHIRE

Architect: Robert Adam.

Marble Hall, Ceiling. Bills from George Richardson and Catherine Richardson appear as early as 1759 in the bills preserved at the house. The Hall ceiling appears in Richardson's *Book of Ceilings*, which is dedicated to Lord Scarsdale. The other decorative plasterwork at Kedleston is by Joseph Rose, but he only charged £29 0s 6d for work in the Hall, which strengthens the theory that the ceiling is by Richardson.

Lit: Kedleston Archives. Bills and account-book, 3R.

Ridley, William (*fl.* 1661)

Of Elvett, near Durham.

1661 DURHAM CASTLE

20 November 1661. Agreement with Bishop John Cosins 'to lath, plaister and seale all and every the roomes and chambers in the Castle of Durham, and the several walles thereof. Sealing of the said severall upper rooms, eleaven shillings the roode, the walls playstring after the rate of seaven shillings the roode.'

Lit: Surtees Society, 1872, Vol. 55, p. 356.

Roane, Thomas (d 1690)

Of Southwark.

His will is P.C.C., 1690, fol. 61.

Roberts, James (*fl.* 1745-79)

Roberts came of an Oxford family and was nephew of Thomas Roberts (q.v.). Advertised in *Jackson's Oxford Journal*, 14 January 1776, 'James Roberts, stucco-plasterer, instructed by the late Thos Roberts over 30 years in Oxford has dissolved partnership with his cousin, William Roberts. Each continues on his own account.' Roberts centred his business 'near Carfax Church', and in the *Journal* for 27 April 1776, he denied responsibility for confusion among patrons between the two businesses.

Roberts, Nicholas (*fl.* 1711-12)

No known connection with the Roberts family of Oxford.

Upper Warden and Master, Worshipful Company of Plaisterers, 1711-12.

Lit: Guildhall Library, London, MS., 6122/3.

Roberts, Thomas (1711-71)

Of Oxford.

Roberts was the uncle of James Roberts (q.v.) and had an extensive practice in the Oxford area. He may well have been in active collaboration with the Danish stuccoist Charles Stanley (q.v.). A fire broke out in his workshop in 1761 (*Jackson's Oxford Journal*, 16 February 1761). For a time his son William and his nephew James assisted him. They then set up on their own at Thomas's death but finally, in 1775, dissolved the partnership. Thomas's death on 21 February 1771, is recorded in *Jackson's Oxford Journal*, 22 February 1771— 'Thomas Roberts, fretwork plasterer died. Some striking work of his in a room at Lord Shrewsburys, Heythrop. Succeeded in business by only son William.'

1738 MAGDALEN COLLEGE, OXFORD

Decorated colonnade of New Buildings.

Lit: W.G. Hiscock, *A Christ Church Miscellany*, 1946, pp. 68-71.

1742 ST JOHN'S COLLEGE, OXFORD

Ceiling of the Senior Common Room.

Lit: Historical Monuments Commission, *Survey of City of Oxford*, 1939, p. 106.

1744 RADCLIFFE CAMERA, OXFORD

Architect: James Gibbs.

Assisted Charles Stanley (q.v.) to do eight ceilings. Witnessed the receipt by Stanley of £232 18s 10d on 18 February 1744/5.

Lit: Oxford Historical Society, Vol. XIII, 1953-4 (1958).

1749, 1760 DITCHLEY, OXFORDSHIRE

Dining Room 'at 17d per yard for plain floating and 2/6d per yard for modillion cornice fully enriched.' Received £33 12s 3d. Roberts also worked at Ditchley in 1760 in the Library, temple in park, etc. Received £24 18s 6d.

Lit: Oxford County Record Office, Dillon MSS., 1/p/3 ab, am.

1750 ALL SOULS, OXFORD

Codrington Library.

Lit: Hiscock, *A Christ Church Miscellany*, 1946.

1752-62 CHRIST CHURCH LIBRARY, OXFORD

In 1752 the work in the Library was entrusted to Roberts and he worked on the ceiling of the Upper Library for fifteen months. He received £663. His name appears in the Building Account in 1759 when he was paid £260 for carving. From 1759 to 1762 he was constantly employed, receiving £537 'for stucco work and carving'.

Lit: Hiscock, *A Christ Church Miscellany*, 1946.

1753 BODLEIAN LIBRARY, OXFORD
Ceiling in the Tower Room. This ceiling is now transferred to the Upper Archive Room.
Lit: Bodleian Library Record, October 1956.

1756 QUEEN'S COLLEGE, OXFORD
Library ceiling. He added 'new ornaments in the Oval Space in the Middle and the Compartments at the Ends'.
Lit: J.R.Magrath, *Queen's College.*

1760 DITCHLEY, OXFORDSHIRE (see entry for 1749)

1764 HARTWELL, BUCKINGHAMSHIRE
Lit: Hussey, *E.C.H.: Early Georgian*, p. 201.

1764 ROUSHAM, OXFORDSHIRE
Great Parlour (£170) and other work. Received in all £266 1s 6d.
Lit: C. *Life*, 24 May 1946, p. 949; Hussey, *E.C.H.: Early Georgian*, p. 160.

HEYTHROP HALL, OXFORDSHIRE
Interior, destroyed by fire, 1831.
Credited with work here on the authority of Mrs Lybbe Powys, writing in 1778. 'In the arches over the doorways', she adds, are 'Fables of Aesop, finely executed in stucco, with wreathes of vine leaves.'
Lit: Passages from the Diary of Mrs Lybbe Powys, 1899, p. 200; *Jackson's Oxford Journal*, cited at head of these notes.
Attributed work:

c. 1745 KIRTLINGTON, OXFORDSHIRE *Plates 72, 73*
May have worked here with Charles Stanley. The Aesop's *Fables* medallions are a prominent feature.

c. 1750 GREY'S COURT, HENLEY, OXFORDSHIRE
Lit: C. *Life*, 30 June 1944. This is not a convincing attribution. The work is mechanical and does not compare in quality with that in Christ Church Library. It does compare with work at Watlington Park nearby by — Swan (q.v.). (The author is indebted to Mr J.A.Kenworthy-Browne for help in this matter.)

c. 1753-8 HONINGTON HALL, WARWICKSHIRE
Hiscock, *loc. cit.*, notes that the entrance hall contains a symbolic design of sunlight which appears to be a replica of the design used by Roberts underneath the gallery of the Upper Library at Christ Church, Oxford. Furthermore, his radiating centre oranment of Queen's College Library ceiling is a variation of the same idea.

Roberts and Charles Stanley (q.v.) collaborated at the Radcliffe Camera and possibly at Kirtlington,

and the work at Honington (Plate 69) has long been credited, somewhat casually in view of the lack of documentation, to Charles Stanley.

1754 NUTHALL TEMPLE, NOTTINGHAMSHIRE
Rococo plasterwork with Aesop's *Fables* motifs. Destroyed in 1929.
Lit: C. *Life*, 18 April, 5 May 1923.

Roberts, William (*fl.* 1760-84)
Son of Thomas Roberts (see above). A series of advertisements in *Jackson's Oxford Journal* is all that is known of him. He presumably helped his father from his teens, and at Thomas's death in 1771 it was announced he had succeeded to the business. On 8 April 1772, he announced in the *Journal* that he continued to do carving and gilding. By 1775 he had dissolved partnership with his cousin James (q.v.), and on 27 April 1776, he inserted an advertisement advising customers to be sure of his address (nr. Worcester College) to avoid confusion with James. By 23 October 1779, he was advertising as a 'stucco plasterer and slater of High Street' and denying a malicious rumour of his quitting the business. He did, however, leave Oxford soon after. His goods were sold on 7 December 1779, and he took over the licence of the Red Lion, Hounslow. On 22 May 1784, the faithful *Journal* inserted his advertisement announcing his return to Oxford.

Robertson, Philip (*fl.* 1736-61)
1736-9 YESTER HOUSE, EAST LOTHIAN *Plate 141*
Worked at the house for 544 days, 1736-9, as apprentice to Joseph Enzer (q.v.).
Lit: Enzer's account-book, Yester House archives.

1759-61 INVERARAY CASTLE, ARGYLLSHIRE
Lit: National Library of Scotland, Saltoun Papers, 1759-60, Box 420. (The author is indebted to Miss Mary Cosh for this information.)

Robinson, John (*fl.* 1724)
Of Malton, Yorkshire.
1724 CASTLE HOWARD, YORKSHIRE
Plain plastering.
Lit: Castle Howard Archives, Building Books.

Robinson, Peter (*fl.* 1768)
1768 THORNDON HALL, ESSEX
Architect: James Paine.
Received £931 3s 0d by 1768.
Lit: Essex County Record Office, Petre MSS. (D/DPA58). (The author is indebted to Miss Nancy Briggs for this reference.)

Robinson, Thomas (*fl.* 1689)
1689 HAMPTON COURT, MIDDLESEX
One of the plasterers working under the supervision of John Grove II.
Lit: P.R.O., Works, 5/55, April, 1689.

Rose, Jacob (alive in 1738)
Of Norton, near Sheffield. Stated by Lord Mansfield to have been a plasterer. Father of Joseph Rose, senior. Living at Norton, near Sheffield, in 1738 when his son was put apprentice to Thomas Perritt.
Lit: Liardet v. Johnson, 1778, law-suit text, cited by Geoffrey Beard, *Georgian Craftsmen and their Work*, 1966, p. 73.

Rose, Jonathan (*c.* 1772-after 1780)
Father of Joseph Rose, junior, and brother of Joseph Rose, senior. Worked with his brother at Wentworth Woodhouse, 1751-63.

Rose, Jonathan (alive in 1799)
Brother of Joseph Rose, junior. Worked with his father, brother and uncle in the family firm.

Rose, Joseph (*c.* 1723-80)
Son of Jacob Rose. Born probably in Yorkshire; living at Norton, near Sheffield, in 1738. Apprenticed on 16 October 1738, for seven years to Thomas Perritt of York (1710-59), with whom he worked on several commissions. Perritt died intestate, and Rose does not seem to have inherited his business. At Doncaster in 1752-3, where he took two apprentices, Richard Mott and John Wright. At this time he collaborated with his brother Jonathan and after about 1760, with his nephews Joseph and Jonathan. Together they monopolized all important commissions, particularly those from Robert Adam (these for convenience are listed under Joseph Rose, junior). Rose was buried at Carshalton, Surrey, on 11 September 1780. He had presumably been living in retirement with his son, William Rose, who was Rector of Carshalton for fifty-two years. His will is P.C.C. 449 Collins, and from a codicil (not executed) we surmise that he was in a position to leave £6,000 to each of his nephews. He left his business to Joseph Rose, junior. There is no positive evidence that Rose visited Italy, but in the sale of his son William's collection of pictures at Christie's on 30 May 1829, there was a view by Richard Wilson of the *Ruins of the Temple of Venus*, 'Painted for William Rose's father by Wilson', and it is stated that Joseph Rose was there at the occasion of its painting (W. G. Constable, *Richard Wilson*, 1953, pp. 196-7.)

In 1768 the architect Sir Thomas Robinson (*c.* 1700-77), of Rokeby, Yorkshire, described Rose as 'the first man in the Kingdom as a plasterer'. Robinson was presumably referring to Rose, senior, as the latter's nephew would have been only twenty-two at this time, and Robinson, as a Yorkshireman, presumably knew the firm of Perritt and Rose very well.
1741-7 TEMPLE NEWSAM HOUSE, LEEDS *Plates 76, 77*
Worked with his master, Thomas Perritt.
Receipted bill on 27 June 1745.
Lit: Leeds Reference Library, Temple Newsam Archives, EA 12/10.
1745 MANSION HOUSE, DONCASTER
Architect: James Paine.
Lit: J. Paine, *Plans, Elevations, Sections and other Ornaments of the Mansion House at Doncaster,* 1751.
1752 CUSWORTH HALL, YORKSHIRE
Architect: James Paine.
Received £226 8s 2d.
Lit: Leeds Reference Library, Battie-Wrightson MSS., A/30; Geoffrey Beard, *Georgian Craftsmen and their Work,* 1966.
1751-63 WENTWORTH WOODHOUSE, YORKSHIRE *Plate 97*
The following entries are from the Wentworth Woodhouse Account Books and Estate Accounts at Sheffield Reference Library. (The author is indebted for this information to Mr R. B. Wragg.)
Account Books:

1751	Mr. Jos Rose plaistering & whitewashing	
Dec. 22. 1753.	Mr. Joseph Rose upon Accot Plaistering	60. 0. 0.
Mar 12. 1754.	Mr. Joseph Rose Great Hall	30. 0. 0.
Jan. 1755.	Mr. Joseph Rose upon Acct. Ceiling of Grand Hall	
July 17 1758.	By Mr. Rose in full for Stucco work done in the Great Hall	£76.11. 3½.
	and another payment of	12.12. 0.
Jan. 3 1761.	To Rose the Plaisterer a Bill.	
Estate Accounts:		
1760 Aug. 14.		50. 2.11½.
	By Mr Jo Rose on Accot for Stucco Work etc.	10. 0. 0.

1762 Jan. 24.	By Mr Jo Rose in full for Plaisterers work done in the Dining Room at Wentworth & in the Drawing, Supping & Writing Rooms	24. 1. 7.
1763 March 28.	By Mr Rose on Accot for Stucco work in the Cliffords Lodgings & Mr. Green.	£31.10. 0.
1763 Dec. 26.	By Mr. Rose on Acct & his Bror. Mr. Jonathon Rose	7. 7. 0.

c. 1752 FELBRIGG HALL, NORFOLK
Architect of eighteenth-century work: James Paine.
Lit: Letters and accounts at house cited by R. W. Ketton-Cremer, *Felbrigg: The Story of a House*, 1962.

1755 ORMESBY HALL, LINCOLNSHIRE
Architect: James Paine.
Worked with an Italian, Pedrola (Patroli, q.v.).
Lit: N. Pevsner and John Harris, *Buildings of England: Lincolnshire*, 1964, p. 370.

1760-1 GLENTWORTH HOUSE, LINCOLNSHIRE
Architect: James Paine.
Lit: Letter from Rose at Sandbeck Park, Yorkshire (see below).
Attributed work:

c. 1740 NOSTELL PRIORY, YORKSHIRE *Plates 78-80*
North and South staircase, Dining Room, Music Room. The medallions are very similar to those at Temple Newsam House (see above), and as James Paine had a share in the design of the house he presumably used his favourite stuccoists.

1758 HEATH HALL, WAKEFIELD, YORKSHIRE
Architect: John Carr.
Drawing Room.
Lit: *C. Life*, 3 October 1968, p. 817.

c. 1766 SANDBECK PARK, YORKSHIRE *Plate 107*
Architect: James Paine.
Lit: *C. Life*, 14 October 1965, p. 966.

Rose, Joseph (1745-99)
Son of Jonathan Rose (see above). Born at Norton, Derbyshire, on 5 April 1745. His father and brother (both named Jonathan) and his uncle, Joseph, were all plasterers and they formed the firm of Joseph Rose & Co., which monopolized the most important plasterwork commissions of the Adam period.
The archives of the Worshipful Company of Plaisterers yield the following information:

1765 November 9.	Admitted Joseph Rose by Redemption.	
	Company	£1.6.6.
	Fine	2.2.0. £3.8.6.

As the means of admission was neither servitude nor patrimony this reduced the chance of finding details of his forbears in the Plaisterers' records, and only details of uncle Joseph's apprenticeship are recorded at York. Joseph, junior, was admitted 'into the same livery' in 1766, in which year two apprentices, Bartholomew Bullivant and James Price, were bound to him for seven years. Rose was admitted into the Court of Assistants. In 1767 he took another apprentice, William Smith, and at the meeting of 5 July 1774, was elected Upper Warden. A year later on 4 July 1775, he was appointed Master of the Worshipful Company of Plaisterers.

To some extent it may be true that this information relates to uncle Joseph, who was more likely, at the age of fifty-one, to be elected Master than his nephew, who at this time was only twenty-eight. Indeed, their careers can hardly be separated, and at uncle Joseph's death in 1780, Joseph, junior, succeeded to the business.

The present author has assumed that Joseph, junior, married Mary Richmond on 15 December 1774, at St Mary le Bone, Middlesex. The witnesses were Edward Webster and Joseph Rose. The family were to be long associated with Middlesex; their premises were in Queen Anne Street East, Middlesex (now London).

It has been shown (Walpole Society, XXXVI, p. 58, fn. 16; confirming Richard Hayward's MS., list, Department of Prints & Drawings, British Museum) that Rose was in Rome in 1768. He gained a classical education which was to stand him in good stead when he worked in the Neo-Classical style for Robert Adam. He subscribed, with his uncle and father, to George Richardson's *Ceilings in the Antique and Grotesque Tastes*, 1776.

Rose's will instructs that £500, a life interest in the residue of his estate and a choice of furniture should go to his wife, and the rest of the furniture should be sold with all 'Books, Moulds, Models, Casts, Scaffolding and every implement which belongs to my business'. The remaining bequests were to his mother, sisters, nieces and nephews. This will was proved on 16 February 1799, five days after his death. The present writer has not traced where he was buried: there is no entry regarding him in the Carshalton, Surrey, parish register, but his uncle and wife were buried there.

Sketch-books

(a) Book, 26 × 16·51 cm (10¼ × 6½ in), in the possession of the Earl of Harewood. Described in an appendix to Margaret Jourdain, *English Decorative Plasterwork*, 1926, pp. 251-3, although some details are omitted. The present writer has re-examined the book and refers to it where relevant.

(b) Book of 331 friezes, RIBA Library, MS., 729.56, presented anonymously in 1836. The title page reads: 'Sketches of Ornamental Friezes From Original Models in the Possession of Joseph Rose. Many of the Models were made from the designs of the most eminent Architects and the whole executed in stucco work by Joseph and Joseph Rose, London. Sketched by Joseph Rose, MDCCLXXXII'. The book is indexed and designs are noted as the work of Robert Adam, Rose, senior, Rose, junior, James Wyatt, James Stuart, Sir William Chambers, Henry Keene and 'Yeman', possibly John Yemens or Yeomans, but more likely John Yenn (1750-1821), a pupil of Sir William Chambers.

(c) Two volumes of sketches, 78·74 × 60·96 cm (31 × 24 in), for his decoration of Sledmere, Yorkshire, are at the house. The author is indebted to Sir Richard Sykes for letting him examine them. No. 1 contains thirty-seven plans and elevations which do not appear to be by Rose, followed by ten, nearly all of which are signed by him. No. 2 contains twenty plans which are not identifiable and twenty-four by Rose.

Portrait

Self-portrait in crayons, 60·9 × 45·7 cm at Sledmere House, Yorkshire. It was engraved by Bartolozzi, and the engraving is inscribed: *Joseph Rose Esqr. Ob. Feb. 11, 1779. A Etatis Suae 53. From a Drawing in Crayons by himself.*

Letters

Preserved at Nostell, Sledmere, Sandbeck and Castlecoole (N. Ireland).

Sale of his Collections

Christie's, 10, 12 April 1799.

Lit: London, Guildhall Library; Worshipful Company of Plaisterers, MS. 6122/3; *Parish Registers of Norton, Co. Derby*, ed. L. L. Simpson (Derby 1908); Harleian Society, 'Parish Registers of St. Mary le Bone, Middlesex'; Rose's will, P.C.C. 138 Howe; British Museum, Department of Prints and Drawings, Richard Hayward, A 59 S.C. MS., containing list of English visitors to Italy.

In view of the many overlapping dates the following list of work is arranged alphabetically:

ALNWICK CASTLE, NORTHUMBERLAND

In a letter of 1763(?) to Robert Adam, the Duke of Northumberland writes: 'I propose Mr. Rose should do the plaistering'.

Lit: Alnwick Castle Library, Vol. 94 (Shelf 22/1), fol. 31, Muniment Room U.I.46 (letter referred to above).

In a 'list of bills and receipts found on the death and in the possession of the late Duke' Joseph Rose is noted as due for £145 10s 1d (23 January 1779) and £56 11s 4d (6 April 1780).

On 29 May 1779, Rose received £3 4s 4d for two half-capitals in the Briesley Tower at Alnwick, but also mentioned an earlier bill of £53 7s 0d. Also received £3 18s 0d from the duke's agent, Mr Butler, for work at the 'House of Messrs Hill and Pitter' (29 September 1761).

Lit: John Fleming, 'Robert Adam's Gothick', *The Connoisseur*, CXLII, October 1958, pp. 75-9; Alnwick Castle Muniment Room, U.I.41; U.I.46.

1769 AMPTHILL, BEDFORDSHIRE

Architect: Sir William Chambers.

Drawing Room ceiling 'by Mr Rose' (from a letter of Sir William Chambers referred to below).

Lit: 5 December 1769, B.M. Add. MS., 41,133.

AUDLEY END, ESSEX

From 19 July 1763 to 2 February 1765, Rose received some £450, and payments to him continued until 1786. Payments were also made in 1769-73 to William Rose (q.v.). Rose also worked for Sir John Griffin Griffin in London, at 10 New Burlington Street.

Lit: Essex County Record Office, Braybrooke Archives D/DBy A 27; J. D. Williams, *Audley End, Restoration of 1762-97* (Essex County Record Office, Publication 45, 1968).

BEAUDESERT, STAFFORDSHIRE

The Rose sketch-book contains:

1. An entablature entitled 'Ld. Pagets'.
2. 'Dineing-room and cove att Ld. Pagets. Mr. Wyatt's desine Aug. 18 1771'.
3. 'Staircase. Beaudesert. Mr. Wyatt's design 1771'.
4. 'Suffeat under the Gallery and string of Great Stairs Beaudesert'.

BOWOOD, WILTSHIRE

Architect: Robert Adam.

Several of the Adam rooms and fittings were sold by auction on 30 June 1955. The details of Rose's work given below include the lot numbers of this sale. The auction preceded the demolition of the Big House at Bowood (Architect: Henry Keene). Rose received £498 and worked here with William Snow and William Pearce.

c. 1763-4 Staircase well, ceiling of room 31 (Lot 42, unsold), destroyed, 6·25 × 5·33 m (20 ft 6 in × 17 ft 6 in).

West Bow Corridor. Ceiling of Room 41 (Lot 75, unsold), 2·69 × 1·52 m (8 ft 10 in × 5 ft).

Corridor ceiling (Lot 82, unsold), 10·36 × 1·83 m (34 ft × 6 ft).

Entrance Hall ceiling (Lot 128, unsold), 9·9 × 6·4 m (32 ft 6 in × 21 ft).

Gallery Lobby (Lot 148, unsold), 2·55 × 1·47 m (8 ft 5 in × 4 ft 10 in).

Dining Room ceiling (Lot 183), 12·19 × 9·14 m (40 ft × 30 ft) and wall panels (Lots 184-9), bought for Lloyd's of London.

The Cube Room ceiling (Lot 198), 5·08 × 5·03 m (16 ft 8 in × 16 ft 6 in).

The King's Room ceiling (Lot 204, unsold), 8·954 × 6·09 m (29 ft 6 in × 20 ft).

Staircase Hall, spandrels (Lot 207), 3·35 × 1·52 m (11 ft × 5 ft).

Corridor, Room 73, ceiling (Lot 284, unsold), 8·3 × 3·35 m (27 ft 3 in × 11 ft).

Lit: Bowood Archives.

1792-7 CASTLECOOLE, N. IRELAND

Seven letters from Rose to the 1st Viscount Belmore are preserved at Castlecoole, together with his 'Estimate of Ornamented Ceilings . . . made from Mr. J. Wyatt's designs'. (The plain ceilings are not included in the estimate.)

In all, Rose received £2,249 6s 4½d for his work between 1794 and 1797. He sent plasterers to Ireland (Robert Shires, Robert Peterson, William Hartley, Thomas Fitzgerald and Thomas Spence were employed), together with eight packing-cases of casts and moulds for the capitals and frieze in the Saloon. Rose visited Castlecoole twice in 1792 and 1794.

Lit: R. Charles Lines, 'Castlecoole, Co. Fermanagh', *Connoisseur Year book*, 1956, p. 17, where one of Rose's bills is illustrated.

CHATSWORTH, DERBYSHIRE

Received £44 3s 3d.

Lit: Building Account, 22 January 1763.

CLAPTON, MIDDLESEX

The Rose sketch-book contains 'Cornices at Mr. Hollis, Solly House, Clapton, Middx. Nov. 22 1813'. This was presumably drawn by a son of Joseph or of Jonathan Rose, junior.

1767-8 CLAYDON HOUSE, BUCKINGHAMSHIRE

Architect: Sir Thomas Robinson.

Sir Thomas Robinson's statement about Rose being 'the first man in the Kingdom as a plasterer' has been mentioned. In July 1768, Rose is reported as saying that he 'can finish the staircase and two ceilings by Xmas'. The walls of the staircase are decorated in Neo-Classical style.

Robinson, who was working at Claydon for the

2nd Earl Verney, wrote in July that Rose was 'better suited to Mr. Lightfoot's work' in the ceiling. Lightfoot is also said to have 'retarded the staircase by not sending [to Rose] the instructions wanting'. 'The staircase', he continues, 'will be very noble and great, Mr. Rose's part very beautiful indeed, and will be one of the great works of Claydon'.

Lit: Robinson's letters were published in *Architectural Review*, June-September 1926, quoted by Christopher Hussey, *E.C.H.: Early Georgian*, 1955, p. 244.

1762 CROOME COURT, WORCESTERSHIRE *Plates 104-105*

The Adam accounts preserved at the Coventry Estate Office, Earl's Croome, mention Rose's work with 'Hopcraft' at Croome d'Abitot Church. This is presumably John Hobcroft (or Hobcraft), the carpenter and builder (H. M. Colvin, *A Biographical Dictionary of English Architects, 1954,* p. 289).

'May 1762—To mouldings at full size for the different cornices and mouldings of the ceiling for Messrs. Hopcraft & Rose'.

Lit: Geoffrey Beard, 'Robert Adam at Croome Court', *The Connoisseur*, CXXXII, October 1953, pp. 73-6; 'The Croome Court Tapestry Room', The Metropolitan Museum of Art, New York *Bulletin*, XVIII, No. 3, November 1959, pp. 79-93.

1770-1 FISHERWICK, STAFFORDSHIRE

Architect: Lancelot 'Capability' Brown.

Destroyed in 1814.

The Rose sketch-book contains:

'North tower room at Lord Donegalls at Fisherwick 1770'

'Lord Donegall's'

'Anty Room, Fisherwick. Staffs. Mr. Rose's desine'

'South Tower Room, Fisherwick' (coloured)

'Dressing Room, 1771'

'Staircase ceiling, Mr. Rose's desine'.

Lit: Rose's sketch-book. For Fisherwick see D. Stroud, *Capability Brown*, 1959; copy of 1814 Sale Catalogue, Birmingham Reference Library.

1765-70 HAREWOOD HOUSE, YORKSHIRE

The Rose sketch-book contains:

'April 16 1769—Sketch of part of ceiling and cover in the second drawing room att Harewood House'

'Best room ceiling, east end of Harewood House'

'Dining room ceiling, Harewood House, 1766'

'Room next dressing room, Harewood House'

'Dressing Room at East end of Harewood House'

'French couch room, Harewood House'

'A stone landing in the staircase at Harewood House, with plaister ornaments'

'1770. Part of Gallery ceiling at Harwood.'
'Room long 77 by 24'. (There is an Adam drawing of 1769 in the Soane Museum for this last ceiling.) Rose's detailed account survives. He received a total sum of £2,829 17s 0d. The account (examined by Robert Adam) is signed by Joseph Rose, junior, 'for the use of my uncle Joseph Rose' on 7 August 1770. It reads:

Stucco work done for Edward Lascelles Esq. p. Jos Rose. Jan/24th 1766 to March 10 1770 vizt.

Dining room	224. 8.	224. 8.
Musick room	130. 3.	
Add to ditto extra work not in the first Estimate viz ornament panels over two doors & two ditto next Picture Frames	35. 5.	
		165. 8.
Library	221. 9.	
Great Hall	333	
Great staircase	206	
Mr. Lascelles Dressing Room 49		
Mr. Lascelles Bedchamber 34		
Lady's dressing room 42	}	163
Occasional Dressing or Lodging Room 38		
Study	53	
Portico ceiling	20.10.	
Circular room exclusive of glass frames	125.0.	
State bedchamber	128	
Principal Dressing room	152	
Ceiling & Cove of Salon	158	
Entablature & sides of ditto	167	} 325
Drawing room next salon	171.10.	
Second or great drawing room	235	
Great Gallery	335	
	2858. 5	

Deduct from Honeysuckles in the Great Drawing room	8. 8	
from the Gallery the finishing over the Chimney not done	20. 0	
	28. 8	
	2829.17	

By cash on acct recd of Mr. Popplewell	2085.13.	
1770. July 13. By Mr. Lascelles Draught	300.	
	2385.13.	
Balance	444. 4.	
	2829.17	

KEDLESTON, DERBYSHIRE *Plate 111*
Architect: Robert Adam.
Rose received £1,107 16s 8¾d, as follows:

Music room	192.19. 8.
Drawing room	345. 6. 5¼.
Library	212. 7. 1¼.
Portico	22.12. 5½.
Hall	29. 0. 6.
Saloon	35. 7. 3¼.
Dining Room	270. 3. 3½.

Lit: Kedleston Archives Book 3 R fol. 64; The Rose sketch-book contains 'Executed att Lord Scarsdales att Kedleston in the Hall, Decr 1775 by R. Mott' (q.v.), Rose's apprentice; 'Hall frieze, Kedleston'; *Connoisseur Yearbook*, 1958.

KENWOOD, MIDDLESEX *Plate 112*
Payments of £200 (4 August 1769) and £276 8s 0d (14 August 1772) are recorded in the 1st Earl of Mansfield's account at Hoare's Bank. It is, however, likely that Rose's work at Kenwood amounted to much more than this but no plasterwork accounts survive (unless at Scone Palace ?). The author is indebted to the Earl of Mansfield for kindly discussing with him the possibility of manuscripts surviving at Scone Palace.

KNIGHT HOUSE, WOLVERLEY, WORCESTERSHIRE
'17 Jan., 1782. Jos Rose on Stucco work £50.
22 October, 1782. Rose plaistering in full £308 11s 6d.
6 Sept., 1786. Jos. Rose on acct of Stuccoing £150.'
Lit: Kidderminster Public Library, Knight Archives, Edward Knight notebooks, nos. 289-90.

LONDON HOUSES
AUDLEY SQUARE
The Rose sketch-book contains:
'Done at Lord Darnley's and Lord Delaware Audley Square.'
House for Lord Percy. Bill from Joseph Rose & Co., to Duke of Northumberland, detailed room by room. Received £145 10s 1¾d. Receipted 23 July 1779.
Lit: Alnwick Castle, Muniment Room, U.I.46.
BERKELEY SQUARE
The Rose sketch-book contains:
'1781. Mr. Thornhills in Berkley Square.'
'Lord Darnley in Berkley Square.'
1786-7 BURLINGTON GARDENS
Rose replaced a plasterer called Pritchard.

Lit: Survey of London, XXXII, 1963, pp. 463-6.

CHANDOS STREET

The Rose sketch-book contains:

'In Chandos Street, Cavendish Square, Mr. Rose's design.'

1771-2 30 CURZON STREET

Architect: Robert Adam for Hon. H. F. Thynne.

The Rose sketch-book contains:

'Domed ceiling at Mr. Thyn's in Curzon Street, Octob. 26 1772'.

DRAPERS' COMPANY HALL

Five drawings for ceilings were among Rose's effects at his death and were sold at Christie's on 12 April 1799, Lot 67.

19 (now 30) DOVER STREET

Architect: Robert Adam.

The Rose sketch-book contains:

'Lord Ashburnham's, Hay Hill.' The house was altered for Lord Ashburnham, 1773-6.

GRAFTON STREET

The Rose sketch-book contains:

'Sir George Warens in Grafton Street, Rose's design.'

GROSVENOR SQUARE

The Rose sketch-book contains:

'Lord Grimstons in Grosvenor Square, Mr. Rose's design.'

'Groynd Ceiling. Ld. Stanleys.'

'Two ceilings at Ld. Stanleys, Grosvenor Square. July 1774. Adam's design.'

In 1773-4 Adam built 23 (later 26) Grosvenor Square (Derby House) for Lord Stanley, later Earl of Derby; the house was destroyed in 1862. One of the six drawings in the Sir John Soane's Museum for ceilings in this house has a note on it: 'this is drawn at large and ready for Mr. Rose'.

c. 1773-5 GROSVENOR SQUARE

Architect: James Wyatt.

Work for William Drake. Rose's charge of £224 16s 7d is included in Wyatt's 'Abstract of Sundry Bills for Alteration and Repair done to a House in Grosvenor Square for Wm. Drake Esq'.

Lit: Buckinghamshire. County Record Office; G. Eland (*ed.*) *Shardeloes Papers*, 1937, p. 135.

MANSFIELD STREET

Architect: Robert Adam.

The Rose sketch-book contains:

'Sir Edward Deerings, Mansfield Street.'

'at Lord Scarsdale, Mansfield Street.'

'Mr. Hobcraft's desine done in Mansfield Street.'

10 NEW BURLINGTON STREET

20 October 1764-8 March 1766: general repairs and plastering. Received £3 18s 4d. 9 July-20 August 1768: received £3 18s 4d. 26 August-2 September

1769: receipt signed John Bullivant, presumably a relative of Bartholomew Bullivant (q.v.) who was apprenticed to Rose in 1766. 11 July 1778-13 February 1779: received £239 14s 2½d for work done under Robert Adam. Receipts signed by Joseph Rose, junior, on 27 March and 24 April 1779.

Lit: Essex County Record Office, Braybrooke Archives, D/DBy.

NORTHUMBERLAND HOUSE

Architect: Robert Adam.

The Rose sketch-book contains:

'Dining Room at Northumberland House.'

The house was decorated for the Duke of Northumberland in 1770; it was destroyed in 1874. Payments to Rose occur in the archives at Alnwick Castle (MSS., U-I-25).

THE PANTHEON

Architect: James Wyatt.

The Rose sketch-book contains coloured sketches described as: 'ornament above ye Pannells in ye Pantheon, att London, June 1770. Burnt in 1792.'

'Cottillion—Room in ye Pantheon 1770.'

PORTLAND PLACE

The Rose sketch-book contains:

'Black Drg Room 16 Portland Place, Mr. R's design. Done 1780.'

'No. 4 Portland Place, Rose's design.'

No. 10

'At Ld Stormont's Portd Place 1776.'

'Done in several houses in Portland Place.'

1776 20 PORTMAN SQUARE

Lit: Countess of Home's account, Hoare's Bank. (The author is indebted to Dr Margaret Whinney for this information.)

3 ST JAMES'S SQUARE

House for the Marquess of Donegall.

The Rose sketch-book contains:

'At Lord Donegall in St. James Square. Mr. Roses desine.'

'Ld Donegall's dineing room, St. James's Square, Mr. Rose's desine.'

'Pannell in drawing room ceiling, Ld Donegalls, St. James Square.'

'Mr. Hobert's Front Drawing room, St. James Square.'

15 ST JAMES'S SQUARE

Architect: James Stuart.

Rose worked here for Thomas Anson, for whom Stuart was working at his Staffordshire house, Shugborough.

Lit: Survey of London, XXIX, 1960, p. 143.

20 ST JAMES'S SQUARE

Architect: Robert Adam.

For work at the town house of Sir Watkin Williams Wynn in 1776-7 Rose received £2,684. The Rose sketch-book contains:

'Groynd Ceiling at Sir Watkin William Wynn in St. James's Square.'

'For Drawing room, Sir W.W.Wynn's.'

'Back Drawing room at Sir W.Wynn.'

'Library, Sir W.Wynn.'

Lit: Wynn Archives, National Library of Wales; *Connoisseur Yearbook*, 1959.

ST MARTIN'S LANE

The Rose sketch-book contains:

'Groynd ceiling and alcove head of window done for Mr. Hamilton, St. Martin's Lane.'

SOMERSET HOUSE

1786-91 Received £1,188 4s 8d. Jobs as various as plastering apartments belonging to the Stamp Office '& Plaistering to the East Water Gate'.

Lit: RIBA, Library, NS., 725.3; P.R.O., A.O.3/1244.

SOUTHAMPTON ROW

The Rose sketch-book contains:

'Duke of Bolton's Southampton Row, London.'

OTHER WORK IN LONDON

The Rose sketch-book contains:

'Done at Chelsea by W. end of Battersea Bridge for Mr. Hatchet.'

1766 MERSHAM LE HATCH, KENT

Architect: Robert Adam.

Adam paid Rose direct for work at this house and then charged the sum in his own account to Sir Edward Knatchbull. In January 1766, Rose prepared an estimate 'for the Stucco, work of the Ceiling & sides of rooms on the Principal Story at Hatch House . . . made from Mr. Adam's designs'. The estimate is detailed, and in reference to the Hall is as follows:

'To finish the Plain work ornaments & Mouldings in the Ceiling after the Design except within the small circle in the centre where instead of the Rose drawn is to be Sir Edwards Arms & instead of the roses in the small circles in the end panels is to be Sr Edwards crest—for the sum of £77.18.9.' The Adam design (*English Houses* VI, Fig. 192) shows the roses which were changed finally for the Knatchbull heraldry. Below the ceiling the 'full enrich'd Dorick Entablature as drawn at Large' is to cost £49 14s 8d and those parts of doorcases and the upper part of chimneypieces not of wood but of composition are to be done for £54 15s 6d. The Great Drawing Room ceiling (*English Homes* VI, Fig. 198) is to cost £111 4s 8d. The frieze below it and the floating of the walls 'for hangings or Paper' come to £68 13s 6d. The work of the

Great Dining Room (so called in the original plan, but 'eating room' in that of 1763) is estimated at £141 7s 3d. At the end of the estimate Sir Edward adds the note 'sent by Mr. Adam'. The first payment to Rose was £50 on account in the following December.

Lit: Kent County Record Office, Sir Edward Knatchbull's account book, 1762-84. Included are five payments to 'Mr. Rose. Plaisterer'. One is listed as 'The Remnant', the other four total £351 7s 0d. The dates are 11 December 1766; 2 and 9 November 1770; 15 November 1771; 1 April 1773.

MILTON ABBEY, DORSET

Lit: C. *Life*, 28 July 1966, p. 209.

1771 NEWBY, YORKSHIRE

The Rose sketch-book contains:

'Dining Room at Wm Weddles Esq., at Newby.'

'Hall ceiling Mr. Weddle at Newby.'

The date 1771 is incorporated in the plasterwork on the west wall of the Entrance Hall.

Lit: Hugh Honour, 'Newby Hall, Yorkshire', *Connoisseur*, CXXXII, December 1954, pp. 246-51.

1766-77 NOSTELL PRIORY, YORKSHIRE *Plate 106*

Architect: Robert Adam.

The statement of accounts which Rose sent to Sir Rowland Winn covers forty-nine pages. He received £1,822 3s 0d. On 25 March 1777, he was paid a first instalment of £1,013 12s 6d, and after much argument about an allowance to be made by Rose for the 'outside Stucco on Riding House etc. which gave way' he received a further £679 6s 9¾d.

Lit: For an analysis of Rose's accounts and letters see *The Nostell Collections*. . . M.Brockwell, 1915, pp. 24-30, based on the Nostell Archives, C3/1/5, 4/2 and 4/9.

PACKINGTON HALL, WARWICKSHIRE

Architect: Joseph Bonomi.

Received £107.

Lit: C. *Life*, 16 July 1970, p. 229.

PADWORTH HOUSE, BERKSHIRE

This house was rebuilt in 1769 for Christopher Griffith by John Hobcroft (or Hobcraft). Hobcroft and Rose have been mentioned in connection with Croome Court, and in Rose's sketch-book some of the designs are stated to be after Hobcroft. Sir William Mount and Mr Robin Mount have kindly provided information about Padworth and Wasing Place (three miles away) built for John Mount in 1760. This latter house was badly destroyed by fire in the Second World War. Sir William remembers that the bills were destroyed in the fire. We may reasonably assume that Rose did the plasterwork at these two houses.

RIDGELEY, STAFFORDSHIRE
Architect: James Wyatt.
The Rose sketch-book contains:
'Done at Ashton Curzon [Asheton Curzon] Esq., Ridgley, Staffs. Mr. Wyatt's desinge in 1771.'
1792 SAFFRON WALDEN CHURCH, ESSEX
Between 31 May 1792 and December of the same year Rose was paid £96 12s 6d for work in the chancel.
Lit: Braybrooke Papers, Essex County Record Office.
SHARDELOES, BUCKINGHAMSHIRE
Architect: Robert Adam.
Between 10 October 1761 and 19 February 1763, Rose received £1,139 18s 0d, receipted 10 August 1764. The account is detailed room by room and includes references to 'An Ornamd. Ceiling as p. Estimate delivered to Mr. Adam'.
Lit: Shardeloes Archives, Bucks., County Record Office; G. Eland, *ed., Shardeloes Papers,* 1937.
SHUGBOROUGH, STAFFORDSHIRE
In a letter of 1766 at Shugborough, James Stuart says: 'Rose thanks you for the money'.
Hussey ascribes work in the Drawing Room and Library to Rose and notes that the coved ceiling of the Great Drawing Room was done under Samuel Wyatt *c.* 1795 by Rose for £800. It has now been established from documentation that some of the work here was done by Francesco Vassalli (q.v.), as attributed in the present author's 'Italian Stuccoists in England', *Apollo,* July 1964, LXXX, p. 56.
Lit: Christopher Hussey, *E.C.H.: Early Georgian,* 1955, p. 81.
SLEDMERE, YORKSHIRE
As a result of Rose's friendship with the Sykes family—his *Self-portrait* is still at the house—he assisted in designing the decorative work for Sir Christopher Sykes at Sledmere (1788-90) and carried out the plasterwork. Two volumes of his sketches are preserved at Sledmere. The plasterwork was destroyed by fire in 1911 and was subsequently restored by G. Jackson & Sons, Ltd., to Rose's original designs.
1762 and after SYON HOUSE, MIDDLESEX
Architect: Robert Adam.
No bill has been traced, but the earl of Northumberland (as he then was) wrote to Adam on 4 November 1763: 'I am glad you have altered some of the Brass mouldings for the Drawing Room chimney piece which I expect will now be finished in a short time and that Mr. Rose will get the ceiling of that room complete before the Frost comes on, so that it may have Time to dry fit to be gilt early in the

spring, by which Time I hope the Paintings will be ready to be fixed up'.
Lit: Northumberland Archives, Alnwick Castle, Library, Vo. XCIV, pp. 44-5, rough draft of the letter.
Work unexecuted:
The Rose sketch-book contains:
'1779 Mr. Rose's design for Judge Wills but not executed.'
Work unspecified:
9 March 1777: 'To Rose, Plaisterer £114.'
Lit: Earl of Harrowby Archives, account-book 337.
Work attributed:
c. 1770 ROKEBY, YORKSHIRE
Dining Room for Sir Thomas Robinson, who employed the Rose firm at Claydon.
FARNLEY HALL, YORKSHIRE
Family tradition ascribes the plasterwork here to Rose. John Carr added a new wing to the house for Walter Fawkes in 1786, and by this time both Carr's favourite plasterers, Giuseppe Cortese and James Henderson, were dead.
Lit: Christopher Hussey, *E.C.H.: Mid-Georgian,* 1956, p. 217.
c. 1790 WOOLLEY PARK, YORKSHIRE
Lit: Leeds Arts Calendar, no. 68, 1971, p. 12.

Rose, William (d 10 April 1829)
Submitted bills at Audley End, Essex (see list above). If this is William, the son of Joseph Rose, senior, he entered the Church and was for fifty-two years Rector of Carshalton, Surrey. There is a monumental tablet in the church.

Ross, Daniel (*fl.* 1738-9)
1738-9 YESTER HOUSE, EAST LOTHIAN
Worked at the house for 161 days, 1738-9, as apprentice to Joseph Enzer (q.v.).
Lit: Enzer's account-book, Yester House archives.

Rothwell, James (*fl.* 1765-87)
1787 MARINE PAVILION, BRIGHTON
Received £272.
Lit: Henry Roberts, *Royal Pavilion, Brighton,* 1939, p. 28.

Rothwell, Thomas (*fl.* 1765-69)
1765-9 HAREWOOD HOUSE, YORKSHIRE
Assisted by his son James. They were in partnership with James Henderson (q.v.).
Lit: R. B. Wragg, *York Georgian Society Report,* 1955-6, p. 59; Mary Mauchline, *Harewood House,* 1974 pp., 68-9.

Rowe (Widow) (*fl.* 1681-2)
1681-2 ST BRIDE'S, FLEET STREET, LONDON
Vestry Minutes:
7 March 1681/2. 'Churchwardens to employ a Plasterer for the plasterwork of the New Gallery and to let Widow Rowe who is an inhabitant of the Parish with her assistants and servants to have the doing of the same.'
Lit: Wren Soc., XIX, p. 13.

Rule, John (*fl.* 1830-99)
Of a firm established in Sunderland in 1830. Worked in fibrous plaster and also did granolithic and fireproof floors and scagliola. A Mr Rule of Durham mastered the method of Gothic plasterwork at Ravensworth Castle, Durham, designed in 1808 by John Nash.
Lit: W. Millar, *Plastering, Plain and Decorative,* 1899, p. 141 and adverts p. vi.

St Michele, John Baptist (*fl.* 1734)
1734 ST BARTHOLOMEW'S HOSPITAL, LONDON
Architect: James Gibbs.
St Michele received £160 for the Great Hall, and a further £32 16s od.
Lit: Hospital Archives, Ha, 19/5/1.

Sampson, John (*fl.* 1673-71)
1673 THIRLESTANE CASTLE, BERWICKSHIRE
Received £229 for work at various of the Earl of Lauderdale's Scottish properties.
Lit: Thirlestane Castle MSS., Scottish Record Office.
1681 YESTER HOUSE, EAST LOTHIAN
Unspecified work, for which he received £13 17s 4d.
Lit: Yester House MSS., Scottish Record Office.

Sefton, Thomas (*fl.* mid-eighteenth century)
'Thomas Sefton, plasterer at Newcastle, the same man who did Mr. Mill's house lately and is recommended by him as a very honest careful man.'
Lit: Harrowby Archives (Sandon), Nathaniel Ryder's notebooks, No. 67.

Sellar, — (*fl.* 1710)
1710 CASTLE HOWARD, YORKSHIRE
Acted as labourer to Bagutti and Plura (q.v.).
Lit: Castle Howard Archives, Building Book, 1702-1720.

Serena, Carlo Ferdinando (*fl.* 1727-8)
Worked in England with his brother Francesco (see below).

Lit: A. Leinhard-Riva, *Armoriale Ticinese,* Lausanne, 1945, pp. 441-2.
1727-8 BRAMHAM PARK, YORKSHIRE
Mentioned in the owner Robert Benson's bank account (Hoare's Bank) as 'Carlo Sereney'.
Lit: C. Life, 27 February 1958, p. 401; bank account cited.

Serena, Francesca Leone (1700-after 1729)
Born at Arogno, near Lugano, Switzerland, on 5 November 1700, and baptized there on 6 November. One of three sons of Domenico Serena and Giulia Cozzi. There is no record of his death. His son (?) Giovanni Battista Serena died at Arogno on 28 October 1774, aged forty-seven and is described as 'son of the late Francesco Serena'.
Lit: A. Leinhard-Riva, *Armoriale Ticinese,* 1945; Registers at Arogno, 6 November 1700, and 28 October 1774.
Serena is said to have worked at the Abbey of Ottobeuren, presumably under the stuccoist Joseph Anton Feuchtmayer (1696-1770), and at the Landhaus, Innsbruck.
Lit: Thieme-Becker; Hugo Schnell, *Ottobeuren,* Munich, 1950, p. 22.
1725 DITCHLEY, OXFORDSHIRE
Worked with Giuseppe Artari and Francesco Vassalli.
Lit: Oxford County Record Office, Dillon MSS., I/p/3h.
1729 CAVENDISH SQUARE, LONDON
Received £30 for a knot-work ceiling done for James Brydges, 1st Duke of Chandos.
Lit: Baker, *Brydges,* pp. 199, 277 fn.

Shann, Robert (*fl.* 1709-10)
Official of the Worshipful Company of Plaisterers.
1709 Upper Warden.
1710 Master.
Lit: London, Guildhall Library, MS., 6122/3.

Shepherd, Edward (?-1747)
According to Vertue (III, p. 51), Shepherd began his working life as a plasterer. Better known as an architect (Colvin).

Shepherd, John (*fl.* 1720-30)
Brother of Edward, above. Subscribed to 2nd edition of Leoni's *Palladio.*
1720 HANOVER SQUARE, LONDON
Sir Theodore Janssen's House.
Received £26 7s od.
Lit: Inventories of the South Sea Company, Vol. 2, 1721.

1728 Employed by James Brydges, 1st Duke of Chandos in London. Lord Chandos accused him in 1730 of being 'drunk from morning to night' and said that he had 'never minded the workmen' at Shaw Hall, Berkshire.
Lit: Baker, *Brydges*, p. 370.
A John Shepheard worked under John Grove II during the Office of Works preparations for William III's Coronation.
Lit: P.R.O., Works, 5/43.

Sherwood, John (*fl.* late seventeenth century)
Worked extensively in the Wren City churches. See the list in Wren Soc., x. Mentioned in Robert Hooke's *Diary* (1935 *ed.*), pp. 14-15, 180, 229, 320, 338, 401.

Sherwood, Thomas (*fl.* late seventeenth century)
ALL HALLOWS THE GREAT, LONDON
Lit: Wren Soc., x, p. 47.

Simmons, Robert (*fl.* 1660)
1660 THE TOWER, LONDON
Worked under John Grove.
Lit: P.R.O., Works, 5/1, November 1660.

Smith, Abraham (*fl.* 1581-99)
Of some twenty-one plasterers who worked on the old Chatsworth and the old and new Hardwick Halls, Derbyshire, Smith was the most talented. He probably came from Ashford in the same county and worked continuously over almost twenty years for Elizabeth, Countess of Shrewsbury, 'Bess of Hardwick'. He was responsible for the frieze and cornice in the Great Chamber at Hardwick, 1599 (Plates 1, 6).
Lit: Basil Stallybrass, 'Bess of Hardwick's Buildings and Building Accounts', *Archaeologia*, LXIV, 1913, pp. 376, 377, 397. *C. Life*, 22 November 1973, p. 1670.

Smith, Samuel (*fl.* 1710-24)
In 1724, at the age of fourteen, Smith was apprenticed to Isaac Mansfield (q.v.) 'of St James, Westminster, Plasterer' in the sum of £10.
Lit: London, Guildhall Library, Boyd's Index to Apprenticeship Registers.
Another plasterer named Samuel Smith was working in 1720-1 at Purley Hall, Berkshire, and was paid 10 guineas.
Lit: Typewritten sheet of *Building Accounts*, 1720-1721 (source unspecified) preserved at Purley Hall. (The author is indebted to Dr Peter Willis for this information.)

Smith, William (*fl.* 1698)
One of the contestants for the job of Plaisterer to Christ's Hospital, Newgate Street, 1698.
Lit: Wren Soc., XI, p. 70.

Snare, Quintin (*fl. c.* 1730)
A York bricklayer and plasterer mentioned in the 1730s in the Ordinance Book of the Bricklayers' Tilers and Plasterers, 1721-52 (York Minster Library, BB5).
1732-3 ASSEMBLY ROOMS, YORK
Received £8 11s od for Stucco modillions flowered with Roses for the Entablature of the Circular Room (June 1732). Plain stuccoed the front of the building and under the portico at 8d a yard (23 June 1733).
Lit: York Reference Library, Assembly Room Minute Book, 1729-58, pp. 58-9.

Snow, William (*fl.* 1762-6)
1762-6 BOWOOD, WILTSHIRE
Architect: Robert Adam.
Received £294. Some work in Cube Room; subcontractor for Henry Holland.
Lit: Bowood Archives. (The author is indebted to Mr J. R. Hickish, the Bowood Agent, for this information.)

Stanley, Charles (Simon Carl) (1703-61)
Born in Copenhagen of English parents on 12 December 1703. In 1718 he joined the sculptor-stuccoist J. C. Sturmberg and worked at Fredensborg Castle. In 1727, after study in Amsterdam under Jan van Logteren, he left for England and joined the sculptors Peter Scheemakers and Laurent Delvaux. He signed monuments to Thomas Maynard at Hoxne, Suffolk (1742) and the Maynard family at Little Easton, Essex (1746). He married firstly Mrs Anne Allen on 21 May 1730, at Eastbourne Parish Church, and secondly Magdalene Margrethe Lindemann on 2 August 1737. He worked until the summer of 1746 in England and then left hastily for Denmark where he had been invited by Frederick V to become Court Sculptor, a post he held until his death on 17 February 1761. His second wife outlived him (d 1763), and his son by this marriage, Carl Frederick Stanley, a sculptor by profession, died at Copenhagen in 1813.
His plasterwork in England presents a confused story. An attempt to explain his career here will be found in chapter V.
Lit: A. F. Büsching, *Nachrichten von den Künsten*, III, 1757, pp. 193-200: Ogveke Helsted

Wellbachs Kunstlerlexikon, III, 1952, pp. 262-4, and entries cited therein; Gunnis, pp. 365-6; K.A. Esdaile, *C. Life*, 2 October and 11 December 1937; *Times Literary Supplement*, 3 April 1937.

c. 1740 LANGLEY PARK, NORFOLK *Plate 75*
'Saloon, Alto Relievo in Stucco, Stanley.'
Lit: Neale's *Seats . . .*, III, 1823.

1744 RADCLIFFE CAMERA, OXFORD
Architect: James Gibbs.
On 5 March 1744, Stanley received £232 18s 10d. The bill was witnessed by Thomas Roberts (q.v.) and is headed 'Plaisterers work done for the Honble Trustees at Dr Radcliffe's Library, Per Charles Stanley & Thos Roberts'.
Lit: 'The Building Accounts of the Radcliffe Camera, Oxford', *ed.* S.G.Gillam, Oxford Historical Society, XIII, 1953-4, (1958).

c. 1745 OKEOVER, STAFFORDSHIRE *Plate 74*
'One thing we must allow of him [Stanley] is your ceiling is well done and cheap.'
Lit: Letter from Joseph Sanderson to Leak Okeover, 9 December 1746 (House archives).

Attributed work:
1728-9 COMPTON PLACE, EASTBOURNE, SUSSEX *Plates 68, 70*
Architect: Colin Campbell.
Stanley was presumably one of four plasterers working under the supervision of John Hughes (q.v.).
Lit: Geoffrey Beard, *Georgian Craftsmen and their Work*, 1966, pp. 32-3; see also chapter V.

c. 1745 KIRTLINGTON, OXFORDSHIRE *Plates 72, 73*
Lit: Geoffrey Beard: *Georgian Craftsmen and their Work*, 1966, p. 34; Metropolitan Museum of Art, New York, *Bulletin*, March 1956; K.A.Esdaile, *C. Life*, 2 October and 11 December 1937.

Stanley is also said to have worked at Barnsley Park, Gloucestershire; Hall Place, Maidenhead; Honington Hall, Warwickshire; Easton Neston, Northamptonshire; and Stratton Park, Hampshire. There is no exact evidence to connect him with any of these houses. The panels at Honington are admittedly similar to those at Langley Park, and Stratton was originally designed by John Sanderson, a possible relative of the Joseph Sanderson who wrote to Leak Okeover (see above).

Stanyon, Abraham (*fl.* 1657-8)
Fined for taking the work of a carpenter, 13 October 1657.
Master of the Worshipful Company of Plaisterers, 1657-8.
Lit: Guildhall Library, London, MSS., 6122/2; 6126.

Staveacre, J. (*fl.* 1708-10)
1708-10 ST PAUL'S CATHEDRAL, LONDON
Worked under Chrysostom Wilkins.
Lit: Wren Soc., XV, pp. 169, 196.

Steede, Miles (*fl.* 1654)
Official of the Worshipful Company of Plaisterers.
1654 Master.
Lit: London, Guildhall Library, MS., 6122/2.

Stevenson, John (d 1692)
His will is P.C.C. 1692, fol. 118.

Stocking, Thomas, senior (1722-1808)
Practised in Bristol and the south-west, where his reputation was equal to that of the Rose family. He applied for permission as a free burgess at Bristol on 29 September 1762, and became one on 20 July 1763, by vote of the Common Council and the payment of eight guineas. He may have been influenced by Joseph Thomas (q.v.).

It has perhaps not been previously noted that his son Thomas was apprenticed to him. 'Thomas Stocking, son of Thomas Stocking of Bristol. Tyler & Plaister put to his said father and Mary his wife for 7 years. 21 Janry 1765.' (Bristol Apprentices Book, 1764-77, p. 23). He was joined in about 1790 by Robert Harding, who carried on the business when Stocking retired. He died on 10 September 1808. *Felix Farley's Bristol Journal*, 17 September 1808, records in its obituaries:

'Same day [*i.e.* 10 September] having borne with fortitude a lingering and painful illness, Mr Thomas Stocking of this city, aged 86; a man greatly esteemed and respected by all who knew him.'

Apart from his son, Stocking had another apprentice, Thomas Dennis, who was put to him for the usual seven years on 31 May 1786.

Stocking did the plasterwork at The Royal Fort, Arno's Court and St Nicholas's Church. His most important commission was, however, at Corsham Court, Wiltshire. Mr Methuen's Day Book shows that between 1763-6 Stocking was paid £570. It is possible that £390 of this was for the very fine Long Gallery ceiling, completed in about 1765.

Stocking must have been responsible for much work in the south-west, and work at Midford Castle, Somerset (*C. Life*, 3-10 March 1944), is attributed to him.
Lit: W. Ison, *Georgian Buildings of Bristol*, pp. 44-5; Bristol Apprentices Book, 1764-77.

Storey, — (*fl.* 1710)
1710 CASTLE HOWARD, YORKSHIRE

Labourer to Bagutti and Plura (q.v.).
Lit: Castle Howard Archives, Building Books.

Summers, — (*fl.* 1670)
1670 ST MICHAEL, CORNHILL, LONDON
Lit: Wren Soc., XIX, p. 46; X, p. 124.

Swan, — (*fl. c.* 1755)
c. 1755 WATLINGTON PARK, OXFORDSHIRE
Lit: Information from Mr J.A.Kenworthy-Browne.

Symonds, Richard (*fl.* 1705)
1705 HILL COURT, HEREFORDSHIRE
Lit: C. *Life,* 27 January 1966. Bills at house.

Tenton, Henry (*fl.* 1670-1)
1670 WHITEHALL PALACE, LONDON
Worked under John Grove II.
Lit: P.R.O., Works, 5/15, June 1670.

Thackham, James (*fl.* 1689)
1689 HAMPTON COURT, MIDDLESEX
One of the plasterers working under John Grove II.
Lit: P.R.O., Works, 5/55, April-May 1689.

Thomas, Joseph (before 1730-77)
Tiler and plasterer of Bristol. Admitted a free burgess on 21 September 1730, being the son of a freeman. In September 1740, was living at 5 Guinea Street, Bristol. The ceiling of 15 Orchard Street may be by Thomas. He died on 6 May 1777. His name does not appear in the Bristol Apprenticeship Books.
1748-50 CLIFTON HILL HOUSE, BRISTOL
Received £406.
Lit: W.Ison, *Georgian Buildings of Bristol,* 1952, p. 198.
Attributed work:
1752 UPTON, TETBURY, GLOUCESTERSHIRE; Hall

Thompson, J. (*fl.* 1708-10)
1708-10 ST PAUL'S CATHEDRAL, LONDON
Worked under Chrysostom Wilkins.
Lit: Wren Soc., XV, pp. 169, 196.

Thorpe, James (*fl.* 1788-9)
1788-9 SOMERSET HOUSE, LONDON
Provided composition ornaments for chimneypieces at Somerset House. Received £61 9s 10d.
Lit: London, RIBA, Library MS., 725.121 (B3); P.R.O. AO3/1244.

Toogood, Arthur (*fl.* 1650-63)
His son Henry was apprenticed to him and was free of the Worshipful Company of Plaisterers, 23 April 1658. Arthur was Master of the Company in 1663.
Lit: Guildhall Library, London, MSS., 6122/2.

Tooley, John (*fl.* 1702-3)
Official of the Worshipful Company of Plaisterers. 1702-3 Master.
Lit: Guildhall Library, London, 6122/3.

Tucke, Anthony (*fl.* 1665)
Possibly father or brother of Richard Tucke (see below). May have been the second husband of John Grove's mother.
1665 He worked under John Grove I at Hampton Court, Middlesex.
Lit: P.R.O., Works, 5/7, September 1665-6. Will of John Grove I, P.C.C. 29 March 1676.

Tucke, Richard (*fl.* 1668-1700)
Tucke's name appears frequently in the Account-Books of the Office of Works as one of the plasterers working under the supervision of John Grove II. He is noted in 1668 at Whitehall, in 1680 at The Tower and in 1689 at Hampton Court, and in 1689 he was one of the plasterers engaged by Grove to prepare work for the coronation of William III.
Lit: P.R.O., Works, 5/12; 5/33; 5/43; 5/55, etc.

Vassalli, Francesco (*fl.* 1724-63)
One of a family long settled at Riva St Vitale, near Lugano. Although little is known of him, and whilst it is difficult to decide if his late work was done by, or in collaboration with 'John Vassalli', there is little doubt of his talent. There seems to have been a connection with Thomas Clayton (see chapter VII).
1724 SUTTON SCARSDALE, DERBYSHIRE
Architect: Francis Smith.
Destroyed *c.* 1919.
Lit: Rising-plate at house; text in Colvin, p. 552; C. *Life,* 15 February 1919, p. 171.
1725 DITCHLEY, OXFORDSHIRE
Architect: James Gibbs.
Lit: Oxford County Record Office, Dillon MSS., I/p/3h.
1730 ASKE HALL, RICHMOND, YORKSHIRE
The Hall and five other rooms.
Lit: Letter from Vassalli 7 December 1730 (see chapter V).
1730-1 TOWNELEY HALL, BURNLEY, LANCASHIRE
Plate 54
This example, documented as Vassali's work, is also in other northern houses and suggests that the

stuccoist moved from one house to the other. Great Hall, Assisted by Martino Quadry.

Received £126.

Staircase. Received £21.

Lit: Lancashire County Record Office, MS., DDTO Q/10.

1736-7 CASTLE HOWARD, YORKSHIRE

Temple of the Four Winds. 'Given to Varcelli for drawing a design for ye finishing ye Temple in Stuco & artificial Marble [scagliola] £2.02.0.'

Lit: Castle Howard Archives, 3rd Earl of Carlisle's Notebook, 1736.

1737 May. To Mr Vasally on Acc^ot of working at ye inside of ye Temple by

recept.	42. 0. 0.	
To Do on the same Accot	31.10. 0.	
To Do	5. 5. 0.	
To Do	5. 5. 0.	

1738-9 To Mr Vassalli ye Ballance of his Acct for work done at ye Temple as by Receipt Mr Vasallei Agre^mt 36.15. 0.

for finishing ye inside of ye Temple	141.15. 0.	
Pd at London	21. 0. 0.	
	120.15. 0.	
Pd at Castle Howard Dec. 1737	84. 0. 0.	
Pd Balance to Vassali by rect.	36.15. 0.	

1751-2 TRENTHAM, STAFFORDSHIRE

Now destroyed. Work in 'My Lords Drawing-Room'.

Received £57 2s 0d.

Lit: Staffs County Record Office, Trentham MSS.; *C. Life*, 25 January 1968, p. 178.

1753 PETWORTH, SUSSEX

Unspecified work.

Lit: House archives (listed by National Register of Archives).

1758 HAGLEY HALL, WORCESTERSHIRE *Plate 98*

Architect: Sanderson Miller.

White Hall. Panel over fireplace, signed bottom left by Vassalli.

Salon, now Dining Room.

Ceiling and walls, roundels, swags and trophies emblematical of the interests of Sir George Lyttelton, for whom the house was built and decorated.

1758-9 CROOME COURT, WORCESTERSHIRE

A 'John Vassalli', who may be the same as or a relative of Francesco, received various sums in 1758-1759, the work being measured in October, 1760. There are two receipts at the Estate Office signed by Vassalli (28 July 1758, £50; 8 October 1759, £50). The measured work amounted to £247 10s 4¼d, and special work in addition, including ornaments

in the stone staircase and 'ye Salon according to my desinge, £47 15s.'. There is another bill, unsigned, but in a very similar hand which reads: 'Stucco work by hand & Plaisterers work done for ye Rt Honble Earl of Coventry at Croom, Worcestershire, 1761.

Measured work	£247. 4. 7½.	
Ornaments by hand		
ceiling of drawing-room	£40. 0. 0.	
ceiling of dining-room	£36. 0. 0.	
wall, ornaments, dining-room	44. 0. 0.	
ceiling of vestibule, passage	19.10. 0.	
other	159.10. 0	
	299. 0. 0.'	

This work would have been largely swept away by Joseph Rose, junior, (1746-99) when working for Robert Adam. (The author is indebted to Dr Damie Stillman for some of this information.)

1763 SHUGBOROUGH, STAFFORDSHIRE *Plate 99*

Dining Room; Library.

Lit: 'Versalli's Stucco here is twice as good as his Performances at Hagley not to mention the Superiority of the Designs ...' Philip Yorke, later 2nd Earl of Hardwicke, to his father, 20, 21 August 1763, B.M. Add. MS., 35351, f.406.

Attributed work:

In view of Vassalli's work in Lancashire it is possible that he was responsible for work at Knowsley; Burrow Hall; Croxteth; the Music Pavilion, Sun Street, Lancaster (Plates 63, 64), and for the vanished Leoni houses, Bold Hall and Lathom, completed in about 1731.

The Ballroom at Lumley Castle, Co. Durham (Plate 61), has similarities with his style. The Hagley trophies (Plate 98) bear resemblance to those at Hatton Grange, Shropshire (*C. Life*, 29 February 1968, p. 467), and Highnam Court, Gloucestershire (*C. Life*, 12 May 1950).

The late Sir Charles Trevelyan maintained that Vassalli worked at Wallington, Northumberland, but confirmation has now been found that the Wallington work is by the Franchini brothers (q.v.).

Walker, Thomas (*fl.* 1705)

Official of the Worshipful Company of Plaisterers.

1705 Master.

Lit: London, Guildhall Library, MS., 6122/3.

Ward, Matthew (*fl.* 1762)

1762 FAIRFAX HOUSE, YORK

'For 9 roses under the stairs. 1762. £2.0.6.'

Lit: Leeds, Yorkshire Archaeological Society Library, Newburgh Archives.

Watson, Grace (*fl.* 1775)
1775 BERKELEY SQUARE, LONDON
House of Robert Child.
General Plastering. Received £6.7.6.
Lit: Victoria & Albert Museum (Dept. of Furniture
and Woodwork), Osterley Archives.

Weatherill (Wetherill), Robert (*fl.* late seventeenth
century-1717)
1682, 1690 ST CHARLES THE MARTYR, TUNBRIDGE
WELLS
Worked with Henry Doogood (q.v.). Together they
received £190.
Lit: Marcus Whiffen, *Stuart and Georgian Churches*,
1952, p. 143.
GREENWICH HOSPITAL, LONDON
Asked to be employed on work there.
Lit: Wren Soc., VI, pp. 31, 56, 58, 62, 63.
BLENHEIM PALACE, OXFORDSHIRE
Lit: David Green, *Blenheim Palace*, 1951, pp. 61, 104,
128.
1716 HAMPTON COURT, MIDDLESEX
Submitted proposals with David Lance to carry out
work in certain apartments.
Lit: P.R.O., Works, 4/1, 6 March 1716.

Wellings, — (*fl.* 1775)
Refused admission to the Painter Stainers' Company
in February 1775.
Lit: W. A. D. Englefield, *History of the Painter
Stainers' Company of London*, 1923, p. 175, fn.

Wenham, William (*fl.* 1808-9)
1808-9 CLIFTON CASTLE, YORKSHIRE
Architect: John Foss.
Lit: Sir John Cowell's notes about the building.
(The author is indebted to Mr Howard Colvin for
this information.)

Weston, Ned (*fl.* 1738-43)
Assistant to John Woolston (q.v.). Fell from
scaffolding while working on the plaster royal arms
at the 1738-43 restoration of Lamport Church,
Northamptonshire.
Lit: C. Life, 10 October 1952, p. 1108.

Wharton, Thomas (*fl.* 1660)
1660 THE TOWER, LONDON
Worked under John Grove.
Lit: P.R.O., Works, 5/1, November 1660.

Whatson, William (*fl. c.* 1728-42)
1742 Apprenticed at the age of fourteen to Thomas
Perritt (q.v.) of York.

Lit: York Reference Library, Apprenticeship
Register, 1721-56.

White, Alexander (*fl.* 1620-30)
c. 1630 THE BINNS, LINLITHGOW *Plate 124*
Lit: Bills at house.

White, John (*fl.* 1627)
£100 was paid to 'John Quhytte' in 1627 at Winton
Castle, East Lothian. He is also credited with work
at Moray House, Canongate, Edinburgh.
Lit: Jourdain, 1926, p. 35.

White, Thomas (*fl.* 1764-9)
Of London.
1764-9 MANOR HOUSE, MILTON, BERKSHIRE
Entries from surviving account-book.
Lit: C. Life, 24 December 1948.

Whitehead, James (*fl.* 1773-80)
1773-80 BARNS HOUSE, PEEBLESSHIRE
Lit: Scottish Record Office, Burnet of Barns MSS.,
Box 17, Bundle 40. (The author is indebted to Mr
John G. Dunbar for this information.)

Whitehead, John (*fl.* 1750s)
1753 EDGECOTE, NORTHAMPTONSHIRE
Received £581 17s 6d.
Lit: Tipping, *Early Georgian*, p. 298; Jourdain,
1926, p. xiii.
1754-6 BRAXTED LODGE, ESSEX
Received £88.
Lit: Essex County Record Office, D/DDCA13,
f.118. (The author is indebted to Miss Nancy
Briggs for this reference.)
1758-9 SOHO SQUARE, LONDON
Architect: Thomas Dade.
Worked for Sir William Robinson at two houses.
His detailed bill shows he received £466 9s 0½d.
Lit: Leeds Reference Library, Newby Hall Archives,
2785A.

Wilkins, Chrysostom (*fl.* early eighteenth century)
Was in charge of many plasterers at St Paul's
Cathedral. He was fined in 1700 for arrears of
quarterage by the Worshipful Company of Plaisterers. His name appears in the subscribers' list
to the 2nd edition of Leoni's *Palladio*. He worked
for Nicholas Hawksmoor at St Anne, Limehouse;
St George, Wapping; St Mary, Woolnoth; and for
Gibbs at St Mary le Strand. He worked at St John
Horsleydown, which was gutted in 1940 and partly
demolished in 1948. He was at St Martin-in-the-

Fields where Bagutti was the stuccoist. In 1709 he was fined for bad materials and workmanship.
Lit: Colvin, p. 231; Colvin, *Arch. Rev.*, March 1950; London, Guildhall Library (Worshipful Company of Plaisterers), MS., 6122/3; 6126, 8 August 1709.

Wilkins, John
Was employed with his brother (?) Chrysostom by Gibbs.
1714-17 ST MARY LE STRAND, LONDON
Lit: Colvin, p. 231. Little, *Gibbs*, p. 37.
1715-23 ST GEORGE, WAPPING, LONDON (St George in the East)
Architect: Nicholas Hawksmoor.
Lit: Colvin, *Arch. Rev.*, March 1950.

Wilkins, William
Of St Benedict's Parish, Norwich. His son was William Wilkins (1751-1815), the architect.
Lit: Colvin, p. 673.

Wilkinson, Richard (*fl.* 1767)
1767 Subscribed to James Paine's *Plans . . . of Noblemen and Gentlemen's Houses. . . .*

Williams, — (*fl.* 1726)
1726 CANNONS, MIDDLESEX
Worked for James Brydges, 1st Duke of Chandos.
Lit: Baker, *Brydges*, p. 149 fn.

Williams, Charles (*fl.* late sixteenth century)
See chapter III for mentions of him in letters at Longleat.

Wilmott, Humphrey (*fl.* 1750-73)
c. 1750 MANSION HOUSE, LONDON
Worked with George Fewkes (q.v.).
1761 In this year Wilmott was fined 42s 'for bad and imperfect workmanship in the Cleansing and Whitening of the plaisterers work by him done . . . [at] the Guildhall of the City of London.'
Lit: Guildhall Library, London, MS. 6126, 5 August 1761.
1767 His son John was bound to him as an apprentice.
Lit: Guildhall Library, Boyd's Index to Apprenticeship Registers.
1772-3 Wilmott was Upper Warden and Master of the Worshipful Company of Plaisterers.

Wilton, William (*fl.* 1722-65)
Father of the sculptor. He died on 27 January 1768, and is buried at Wanstead, Essex.
Lit: Parish Registers. Information from Colonel J.H.Busby.

1722 STANMER, SUSSEX
Architect: Nicholas Dubois.
Entrance Hall.
Lit: Hussey, *E.C.H.: Early Georgian*, p. 56.
c. 1740 FOUNDLING HOSPITAL, LONDON
Lit: L.Turner, *Decorative Plasterwork in Great Britain*, 1927, p. 224, pl 299.
1765 LINLEY HALL, SHROPSHIRE
Worked with Thomas Collins (q.v.), his apprentice.
Lit: Bill at house. (The author is indebted to Mr Howard Colvin and Colonel J.H.Busby for this information.)
Attributed work:
c. 1750 FIRLE PLACE, SUSSEX
Library.
Lit: C. *Life*, 3 March 1955, pp. 621-2.

Wolstenholme, Thomas (*c.* 1759-1812)
Of York. His nephew John was a wood-carver who worked extensively at York Minster. Thomas made his name as a maker of composition plaster. His houses at 3/5 Gillygate, York (built in 1797) have the ornament in most rooms and on the facade. The composition has been found in several houses in York and district, such as 53/5 Micklegate and Ripley Castle.
Lit: David Black in York Georgian Society *Report*, 1968-9; R.C.H.M. volume *City of York*, vol. III, 1972, p. LXXXV. The author is indebted to Mr Black, Major J.D.Williams, Mr John Harvey and Dr Eric Gee for sharing the result of their researches made on behalf of the Royal Commission on Historical Monuments.

Wood, John (*fl.* 1782)
1782 COURT HOUSE, NORTHALLERTON
Architect: John Carr.
Lit: R.B.Wragg, *York Georgian Society Report*, 1955-6, p. 60.

Wood, Joseph (*fl.* 1778)
Freeman of York, 1778.
Lit: Surtees Society, Vol. 102.

Woolston, John (*fl.* 1738-40)
Of Northampton. Became an Alderman of the town.
1738 LAMPORT, NORTHAMPTONSHIRE
Plasterwork in the Music Hall and over the staircase; Library ceiling.
Lit: Northants County Record Office, Isham Archives, M.D.Whinney, *Arch. Jnl.*, 1953, CX, p. 205: C. *Life*, 3 October 1952, p. 1023.

1740 LAMPORT CHURCH, NORTHAMPTONSHIRE
Interior classicised to designs of William Smith.
Lit: Whinney, *Arch. Jnl.*, 1953, CX, p. 206.
Attributed work:
EASTON NESTON, NORTHAMPTONSHIRE
Dining Room.
Lit: Whinney, *Arch. Jnl.*, 1953, CX, p. 210.
ALTHORP, NORTHAMPTONSHIRE
Work in the Entrance Hall, *c.* 1733.

Worrall, George (*fl.* 1724-61)
Possibly the son of William Worrall (see below).
Was Master Plasterer, Office of Works, from 17
March 1724/5-1761.
DRAYTON HOUSE, NORTHAMPTONSHIRE
Chapel.
Lit: Drawing with attached bill (Coke MSS.
Melbourne, Derbyshire.) The author is indebted to
Mr Edward Saunders and Mr Gervase Jackson-
Stops for this reference; *C. Life*, XXXI, p. 944; N.
Stopford Sackville, *Drayton*, 1949.

Worrall, William (?-*c.* 1690)
Of St Giles, Cripplegate without London. During
his lifetime accumulated enough money to purchase
estates and endow by will a London charity.
Lit: East Sussex County Record Office, Add. MS.,
3573.

Wright, John, and others
A John Wright of Southwark was apprenticed to
James Ellis (q.v.) on 2 April 1703 (Guildhall
Library, MS., 6122/3), and another of this name
was apprenticed to Joseph Rose, senior, in 1753
for seven years. Rose was then living at Doncaster.
Lit: London, Guildhall Library, Boyd's Index to
Apprenticeship Registers.

The John Wright who worked at Stanford Hall,
Leicestershire, in 1743 and received £270 12s 1d
may have been a relative. It is difficult to believe they
were the same in view of the apprenticeship dates.
Lit: C. Life, 11 December 1958, p. 1410.
A John Wright worked for John Thorold at Syston
Hall, Lincolnshire, and received £391 16s 9d,
although he charged £398 17s 6d.
Lit: Lincolnshire County Record Office, Thorold
Archives, VI/III/5.
A 'Mr Wright' described as 'the ornament man',
'ornament plasterer' and 'Stocco' was employed by
James Paine at Thorndon Hall, Essex, in 1768, and
Thomas Wright was fined for using bad material
at the Grocers' Hall in 1771.
Lit: Essex County Record Office, Petre Archives,
D/DPA58 (the author is indebted to Miss Nancy
Briggs for the Thorndon information); Guildhall
Library, London, MS., 6122/3; 6126, 5 August
1771.

Wright, Thomas (*fl.* 1657-62)
1662 LONDON
'Mended the frett ceeling in the Queen's Chappell',
etc.
Received £67 9s od.
Lit: Public Record Office, E351/3276; P.R.O.,
Works, 5/3.
Wright was fined in September 1657, for keeping
four apprentices instead of two, as the Worshipful
Company of Plaisterers rules decreed.
Lit: Guildhall Library, London, MS., 6126.

Yeape, William (*fl.* 1660)
1660 THE TOWER, LONDON
Worked with John Grove I.
Lit: P.R.O., Works, 5/1, November 1660.

Bibliography

The following is a list of books and articles on plasterwork. Reference should also be made to articles cited in the *Select List of Plasterers* and the notes to the text.

Adderley, J. 'The Pargetter's craft in Essex', *C. Life*. 1914, Vol. 34, 11, 167-9.

Ayscough, A., Jourdain, M., and Sitwell, S. *Country House Baroque*, 1940. (Contains excellent detail photographs by Ayscough, an introduction by Sitwell and notes on the plates by Jourdain.)

Bankart, G.P. *The Art of the Plasterer*, 1908.

Beard Geoffrey, 'Italian Stuccoists in England', *Apollo*, July 1964, pp. 48-56.

—— 'Italian Masters of Stucco, *C. Life*, 24 November 1960.

—— 'A family's 50 year supremacy' (the Rose family of Plasterers), *C. Life*, 8 December 1960.

—— 'The Rose Family of Plasterers, with a catalogue of Yorkshire work', *Leeds Art Calendar*, No. 54, 1964.

—— 'The Rose Family, with a catalogue of their work', *Apollo*, April 1967.

—— 'Plasterers in 17th century Scotland', *C. Life*, 10 April 1969, p. 909.

Bassey, G.E. 'The maintenance and repair of Regency painted stucco finishes', *RIBA, Jnl.*, v. 57, pp. 143-5 (February 1950).

Brooke, Iris. 'Riddle of the Devon plasterers', *C. Life*, 29 December 1950, pp. 2214-16.

Curran, C.P. 'Dublin Plasterwork' in *Jnl. of the Royal Society of Ireland*, Vol. LXX, Part I, 1940.

—— *Dublin Decorative Plasterwork in the 17th and 18th Centuries*, 1967.

Deveboise, N.C. 'The origin of decorative stucco', *American Journal of Archaeology*, v. 45, January-March 1941, pp. 45-61.

French, Cecil. 'Plaster ceilings in Devon', *C. Life*, 15 March 1956, pp. 468-9.

——'West Country plasterers', *ibid.*, 8 December 1955, p. 1386.

—— 'Symbols on ceilings', *ibid.*, 1 May 1958, p. 935.

—— Letter (commenting on the article 'A 17th century Plasterer, John Abbot of Barnstaple), *C. Life*, 19 January 1956, p. 116.

Jack, J.F.S. 'Notes on the repair and preservation of decorated plaster ceilings', *RIBA, Jnl.*, v. 57, September 1950, pp. 416-9.

Jourdain, Margaret. *English Decorative Plasterwork of the Renaissance*, 1926.

Longfield, A.K. 'The manufacture of "Raised Stucco" or "Papier-Mâché" papers in Ireland', *Jnl., Royal Antiq. Soc., of Ireland*, LXXVIII, 1948, I.

Lyman, D. 'Examples of ornamental plasterwork of the English lowlands', *Architectural Record*, v. 32, September 1912, pp. 251-5.

Millar, W. *Plastering, Plain and Decorative*, 1897.

Raley, Robert L. 'Early Maryland plasterwork and stuccowork', *Society of Architectural Historians Journal*, v. 20, No. 3, October 1961, pp. 131-5. (Useful for lists of plasterers, mainly Irish, who worked in the eastern part of the United States in the late eighteenth century.)

Stebbing, W.P.D. 'The Adam brothers and their plaster', *RIBA Jnl.*, 12 September 1938, Ser. 3, XLV, p. 991.

Thorpe, W.A. 'Portrait of a Roaring Girl'. Article on the plaster panels *c.* 1632 from Hilton Hall, now in the Victoria and Albert Museum, London, representing Mary Frith, the heroine of Middleton and Dekker's play, *The Roaring Girl*, in *C. Life*, 6 December 1946, pp. 1070-2.

Turner, Laurence. 'Plasterwork', *RIBA Jnl.*, Ser. 3, v. 13, 1905-6, pp. 317-34.

—— *Decorative Plasterwork in Great Britain*, 1927.

Index of Places

Index of Persons

B7